P9-DUQ-505

Sa

Talking with the Poets

Edited by David Meltzer

CITY LIGHTS BOOKS

SAN FRANCISCO

© 2001 by David Meltzer

Cover design: Stefan Gutermuth
Book design and typography: Small World Productions

Library of Congress Cataloging-in-Publication Data

Meltzer, David.
    San Francisco Beat: talking with the poets / David Meltzer
        p. cm.
    ISBN 0-87286-379-4
    1. Poets--American--California--San Francisco--Interviews.
2. San Francisco (Calif.)--Intellectual life--20th century. 3. Beat generation--
California--San Francisco. 4. Poets--American--20th century--Interviews.
5. San Francisco (Calif.)--In literature. I. Title.
    PS285.S3 M45 2001
    811' .5409979461--dc21

                                                    00-065640

CITY LIGHTS BOOKS are edited by Lawrence Ferlinghetti and Nancy J. Peters
and published at the City Lights Bookstore, 261 Columbus Avenue,
San Francisco, CA 94133. Visit us on the Web at www.citylights.com.

Contents

Preface   v

Acknowledgments   xi

Diane di Prima (1999)   1

William Everson (1971)   22

Remembering Everson (1999)   61

Lawrence Ferlinghetti I (1969)   68

Lawrence Ferlinghetti II (1999)   96

Jack Hirschman (1998)   107

Joanne Kyger (1998)   122

Philip Lamantia (1998)   133

Michael McClure I (1971)   150

Michael McClure II (1999)   177

David Meltzer (1999)   188

Jack Micheline (1994)   216

Kenneth Rexroth (1971)   228

Remembering Rexroth (1999)   266

Gary Snyder (1999)   276

Lew Welch (1971)   294

Philip Whalen (1999)   325

Bibliographies   352

Preface

Nothing is hidden;
As of old
All is clear as daylight.
—Anonymous haiku, 16th century

San Francisco Beat: Talking with the Poets reaches back to the late sixties, early seventies. And back up to the late nineties. Everything and nothing has happened.

Power continues more rapidly and digitally to concentrate its manna into fewer, fatter virtual and actual hands in the arcane splendor of bottom-line commerce. Many poets have died in obscurity while others are elevated to billboard magnitude. Myth and debunk dance together in the spectacle. Reality is fought for and against in virtual versus actual; spirituality is reclaimed as a bridge out of the tangle and sustains as it comforts.

History is not only written by the winners but also the survivors. The Ur text of the present book—*The San Francisco Poets,* whose five interviews are included here, along with eight recent ones—was published in a period of immense social, political, and spiritual struggle. The war in Vietnam still had a couple of years to go but was, we were assured, "winding down"—but not before massive bombardment of North Vietnam the day after Christmas. Nixon was president, and William L. Calley Jr. was convicted of the premeditated murder of South Vietnamese civilians at Mai Lai. There was the Attica prison riot, where twenty-eight prisoners ands nine guards held hostage were killed in the onslaught of 1,500 state police in the air and on the ground. Rev. Philip F. Berrigan was indicted with five others for conspiring to kidnap Kissinger. The Weather Underground ignited a bomb in a restroom in the Senate wing of the Capitol. Thousands of antiwar demonstrators were arrested in Washington. Daniel Ellsberg made *The Pentagon Papers* available. Watergate was a year away. George Jackson was killed in San Quentin. Jim Morrison and Igor Stravinsky died. Charles Manson and his family were convicted of the 1969 murders of Sharon Tate and six others. And the Bollingen Prize for poetry, once awarded to Ezra Pound while he was incarcerated for treason in St. Elizabeth's, was split between Richard Wilbur and Mona Van Duyn.

The San Francisco Poets was published as a mass-market paperback; it contained interviews with Kenneth Rexroth, Lawrence Ferlinghetti, Michael McClure, William Everson, and Lew Welch. Richard Brautigan declined to be interviewed but submitted a statement about himself. Only two of the poets interviewed—McClure and Ferlinghetti—are alive today. The others are gone. Two by suicide.

At the time of those interviews, I was thirty-three years old, married with three young daughters, and living on the margins. Today, three decades later, my daughters are middle-aged; a son was born in the interim and is in his early twenties; I'm sixty-three and still living on the margins. How's that for progress? All the poets interviewed for *San Francisco Beat* are like me, a step or two before or after Social Security kicks in. Not geezers, still creative and vigorous in their relation to the world around and beyond them, but now perceived and received as elders.

The reclamation and reinvention of the Beats and Beat literature in the nineties is an international phenomena that at once recognizes the dissident spirit of the Beats and removes it from historical complexity, makes it safe, and turns it into products and artifacts. The more removed from history's discomfort, the easier it is to imagine and consume history without taking on its weight. The books of that time recirculate in new hipper covers, along with all the dreadful accoutrements of the postwar middle-class suburban diaspora, the kitsch and crapola. It's the "look" that dot-commers yen to trophy their nouveaux pads with. It's more to do with style than bile. Fictive history can be owned and displayed as the fifties' ultimate product: stuff. Both radically disruptive stuff and suburban kitsch are easily embraced by the neo-con techno-cart. The pervasive postwar advertising seduction of selling standardized goods to consumers as an act of claiming individuality and choice deeply insaturated itself into the American psyche.

Conformity is the rule, though the fantasy of individuality is the carrot. Your pubic goatee and antique shades complement your acquisitions (the vintage butterfly chair, free-form plywood coffee table,

naugahyde-tufted home bar and bar stools) ar
buddies can caw "cool" at your trophies that were
machine from the great age of conformity-through-
rule of realm makes inevitable and desirable such
and "brands" and "branding." A voluntary slave cl
For many of the new class, what seems familiar ar__ ..ievitable is a
kind of truth, what some folks call "comfort food" like Big Macs and
Starbucks and Barnes and Noble and Amazon.com. A predictable and
paternal corporate company whose zeal to standardize reality, realize
unheard-of profits, reaches out across the globe, globalizes, plants the
undeniable triumph of Coca-Cola over Dr. Pepper.

If the New Agers have their goddesses to worship, the pomo-techno
boy's club have the Beats and their writings: great sizzling prose of
male flight and fraternity—not only running away from hearth-bind-
ing lives but often from immaterial materialism. In *The San Francisco
Poets* there was very little talk about the fifties and the Beat but much
talk about poetry as a life practice and of being a poet-citizen. In the
intervening years, the Beat has taken on an independent and indus-
trial life of its own, and, more than anything else, has become em-
braced by the academics at the same time they bear-hugged
L=A=N=G=U=A=G=E poetry and the New York School.

Where the Beats and New Yorkers produced work in retaliation to
the aridity of poetry's institutionalization by using a highly charged
vernacular approach to express both visionary and ordinary moments
in stylishly direct and often experimental writing, the Language cad-
res never truly left college. They've always been good students, and
now they're excellent teachers. The professionalization and rational-
ization of poetry in the academy took hold and routinized the teach-
ing and writing of poetry, canopied under the assumption that poets
who write the right stuff will be able teach it too. Almost all American
colleges and universities have writing and poetry degree-track pro-
grams that adhere pretty well to the standard Ohio workshop model.
On the other side of the poetry divide are the Jack Kerouac School of
Disembodied Poetics at Naropa in Boulder, the New College poetics
program in San Francisco, and the University of Buffalo's graduate
program in poetics.

Since then, poetry, like Plastic Man, has elastically sought new modes of expression, communication, and production via "spoken word" performance poetry (matrixed in the Nuyorican Café in Manhattan and Café Babar in San Francisco), hip-hop, poetry slams, and the omnipresent endless page of cybervoid. The divide between the Castle culture and what Jack Hirschman calls "the street" remains large in most aspects or sectors of American society.

In the twenty-first century, postmodernism happily coexists with Beat retro nostalgia. In the fix of the mix the tricks get obvious and ironic and therefore manageable. Computer technology, if anything, makes the metaphor of mind revealed in all its complexity and non-sense, and struggles to still the roar and make it one-dimensional and commercially viable. On the other digital hand, the Net allows for all kinds of rebellion in real or imaginal terms.

Why be a poet? Especially in the U. S. of A? You can be workshop bard of lawnmowers and soccer moms; you can share and heal through an automatic wound; you can rage against dial tone and roar, rap your resistance, confound the founding fathers who truly were motherfuckers; you can gauze out a perfect world without passion with vaseline-coated lens; you can splash your Web site with verse, epic or minimal; you can publish yourself and your friends; organize poetry readings and hope somebody shows up. . . .

In *The Red Shoes,* a fifties British film directed by Michael Powell, Anton Wolbrook, typecast as a Diagheliv-like ballet impresario, asks ballerina Moira Shearer, "Why do you dance?" "Because I must," she answers, sealing her fate. The poets chosen for this book represent a divergent yet socially and historically connected weave. Philip Lamantia was America's Surrealist prodigy and a participant in the legendary Six Gallery reading, October 7, 1955. (His work from that time on is brilliant, romantic, polemically visionary and deeply sensitive to the details of the natural terrain; in many ways, he's like his mentor Rexroth, a great nature poet.) Philip Whalen also read there, as did Michael McClure. (Allen Ginsberg read "Howl" that night; Kerouac was loudly in the audience.)

As in all free-floating nonlegendary communities of young artists and poets, there was constant interaction, competition, rivalries, gossip, support; the young artists jammed into the sardine can of Beat were the least able or willing to get derailed into such freeze-frame reductivism in that time. They were too busy surviving and learning their arts.

Diane di Prima, a homey from Brooklyn, has been politically and artistically a natural activist and matrix for others to allow and resist. Her large body of work attests to the range of her poetical and practical intelligence.

Jack Micheline, like Jack Hirschman, was from the Bronx; he died before the book was realized. I wanted to include Scott Thompson and Rebecca Peters's interview with Micheline because he was like a club fighter, pugnacious and contentious, tender and romantic, a self-professed poet and champion of the margins and a pit bull for and against Beat hierarchies of razzle-dazzle.

Joanne Kyger, like her mentor Whalen, is a poet of transparently easy and immediate wisdom that, in its dispatch, is gracefully disarming and ultimately immensely profound.

Roshi Phil Whalen is an amazement, a one and only, whose "mind graphs" are a treasury of an erudite, whimsical, all-too-human, spiritual gourmet and trickster of serious fun at its most sublime heights and depth.

Jack Hirschman is an occulted major American poet who chooses, because of his politics, to publish through the American way of samizdat and the occasional small press. A Communist, he enjoys more credibility and admiration in Europe than in the States.

Gary Snyder, whose anarcho-Buddhist élan has been synonymous with the Beat movement, has been immensely effective and present in the ecology and sustainable economy politics and consciousness.

Returning some thirty years later to the two surviving poets of the first book was a lesson in growth and process. At the time of the 1999 interview, Lawrence Ferlinghetti was in the last month of his term as the first poet laureate of San Francisco; he was eighty years old, but no one could even remotely guess it. Trim, hearty, an almost daily swimmer, he crackled with energy, wry wisdom, and playful certainty.

Michael McClure was an elegantly down-to-earth participant and custodian of key elements of Beat and post-Beat history; his admirable and impeccable memory were graced with a new involvement with Zen Buddhism. (Both McClure and Snyder retain informed and open-ended involvement with ecology and biology as complements to the weave of their intellective and creative work.)

Then I was fortunate to interview Robert Hawley about his association with William Everson aka Brother Antoninus. Bob is the editor and publisher of Oyez Books, which in the late sixties and seventies published essential works by Everson, Robert Duncan, Larry Eigner, Mary Norbert Korte, Charles Olson, Lew Welch, Michael McClure, Samuel Charters, and others.

The informal Rexroth colloquy at Berkeley's The Musical Offering café (orchestrated by my editor James Brook) was made rich and valuable by the presence of Ken Knabb (noted editor/translator of *Situationist International Anthology* and author of *The Relevance of Rexroth*) and Morgan Gibson (activist and scholar, author of *Revolutionary Rexroth*).

All these poets are my peers and mentors and were gracefully generous in their welcome and availability. The dissident egalitarian poetry of the postwar fifties, as distinguished from the formalist monasticism of the academy, provoked and allowed an ongoing permission. All of the poets herein are unique exemplars of their devotions, passions, intelligence, and questing spirits.

The new interviews include poets who were geographically unavailable in 1971, who are part of the Beat continuum, but whose work has moved beyond that. I am deeply privileged and honored to present these conversations to survivors and go-getters of this new century. These interviews are about being a poet in America, a country that has never executed a poet for his or her writing. I don't know what this says about the life of poetry in American culture, but for too many it's not a matter of life or death. Why should it be? And why isn't it?

Acknowledgments

San Francisco Beat: Talking with the Poets is a new book, with some odd and old twists. In 1998 and 1999 Marina Lazzara, James Brook, and I made the rounds of the Bay Area to interview Diane di Prima, Lawrence Ferlinghetti, Jack Hirschman, Joanne Kyger, Philip Lamantia, Michael McClure, Gary Snyder, and Philip Whalen.

Christopher Winks consented to grill me about my own past and prejudices so that I could put in a reluctant appearance in the book. He has taught Caribbean, African American, African, and other literatures at New York University and the City University of New York. He's working on a study of utopias and dystopias in Caribbean literature.

The Jack Micheline interview, by Scott Thompson and Rebecca Peters is, for my money, the most balanced encounter with a notoriously disruptive and contentious free spirit. It's a durable memorial. Scott Thompson is Director of Research for the Walter Benjamin Research Syndicate (www.wbenjamin.org) and a political activist and pirate radio talk show host. He is also the translator of Goethe's *Tales for Transformation* (City Lights Books). Rebecca Peters is a film researcher, and she works in the animation department of Academy of Art in San Francisco.

San Francisco Beat reprints five historic interviews from *The San Francisco Poets*. The 1969–1971 interviews with William Everson, Lawrence Ferlinghetti, Michael McClure, Kenneth Rexroth, and Lew Welch have been lightly edited to correct typographical errors and a couple of errors of fact. Otherwise, they are faithful reprints—without additions or subtractions or any higher math—of the interviews as originally published in *The San Francisco Poets* (New York: Ballantine Books, 1971) and then in *Golden Gate: Interviews with Five San Francisco Poets* (Berkeley: Wingbow Press, 1976).

What I wrote thirty years ago in acknowledgment of the help I received with *The San Francisco Poets* still holds:

> Jack Shoemaker, first of all, helped beyond measure. He pro-
> vided transportation, since I don't drive, into the city, & was an

important voice in many of the interviews. . . . His encouragement, his useful ideas, helped direct the book's outcome as much as anything. [Jack later became editor-in-chief at North Point Press and is now editor-in-chief at Counterpoint Press.] Liz Pintchuck toiled more than anybody else & worked out of the goodness of her heart—certainly not for the criminally meager money offered her. Poor Liz had to transcribe the interviews, usually poorly recorded, onto paper using a clumsy plastic portable typewriter. . . . My wife Tina paid her dues listening to me rage & holler when things went wrong, snarled & tangled, & she also patiently went over the final draft for last minute corrections & proof-reading.

In an attempt to bring the historic interviews up to date in 1999, we conducted follow-up interviews with Lawrence Ferlinghetti and Michael McClure, and we also interviewed people who had something to say about William Everson and Kenneth Rexroth.

Robert Hawley, of The Ross Valley Book Co., Berkeley, gave generously of his time to provide some perspective on the life and works of William Everson.

Morgan Gibson and Ken Knabb volunteered to speculate on the import and afterlife of Kenneth Rexroth, whose influence was formative on the San Francisco scene. Morgan Gibson has taught at a number of universities in America and in Japan, where he now lives with his wife and son. He is the author of *Kenneth Rexroth* (1972), *Revolutionary Rexroth: Poet of East-West Wisdom* (1986), and several volumes of poetry, essays, and translations. A revised and expanded version of *Revolutionary Rexroth* is available at the Light and Dust poetry Web site (www.thing.net/~grist/ld/rexroth/gibson.htm). Ken Knabb has lived in Berkeley since the sixties. He is the translator of *Situationist International Anthology* (1981) and the author of *The Relevance of Rexroth* (1990) and *Public Secrets: Collected Skirmishes of Ken Knabb* (1997). Updated versions of all these texts are on line at his Bureau of Public Secrets Web site (www.bopsecrets.org), which also contains many texts by Rexroth and links to other Rexroth-related sites.

My editor at City Lights, James Brook, another poet—and translator—burdened with too many day jobs, was the commissar of the project. He was the organizer of countless details and the shaper of both manuscript and book. His collaboration was indispensable through all phases; he is very much co-author of this work.

Marina Lazzara, a poet and musician, recorded and transcribed most of the new interviews in *San Francisco Beat*. She was paid in peanuts and love.

Now roll the nonhierachically arranged credits of others who in some way or another gave succor, direction, help, sympathy, advice, insight, etc., in fashioning this document: Steve Jones, Nancy Peters, Owen Hill, Alastair Johnson, my students at New College of California who had to put up with strange gaps in class continuity, Anne Charters, Aya, A.D. Winans, Michael Rothenberg, Steve Dickison, Joyce Peters, Giovanni Singelton, Tish Parmeley, Kristine McKenna, Josh Kuhn, Ali Baba's Cave, Lorenzo Thomas, Gloria Frym, Sheila Tully, Christian Parenti, Bob Callahan, Danny Cassidy, and more.

My agent, Victoria Shoemaker, pulled the Big Deal together.

Don't get me started on my P.S. of poets I wanted to interview but who weren't identified with the Beat thing while sharing the same historical time frame and choosing other equally defiant poetics.

OK, one P.S. A major motivation for *The San Francisco Poets* was that I wanted the poetry of Lew Welch to receive greater recognition; unfortunately and ironically, before the book was published Lew took (or gave) his life away. His widow, Magda Welch, compiled a lovely tribute to his life, *Hey Lew!*, which reminds us of his life and updates it to this disjunctive yet familiar present.

David Meltzer
Richmond
February 2001

Diane di Prima (1999)

© Sheppard Powell

July 21, 1999: Marina, Jim, and I meet up at the BART station close to Diane's apartment in San Francisco. Her partner, Sheppard Powell, opens the door for us, and we walk up to the second floor into a book-filled living room. The usual awkwardness about where to plug in the tape recorder and set up the microphone. Diane asks if we want tea or coffee, and once everyone is settled, the interview commences.—DM

Diana di Prima (**DD**)
David Meltzer (**DM**)
Marina Lazzara (**ML**)

DM Your grandfather introduced you to Dante. Was that your earliest encounter with poetry?
DD Yeah, I was about four or so. He took out this old paperback . . . one of those European ones . . . and told me that this book had traveled around the world. I thought, oh, that's why it looks so beat up. I pictured housewives in the Bronx reaching from one window to another like they would pass food and, instead, passing the same book all the way around the world.
DM Around the clotheslines.
DD Around the clotheslines, right. Dante on the clothesline! Yeah, that was the first poetry. We also listened to a lot of opera together. He

was forbidden opera because it was bad for his heart. He had heart trouble and he'd get so worked up about the opera.

DM You say you'd made a lifetime commitment to poetry at the age of fourteen. What happened to lead up to that?

DD In order to stay sane, I found the public library, or my father actually showed me how to walk to the library. Girls weren't allowed out much. I was allowed to go to the library. And I read my way. . . . I found that if you were caught in the adult section, they told you that you couldn't be there. But if you got the books to the counter, they checked them out for you. Everything was a double message. So I was reading my way through philosophy. I had written answers to Plato in all the margins of the Jowett translation, when I was eleven, twelve, thirteen. I fell in love with Schopenhauer. I was sure Schopenhauer would have been happier if I would have been with him. Meanwhile, I was also reading novels. [*laughter*]

ML Was that your first crush?

DD One of my very first crushes, yes. I had a pretty big thing for Spinoza, too. Anyway, somewhere in that reading there was a Somerset Maugham novel—maybe it was *The Razor's Edge*—where he quotes Keats: "Beauty is truth, truth beauty." So I went looking with my little library skills for this person named Keats, and I found the poetry section. Whereupon I began to read nothing but poetry. I couldn't understand why anybody would bother with philosophy because clearly any point you had to reach consistently couldn't be completely right. Any logic couldn't be completely right, and poetry could hold all the contradictions.

So then a lot of poetry . . . the people who were my people at that point were Romantics, Shelley and Keats mostly. And reading all of Keats's letters, which I was doing when I was age thirteen or fourteen. And finally one day it hit me that this wasn't just out there, it wasn't just heroes, other people, it was me. I could do this. I could do this. I cried a lot when I realized that. I was very sad because with it came the understanding that I was going to have to give up a lot of things regular people have. I wasn't going to be able to snuggle into regular human life. I don't know how I knew all that, but I did. And that's when I made my commitment to poetry. I was sitting in my backyard, and it hit me. Like that. If that's the case, then I better start writing every day. So I bought a new notebook, and every day I wrote something. By then I was in high school.

DM In high school was there encouragement for this?

DD Yes. I was in Hunter High School, which in those days was for women only. And you got in by exam, so there were the brightest women from all kinds of backgrounds. And in my age group, in my class, there were about eight of us who wanted to write. By the time we were sophomores or thereabouts, we would get together in the morning and go to one of the home rooms a little early and read what we'd written the day before. A few of the teachers were very encouraging—very interesting women teachers dedicated to teaching women.

I graduated in '51. One summer I went to summer school because people had these crazy notions back then that it's better to do everything faster. . . . I skipped a grade in grammar school, which made life miserable in grammar school—all the kids hated me. At summer school, there was an off-the-wall teacher, a crazy man in a beret named Anton Serota who I let read one of my poems, and he had me read it out loud to the class, and he was very encouraging. And also very helpful about the way you write when you're young, with so many abstractions. "This part works because I can make pictures in my mind; this part doesn't work." It was just one summer, but it was a really helpful and close friendship. Those things happen. Then I went to Swarthmore College and got the opposite of encouragement.

I wanted to major in Greek and Latin. I'd gotten a city prize for Latin translation. I was in the top two percentile in math and physics. There was a lot of propaganda that the U.S. needed scientists. So their little claws were out there: come and be a scientist. I majored in physics at Swarthmore. However, they weren't equipped. They were teaching nineteenth-century physics; nobody was teaching relativity. So it was very boring and didn't work, and I dropped out of school when I was a little more than eighteen.

DM What were your feelings as a young person growing up in the Second World War and then in the aftermath of the war with the unveiling of the atomic bomb and the Holocaust. How did that affect you—or did it?

DD While we were growing up, there was no war news in the house. Before the war started, half of my family went back to Italy. My father's father's brother and his half of the family went back, but my paternal grandfather stayed. We all went down to the boat, and half of them sailed off. We never traced that part of the family again. Rudi, my oldest son, recently tried. There was this feeling of enormous Greek tragedy going on. And it would be an understatement to say that my mother and father were very controlling. We never saw a paper, we never heard the news, we never read a comic, and we never went to the movies except for about four Disney films until I was in high school. As far as the war went, it was blocked out except for the nuns having us pray for all the children—on both sides—at school.

I write about a lot of this in *Recollections of My Life as a Woman*. I remember the day the war was over and everyone was waiting with their boxes of confetti to throw them out the window, and all that . . . there was a feeling of horror for me in that. My neighborhood was very primitive, and everybody had something like doll's heads on sticks with slanted eyes painted on them. They were running up and down the street like that. In my neighborhood, they burned politicians in effigy from lampposts when they lost elections.

The bomb fell on my eleventh birthday. August 6. And that was a moment that I talk about in the book. My father came home. We were waiting for him for the birthday party, and he threw down the paper and said, "Well, we lost." He said, "Whatever we do now, we've lost." I remember that. Consciousness flooded in with the dropping of that bomb. Consciousness of the war. But then it was only two weeks more and the war was over. But I don't remember the slow unveiling, as you put it, of the information about the concentration camps.

DM We used to go to newsreels a lot. Everyone in the neighborhood was also a newspaper junkie. We'd sit on the stoops talking politics.

DD Yeah, I remember the stoops. . . . But, no, the discourse didn't happen around the kids. It's nuts. I was eleven, and two years later I'm in high school and there's a whole world of God-knows-what kind of conflicts going on that you had not heard a word about. I'm sure they talked about the war in Italian, but I was only interested in whatever intrigue might affect me and my brothers in terms of who was mad at who, and what was going to make another blow-up happen in the family. So the war was a metaphor for the other war.

DM So you leave Swarthmore at eighteen? How did this come down in terms of your relationship to your family?

DD It was very traumatic for them.

DM Did you go back home?

DD Yeah, I was home for the Christmas holidays when I decided that I wasn't going to go back to school. I had a group of friends at Swarthmore, and everybody I was close to was dropping out. It was just too straight and precious and protected—class-conscious and definitely not my class, not my kind of place. Two of my friends, women who were lovers, asked me to join them in renting an apartment in New York. I said yes. It turned out that one of their mothers threatened them both with the police because between the ages of eighteen and twenty-one your parents could bust you for being homosexual . . . your parents could call the police. You had no rights then. One of them decided to do what her mother wanted and went on to some school in Connecticut, so it was left to me to get an apartment alone. Really no regrets. I mean there was nothing happening for me at Swarthmore.

DM What was it to be alone for the first time?

DD It was great. I wasn't terribly alone, because of lovers and friends, but having your own say over your own place was heaven. I got a place on Fifth Street between Avenue B and Avenue C. In those days women weren't doing that. It was 1953. Forty-five dollars a month. A nice-size room and a little room, a kitchen, and bathroom. I was the only woman living alone in that block that I know of. People thought I was a whore.

DM When did you seek out a literary community?

DD Well, there was already the people from Hunter and a couple of friends from Swarthmore. I used to go hang out in the first coffee shop that opened that for us—the Rienzi. I used to hang out there some, and I hung out in Washington Square Park. I wasn't so much looking for poets or writers as looking for artists of any sort. Writers talk too much. I liked creativity that was more intuitive, so I hung with painters. Took dance classes. Did that for a while. Actually, ever since my parents first let me out of the house. Not having been able to play actively as a kid made my first dance classes a matter of reclaiming the body. I became friends with dancers and painters and met people from the Arts Students League and Ballet Theater and the New Dance Group, and took classes all over the place. At the New School of Social Research. I took some classes at Brooklyn College at night and some at Hunter and some at Columbia.

DM What kind of classes were you taking?

DD I was still very interested in math. I loved math. Pure math. I took integral calculus in Brooklyn and theory of equations at Columbia. And took Greek at Hunter, classical Greek, and just whatever I wanted, rather than going for a degree. At the New School it was really more like theater because they typecast their professors. The Russian literature professor was a guy with a shock of gray hair and he "suffered" a lot in the classroom. The existentialist professor had a very thin profile and blond hair and a French accent, and he'd show us his profile. But it was fun. For me, it was learning about other literatures and all that. Everywhere I went I met people—and people talked to each other in those days. I have a daughter who moved to New York recently, and it seems like people don't know how to meet each other anymore. Back then you would sit on a park bench, and someone would sit down next to you, and you started a conversation. And then you went somewhere and drank coffee and continued. It wasn't necessarily about picking people up. It was more like: who are you and what's going on?

DM How'd you make a living?

DD The first year I worked downtown on Wall Street doing an office job. I didn't need to work that much, but I was helping one of my gay women friends with some of my money. The next thing was a part-time job at Columbia at the electronics lab. I got security clearance! That gave me access to free classes at Columbia. And then one day I was in Washington Square, and the painter Nicolai Cikovsky came up to me, one of the Eastern Europeans who migrated just before the war, and asked me if I would model for him. I said sure. His studio was right off the park there, and other painters came to visit. Those guys passed their models from hand to hand. That led to years and years of just modeling for painters for a living. (There's one of Raphael Soyer's paintings over there on the wall.) We were making $3.50 an hour in

1953. . . . That would be like $50 an hour now. All under the table, all in cash. We worked two-hour shifts. I wound up working twenty hours a month. The rest of my time was for writing and studying and filling in holes in my education. I went to movies at the Museum of Modern Art almost every day.

DM Did you ever go to the Thalia?

DD Went to the Thalia a ton. I used to bring my lunch and see the same movie over and over, and if I didn't want to see the second feature, I'd go sit in the lobby and read during that one.

DM You hadn't been allowed to go to movies as a kid and started going to movies at eighteen. Do you remember what that opened up?

DD It's hard to express it, but a whole sense of manipulation of light and time, like the heart of magic, the heart of art. The first film I saw—besides Walt Disney and one Shirley Temple film—the first film I consciously saw was Cocteau's *Blood of the Poet* when I was fifteen in a little theater on Irving Place, when I was going to summer school. From then on, it was all the Cocteau movies. . . . The Museum of Modern Art would show series. They'd show everything that Von Stroheim ever directed, for instance. You got a total education without anybody blathering at you, lecturing. Everything by Carl Dreyer. All the movies Garbo was ever in. One thing after the other. You got a pass. It was $3 a year if you were an art student. And Raphael Soyer always signed that I was an art student. You could go to the museum every day for a year. I was busy trying to fill in the holes in my information as an artist.

DM Can you describe your writings at that time?

DD Some of the stuff that's in *Dinners and Nightmares* was written around then. I was very interested in making it as sparse as possible— I was influenced by Hemingway, among others. Also by the Matisse line drawings that came out in a Dover paperback around that time. I noticed that there was not only dimensionality but color . . . a hint of color to the eye from those black-and-white line drawings. I wanted to know how much information you could give with how few words, just like the lines in a Matisse drawing. And so I would cut and cut and cut. The first book has some of that stuff—*This Kind of Bird Flies Backwards*—and the "More or Less Love Poems" that are in *Dinners and*

Nightmares. I was reading a lot. When I left Swarthmore I charged a lot of books the day I was leaving. One was *The Cantos.*

DM To the library?

DD No, I charged them in the bookstore at Swarthmore and paid the bill off about thirty years later. I got Auden and cummings and those people you would expect. But I got *The Cantos* and *Personae,* too.

DM Was Pound informing at that point?

DD The most. I read and did what he tells you to do in *ABC of Reading.* I was doing a little Homeric Greek. I had some wonderful books of the troubadours with glossaries in the back and that kind of stuff. I didn't really meet the poets or start meeting the literary community until '56. So there's three years that were more dancers and painters and Actors Studio people. My friend Bret Rohmer was a painter. Bret had been a child actor. He was friends with all those Actors Studio guys— Bill Gunn, Marty Landau—so they would come over. Allen Ginsberg came through town in '56, early '57, maybe.

DM What was the impact of Allen?

DD Well, I had been writing all this slang from '53 on. I loved the street language. My friends who I lived with and other serious artists were saying, no, you can't do that. Nobody's going understand it in ten years. People were pretty down on me in my group. We were all nineteen years old. There was an argument about whether or not you could use the vernacular. But my friend Joan O'Malley said no. At one point, somebody got upset. We had a whole wall collaged full of photos of the artists and actors we loved. We all started tearing down all the photographs, yelling that we weren't worthy of these people if we had these terrible ideas about art. So in a way it was like oil on troubled waters to see *Howl* published. It legitimized things that were already happening in my work.

Within a year after Allen came through, people started looking me up. People started showing up at my house, and that would be anywhere from people of my age like LeRoi Jones to Edward Dahlberg and Kenneth Rexroth. Dahlberg and Rexroth acted like lecherous old guys. In the world I was in, all of that seemed quite natural. I didn't wonder what piece of the woodwork they had come out from or why they had looked me up.

DM Besides being lecherous, did you learn anything from Rexroth?
DD I love Rexroth. I love Rexroth. He was valiant and wonderful and helped me many times, especially in terms of my political writing or information that I had or thought I had or wanted to find out about in history. He sat in on a workshop once of mine that was called History as Paranoia. Everything I said, he would answer from the back of the room, "And furthermore, did you know that . . . " and he'd add six more things. He was quite wonderful. It's just that I don't think guys of that generation had ever encountered a girl who was writing but wasn't particularly on the make. I slept around a lot, but I wasn't on the make when I met a guy who was a writer. So it took them a little while to adjust. They did good. [*laughter*]
DM OK. Let's see . . . what about the Beat movement?
DD Yeah, what is that thing rumored to be the Beat movement?
DM Help me. I'm having a crisis here. You're known as an important writer of the Beat movement. Do you want to tell me what it is or was?
DD I and people I knew were disgusted with the whole thing of a label, and the label came late, and the label brought all those little girls from Jersey with their eyeliner and their black tights, and you had to take care of them because they were going to bed with the wrong people, and they were going to get hurt. Do you remember those girls from Jersey?
DM I remember the girls who came to North Beach from the suburbs.
DD Same thing. When did you move out here?
DM Let me see . . . maybe '60, '61.
DD Those girls were showing up by about '57 or '58.

I have no idea about the Beat movement. To this day, I find it very difficult, as I'm sure you do, or anyone does, that people assume that whatever we were doing then we are doing now. What I'm doing now is what I'm doing now, and if you want to read *Loba* as a Beat poem, more power to you, but it doesn't make sense to read it that way.
DM To what do you attribute this great renewed fascination by primarily young males toward what they imagine was the Beat? It seems to be almost exclusively a male fantasy.
DD This is such a repressive age we're in right now. It's really disgusting right now. So the idea of a time when it was OK to blah, blah, blah.

DM For guys.

DD For guys. Not just for guys. It was OK for me. Look at how awful it is right now for everybody. I mean, it is fucking difficult. Drugs have been given a bad name. Traveling freely on the road would be a form of insanity. Money is so tight, nobody works twenty hours a month and studies their art. You know Edward Dorn's phrase, "crazy with permission," from *Gran Appacheria?* There was some kind of wild permission that we took. It certainly hadn't been handed to us. McCarthy didn't hand it to us, nor did our parents. But the biological facts of life weren't against it. We weren't going to die if we slept around. Which you might now.

Robert Duncan used to say all the time that when something is leaving the planet it enters the realm of the imagination. When Dante wrote about the Church, the Church was failing—and so it *could* enter the realm of the imagination. Maybe that's part of it now. Real life, as we lived it, is fading, so there's this terrific Beat fantasy.

ML Spoken word poetry might be inspired by the Beats, don't you think?

DD Not to me. My experience of the whole thing was not an experience of the public arena much. I would read if people asked, and friends were doing it, at some of those places along the Lower East Side, but the heart of it for me was making my first book and editing *The Floating Bear*. It was always the word on paper and getting it out, much more than it was performance per se. Performance was the theater. We had the theater. . . .

DM The New York Poet's Theatre? Could you tell us a little bit about how that originated and what it did?

DD Yeah, at that point I was married to a guy who was a performer, Alan Marlowe.

DM That's a great actor's name.

DD Yeah, but his name was Meyorwitz, but he didn't even find that out until later. We did one-act plays by poets, with sets by painters. People who weren't directors directed—choreographers and dancers or whatever. George Herms did the set for McClure's *The Blossom, or Billy the Kid*. Alex Katz did a set for a James Schuyler play. Peter Agostini sculpted the hanged man for *Three Travelers Watch Sunrise* by Wallace

Stevens. We had some beautiful, beautiful things. It ran for about a four-month season each year over a period of four or five years.

DM Where was the theater located?

DD Different places, different years. We would rent different spaces. The plays would run on the weekends, and during the week there'd be contemporary music night, a dance night, an experimental film night, something else. Different people would run those. And then on Sunday afternoons, before the evening play, we would have poetry readings right in the set of the play. We did a whole series where we invited poets to come and read their favorite poems by others. Red Grooms made a set for Kenneth Koch. It was exciting and beautiful. *That* was the performance thing. By the time the coffee shop thing got big, it was it was a little too raucous for me. There's a part of me that prefers being able to read poetry in a more subtle and quiet way. I never was really into the "performance" part of all that, although I read with musicians a few times. I worked with the Chicago Art Ensemble at the University of Chicago, for example.

DM When did you have your first child?

DD In '57.

DM Were there difficulties?

DD Yeah, there were a lot of difficulties. I had decided I wanted a kid, right? I decided I didn't want to live with a man. My family experience of growing up made me think that living with men wasn't a nice idea. I had lots of lovers, and I asked people if they wanted to father a kid, and everybody thought I was insane, and finally I didn't ask—I just got pregnant and had Jeanne. That part was not a problem. The problem was, for example, I didn't dare let people at the hospital know that I wasn't married, because they were looking hard for white babies to put up for adoption. They had babies of every other color under the sun, but if you were a single parent with a white child the pressure put on you to give up that baby before you left the hospital was enormous. So I made up a husband for the birth certificate. A lot of problems like that.

Of course, my family, my poor family, was completely freaked out already about this. It wasn't hard for me in the sense of daily life because I just worked at home. I had bought a mimeograph machine, and

I made a home business. I did the scripts for the off-off Broadway theaters. I would do them at the house, and people would come and pick them up. That was fine. I tried getting not welfare but child care so that Jeanne could be somewhere when I did this work, and the only way you were allowed Social Service child care was to be on welfare, and if you were on welfare, you had to turn in the name of a father. None of which was of any interest to me. So Jeanne just stayed home and played. I worked at the Phoenix Bookstore when she was two, and she'd come in the stroller and play in the back. I did that for about two years.

DM You had more children and sometimes had more than one to deal with.

DD Having one, you take her everywhere, do everything together. She used to sleep backstage when I was at the Living Theater, when I worked there with Jimmy Waring. Having two meant you had to arrange things. But it was so difficult anyway between me and Roi after I had Dominique. I left for the West Coast with Alan Marlowe, who was breaking up his affair with Fred Herko. Alan had money coming in from TV residuals. For some reason, and I'm not sure what his reason was, he wanted to marry me. I knew that he was a man I'd never fall in love with, so he seemed like a good person to marry. I had two kids with him, Alex and Tara, over six years. But most of the time, we weren't even sexually involved. It was an open marriage, and he was mostly with guys. We ran the theater and we ran the press. I really wasn't alone with more than one child that much. Although the men weren't much use in terms of taking care of the house or taking care of kids or making money. Once the residuals stopped, Alan had no idea what else to do. He could raise money for the theater for a season, but he had no idea about day-to-day things like rent.

DM I'm interested in *The Floating Bear* project—it had a lasting impact in the strange history of poet-produced bulletins. It came out in mimeograph form and was an incredible repository of poetry and poetry news, reflecting a coast-to-coast poetic network. I wonder if we could talk about the whole process of co-editing with LeRoi Jones, Amiri Baraka. How were the editorial meetings?

DD Roi and I had gotten together as lovers about a year before we got together as editors. A.B. Spellman and I were going to do a magazine called *The Horse at the Window.* We had this whole stack of interesting manuscripts, and A.B., the first time he had to reject something, decided he couldn't be an editor because he couldn't reject anybody. So we had this whole stack of manuscripts, which I think he then gave to Roi, and then Roi approached me about the idea of a newsletter. At first, it was an every-two-week thing. Later, it got to be once a month, and very much later it got very big and came out only a few times a year. But when Roi and I did it the first year or so it was every two weeks.

We started out with the addresses in our two phone books. One hundred seventeen people got the first issue. It was always free. It always broke even. People would send contributions and things. Painters gave us money. Painters had lots of money in those days. In terms of the editorial meetings, there were a lot of ways that Roi and I saw eye to eye about literary stuff, and a lot of ways we didn't at all. There was a lot of hard-edge macho stuff that he loved a lot more than I, like early Dorn, and there was a kind of mystical work, like Robert Duncan's stuff and other work, that I liked more than he. But we just put both in. That gave the *Bear* its odd flavor. It was an amalgam of the two kinds of taste. We basically trusted each other's point of view or taste. I did the typing, everybody did the proofreading, and we would have collating parties. Roi did most of the correspondence and staying in touch with the writers.

After I married Alan, Roi resigned. For personal reasons, he said. I kept going with the *Bear* 'til '69. I had some guest editors. John Wieners edited one issue.

DM You say in '65 you went up to Millbrook, Timothy Leary's psychedelic community. Could you describe what that was like?

DD I visited it in '65; I lived there in '67. It was wonderful, amazingly wonderful. Tim had this idea that he wanted to gather a lot of very creative people in one place and give them all the acid they could possibly take and make sure they had no worries or responsibilities and see what happened.

I and my kids and Alan Marlowe had kind of a house. It was the upper floor of this place that was built like a Swiss chalet. The lower floor was a bowling alley, and the upper floor was meant to be a huge billiard room, and that's where we lived.

Tim's plan was that we were not supposed to want for anything, we weren't supposed to worry about anything. If there was anything we needed . . . I mean, if I had the vague idea or mentioned to someone that I might like to try watercolor painting, an elaborate watercolor paint set would show up on my desk by the next day. It was very unnerving, because I was used to struggling. Very hard to get used to not struggling. The place was set up with the basic rule, which I broke all the time, that you were supposed to trip once every five days. Nobody was supposed to go more than five days without tripping. Now this gets very boring after a while.

DM And exhausting.

DD And exhausting. So I would take my LSD and say thank you very much and stash it. It wasn't hard to act as if you were tripping. Nobody knew the difference. That was the main rule, but since everybody was tripping every five days, nothing ever was the same in the community two days in a row. We'd figure out how we were doing the meals. We'd figure it out again different the next day. I did the cooking there for the first month or two. Which was nice because I couldn't give up on taking care of business. Tim's group on the top floor ate meat and wanted lots of alcohol. Then an ashram moved in while I was there, and they wanted lots of milk and white bread and sugar, and then there were the macrobiotics. Jean McCreedy's children were crying because there was no Campbell's soup for them. You learned a lot. You also had incredible space.

There was a place called the Meditation House. I'm sure people have written about this. It was a one-room house, with windows all around. The sun came up on one side of the room and went down on the other side. We took turns being "the spiritual watch" for the place. You were there, doing solitary tripping for twenty-four hours, and the guard was changed in the evenings. We all came and meditated with the person who had been tripping, and then the next person moved in and took her post as watcher. Usually you were on watch for twenty-four hours, but once I did it for three or five days just before I left Millbrook. It was like indigenous American religion just beginning to grow. The nights as the trip came on . . . it was incredibly lovely and very deep. With the support of the whole place, unspoken around you, with ten square miles of property between you and whatever was trying to stop this whole thing from happening. There was a leather-bound blank book in the Meditation House. Everybody either left a drawing or a message or something from each trip. I wrote "Rant from a Cool Place" while I was there tripping. Later, I published it in *Revolutionary Letters*.

DM I'm interested in your long-term involvement with the hermetic and, then later, with Buddhism.

DD There was an involvement with the hermetic at Hunter. This often happens with adolescents, both girls and boys, if you let it. I and my writer friends, including Audre Lorde, would work with things like ESP and trance and trying to have séances. And then Buddhism. I read a lot of Eastern stuff from around 1960. Zimmer, *Philosophies of India*. I met Shunryu Suzuki Roshi in '62 when I was out on this coast with Alan Marlowe. Suzuki Roshi married us.

DM I remember.

DD I don't remember who was there. There were only twelve or so of us. Marilyn Rose was there, Kirby Doyle was there, you were there, Dee Dee Doyle was there. And a whole lot of Suzuki's wife's friends. Because it's so auspicious to have the place full for a wedding, they invited all these Japanese ladies.

I started sitting then. When I met Suzuki it felt like the first time in my life I had met somebody I could really trust. That was an interesting thing for a Brooklyn girl. And so I took home a cushion, got some basic instruction, and wrote Dick Baker once or twice a year to say this is what's happening. He would tell Roshi, and sometimes I'd get a message back. Whenever I was on the road and I was here, I would hitch to the Zen center and sit in the morning with them. Zen practice began in '62. I had been playing with stuff before that. I had been playing with *The Six Yogas of Naropa* from Garma C.C. Chang's book and stuff like that.

New Year's Eve '63 was when I took my first acid. What happened to me on that first acid trip was that a whole lot of stuff I'd been reading about became clear as day. About time and about emptiness—I could just see it. So that put things in a different light, as it were. Probably this is where the mysticism starts to come back into the poetry in a much more clear way. Although in '59 there was a peyote trip, and that's when the poems broke open to long lines like those in *The New Handbook of Heaven*. That book started after the peyote trip in '59 in my apartment on the Lower East Side. Jimmy also helped as a teacher of mine—James Waring. He said to follow precisely wherever the poem went—"the graph of the moving mind" (that's Philip Whalen's phrase), rather than this thing that I was doing earlier of cut, cut, cut, and make it sparse. I think I was doing that to learn certain techniques. This wasn't about technique now, it was about really following and being obedient to consciousness, as Robert Duncan liked to put it. That started in 1959.

DM You've been involved with Buddhism as well studying the Western hermetic tradition for twenty-five, thirty years.

DD Oh, easily. Easily. If you don't count the séances. It's about thirty-three years of Western studies. I would say around '66 I started really studying the Tarot.

DM Because of your earlier background in physics and math, did the alchemical material make more immediate sense?

DD Could be. And my anarchist grandfather used to run a pharmacy, even though he didn't a have a license—his son-in-law had the license. I remember hanging out with all those glass bottles of herbs and powders and scales. Grinding things for him. I started to work with the cards when I lived in New Mexico in '66. I'd just hang out with a card—I was using the Waite deck then—and fall asleep nearly every afternoon. And I'd have a dream about that card. It seemed very simple. It wasn't like I was trying. Within the next few years I got hold of the tool of the Tree of Life, as it's used in Western magic, then everything fell into place. That was '71.

DM Do you mean a combination of the various symbolic systems?

DD The using of the Tree as a way to synchronize the systems.

DM And is that compatible with Buddhism?

DD You know, in Vajrayana Buddhism there are two truths. There's absolute truth and relative truth. Absolute truth is emptiness, but it's luminous, creative, constantly moving and changing. But it's empty. Or we call it mind. Big Mind. It's the same thing. Relative truth is *kundzop*, which means costume. It's all the costumes of the empty, and they're seen as inseparable from the absolute. Throughout the world there are techniques of working with and sometimes, yes, even manipulating relative truth, as in Western magic. I have a Buddhist shrine room and also a Western magical shrine, which is a landing place (and launching pad) for all the elemental forces. But it's not a place where I meditate, in the Buddhist sense.

I had this same question for Suzuki Roshi one of the last times I saw him. I said exasperatedly, "I'm a poet. I want images, and here Zen is supposed to be empty!" He said, "Two sides of the same coin." He was telling me the same thing that I learned again in Vajrayana. He said: "You have image, you write. But when you do zazen it should be like going to sleep in your mother's arms."

DM When did you first meet Robert Duncan?

DD I met him at Michael McClure's in 1961. Michael invited Robert to meet me. Invited him over for breakfast. Robert was clearly not very interested in meeting me. And at one point, I was barely awake, I went over to the window and started brushing my hair, which was very, very long and very, very red. All of a sudden Robert looked up and said: "You have the most beautiful hair I've ever seen! Will you come to lunch?"

DM Could you tell me what you learned from him as a mentor?

DD It sounds odd, but I think Robert was probably one of the closest, most intimate lovers I ever had, even though we never had a physical relationship. I learned a lot of different kinds of things from him. One of the things I learned—in a way no teacher of Buddhism ever showed me—was how precious my life was. How precious the whole ambience of the time. A real sense of appreciating every minute. He used to come and do Christmas with us and eat hash brownies and talk. All Christmas morning. He would come up and stay with us in Marshall on Tomales Bay, and there was something about that—more than all the exchanges which were about hermeticism and one thing or another. Something about this ineffable quality of the time and the energy that was there—I can't describe it. He trapped me into a whole field of study. Remember that first year of the New College poetics program that we did? I was supposed to be chairwoman that year and tell everybody what they should teach—not that anybody ever managed to tell anybody what to do in that program. I said: "Robert, I think you should do a course that covers nonorthodox threads of thought in the West, maybe from the caves to the present. Give us some sense of continuity, how it all relates to one another, Gnosticism and the heresies and this and that." He said, "I think you're supposed to teach that, dear." I said, "Robert, I don't know anything about it." He said, "Well, that's why we teach, isn't it?" Of course, after I taught it for two years, everybody was on my neck. "You have to stop teaching that."

DM What was the New College of California poetics program all about in those days?

DD It was whatever Robert thought it was. He felt that it was time to make a model, as he probably said a million times to all of us, of what a curriculum in poetics—as opposed to one in writing poetry—would be and what it would constitute. Not that he thought we had to do it forever or push it through and make it happen, but that we had to make a *model* that would exist for future times. I think that was what mainly it was about. I took that as my permission when I and some friends, Sheppard Powell and Janet Carter and Carl Grundberg, started San Francisco Institute of Magical Healing Arts. Again it was Robert's idea of making a model of what would it be to teach Western hermeticism.

DM How does it feel to write an autobiography?

DD You know, I started that book because I wanted to write something for my daughters, especially about the stupid things I did because of myths I bought into about being a woman. But it just changed and grew. It feels like . . . deep diving. You don't know that you remember the thing you remember until you're writing it down, and then later you don't remember that you remembered it. It's been very helpful. Part of it is about what women do that they don't really have to, because they think they should. Part of it is an exploration of my Italian American roots, and a lot of it is the dance of being an artist with all these guys, and the problems of having kids on your own in the 1950s. It stops in '65 when I'm thirty-one years old.

DM Is there a second volume?

DD If I get around to it. I'm sixty-five, and at first I thought there's definitely going to be a volume two, but I don't know if I feel like doing that again. I'm not sure I'd do it with a big publisher. I hate working with New York. It's unpleasant. It's all about money and stardom, and the legal department wants a list of everybody in the book and little marks next to their names, are they alive or dead? I told them let's wait a while till everybody's dead, so then you don't have to have this list. But writing the book itself was great. It's an imagination of an autobiography.

DM We didn't talk about the sixties. . . .

DD There were two reasons to move out here: to study with Suzuki Roshi and to work with the Diggers. I came out in '67 with John Braden, who was a lover of Alan Marlowe's, to perform. We did poetry readings and music. He was a song person. And we stayed with Lenore Kandel. She was right in the thick of it. Lenore was wonderful as the woman on the scene, the matriarch, and she made it so clear that I was welcome; otherwise, it could have been very different.

Moving out to California was very much talked about during that trip. Peter Berg said, "You did the ground work, now come and enjoy the fruits." Fruits, I don't know about. I enjoyed something, but it was pretty chaotic. Yet I had always wanted to live out here ever since I first saw it. There was no place else I wanted to live.

We found a house on Oak Street. It was fourteen rooms at $300 a month, with an in-law apartment, a big yard, two-car garage. On Oak between Cole and Schrader. Built in 1914 or 1915. John Braden flew back out and found the house. We rented it immediately. And then we got all these people. A whole slew of grown-ups, some of them crazy, some with children. I had a VW van with rifles and electric typewriters. People decided that's what I needed, so at my going-away party they gave me rifles and electric typewriters. Alan Van Newkirk drove them all out, together with some of my kids.

Our new VW van was used by the Diggers for food pickup and delivery. Our house did two vegetable runs and a fish run every week, and delivered to twenty or twenty-five communes. That was our gig. I wrote lots of *Revolutionary Letters,* and they were going out through Liberation News Service to all the underground newspapers in the country. It was nice because I always had the feeling that I could believe this stuff but there was no way I could ever actually *do* anything, because it was McCarthy time and the FBI was chasing some of my friends because they were here without papers. Everything was like that in the '50s. Suddenly to be able to be out in public and do anything, delivering food, having be-ins—it just took a weight off your heart about having kept your mouth shut too long. So it was great. It was really great.

DM How long did that last?

DD We got out here in June of '68, and by the fall of '69 the FBI was at the door every day. People from the White Panthers were staying with me; they were wanted, of course. The Black Panthers were in and out of the house. . . . We really didn't know what the FBI was after, but there was somebody knocking on the door just about every day. So we went up to Black Bear Ranch. Elsa and Richard Marley invited us up. I forwarded all my mail to a dead-end post office box where nothing was traceable. Keith Lempe picked it up and readdressed the mail to "Lucy Fur" and sent it on in a plain envelope. We came back a year and a half later. The FBI was still coming to that house, which by then had passed through other hands and a series of other communes. They were still looking for us at that house.

DM What do you think led to all that?

DD Well, I think partly we were set up. We were naive as hell. We're still (as a generation) naive as hell or we wouldn't have let KPFA get into such a bad situation. That's been going on for years. We are heads-in-the-sand people. There were too many people with no survival skills at all who came to San Francisco and needed too much for the small number of people who had real vision and really wanted to do something. I think any time that anything interesting happens, heroin is dumped into the scene. Besides our being naive and besides the dope and besides the too many kids who didn't know how to take care of themselves, none of us knew how to deal with our own egos. There was a big revolutionary ego game. With those same egos and a sense of humor, maybe we could have made something work.

DM Well, if you had a sense of humor you wouldn't have those big egos.

DD I remember Ginsberg saying to Leslie Fiedler about Vietnam, "I, Allen Ginsberg—single-handed—will stop it!" It was that "single-handed," you know. We were crazy like that, but it was a good kind of crazy. And, of course, the women-and-men thing was impossible.

DM Do you want to discuss that further?

DD No, I think we've talked about it. It will be volume two of my book!

DM Isn't it interesting that in all these radical social movements from the turn of the century, the early twentieth century, the sixties, sex politics falls into that same kind of male-privilege model?

DD Still doing it right now, this minute. Many of the young artists, couples that I could name, they think they're being fair and equal, and yet the girl's still doing all the money work and housework as well as trying to do her art, and the guy goes up to the attic and just does his art. Still.

You need centuries of change. In the sixties it was a kind of mythologizing: the women had the babies and the men went out hunting. They got very mad at me at Black Bear because I moved up there with not one but two men. And the men chopped wood and carried water. They said those are women's jobs, you're not supposed to be doing that. They got Grant Fisher very upset because he wanted male approval so badly. I said if you don't do some work, you're leaving. So he was doubly upset. Poor guy! The other thing is we didn't and we don't know any history. We don't know what worked and didn't work.

DM What works, then? What can a poet do to reach the world?

DD It's important to self-publish and make your work available. Form small collectives. Start small. You have to remember, you don't have to think of going national. Each small city and its surrounding area is the size of a country from a long time ago. Handle it that way. If you can get books from here to L.A., that's good. Part of what we're hypnotized by from the media is that we have to hit millions of people at once. Back then 117 people got the first *Floating Bear*. And I sold 1,000 copies of my first book out of the stroller wheeling Jeanne around New York. They all went in less than a year. Two years later somebody came to me from one of the federal prisons and told me that twelve carbon copies of that first book had been typed in prison and passed around. Which to me was a bigger honor than any Pulitzer Prize.

William Everson
(Brother Antoninus)(1969)

© Jim Hair; courtesy New Directions Pub. Corp.

Fall 1969: Bill Everson hiked up the redwood canyon trail, crossing three footbridges in an ascent that passed a waterfall or two (if the rainy season was ample). Following behind him, like sherpas bearing foodstuffs and wine, were Robert and Dorothy Hawley. They entered our Mill Valley tree house. Victoria and Jack Shoemaker had arrived a little earlier. Everson, a tall man, lumbered into the living room: he was dressed in buckskin, and a necklace of what looked like animal teeth, beads, and feathers hung around his neck. His gray hair was long and wild, and he had a big full beard that made him look like a cross between Moses, John Brown, and Davey Crockett. He was eager to begin the interview and so, after a glass of wine, we began. The crackling fireplace was the main source of light, which sometimes created dramatic lighting effects when Everson would pause, intensely, to ruminate on his life and recent leaving of the Dominican priory where he'd lived as a lay brother for many years.—DM

William Everson (**WE**)
David Meltzer (**DM**)
Jack Shoemaker (**JS**)
Tina Meltzer (**TM**)

1

WE Leaving the order was more of an upheaval than a decision. That's one reason I'm still at sea. I just plunged out. I should have waited for the expiration of my temporary vows next October when I would either make final profession or leave legitimately.

The reasons I didn't are really personal ones and would take too long to lay bare. I've been too close to them to analyze them. I . . . Susanna . . . when the father of her child, you know, that off-again, on-again thing . . . when that wouldn't resolve, when they really couldn't find their way to make a life together, it kept throwing me back into the picture as a—as a what? Not an alternative, certainly. I was in her life before him. I think, really, that her bid for a marriage with him was an attempt to find an alternative to me. And when it didn't work out—even with the arrival of their baby, no marriage was forthcoming—I began to sense that my number was up. So I went to Europe last summer, really an attempt to get away, to change the focus so as to allow every opportunity for the other thing to prevail. Then I came back, and it hadn't and it didn't and it wasn't. In November I went on my regular eastern tour. By the end of that month I realized that what I was returning to was something permanent, that I could no longer delude myself that this was a transitional involvement. That did it. I moved then to make the break with the order. At my final reading at Davis in December I closed by pulling off my habit and leaving the stage. The price I must pay, of course, is that I am out of the sacraments.

JS That must have played some part in influencing your decision. You knew before, didn't you, that you would be out of the sacraments? Will you attempt to get some dispensation?

WE Yes. It seems we may be able to marry in the Church. At least, that's my hope.

DM You really haven't left the faith as much as the order?

WE That's right. I'm still a Catholic.

JS Why don't you bring us up to date by telling us a bit about your life prior to your initial conversion experiences? When you were William Everson, the printer. I guess that's what I heard about you first.

WE Well, actually, printing came late with me, although I was born in a print shop, so to speak. Being the son of a printer, I experienced the atmospherics of it very early. But what with the powerful presence of the father, and being in one of the basic Oedipal situations . . . man, I got out of there fast! So it wasn't until after I became a poet that I began to recognize my lost opportunities. But the printing really didn't develop until Waldport. We needed a press badly up there and when we got one I began to print in earnest.

DM Waldport . . . the CO [conscientious objector] camp?

WE Yes.

JS Did you go there out of high school?

WE No, no. I was thirty years old. High school was the Depression. I graduated in 1931, down in the San Joaquin Valley. Then I tried a semester at Fresno State and dropped out and went back home. My only work was summer work at the Libby McNeil cannery, as a syrup maker, with idleness in the winters, pretty much trying to find myself. In 1933 I entered the CCC [Civilian Conservation Corps], and a year later left that to go back to Fresno State. This time I encountered the work of Robinson Jeffers and at last came to terms with myself as a poet.

DM Were you writing then?

WE I only began to write in earnest after I found Jeffers. Before that, it could have been music or art or literature. I was trying all three. But when I encountered Jeffers suddenly everything coalesced. I found my voice, began to speak in my own right. I left college to go back to the land, to get married, and plant a vineyard. I put my roots down and was making a life of it. But the war pulled me out of that. And it was the war that really forced me to shape up. I don't know how else to put it. Being uprooted was a crushing blow, but it proved to be the breakover point I needed. In retrospect, I can see that I had to get out of the Valley. But I couldn't see it then.

JS And you were arrested and tried?

WE No, my claim for conscientious objector status was accepted. I went right into the camp as part of the regular CPS quota. Civilian Public Service, that was the euphemism.

JS So you were called to alternative service?

WE They sent me there. I didn't choose it. They sent me there.

DM I guess that really was the only legitimate alternative to military service?

WE No, there was what was called Detached Service, work in hospitals and on dairy farms. I didn't opt for that. Actually, there were three alternatives. One was lAO in the military service, noncombatant. This is the one the government wanted us to do, made every effort to get COs to accept.

DM You mean medic . . . ?

WE Yes. Then there was Detached Service, work at specified mental hospitals and dairy farms. And finally there were the camps, work with the Forest Service.

JS And that was what Waldport was?

WE Yes.

DM You were kept there in a restricted kind of environment?

WE There weren't any guards or barbed wire, but if you left, the FBI was after you. When you were caught you went to prison. Mussolini did the same thing with political dissidents before the war—sent them to work camps in the mountains and, if they left, clapped them in prisons. The comparison is only approximate because ours was a true alternative to combat duty. But the injustice lay in the fact that there was no pay. Under the Emancipation Proclamation, involuntary servitude is outlawed. No citizen can be made to work without pay except as punishment for a crime. The draft did call for equal pay with the armed forces, but Roosevelt feared a pacifist resistance movement and saw to it that Congress never appropriated the money. And it never has.

DM Weren't there several other artists and writers there?

WE Actually, a good deal of what later happened in the San Francisco scene had its origin right there in Waldport. The Interplayers began there. Adrian Wilson, one of our ablest printers, got his start there. James Harmon, who later edited *The Ark,* was there.

I never think of Harmon without recalling an episode that is still, as they say, etched on my memory: the encounter with Dreiser. It was on my first furlough, the furlough of 1943. Harmon and I got leave to go down to San Francisco. We took the coast stage south to Marshfield where we had to lay over in order to pick up the Portland bus southbound for San Francisco the next morning.

As we boarded the bus in Marshfield I noticed a man who seemed familiar. I said to myself, "That man looks like Theodore Dreiser." Harmon said it couldn't be, but Jeffers had spoken of Dreiser as a "tough old mastodon," and that's just the way this character looked. Hulking shoulders. Slack jaws. Strangely inattentive eyes that missed nothing. Even in his photographs his configuration was unmistakable.

During the war the bus travel was simply awful. In order to save rubber the law held their schedule down to thirty-five miles an hour, but the drivers went like hell between stops and waited at the next depot for time to catch up. So we had plenty of opportunity to look each other over.

At Gold Beach, Oregon, we pulled in for lunch. By this time I was sure it was Dreiser. As Harmon and I got ready to sit down, Harmon forgot about lunch and followed the man into the lavatory. He came right out as if he'd really found gold on that beach. "It's him!" he exclaimed excitedly. "Its Dreiser, all right. Come on!"

Even as I got up I had my misgivings, but curiosity got the better of judgment. Dreiser was standing at the urinal relieving himself, and not knowing what else to do I began to talk. I had never read any of his books, so I began with us. It was a fatal mistake.

"Mr. Dreiser," I began, "we're two poets on furlough from a camp in Waldport. We are going down to San Francisco. We hope to meet some of the other writers there and renew our acquaintance with the literary scene. . . ."

Dreiser looked at me, and I suddenly discovered I had nothing more to say. He slowly buttoned his fly, and as he turned to wash his hands, he said two words with extreme irony: "So what!"

Then he started in. Ripping a paper towel from the rack, he crumbled it in those fearsome hands and proceeded with contempt. "There are thousands of you. You crawl about the country from conference to literary conference. You claim to be writers, but what do you ever produce? Not one of you will amount to a goddamn. You have only the itch to write, nothing more . . . the insatiable itch to express yourself. Everywhere I go I run into you, and I'm sick of you. The world is being torn apart in agony, crying out for truth, the terrible truth. And you. . . . " He paused and his voice seemed to suddenly grow weary. "You have nothing to say."

I turned to go. Harmon was already gone. Opening the door into the restaurant, I looked back to let him know how sorry I was that I had accosted him, but I couldn't open my mouth. Then Dreiser stepped past me, as if I had opened the door only for him. For a moment the contempt seemed to fade from his face and a kind of geniality gleamed there. "Well," he said, "take it easy. It lasts longer that way." Then he was gone.

Not really gone. His seat was ahead of ours, and we had already noticed that he was traveling with a young woman. After Gold Beach, aware of our presence behind him, he kept stiffly aloof, conversing with her circumspectly. But far down the coast, at the end of the long hot afternoon, when everyone was collapsed with fatigue, she could stand it no longer. Reaching out her hand she stroked with tender fondness the balding head. Dazed with exhaustion, he accepted it gratefully until he remembered us. Suddenly thrashing his head like a mastodon caught red-handed in a pterodactyl's nest, he flung the hand from him. She never tried that again.

DM Fantastic. . . . But getting back to Waldport, how did so many artists happen to arrive there?

WE The setup was like this. In 1940 when France fell, the draft was instituted here, although the country had no expectation of going to war. The law allowed for conscientious objection based on religious conviction, categorically defined as membership in one of the "three historic peace churches." Actually, individual draft boards applied it more broadly.

In order to avoid the merciless treatment of COs in World War I (and cummings' poem, "I Sing of Olaf," gives us a glimpse of that), the peace churches stepped in and proposed an alternative along the lines of the CCC, which was still in operation, and which provided a good model to follow. In the CCC operation the army reserves ran the camp program, and the Forest Service ran the work program. What the peace churches proposed was that, if they could run the camp program, in place of the army reserves, they would pay for maintenance out of their own pocket. And this is what the government accepted. But it meant we had to go into a religiously oriented camp, and many of us didn't like that because we were not orthodox Christians.

So we arrived at these camps under the authority of some church group—either the Quakers or the Mennonites or the so-called Brethren, historically the Dunkers. The Quakers were the most favored by nonconformists because they were the most liberal. The Mennonites were the most disliked because they were the most conservative. The Brethren camps were ranked somewhere in between, and that's what I found myself in at Waldport.

The churches early began setting up special schools in certain camps so that men interested in a given project could transfer there and participate in that activity. The government didn't object so long as the work program wasn't affected. Before Waldport, the special schools were for such studies as Cooperative Management, Pacifist Philosophy, etc. At Waldport we proposed an arts project and were accepted. On the basis of this we began to attract artists from camps all over the country. That is, until the Forest Service Director put the kibosh on it when he saw that most of them were goldbrickers as far as his work project was concerned. But by that time, we had our nucleus.

DM You established a press there?

WE Yes, the Untide Press. Actually, before it was over three publications were coming out of Waldport. The *Illiterati* came to us from Cascade Locks in Oregon, and *Compass* magazine came to us from Maryland. Each kept its editorial distinctness.

DM Did you do a lot of printing for the Untide Press?

WE Yes. Our big problem was, of course, the presswork. Eventually, we received by transfer a real printer, a pressman, from Michigan. He had no love for the arts program (an incredible suspicion and hostility to these special schools prevailed among the camps generally, a real anti-intellectualist bias), but Kalal helped us. I pumped him for everything he knew about presswork, and he knew plenty.

JS Did they allow you to do presswork instead of project work?
WE No, this was work done after hours.
JS You would work a full day and then go and do presswork?
WE That's right. Nine hours of project work each day and then to the press to work in the evenings
DM *These Are the Ravens* is your first book. Was it published at the camp?
WE Much earlier. It was printed over in San Leandro in 1935. There was a vanity publisher there, Hans A. Hoffman, who had a little mag called *Westward*. He printed conventional middle-class poetry. Ladies with three names, that sort of thing. But he accepted some of my open-form poems, and I was jubilant, my first magazine publication off campus. When he announced a pamphlet series, I wrote to him about it. The uniform format called for an edition of 1,000 copies to sell for 10 cents each. The author paid $30 for the job. The publisher kept half the edition to sell, paying the author ½ cent per copy sold. The author kept the other 500 copies to sell for himself. Thirty dollars was a lot of money in 1935, but I was making syrup at a cannery in Sunnyvale that summer, and I swung it.
DM How long were you interned at Waldport?
WE Three-and-one-half years.
DM When you left Waldport, where did you go?
WE Right back here to San Francisco because of Rexroth. You see, when the war was over and they began to demobilize, they could have closed the entire system of CO camps right off. But because of their notions of equity and the political instinct to prevent the complaints of re-turning GIs that we got first crack at the jobs, the government made us wait until they could demobilize those thirteen million fighting men. We found ourselves waiting interminably. VJ day was in August of 1945, and I was not released until late in July 1946, and I wasn't the last by any means. And the only reason we were kept that long was so that we would not be released ahead of the men who were inducted at the same time as we were.
DM When did you first come in contact with Rexroth?
WE Let's say about 1944. I got a letter from him when I was in camp. Somebody had sent him one of my CO pamphlets, *The Waldport Poems*

or *War Elegies,* I don't remember which. On my next furlough (we got furloughs on the same basis as the soldiers), I came down to San Francisco to meet him, and his presence here was the real reason I returned after the war. Not only was he the acknowledged leader of the new literary ferment, but as soon as I read his new poems, *The Phoenix and the Tortoise,* I took him to be the best poet of his generation. I've never really doubted that. It was a tough generation to be born into, because following the brilliant coterie of writers born in the nineties—the Hart Crane generation—those born in the first decade of this century couldn't sustain that kind of esprit de corps, and the baton went to England: the Auden-Spender generation. But of the Americans, Rexroth remains the best. Better than Eberhardt, who has won all the awards. Better than Kunitz, the supertechnician. Better even than Roethke, who is, of course, the ranking poet of that generation.

Both Roethke and Rexroth were born in the Midwest, but whereas Rexroth came west, Roethke went east. It was fatal for him. He could have been—ought to have been—the Theodore Dreiser of American poetry, but he opted instead for prestige and technical proficiency. The prestige he got, but the proficiency remained very limited, actually. He constantly celebrated rapture but could never let go. He mastered certain forms, and these are impressive, but his open-form experiments of the later years were not. In contradistinction, the open form of Rexroth is brilliant and vivid, his sense of the earth is immediate and pungent. Gary Snyder, for instance, the best earth man now writing, stands squarely on Rexroth's shoulders. Rexroth is more uneven than Roethke, granted, but that's because he risks more, attempts more. Though in the modernist tradition, actually his classical sense is far more haunting and evocative than Roethke's doctrinaire aesthetic classicism. His masterpiece is the title poem of *The Phoenix and the Tortoise,* in my view the best poem of World War II. Unless Lowell's "Quaker Graveyard" is really that. I've long wanted to do a piece on Kenneth, but his erudition is overwhelming. I'm not capable of coming to terms with it. Anyway, it was his presence here in San Francisco that drew me when the camps finally closed.

Of course, there was the fact that my wife was here. But we were so estranged by that time, it was hopeless. Sometimes she came up to

Waldport, but we were never able to straighten it out. She fell in love with a young friend of mine even before she left the Valley for San Francisco. That affair went on all through my time in camp, and it was this that I couldn't abide. "Chronicle of Division" in *The Residual Years* spells it out. So by war's end there really wasn't much hope of salvaging the marriage. When I look back on it, I think we could have resumed our life together, but I was sensitive and proud and very, very hurt. I'm certain now that she was ready to take up the relationship again, but I was just too proud, just too hurt.

JS Did you go back to cannery work?

WE No, I came down here and joined a group on a farm outside of Sebastopol. We were going to make a life on the land together—the commune idea that's so fetching now with the hippies. Rexroth was going to join us. I actually moved my hand press there and installed it in an old apple dryer, but I met Mary Fabilli, and as soon as I met her I fell in love with her. I left the farm and followed her back to Berkeley. The poems in the third section of *The Residual Years* are all the product of this change. In Berkeley I got a job as the janitor at the University of California and then moved the press back and began to print my poems.

DM Were you a Catholic at that time?

WE Lord, no. I was anti-Catholic. It was Mary who converted me. She was fallen away herself but had already begun the painful process of struggling back. You might say I was her last fling!

DM Did she actively try to convert you?

WE God, yes! Mary dominated the relationship to the end. She's a powerful personality, and I was confused, lost within myself, and really looking for anchorage. It was her strong hand, no doubt about it, that drew me into the Church.

On the other hand, in my own defense, I'm not saying that a masterful woman simply got me by the nose and pulled me into this monolithic religion. I was really looking for what the Church is, though I didn't know it. I didn't know I needed the sacramental life. She brought me that, and I've never regretted it.

DM The ritual, the structure. . . .

WE Yes. If you are a religious man without a religion, you're in trouble.

Mary gave me that religion, the vocabulary, the conceptual background. And also the faith, the belief. It was really the great turning point in my life.

DM Do you think that initially it was a philosophical conversion and later an emotional one?

WE No. The other way around. It's possible that I sensed a whole new field of engagement remaining untried even as I met her. Certainly my pantheism had reached its term. In the breakup of my first marriage I would cry out to God, and there just wasn't any answer coming back. Pantheism is really a great concept, but there's not much help from it when your life needs help most. It just isn't personal enough to meet the absolute demand of the spirit.

JS In conversion, you generally think of the mind leading or the heart. . . .

WE Well, this was a conversion of the heart, but with the mind running like crazy to catch up. I went into the order to enable the mind to catch up with where the heart was.

DM Then you and Mary split?

WE Not just to enter the order, I would never have done that. But before I could be baptized, we had to separate because of the validity of my first marriage. And, of course, her first marriage was valid, too. She married Grif Borjesen in the Church, even though she was no longer a committed Catholic. In order to satisfy her parents. Which is foolish. But that's the way born Catholics do.

JS So you couldn't get special permission to . . . ?

WE The norms then were so tight, so legalistic. To get an annulment you had to produce legal evidence of coercion or of nonbelief. Apparently, the Church is more willing to take your word for it now.

JS You were both struggling Catholics, and yet they wouldn't allow you the sacrament?

WE Not as long as we stayed together. We tried to get permission to live "as brother and sister," as it's called, cohabitation without sexual intercourse. But they said we were too young. And we were. They were right! [*laughter*]

DM After all this trouble, what did you and Mary decide?

WE It wasn't a matter of having to agree to enter an order or anything like that. We just had to separate to receive the sacraments. Once we were not living together, she was free to reenter the sacraments and I was free to get baptized, which I did. I stayed on in Mary's house because my press was there. She was most generous about that, renting another room for herself and letting me stay on alone there. And as luck or grace would have it, my Guggenheim came through at that moment. Boy, that was a beautiful year, in spite of the pain of another separation. I worked that Guggenheim year! I was printing and binding and writing like crazy, just like crazy! Nineteen forty-nine. Twenty years ago! Oh, man!

So I didn't travel on my Guggenheim, which actually I should have done, from the point of view of tactics. New Directions had published *The Residual Years* the year before, and if I'd used my Guggenheim to go east and stump the campuses, that book would have sold. But I hung right in there and wrote. I wrote so much some of it is still unpublished.

I bound *The Privacy of Speech* that summer, and in the fall was getting ready to print *In the Fictive Wish,* but my need for a more structured religious life was beginning to assert itself, and instead I began to search for an order.

I couldn't find one to meet my needs. The Dominicans were there, but I never approached them. They didn't seem reclusive enough for me. I talked to the Benedictines and the Franciscans. I didn't go to the Trappists because Merton was there, and his *Seven Storey Mountain* had made that route a bit too faddish at that time. Besides, their entrance requirements were strict, and with the impediment of a marriage in my background, I stood little chance of acceptance. So I talked to the Benedictines and the Franciscans, but neither would satisfy me as to my own creative needs. I would ask, "What about my literary career? What about my capacity as a poet, my talents as a poet?" Each one told me that I would have to put that matter aside on entering. If in the decision of my superiors those talents were useful, well and good, but I could claim no mandate. Well, I could understand but couldn't accept it for myself. I knew the necessity to write was too deeply founded in me to renounce.

When my Guggenheim year came to a close in the spring of 1951, I applied for an extension, which was denied. I didn't want to go back to my job. Instead, I ended up in a Catholic Worker House of Hospitality down on Skid Row in Oakland helping indigent men. But the real event there was meeting an ex-Trappist monk who taught me how to pray. He watched me for a week or so and finally approached me and said, "You aren't praying enough." "Why," I protested, "I pray three rosaries a day!" He said, "Three rosaries a day. That's nothing. That's chicken feed!" [*laughter*] So he said, "You follow me. You pray ten rosaries a day for ten days, and I'll guarantee you results!" [*laughter*]

So I began to pray those ten rosaries a day. I did. I really began to bear down on those beads. Ten rosaries a day is a lot of prayer. But by golly, before those ten days were up we were praying fifteen and twenty rosaries a day. That's around eight solid hours of prayer. [*laughter*] I took it on because I had read of the "Jesus Prayer" of the Russian pilgrims, repeating the holy name hour after hour as they walked. I mean, we would walk around Skid Row jumbling those beads like a couple of idiots. I'd say "Hail Mary full of grace . . . " and he'd be right behind me with "Holy Mary Mother of God!" [*laughter*] The winos thought we had gone out of our heads.

Well, on the tenth day we went to mass that morning, and I was almost sick with fatigue. But right out of the tabernacle came a bolt from the blue. I'm telling you it was my first great mystical experience, and the primary one. It hit me right in the heart like a sledgehammer. I went down like a poleaxed ox. I dropped in my pew, and the tears poured down my face. It was so great, so beautiful. From that point on I knew. Up to then I had been searching, but from that point on I knew. And I still do. After twenty years nothing can erase the awful reality, the terrible truth of that experience.

Well, to get on with the story. On the strength of this experience, the parish priest sent me to a Dominican. "This stuff," he said, "is too strong for me!" [*laughter*] He never cottoned to all those rosaries in the first place.

The Dominican listened carefully and asked me a few questions. They were the right questions. When I answered as best I could, he nodded his head and said, "Yes, that's real. That's true." After a few months' work with him, I began to read Dominican books. From them and from what I sensed in that Dominican priest, it began to dawn on me that maybe the Dominicans were where I belonged. But there still remained the problem of the literary career and the poetic faculty.

He was dubious about my being a Dominican. I seemed too far out to fit into the local community, at least. But he sent me to another priest, a theologian. When I asked him the telltale question about the talents, he never batted an eye. "Of course, you will develop your faculties," he said. "Saint Thomas insists that the talents are God-given. I once had a superior who claimed that if the order accepted a man with a fine tenor voice, it was obligated to develop it, even if it had to build him a soundproof room!" I stared at him in disbelief and exclaimed, "Let me in!" [*laughter*]

2

WE The thrust toward hand-press printing really began at Waldport when I found that even with Kalal's help I couldn't perfect the printing process. I wasn't enough of a mechanic. The mechanical press is a true machine, and I am not adept enough with machinery to produce the work I desired.

I remember reading somewhere that the printing device par excellence is the hand press, that the greatest books of modern times have been produced on it—the Kelmscott Press Chaucer, the Dove Press Bible, and the Ashenene Press Dante. Then, too, I knew of Eric Gill's work because my first wife was a sculptor, and among her collection she had Gill's books. Of these the most impressive was the *Autobiography*. I read there of the relation of printing to life, of a craft lived as a poetic vocation is lived.

When I came down to San Francisco on that furlough of 1944, I found a giant hand press in a printing equipment shop, a fantastic press. I cashed in an insurance policy to buy it and persuaded the shop owner to keep it for me till I could get released. Then I hauled it to Sebastopol and, as I said, back to Berkeley. I had me a press, but I had no idea how to make it work. That was something I had to learn from old printers' manuals.

Janitoring at the University of California, I had access to a great typographical library, Sam Farquhar's library. I'd get my work done early and go up there and immerse myself in that library. The night shift was good for me, because it allowed me to get up in the morning fresh and plunge into either printing or writing. My janitor's shift ran from 4:00 p.m. until midnight. That's the way I worked until the Guggenheim came through.

DM Did you carry the same press along with you when you went into the order?

WE Yes. First I moved it down to Skid Row, though. My Dominican guide insisted I had to resume my craft, that I couldn't go on driving myself nuts with all that prayer. When I entered the order in 1951 I moved the press to Saint Albert's and began to print the *Psalter*.

JS The *Psalter* is the major project?

WE Yes.

DM Did you translate the *Psalter* as well as print it?

WE Oh, no. I used the *Novum Psalterium PII XII*. It was the first approved version of the psalms in 1,500 years and seemed like a great opportunity for a printer.

JS It's a beautiful piece of work. How many copies did you do?

WE I think forty-eight were bound. I tried for fifty.

DM You didn't bind them yourself?

WE No. I meant to. But when I abandoned it to try for the priesthood, I sent the sheets to Dawson's Bookshop in Los Angeles, who passed them on to Mrs. Estelle Doheny, the great collector. She sent them to the Lakeside Bindery in Chicago to be bound. Some people say she must have paid $75 a copy to have them done.

DM So you abandoned the project to go into the priesthood?

WE Yes.

DM Were you finished with printing?

WE No.

JS So the bound *Psalter* is just a third of it?

WE Right.

DM What occurred when you decided to go into the priesthood?

WE Well, when the novitiate period began in the fall of 1954, I went over to Kentfield and began the life of a clerical novice. This lasted six months. I blew up and went back to Saint Albert's in Oakland.

DM When you say "blowing up," does that mean you couldn't endure within the structure?

WE I couldn't maintain the regimen.

DM What was it about the priesthood that you weren't able to contain within yourself?

WE The emphasis on formal study. It was really the same reason I dropped out of college to become a poet. I couldn't master the formal intellectual application. The monastic life was the same. But for my writing and printing I now had to substitute study. Sheer unadulterated study. My psyche couldn't tolerate it after a while.

JS How long was the proposed course of study?

WE Seven years.

DM During this period had you kept in contact with poets in the Bay Area?

WE No. Rexroth and I had split. We had a falling out back in 1948, before I entered the Church. When I entered the order, we were still out of communication.

DM Were you in contact with any of the poets you knew earlier at Berkeley and at Waldport?

WE Not during this period.

DM When did you first meet Robert Duncan?

WE I met Duncan way back before I went to camp. There was a magazine in Woodstock, New York, called the *Phoenix,* devoted to the memory of D.H. Lawrence. It was my interest in Lawrence that led me to send a contribution there. Duncan was in Woodstock with Sanders Russell beginning another magazine, the *Experimental Review,* and he saw my contribution and wrote to me. I responded, and when Duncan returned to California, he came down the Valley and dropped in for a visit with Edna and me on the farm. This was when I still had the land.

DM He came on to settle in Berkeley?

WE Yes, he studied at Cal.

JS Did you know Mary Fabilli?

WE He did but I didn't. He introduced me to Mary Fabilli's painting before I ever met her. I bought a drawing of hers, and I had it on my wall long before I ever knew her.

DM She designed his first book, *Heavenly City, Earthly City.*

WE Mary did the illustrations for it. But that was after I was with her. We were in our most intensely sexual period, and that's why her rendition of Apollo in the cover illustration turned out to be so nakedly strong.

DM What were the aspects of D.H. Lawrence's work that attracted you?

WE The affinity to nature and the celebration of sex as the central archetype of the natural. The first great impact in my creative life was Jeffers, the celebration of nature as divine, the divine made concrete, a kind of agonization of divinity in the concreteness of natural forms, what I would rather recognize as incarnation. Then in 1937 someone, some friend, smuggled into the country a copy of *Lady Chatterley's Lover*. Lawrence delivered sexuality from the torment of Jeffers and sang of it in its joy. With this book I adopted him as my number two formative master. Both the Jeffers and Lawrence interests led me to Lawrence Clark Powell, and through Powell I encountered Henry Miller. All this before the war.

Powell told Miller about me, and he came up the Valley from Los Angeles with Gilbert Neiman and stayed at our house overnight. Edna and I had read all his books before we met him. They were quite unknown in this country except by hearsay. Powell had lent us his copies, until a Trotskyite seaman in Fresno named Carl smuggled in pirated editions from Hong Kong. As a revolutionary, Carl repudiated my pacifist stand, but the poor devil was torpedoed in the Caribbean by a German U-boat and never seen again. I remember how impressed he was with the purity of Chinese whores. When they ganged up on you in port you could scatter them just by saying, "Suckee! Suckee!" But the first pirated edition of *Black Spring* that Miller ever saw was a copy Carl got for me.

DM Was Miller's work influential?

WE Not in any stylistical way. What Miller taught me was . . . how shall I put it? Not just the desirability, but the *necessity* of going for broke. And not just in the aesthetic sense.

With both Jeffers and Lawrence there was always the primacy of the aesthetic. Traditional literary values were used to orient the mind into violational areas, sexual explicitness subsumed in the aesthetic intuition. Miller taught me the truth of going for broke even without the blessing of the aesthetic. Just the raw force of language humping you through, that pre-aesthetic draft into the unconscious, the sexual surcharge lifted out of the pornographic, not by aesthetics as other writers had done, but by the naked energy invested in language itself. That alone. I never attempted it for myself, but at last I began to realize what was possible. With those three masters behind me, I was set up for the work I had to do.

JS You met Lawrence Clark Powell through your interest in Jeffers or your interest in printing?

WE The Jeffers interest, before the printing. I read Powell's book on Jeffers, then a mutual friend sent him my poems, and we began to correspond. . . . But our relation was one of sharing inner thoughts rather than of stylistic influence or derivation either way. We corresponded monumentally.

DM It's interesting that Miller wrestled with Lawrence's work and tried to write a book on him and failed, whereas Anaïs Nin, who figures importantly in Miller's formative time in Paris, wrote an excellent study on Lawrence.

WE I never read that.

DM She perceives Lawrence and his work as a woman, and it is the feminine responsiveness to it that makes her book so valuable.

WE I met Anaïs Nin and felt very attracted to her—a beautiful woman. Did you know that Duncan was once her secretary? They quarreled, however. When I met her she was so furious with Robert she wouldn't speak to him.

Duncan was often difficult in those days. He is mellower now; success has made him more secure. But when he wanted to, he could be a real son of a bitch. (I say this affectionately.) But he was so childlike, so childish, that you just had to make allowances for him and accept his friendship for what it was. When he became insecure in a group he would try to overcome it by talking above his head. Voice raised. Eyes dilated. He would expatiate in the most astonishing way. Often he was brilliant, but other times he would soon have hardly any friends left in the room. But I always admired him as a comrade and friend, and I always believed in him as a poet. Because he is a lovable person.

JS Were you seeing him and having literary contacts outside the monastery?

WE No. I wasn't seeing Duncan at all. He'd gone on to Black Mountain, I think, following Olson there. I met Charles Olson in 1947. He came out here to the West Coast with his first wife. I believe *Call Me Ishmael* was just out. He was looking for another project and was going to the Sierras to check out the area where the Donner party starved to death. But it didn't turn out. His wife went back east, and he stayed out here for a winter.

There's a story regarding Olson and me. He came to our house one night and waited for me to come back from my swing-shift janitor job. Charles chucklingly recalls that in the middle of the night, when I finally got home, I had to take my wife upstairs first thing and get laid before I could come back down and be sociable.

Well, in the first place I simply wouldn't be capable of that. What really happened was he arrived hoping for a spot for the night, and Mary Fabilli was quite uptight with him. He's an enormous man, you know, a whale of a man, and they sat there eyeing one another. He's a lapsed Catholic, and Mary was already gung-ho about Catholicism, struggling back to the faith, and all. I don't know what he said that got her going. But anyway, when I arrived home she was upset. And her Maybeck house doesn't have any privacy, really. The whole lower floor is built so you can hear everything in every room. So Mary gave me the high sign and led me upstairs to the bedroom. "Get him out of here," she told me. "I can't stand the man!" It was by then one o'clock in the morning, and I knew Charles had no place to go, but I had to tell him that I was sorry. Women are like that. Bleeding hearts over a wounded bird, but with their husband's cronies they can be flint. Poor Charles shambled off into the night. But I wouldn't be capable of making out, like he thinks I did, not with a friend waiting downstairs.

DM Did you have any contact with Patchen during that time?

WE We did a book of his with Untide at Waldport during the war. *An Astonished Eye Looks Out of the Air,* his antiwar poetry. We had difficulties, the relationship broke, and I never had much to do with him after that. It wasn't until 1960 or so that I met him in Seattle, and we were friendly, I'm glad to say

Duncan had warned me that Kenneth Patchen is the poet little presses fold on. You begin with having a Patchen book as a wonderful prospect. The next thing you know he's breathing down your collar. And suddenly he's reaching over your shoulder. It's impossible.

Jack Stauffacher once started a book with Patchen. Jack is a meticulous printer and likes to proceed at a reflective pace. He thought he had an understanding with a genial poet that would make an interesting project to do. But he hadn't got on very far with it when the door would open and this figure would be standing there with accusing eyes. "How are you coming with my book . . . ?"

But I do believe in Patchen's witness. I don't cotton to his poetry the way I do that of Rexroth and Duncan. But I do believe in his witness.

3

DM You were one of the first poets I heard when I came to San Francisco. They were having an arts festival in North Beach, and there were readings at Fugazi Hall during the day. You were reading with some other poets, and I remember you had a black suit on. The hall was relatively empty, and we were all sitting on wooden benches. I remember I was listening for the sound of what poetry should be. And I remember the impact and power of your reading, even though, at that time, I had never heard of you.

I remember I came to San Francisco to seek my poetic identity and found a lot of people just sitting around. Not the archetype, but the stereotype media created in multitudes. What did emerge at that time was the rise of poetry into more of a public art . . . the poet as spokesman, the poet as conscience, as well as the poet as entertainer.

WE Exactly. That's why I always identified with the Beat Generation—the point you're making just now. I'd never let any kind of negative aura around the Beat image deter me from the primacy of that fact. It put poetry back on the platform. We had been trying for a whole decade to get something like the Beat Generation going. We tried it back in the late forties with Rexroth, and were successful enough to get attacked in *Harper's*, as "The New Cult of Sex and Anarchy." But the nation as a whole wasn't ready for it, what with the postwar preoccupation and the Cold War freeze. It took Korea and the second Eisenhower administration to make the country ready. It took the man in the gray flannel suit as the national image and the crew cut as the prevailing college mode. The tranquilized fifties. I remember that *Life* magazine titled its big feature on the Beats "The Only Rebellion Around," almost begging for dissent. Now they've got their belly full of it.

As I say, out here in San Francisco we were ready for it long before the rest of the country, but we couldn't have pulled it off alone. It took something outside ourselves, something from the East Coast to make a true *conjuntio oppositorium,* a conjunction of the opposites. As it turned out, Allen Ginsberg and Jack Kerouac provided the ingredients. They came to San Francisco and found themselves, and it was *their* finding that sparked us. Without them, it would never have happened.

DM What made you emerge from seven years of a rather closely regimented monastic life?

WE I was called out, really. The Beat Generation broke with the second issue of the *Evergreen Review,* the feature that announced the San Francisco Renaissance. Our poems were there, but more importantly our photographs were there. Harry Redl's portfolio of portraits was added to that issue almost as an afterthought, but in my opinion it made the issue. It's astonishing how a photographer's point of view can give to a group a collective identity it doesn't actually possess. I'd never even met Ginsberg or Kerouac, but under Redl's somber lens we all looked like brothers. Soon requests for readings began to come in. My superiors would evaluate each one on its own merits, then give me the permission to take it. And actually it wasn't the readings that got me in trouble, it was the interviews.

JS How was that?

WE Well, the image of a Roman Catholic religious poet as an exponent of the Beat Generation was sensational enough to attract the press. It was this image more than anything I actually said that set the hierarchy's teeth on edge. After the *Time* feature on me in 1959, the archbishop lowered the boom. I'll never forget him. John J. Mitty, Archbishop of San Francisco. His clergy didn't call him "Cactus Jack" for nothing.

DM You mean he silenced you?

WE He tried to. He silenced me locally and tried to silence me nationally. My superiors had to go along with his wishes as far as his own diocese was concerned, and they began to be more choosy about where I could read. They made me stop giving interviews to the press. And they denied me the use of the religious habit on platform. Lord, I suffered during this period. I thought they should stand up and fight him, but they said they couldn't possibly win on an issue like that. I submitted. Within a couple of years he was dead, and the ban was lifted. I saw his death as divine retribution. [*laughter*] But I had a beautiful Mexican friend named Rose who saw it otherwise. Unshakably loyal to both the charismatic and institutional aspects of the Church, she declared: "This lifting of the ban proves that his grace is already in heaven and moving to correct the natural mistakes of his episcopate!" [*laughter*] Meantime, we had a new provincial, also. The ban was lifted, and I was back on platform, interviews, religious habit, and all.

DM It must have been unusual to leave that closed life and find yourself on the platform with people you hadn't seen for seven years.

WE In the beginning all I could do was just get up there and lose myself in the voice, let the voice itself carry me through. That's what you heard in Fugazi Hall.

JS How did this influence your poetry? Did it happen to occur at a time when you needed something?

WE Well, the poetry had dried up, all right, but that was in the novitiate studying for the priesthood. *The Crooked Lines of God* was finished there in 1954, and I didn't write again until 1957. It was the crystallized monastic ego that dried the poetry out of me. Heap big monk. I had no way through until the summer of 1956 when I underwent a real psychic break, a real invasion of the unconscious. This took me into depth psychology. Out of this inner break, almost as a lifesaving thing, the poetry began to flow.

JS What do you mean by depth psychology?

WE Jung. I began to study Jung. I took up the analysis of dreams. The years between 1956 and 1960 were spent primarily on dream analysis. At the same time, I was writing *The Hazards of Holiness*. But the main force of my thought was in depth psychology, in dream analysis. Jung was the master who showed me the way through that.

DM It seems your creative cycles are always led by a master, a guide.

WE That's right. When I need knowledge the masters always appear to guide me. But in terms of instinctual impasse, the guide is usually a woman.

DM How about some of the younger poets here in 1959? Did you get to know any of them well?

WE No, I wish I had. But my image of a monk was such that when we occasionally met we were never really free with each other. The fault was mine. As you say, to come out from so many years of monasticism wasn't easy. My first meeting with Allen Ginsberg was not a happy one. In those days, he used to come up to anyone having a religious orientation and open with, "Have you had any mystical experiences?" I shouldn't have let it turn me off, but I couldn't be so free about such matters.

I'll always remember a story about Allen seeking across India for the absolute guru. Finally, he found this ragged holy man, half gone with visionary rapture, sitting by a path in the lotus position. Allen rushed up to him and in broken Hindi stammered: "O Master! I have come all the way across the ocean to find you! Tell me, have you experienced the *Paranirvana,* the nirvana beyond nothingness?" The old adept opened his eyes and focused them blankly on Allen for a long moment. Then he replied in perfect English: "None of your fucking business!"

That's really unfair. Allen Ginsberg is one of the crystallizing forces of this time. His poem "Howl" remains what Rexroth first called it: "The confessions of faith of a new generation." Few people yet grasp how so much of what is happening now goes back to the writing of a poem in the Drake Hotel cafeteria on Powell Street in San Francisco.

4

WE It was in 1963, after twelve years in the order, that I finally re-turned to Kentfield Priory to begin my novitiate as a lay brother. You see, I entered the Dominicans as a donatus or oblate, as the Benedictines term it: a monk without vows. This was because my previous marriage constituted a canonical impediment to profession, to vows taking. I immediately petitioned the order for a dispensation, but they asked me to wait. I kept trying, though. I must have petitioned four or five times all through the fifties.

DM And did they continue to refuse?

WE The first two provincials did, and I quit trying. Then a new provincial in 1960 came to me and said, "Antoninus, you've earned your spurs. You've had ten years on a broom. I'm going to take you off that and let you do your own thing." So finally I was free to devote my entire time to writing and the poetry-reading circuit, which was cresting then as a big thing on the campuses. This is why I stopped petitioning them on the matter of vows. It was pointed out to me that had I been in vows they probably would not have allowed me so much liberty.

It was about this time that I met Rose and began to write *The Rose of Solitude*. She had been born Rose Moreno in Austin, Texas. She married very young, one of those German Catholic Texans, and ended up in San Francisco, divorced, with three children. I met her through a friend in the order, and she began to come to me for counseling. But the situation reversed very fast. I fell in love with her, and placed my life in her hands, so to speak. That's not so unusual a thing as it seems, actually. Saint Catherine of Siena and Saint Teresa of Avila were each the spiritual advisers to many priests and religious. I had had a rift with Mary Fabilli after she rejected an autobiography I had written. The order said she had to approve it before it could be published, and she refused. It caused a break between us, left me hanging, so to speak. . . .

DM Why did she refuse?

WE Deeply personal reasons. Ortega y Gasset says it's the nature of man to express his intuitions, the nature of woman to contain them.

JS You mean you have a completed autobiography that's never been published and can't be published?

WE It's just as well. It was too apologetical, really, and after Vatican II that emphasis went out. But to get on, Rose brought a new dimension into my life, a new version of woman. Beautiful and ardent and adamant, she took over after Mary, and for five years my life was hers. Not that Mary was not beautiful and ardent and adamant in her own right.

She was and is. But Mary is an Italian and an artist, while Rose is a Mexican and a mystic—an altogether more primitive sensibility, capable of fanatical Mexican asceticism, spikes in the flesh, that sort of thing. Yet with an overlay of sophistication that was like nothing I had ever experienced. She never missed daily Mass, but her perfume was My Sin!

I did not introduce her into the literary life around San Francisco, even though I was now moving through it again. It had been my world with Mary Fabilli, and I wanted to learn Rose's world. Oh, I took her to one of Kenneth Rexroth's annual birthday parties, and she was sensational there. And I once took Phil Whalen and Don Carpenter by her house and basked in the effect she created. But her meaning in my life lay elsewhere, and I prefer to keep these things separate.

For as I say, she led me out into that world of café society which I had never known, had feared and disdained. She was preparing me for the cocktail rounds every poet has to survive as a literary lion on the lecture circuit. After the red wine of the bohemian period, I learned to drink scotch and daiquiris. And she taught me the art of holding a contemplative life in the midst of the social whirl, the mystic encounter with people in a highly transitory social milieu, how to go the limit until you collapse, then bounce back and keep moving, keep swinging. Rose is a swinger, and watching her I saw how it's done.

Then in 1963, out of the blue, she told me the time had come for me to petition again to take vows. This threw me. I did not want to forfeit the freedom I had gained so arduously in the order, and besides I was cresting at that time on the poetry-reading circuit, and I wanted to keep hammering away while the iron was hot. I had had too many instances in my career of changing course just on the threshold of a real triumph. But Rose was adamant. The request was granted immediately—an instance of her mystic intuition. That fall I found myself off the lecture circuit and back in the novitiate at Kentfield, locked up.

That was the end. When you leave a woman's life you leave a vacuum behind you, and somebody's going to fill it. It happened with Edna when I was drafted. It happened with Mary when I entered the order—though in her case I was not supplanted by another lover but by a father confessor. And now it happened with Rose.

The thing about Rose is that once a man goes out of her life, she never turns back. It's that stone knife in the Aztec heart, that Capricorn heart. I saw it happen with others, and I knew when it happened to me. You know, in my horoscope I have an afflicted moon. The interpretation is that the women in your life will always somehow fail you, and sure enough, they have. But each has brought me a new kind of realization that I needed, so it's not really a matter of failure. A man has to make his defeats with women the building stones of his perfection.

So at Kentfield I found myself on my own again. When the novitiate period was over and my first vows pronounced, I hit the road. Rather than sending me back to Oakland, I was kept stationed in Kentfield as home base. Then in 1968 they sent all us lay brothers back to Saint Albert's as part of a new policy.

DM What is the difference between the priesthood studies that you undertook at Kentfield ten years before and the studies you took on as a lay brother novice when you arrived in 1963?

WE Well, the lay brother novitiate these days is the same as that of the clerical novitiate, but at that time they were different. The lay brother novitiate then was still largely a period of learning to live the monastic life through prayer and work. That's why it was unfair to send me back after being in the order for twelve years. They could easily have got a dispensation for me. They'd done it with other oblates before me.

JS Do you know why they didn't?

WE Well, they said that having petitioned Rome for one dispensation, my marital dispensation, they did not want to press their luck with a second one. But that really doesn't figure. I think it's some kind of archetypal suspicion of the poet, the distrust of the cleric for the poet. When I left the order, the president of Saint Albert's explained to the press that I was always more the poet than the theologian. Almost as if to say, "We told you so."

DM Were there any beneficial characteristics in those two disruptions?

WE Yes, the overall result was clarifying and resolving. You never know if you're meant for a thing until you've tried it, and even if it doesn't prove out, there's an inner liberation, as of something settled or confirmed. I was happy at Kentfield after Saint Albert's. It's a smaller house and more removed. There's more nature there. Marin County is heaven after Oakland! I was in a better position to live out the loss of Rose, a better place to lick my wounds. And it was there, in 1965, that I met Sue. Some will say cynically, "on the rebound," but rebounds don't last. If they last, they're not mere rebounds. And I gave this one four years before I trusted it. So you can't call it a rebound. Anyway, at Kentfield the new fate began. I can see by hindsight that the ground was being laid for my transition out of the order.

DM Is it true, that in the week between your leaving the order and your formal marriage to Sue, Rose showed up at Stinson Beach to dissuade you from it, to make you return to the order?

WE She did.

JS Would you care to talk about that?

WE No.

5

DM During all these disruptions you were spending a great deal of time on the reading circuit. How did you regard that experience?

WE I regard it always as a witness. On the college campuses the emphasis is on communication, what you know. I can communicate, but the witness is greater. It's something like this: what you can communicate maintains the point of contact, but it isn't the essence of your total effect, which is witness. By witness, I mean a personal confrontation, a personal encounter, a psychic crisis deliberately precipitated to produce a change in attitude, a new center of gravity, a displacement of consciousness from cognition to faith. I don't mean faith in the Catholic sense. I never proselytize. I mean faith in the sense of commitment to life and to living. To live my faith, rather than by the mental thing that our education inculcates. To enter via the ideational world, yes, but to move through it. To be able to field the questions as they come to you and at the same time to throw back into the questioner a different principle of life. We are familiar with this from the example of the Zen masters, but my point of orientation is not Zen.

The Beat Generation began it back in 1959. And it took, you know, it really took. It took more than any of us thought possible. Certainly the image took. The credit is usually given the Beatles, but the Beatles can't be compared with the Beats. They were the middlemen between the Beats and the rising generation, because the Beats alone could never make that image all that popular. Nevertheless, it began in a different place, another point in the psychic hemisphere. Not Liverpool but San Francisco.

JS Is the platform also a testing ground?

WE Not really. I never considered it that way. The testing ground was back in the monastic cell, where the inferiority of vision was fought out and preserved. The testing ground was in the writing of the poem, not its utterance on platform. Once you are on platform you have to be absolute master or you're lost. The long periods of withdrawal build, they build fantastically. They fill you up, and you move out into the world. And at the point of contact, the crucial issue, you respond. It's not that you have it programmed like a good debater, all the answers, etc. It isn't that at all. It's just that when the point of issue actually occurs you are there to meet it. And you do meet it. Because you know what you are. There isn't any other principle, really, than that.

For me, this will go on. It's not something that will end with my change of life. True, I learned it in the monastery. I learned what it is, the meaning of it, and its tremendous value. From the monastery I brought out to the world an image consonant with its essence: the religious habit, the robes. But now that the robes are gone, the same thing will go forward, and in going forward a new image will emerge. I don't know what it will be. I won't know until the first encounter.

The monastic life gives you terrific capacity for reflection. There is awesome power in it. Separation from the world really constitutes a kind of power. I'm sure that the orders are by no means finished. It's just that so few in the orders ever discover how to utilize the power they possess. The shift in Western culture from a religious orientation to a secular orientation has left them in a kind of backwash, and they haven't been able to free themselves, because their parochial constituency prefers them as fixated security symbols in a transient world rather than moving and living dynamic charismatic entities. As a brother, I really feel that I perfected the accommodation of that religious power to the point of issue in the world of today. Perhaps that's why I left. As someone has said, "What you've perfected, you've condemned."

As I look back on it . . . and I hope I'm not bragging, only just musing about something that is no more . . . it seems my approach was an almost perfect equation between the monastic life (the principle of reflection) and the point of application that youth was asking for on the campus. If it wasn't absolutely perfect, it was because it took so long to perfect it—ten, twelve years. As you yourself saw me there in the beginning, in Fugazi Hall in 1958, it was so utterly stark. There was no point of mediation except the primal voice of the poet. But after a while I began to orient myself.

I'm just wondering what's going to happen now. This great break that I've made, I can't justify it. Not in terms of my Catholic beliefs. But I feel God has something in store for me that I could not accomplish in the context of the order. What it is I don't know. It remains to be discovered.

DM You were inside the monastic life for sixteen years?

WE Eighteen, almost nineteen years. Even though I was out of the monastery a good deal on reading tours, nevertheless the monk was always there. What's going to happen to the monk?

I find there are two different worlds, the domestic world and the monastic world, with the prophetic role bearing the same relation to each. The domestic world is much taken up with trivia, and the Church ranks the monastic life higher because its detachment from trivia renders it so accessible to spiritual infusion. But it seems to me that once the domestic life, the life of trivia, is constituted as a permeable reflective form, then the prophetic role, the poet's role, may draw on it with the same accessibility as it does on the monastic life. What I'm saying is that, monasticism or domesticity, the prophetic function must go on.

Yet it's difficult, for I don't know the world, really. I don't know how much money you need to live, to get by on. I don't know anything about that. And I don't know where to throw my energies in terms of it. Before the order I was able to constitute the domestic life as a permeable reflective form, but I had no children. Very likely that was the reason I feared children, why I became a monk. But now I have a boy to raise to manhood. So the life of a parent, the life of responsibility in trivia, confronts me.

DM Do you plan to continue your reading tours?

WE Well, I announced that I was going to stop for a while, but my agent asked me to keep going, to honor the contracts I had already signed.

DM You'll now be reading without your religious habit?

WE Yes.

JS Will you read in your black suit?

WE I don't know. Sue doesn't want me to get into that black suit again!

JS It would be interesting to see you reading in buckskin or corduroy.

WE I'd like to wear buckskin. But it just seems like too much. It's the Virgo in me that hesitates to go that far. But Virgo has to learn to jump through its own shadow, and maybe that's what I will eventually do.

JS What made you announce that you were going to stop reading?

WE Taste, as much as anything. That and the natural reluctance to exploit a denial of all you stood for. It would seem to require an absolute break. Also in order to go through a period of silence and withdrawal to prepare for a new phase. I think all great things should be prepared for by a period of withdrawal. I really feel that. But not seven years . . . ! [*laughter*] Actually, I'm ready to go back on platform. I can tell by talking tonight that I truly am.

JS David and I have many times talked about Lew Welch's once proposed magazine, *Bread*. It was planned to present a variety of essays and poems dealing with the poet's considerations about trivia—about how to get along, how to pay the bills, how to keep the lights turned on, the children fed, the wife happy. It's interesting to hear of your encountering these problems after having them somewhat solved for you.

WE Yes, in the monastic life everything is provided for you. That's the great thing about it, but also the reason why so many lay people call it a cop-out. What they don't see is that you pay plenty for it in terms of restrictions, and that these restrictions are the prime ingredient in enforcing the inferiority that is the purpose of the life. Anyone who thinks the monastic life is a cop-out is welcome to go and try it. He'll find out.

Actually, in the monastery I went my own way as a writer. It took ten years on the broom before I was free to rove as a lecturer, but that kind of submission eventually proves that. In the end, I had it like no one else: free to write, free to lecture. I can hear someone say, "Yeah, and he hung himself. They gave him enough rope and he hung himself." I guess I did, but the process was a true working-out.

DM How do you find the world?

WE Tough. I'm still smarting from my break, and I dare say I'm not yet seeing things as they actually are. A routine dental appointment came up last week, one I'd made while still in the order. I've known this dentist for fifteen years. I hesitated to go back there after my break, but it seemed cowardice not to, since he knows my teeth inside out and put a lot of time into them free of charge. He is a conservative, a Republican, an ex-navy man, a staunch Catholic, and I knew he would be offended at my leaving the order. But I also thought it was something we could talk about. I should have sensed something from the receptionist's attitude, but I was totally unprepared when he emerged in the sitting room and announced in front of the others waiting there: "For my own reasons, I don't want you for my patient!"

One of the fondest items of liberal polemics is that of the clergy as a high-placed nucleus maintaining position at the laity's expense. Actually, the laity invests fantastic emotional security in the image of the priest and the nun, fixating them in rigid personas and denying them the full ambience of their humanity. The gun at the head of the clergy is the crushing burden of responsibility thrust upon them by these "little ones." Anyone who has seen pictures of the Pope being mobbed by weeping, pleading supplicants, grown men and women who touch his robes and kiss his hands, can see what every priest is up against, and every monk and nun, too.

In the spring of 1968 I took Susanna to my favorite restaurant in San Francisco, Tadich's Grill. It was on this occasion that she told me she had fallen in love with a young man who had recently taken lodging at her rooming house, and who in the course of impending events was to become the father of little Jude. She was so radiant and daughterly that I could only rejoice for her. Although I was in mufti at the time, it so happened that I was recognized by an entering family of Catholics—no one I knew, but the fact of recognition was evident. Normally, I would have conducted myself prudently, but in view of what Sue had just told me, and since it was apparent that this occasion was to be one of farewell, I would not think of being anything less than true to the state of poignancy and relinquishment we were experiencing. So I took her hand and gazed, with all the meaning I could muster, into her eyes as we shared that meal. The Catholics were disturbed. They stared at me disapprovingly, in fact, incredulously. Yet we did nothing wrong. It was only that I had violated the convention of how a celibate is expected to act publicly. At bottom, it is the Catholic laity who provide for the sustenance of the monk, and they let you know if your need for latitude conflicts with their need for security, with its heavy investment in your decorum.

DM Have you had the opposite kind of reaction: have you had people welcome you with open arms?

WE Very much. The response from that quarter has been gratifying. Sometimes not too much understanding of what you put into it and what it cost you to go. I find myself disturbed by people who exclaim, "Welcome back!"

TM Has anybody said, "Where have you been?!" [*laughter*]

WE Actually, it's more the practical problem of how to restructure your life on a daily basis after so many years of monasticism. The problem of adjusting to the child has been a big one. If it were just the erotic relationship . . . I've been through that before. But when a child comes into it, every time you make love, there's a third person to consider.

DM How old is he?

WE Ten months.

DM Are there any problems of making a living at the moment?

WE Sue has an income, so that's not the main problem right now. I can supplement it, of course. One reason I must get back on the road and carry my own share, as they say. I've begun a new sequence of poems, and they should be ready by fall.

DM You must have imagined at times, in the monastery, being out, didn't you?

WE Yes, but not seriously. I had every expectation of ending my days in the order. Even after finding myself in love, I didn't want to give up that image of the monk. That was the hardest thing, because I had perfected it and knew how to use it. Not that I didn't live the monastic life; I did in the beginning, I used to crawl back from being on tour as a hermit crawls back to his cave. But eventually I learned how to keep my spiritual balance, even on the road. Rose taught me that. But what I didn't want to give up was my pride, my image. Oh, the sweet power in that image!

By leaving it I did, though only a woman could have dragged me from it. That was the most terrible thing to forsake, that beautiful image, that beautiful habit and the power in it. I know this sounds power-thirsty, and I won't minimize it. But if you're a prophet and have not completed your work in the world, to relinquish a power you have perfected in order to start all over again is terrible.

6

WE I distinguish between the poem written and the poem read. The poem read is the confrontation with the world, but the poem written is the confrontation with the self, the unknown part of the self, which is hidden. This is carried on at an entirely different level than the blazing confrontation which the world exacts. We begin as introverts, the reason why so many poets are poor readers. For the art of the platform is an art of extroversion. You master the problem by throwing a more challenging confrontation back to the world than it is prepared for. This enables you to survive even as you insist on your own terms. For this reason, I will sometimes outrageously exploit my poems when I read. Whereas when I write, it is as private a thing as my love life. There is all the privacy of the bedroom about it. Procreation and insemination. Except that the dialogue is with the self, the unknown self. In the act of creation we find the pagan in ourself, the primitive. We find him or *her* or it—whatever it is that has not yet yielded to formality.

And it taunts us and rebukes us, mocking us with the limitation of formality, suffering itself to be accepted only under the most specifically appropriate terms. And so the poem emerges, the ritual in which the dialogue with the mysterious self is consummated.

These truths are weapons. I have this knowledge, this secret knowledge. And it is the knowledge that enables me to confront the world, convert my introversion into a true extroversion. What I have achieved is irreducible. No one can take it from me. Nothing that happens out there can nullify it.

And the heart of encounter, as I said, is witness. Witness is the passion that propels me, as monk or citizen. A man is seldom honored for that. The world wants to be entertained. You have honored me when you spoke of the primacy of the voice at that Fugazi Hall reading, but a poet can take an audience to the depths and have it spit in his face. That is what being a prophet means. No performer alive can hold such power over a people, for the poet is the archetype of the performer. But that power brings pain. Any psychiatrist, any counselor or confessor, will tell you the same thing. A psychiatrist will wait weeks for the moment he can truthfully tell what he has truthfully discerned. The patient leaves his office exalted with a kind of received wisdom. But the next day he is back glaring and muttering accusations. "Human kind," as Eliot has said, "cannot bear very much reality." The same thing goes for your audience. You can shake them to the bone, move them with a religious revelation they never before experienced. But the responses the next day are mixed, and the reviews, if you are lucky enough to get any, say "excessive" or "emotional." Or they speak of the performance as "uneven." Uneven! Good God! I seek perfection, in my life and in my craft, but I will jeopardize it if need be, and sometimes sacrifice it deliberately, in order to touch, to move, to change attitudes, confront lives. This is the meaning of witness.

"Ah, yes," the critic replies, "but it is not art!" I deny the distinction. In his *Essays on the Philosophy of Art,* Collingwood spells it out: "The artist must prophesy not in the sense that he foretells things to come, but in the sense that he tells his audience, at the risk of their displeasure, the secrets of their own hearts."

I have emphasized the prophetic role of the poet because of the relevance of the prophet's moral confrontation as it derives from our Old Testament heritage. But now that I'm out of the order and experiencing the recovery of nature (not so much probing it as letting it invade me), I feel that those young San Francisco poets who localize the matter in the image of the shaman are closer to the truth for our time. The more you study the function of the shaman as archetypal creator and poet—as seen, for instance, in those fantastic bison preserved for us in the Altamira caves: figures replete with that unbelievable delicacy of abstraction that could only have come from sources of the utmost psychic cruciality (even if, unfortunately, the performance was "uneven"!). A function brought right up to our own times in the tribes out here on the Coast, for whom the shaman served as tribal psychic stabilizer as well as master of ecstasy in the dance and the peyote cult. So I am becoming more aware of the deepening relevance of the shaman for our time and the poet's archaic connection with him. In fact, come to think of it, the first time I ever read the term was in Duncan's poem, "Toward the Shaman," printed in the *Experimental Review* before the war.

And the more I reflect on what actually happens on platform, the more I am convinced it is shamanistic rather than prophetic—the trance-like rhythms, the unspeakable silences, the incredible psychic polarization in the audience—these are all ingredients of the shamanistic syndrome. Of course, this function has now been largely taken over by the rock band. The infusion of Oriental tonalities into rock in the sixties is the clearest indication of its appropriation of the shamanistic role. We Beats were a manifestly poetry-oriented generation, whereas the voice of the succeeding one is indubitably rock, so that poetry is relatively unemphasized right now. I think this is to be expected, while the implications of rock are being extended. But this does not mean that the place of poetry has been altered. Pure tonality augments but does not supplant the primacy of concept, for it is founded on the priority of inception: "In the beginning was the Word. . . . " I believe that in the field of expression, music emerged and developed as an augmentation and extension of the Word's latent nuances, which poetry's limited tonalities of necessity could not articulate. Sometimes the Word must retire in order to let these latencies find their activation. But it can never be a matter of primacy. I have experienced too much on platform to fear that any music can usurp the poet's place in the field of man's awareness. For his verse clinches the point of cognition, the bone-cold nucleus in the vast connotative flux. What poetry concedes to music in the area of the implicit is more than recovered in the area of the explicit, where music never can challenge it.

Anyway, it's this consideration, this complex of considerations, that makes me feel the transposition from the religious habit to, say, buckskin, if that's the way I am meant to go, has an unconscious validation that authenticates it as something more than affectation. The deep work now confronting man is to touch the roots of his symbolic motivation. It was shaman's work once and it is the poet's work now, and it will be met.

Thinking of this struggle, I remember that I listened to you both read on the same program at Santa Barbara a little less than a year ago. David, I could see, had had more experience on platform, and had through pain been liberated into a direct feeling-rapport, a true discursive, with the audience. Whereas you, Jack, had not had so much exposure. The audience had not yet clarified you and purified you through the suffering of your prophetic witness as poet, or I should say your shamanistic witness. For the shaman this purification was done in solitude, immersal in the wilderness. The wilderness was then man's problem, and deliverance comes only from being swallowed up by your problem, like Jonah in the whale's belly. But it is increasingly evident that such solitude is no longer feasible, for the wilderness is no longer man's problem, except how to preserve it.

What is truly his problem today is the wilderness of the race itself, the vast, anonymous, terrifying, and inscrutable population that everywhere surrounds us, and which for the poet is symbolized by his audience. For him, paradoxically, the solitude and the suffering are undergone on platform.

I know this contradicts what I said earlier in answer to your question of whether or not platform constitutes a testing. I was struck cold by the realization that the platform is too late for testing. It is the arena. And yet so was the wilderness for the shaman. The platform for the poet, like the wilderness for the shaman, is not a place of testing. It is a place of survival. For me, my testing was my solitude, and my solitude was my cell, and that solitude formed me. And yet that is nothing compared to the terrible solitude, the isolation one undergoes on platform. I think it is crucial to see the audience as the active force, the dangerous unconscious force. Then the audience as the bull and the poet the matador. Until you have been gored a few times,

your vocation has not been confirmed. We wait always for the baptism of blood. In her book, *Waiting for God,* Simone Weil quotes with approval the saying of French craftsmen, that until an apprentice has been hurt by his tools, "the craft has not yet entered into his body."
DM Your view, then, that in his platform role the poet accommodates to a persona, or mask, which in your case the religious habit confirmed and which, as you say, the transposition might well extend—this is a different thing, as you have indicated, than the creation of the poem itself.
WE Actually, I believe that in every response, the psychic element we designate as the persona is in play, that it is not only an indispensable factor in the creative process but in the psychic process itself. It complicates, but in some strange way it precipitates cognition. Among the implicit criteria of sanctity in our time, the one that presupposes a totally unstructured awareness, pure spontaneity responding without inhibition or equivocation or any suggestion of predetermination. Thus I have heard Allen Ginsberg called "our only modern saint" because of his apparent liberation from our collective taboos. But this assumption is one of our myths; insofar as it is entertained as an ethos or value it is itself memorialized as a constitutive persona. Let's say that the persona is the ineluctable concomitant of concept, which is attitude. Persona is the prism through which subjective attitude is conferred on objective reality. It is only objectionable when it is not really one's own. The poet might as well accept its presence as something given, something ineradicably present in the creation of his poem.

It's harder to speak of what happens in the writing than what happens on platform, because in the writing everything is introjected. The creation of a poem is like a love word uttered; you are not aware that you have spoiled it until it is too late. If when you speak to your beloved you are unsure, it is implicitly revealed in the signature of the inflection. Then you find trueness in yourself, maybe out of your experience, certainly out of your suffering, always, if you do, the grace of God, and the uttered word comes true, not a quiver of uncertainty . . . and you and your beloved understand each other. So it is also with the writing of the poem, only the achievement is permanent.

This makes it terrible. From one point of view it is horribly like photographing your beloved in the moment of giving herself to you. Who would do that? Yet as a poet you do it. Except we deal with more intangible forms.

For there is this inscrutable character of the language, its capacity to both withhold and manifest at the same time. This is so strange. Everything that happens in a poem happens in terms of language. You cannot exceed the language. You can never say more than it says. The collective nature of the language is the boundary you can never cross. Your personal language, yes, you can rattle off. The baby babbles. But the collective nature of language remains intransigent. You finally begin to realize that the other self—the *he* or *she* or the *it* whom you address—is your collective self. This mysterious one is really all men. We talk about it as the most deeply personal self, and so it seems. But who does it turn out to be? It turns out to be the race! This is the explanation of craftsmanship, and why it works, why it is necessary. It liberates the impersonal through efficiency. But if it is merely effectual, it's like the lover who is merely skilled. Who ever heard of an efficient lover?

This is why it's easy to write the first poem. A minimal craftsmanship is endowed in your tongue. The problem is how do you keep doing it. Again, it's like in love. It's easy to make love the first time. The act is so much its own motivation that it blows your mind. But making love the five-hundredth time? My first true poem was written with tears pouring down my face. Then the tears turned to sweat.

DM You say you have begun writing a new sequence. Do you have a sense of the work's direction?

WE Actually, I write out of the crises in my life. For Virgo, this is the permanent condition, since it is the sign of crisis. We see this in Lawrence, a true Virgo, the condition of the sensibility in permanent crisis with itself, from which his art could not deliver him, and which burned him up. But my sensibility is not all exacerbated, and my religion came in my life at a time when the crisis became absolute, and gave me comfort. Nevertheless, the contour of crisis constitutes the contour of formality in what I do. The only sense of direction is the sense of crisis engaged.

However, I simply wasn't prepared for this terminal break with the order. As I say, leaving was more of an upheaval than a decision. Now that I have truly begun again, I rejoice. Because I see how right it is. I don't mean in the moral sense. I only mean I am delivered from having to elaborate what no longer required elaboration.

For in beginning again, right or wrong, you are restored to fundamentals. Nature, love, the touch of woman, Susanna. And something never before in my life, or in my poetry: the child. Little Jude makes it all new.

Remembering Everson (1999)

September 27, 1999: Jim and I meet at Hawley's Ross Valley Book Co. in Berkeley in the morning. During the sixties and until Everson's death in 1994, Robert Hawley was not only a publisher and editor of Everson's work via Oyez press, he was also an ally of the man, as this interview shows. His bookstore specializes in new and used Western Americana books and artifacts. Saddle blankets, Indian baskets, nineteenth-century and early twentieth-century photographs, paintings, dime novels, ethnographic tomes on Native American tribal cultures, books on California history, chromolith posters—time-machine escapees. As we enter, an audiocassette tape of cornetist Ruby Braff in dialogue with pianist Ellis Larkins is playing.—DM

Robert Hawley (**RH**)
David Meltzer (**DM**)

DM When I interviewed Bill Everson for *The San Francisco Poets*, he was in transit. He was leaving the order and talking about how he needed a new costume. He said the robes of the monastic order were a great costume. And then he transformed himself into Buckskin Bill, letting his hair grow long, wearing jeans and a big buckskin jacket with fringes, a necklace with animal teeth, projecting this frontiersman prototype.

RH He always had to have a costume. In the thirties, he was the struggling vintner, then it was the jeans-clad conscientious objector when he divorced Edwa, then he was the . . . Mary Fabilli has some photographs of Bill in the forties. . . . You know, I never called him Bill. I called him Brother. In this photo, he was wearing a slouch hat and a cape, looking like Ezra Pound in 1924 or something like that. After '69 he adopted the mountain man persona, and he became friendly with two Native American hustlers . . . he was vaguely interested in Native American art. He had a wonderful archery guide, a bear claw and eagle claw necklace—both are illegal. A great leather coat. A flat Montana-style cowboy hat. I gave him a big Apache basket with turtles around it, and he had it about six months, and I wasn't aware of where it was or what they were doing with it. It was a piece that was very important to me. I went down there, and I guess I was going to the bathroom or something, and off a closet it was sitting on the floor with umbrellas in it. And just falling apart. A $750 basket. I'm not aware of a single piece of representational art.

DM Wasn't Mary Fabilli a Dorothy Day Catholic Worker activist?

RH Yes . . . now Mary is approaching sainthood. Living for the Church, she persuaded Brother to go, too . . . But Brother never took his final vows. There was poverty and chastity. We visited him, had lunches with him over at Kentfield Priory. I think he was a serious Catholic, but I think he could question his total commitment to the order. I know of at least two women he was involved with. His relationship with Susanna was four or five years before he went to the order.

DM He had a very powerful platform presence and was very theatrical. I remember during the week-long San Francisco Rolling Renaissance—Jack Shoemaker and I curated a five- or six-night poetry reading series at Glide Memorial Church, and I think he was in one of the last groups of people to read. He was wearing the robes, and he was in a church setting, and there was a pulpit and candelabra beneath it. In the midst of one of his poems he reaches down—a gaunt posture, this sort of strange crow-like figure, reaches over and puts his hand over and closer to the candle like G. Gordon Liddy and stared down the audience that's staring at him. Wonderful.

RH I don't know when he got the confrontational style. I talked to Alan Campo, Steve Eisner. Steve was kind of his Midwestern rep—he set up readings for him and things like that. And they weren't aware of that early on in the sixties. Maybe when he went plebian, went out in the real world again. When they had that big reading at the Bancroft, he was that way. I was always a little embarrassed.

DM There was that aspect, too. His was often a difficult persona to cuddle up to.

RH When I look at Brother, I have a great love and respect for what he was doing. I could question maybe some pretensions, some of the costumes, things like that, but within that very large body of work is some tremendous stuff. I think of *Archetype West, River Root*. In '47 to '48, with some critical advice from Kenneth Rexroth, New Directions published his *Residual Years*. Rexroth had taken out all the Dionysian quality of the verse. Brother was unhappy with that, and later we did *Single Source*, which was essentially the collected early work that was more his choice and not under Kenneth's influence.

DM Brother was obviously affected by a variety of belief systems, and he embodied them during different stages of his life.

RH He was an ardent astrologer. I have a horoscope that he did for me. He corresponded with Dane Rudhyar and some other well-known astrologers. Brother was influenced by Gavin Arthur, locally. And then Jungian philosophy and depth psychology.

DM I knew that he was involved with astrology as an ordering symbol system. I know too that he became deeply involved in Jung and started reframing his relationship to his life and to the world in Jungian terms. And I know that you were working at Holmes Book Co. and were very generous in getting him supplied with the Bollingen books and all the rest of it. . . .

RH I'm not good at speculative reasoning at all. Philosophy, psychiatry, psychology. Generally, I don't understand them. I don't know the terminology. I've never studied it, and it doesn't interest me. I've been in rooms with Brother as he was expounding on Jungian philosophy and its importance to him. I don't think I ever understood it.

The relationship began as author and publisher. I liked him immensely. He seemed to put up with me like a retarded nephew or something. But we had absolutely great times together. I came to love him as a friend, respect him as a man and a poet, and he was very, very important to me. I think the body of his work is really splendid; some of it is a bit self-indulgent. The *San Joaquin* poems at least are honest and a decent response to the environment. The *Kingfisher Flats* poems are major works. A little bit of the religious work—*At the Edge*, *Rose of Solitude* . . . and *River Root* is just tremendous, one of the great erotic poems in the English language. I don't like his earth poems in particular, or prose, but *Archetype West* is a splendid book. I don't know, David, I miss him. I miss him tremendously.

DM: You were there at the time of the illness. Do you want to talk some about that and what that meant? Was it difficult dealing with his deterioration from Parkinson's?

RH When we were proofreading at Kentfield Friary in '65, there was a very modest tremor. It became increasingly worse, and by '70 or so it got so that he couldn't type. I did some typing for him, Bill Hotchkiss did typing for him, and his handwriting became difficult to read. Susanna was very, very supportive, but there was . . . it was so painful . . . there was this man who was six-foot-five suddenly shrinking to five-foot-nine. It became important to maintain a very spirited and cheerful relationship with him.

We would make these pilgrimages with my wife or with girlfriends or boyfriends, go down there and stock up his pantry. We'd get liquor and wine and delicatessen food. Susanna would make sandwiches in bite-sized pieces so he could pick them up and eat them. And we were being very, very cheerful. There were great laughs in there, and we were drinking Jack Daniels, and in a taped session we made, you can hear the clinking of the glass. But he was supportive and positive. In the last five or six years a group of former students and friends from the Santa Cruz area attended to him . . . a lawyer whose name I can't recall, an artist named Dan Stolpe, a young man named Steve Siboly, who became almost a secretary for him. A great group of people. And when there was a birthday party for Brother—his seventy-fifth birthday, I think—there must have been 150 people there. Former students, editors, and other authors who were associated with him. You could see his disintegration and that was very, very painful, but we handled it. He did and we did with good spirits. We had good times, and he kept up until the very end when he was so pathetic, so weak, got pneumonia. . . . He was talking about tomorrow, what he was going to do. And friends really rallied around him.

DM In the poetry-related conversations you had with Everson over the years, who didn't he like to read?

RH He couldn't understand Ezra Pound and Yeats and the collected Dylan Thomas. There were about five Dylan Thomas poems but two or three Tennyson poems. I don't want to be in a world that doesn't have those. But he challenged me. He didn't like Yeats too much. His big love was Jeffers. He felt that Robert Duncan could do good work but wasn't doing it. He could not handle the whole gay scene. Robin Blaser, John Wieners, Stan Persky, George Stanley, he just rejected it.

He didn't like Weldon Kees, but he liked Maddie Gleason. He liked Allen Ginsberg. We took him twice to Ginsberg, who would stay in the office above City Lights. We'd take him to Tadich's, our favorite restaurant, and sit there and talk for hours and have this incredible meal. There's a body of Ginsberg's work that he'd speak favorably of. They spent more time socializing. It wasn't aesthetics. It was, "Where were you at?" "Did you hear who's doing what?" "Where are you reading next?" Naropa was just getting started, and Brother was curious about that because they never asked him there. He loved the writing of Thomas Merton. Young poets would send him books, and he had quite a collection.

He was always talking about himself and his own poetry and what he intended to do, and when he was at Santa Cruz, he showed some things of the students. Some of it was all right. He turned out some really fine printers. I had done two or three small books of Mary Fabilli, and he spoke very favorably of all of it. He liked your writing. He liked Michael McClure—*Dark Brown* was probably the best erotic poetry of the whole Beat scene. And Brother responded to your erotic writing. I thought Michael had done a good body of work, especially *The Beard,* which I think is a work of comic genius. Brother didn't like *The Beard.* I didn't always understand his response to things. Frequently, there wouldn't be an explanation.

DM: How did he feel to be identified with the so-called Beat movement?

RH He was pleased. He was really pleased. I don't remember this, but I was told this: there was an article in *Time* magazine referring him to as the Beat Friar. Which pleased him. But then Annie Charters did *The Portable Beat Reader,* and he's not in there. He didn't understand why. I thought it was a chronological association and geographical association, and I didn't see any relationship between what I see as the aesthetics of the Beat, the intentions of the Beats, and what he's doing. I think Ginsberg, of all those people who were writing as Beats, did some of the best work. Kaufman, had he lived, would have been very good. I like a lot of Diane di Prima's writing. LeRoi Jones is a masterful writer. Overall, I don't think the movement produced a great body of literature, especially of poetry.

DM Who were the stalwarts in Brother Bill's pantheon of poetry? Besides Brother Bill. [*laughter*]

RH Jeffers is very much at the top. I like Ezra Pound. The short poems, the lyrics, the Asian things. Magnificent writing. Some of *The Cantos* is worthwhile. He did not like Pound. He would take Yeats with a grain of salt. He didn't seemed to like any of the women poets, unless he'd met them. Mary Korte or Lenore Kandel, Joanne Kyger. He liked a poet and friend of his, I think he teaches at Sierra College, named Bill Hotchkiss, who had written some books about Native Americans and some big books of poetry. He liked Denise Levertov. Denise was at Stanford for a number of years. He liked Edna Millay, Louise Bogan, Muriel Rukeyser, Conrad Aiken, Ciardi, Lowell . . . he didn't like most of the academic poets.

DM It's amazing that he kept up with it.

RH Where they lived in Santa Cruz there was a cottage: living room, kitchen, tiny bedroom, bathroom, tiny bedroom. That's where they lived. An old A-frame garage was sealed off and a small heater put in there where he had part of his library and his printing press, equipment, some things on the wall. There was a bunk house that probably would've slept about eight to ten men. It had been a fire station, and there were three walls with three or four shelves filled with books of poetry, mostly paperbacks, mostly presented to him. There were things from Allen Ginsberg, Gregory Corso, people from the fifties and sixties who had maybe touched him. Some academic poets. Review copies. James Laughlin sent him everything that New Directions published. People who stayed there ripped him off—let me say that other people were staying there and books disappeared. Souvenirs. He didn't take care of them. He had a number of very important press books, but they were frequently in areas where there was dampness. As he developed Parkinson's disease tremor, he frequently dropped books, or couldn't get them back on the shelf, things like that. So there were great books there but not in the best condition.

DM What do you think will be Everson's life after death, as a writer and a poet? Because you know how these things work, how suddenly people who were so present in one time have this way of absenting themselves for a period of time and then reemerging.

RH Well, I think of Everson as I do now of Duncan. We sort of dismiss them as regional poets. *The Norton Anthology of English Literature* doesn't have any Everson in it. I can think of three or four poems of his that are as good as, say, Richard Wilbur's and some of the other people they have in there. It's hard to find Duncan anthologized. I don't know any serious criticism on Everson.

DM But in a sense Everson made much use of regionality, California landscape, and both the low country and the mountains. Rexroth is another—what would you call them?—not regional but nature poets, which I think encompasses a larger domain.

RH I couldn't understand why Brother was not included in major national anthologies. Why he was not getting serious reviews. Just a mention in *Poetry Magazine* or something like that. And then he was—there isn't that much difference in our ages—maybe he was twenty years older than me, but he felt a loss of his contemporaries. Parkinson, Duncan, Adrian Wilson. People who were important in the late thirties, forties. Rexroth. All gone. There were times when he seemed to feel very alone. That's when he'd hug me, or we'd walk about a hundred yards out from his place where there were small falls with very cold water. We'd sit there, dangle our feet in the water, and talk. Very important. Even with Susanna as supportive as she was, the people who were significant in the thirties, forties, fifties, and sixties were no longer there.

Lawrence Ferlinghetti I (1969)

Spring 1969: Jack Shoemaker and I drove to Ferlinghetti's San Francisco house in the Potrero Hill district, a warmly worn and comfortable home filled with art and books. We sat in the living room for a while, chatting, sipping wine, and then Lawrence took us upstairs to the attic garret where he had his office. Its windows looked out over the city. He was forthcoming but also playful; sometimes I thought he was putting us on, a sly trickster with ice-blue eyes. As the interview proceeded, the sun began a spectacular descent behind the city skyline. Afterward, we went downstairs where Kirby, his wife, had made supper for us, which we ate with much wine and wonderful conversation and laughter.—DM

Lawrence Ferlinghetti (**LF**)
David Meltzer (**DM**)
Jack Shoemaker (**JS**)

1

LF I have nothing to say. I haven't got my crystal spectacles on.
DM You just published a book? [*Tyrannus Nix*]
LF I don't have anything to say in relation to all these other poets. I don't feel myself to be part of any scene now. I never went in for the regional point of view. I don't know anything about anything! That's the way I feel. I am living in Big Sur a lot of the time, and I really don't have much to do with what is going on now.
DM Is this a transitional period for you?
LF Definitely. When isn't it? In the summer I'm a nudist anarchist; in the winter I'm a Buddhist socialist.
DM Your new book of poems . . . can we consider that to be a statement of your concern?
LF It is the old political bullshit. Politics is a drag, but every once in a while you get dragged into it and have to sound off. But it is not my idea of an ideal kind of poetry.
JS It is not your constant concern . . . ?

LF No. I keep getting dragged into that bag, and I get classified as a political poet. I had another book that came out this year called *The Secret Meaning of Things,* which is generally not political at all.

JS You have written a poem now about every president since Eisenhower. . . .

LF That is just what Snyder said.

JS It seems you have an overwhelming historical concern. . . .

LF No, I haven't. I wrote a poem about Eisenhower, and I wrote this one about Nixon. It seems to me there were very few presidents in between. I wrote about Fidel Castro in between. The last president of the U.S.A. was really Fidel Castro. He ran things from down there in Cuba even when Kennedy was president. Castro was acting, and the U.S.A. was forced to react according to its already well-established guidelines for Christian behavior and, therefore, had to react strictly according to the American way of life, which he threatened. Castro may still be president. Nixon is sort of a bush-league stand-in.

The Cuban Revolution was the Spanish Civil War of my generation. The thing that turned on the writers in the thirties was the Spanish Civil War. It would be interesting to pin down some of the other poets you have interviewed as to what their actual position is on Castro. I find a good many of the poets around are quite rightist, if not reactionary, and most of them are politically illiterate. Great Kerouac is not around anymore, so we won't go into him. But there's a Hemingway parallel there.

I recently received a list of award winners from the National Foundation of the Arts. Many poets and little presses in the country have received grants from them. This is government money in the form of grants from either the National Foundation of the Arts and Sciences or the Coordinating Council of Little Magazines and Small Presses.

Jean-Jacques Lebel and I had a running argument over the last six weeks while he was staying here. He considers himself a revolutionary, and he proposed that a young poet he met in Berkeley get a $1,000 grant from this foundation. There was a scout in town, Gus Blaisdell, from the University of New Mexico. He was looking for people to recommend for government grants. Jean-Jacques Lebel suggested Blaisdell recommend the young Berkeley poet. It happened that

Blaisdell didn't dig this fellow's poetry. That wasn't my point.

My point was that it surprised me that someone who considered himself a full-blown revolutionary would be the first to accept government money. Even though I dig that using establishment money for anti-establishment ends *is* subversive—part of the cultural "rip-off." The Kayak Press in San Francisco, for instance, took $10,000 two years in a row. One of the editor's justifications was that he would sponsor a prize for the best poem on Che Guevara. The *prize* for the best poem on Che Guevara was $400, I believe. I have heard that the Kayak editor, George Hitchcock, was a radical in the thirties, and it seems to me that this is sort of what happened to the whole old liberal movement in this country. The labor unions were bought off. They loaded the ships for Vietnam. From my point of view, which I admit is disputable, poets and little presses are also being bought off. Any one of them that took the money would say, "No, that's not true. We are free to do anything we want with the money." But it's logical that if you're a real bad boy the first year, you won't get the grant renewed. And then, too—someone in another country—a radical in France or Germany—reads about your taking this money and they don't see the rationalization and the various gradations of your reasoning. All they see is the fact that you took the U.S. government money. . . . I guess mine is the "pure" purist position—though I hardly consider myself "pure"—

JS Perhaps what happens today is that most poets of David's generation and the younger poets of my generation don't take the whole thing that seriously. And free money is. . . .

LF Jean-Jacques's argument was that it depends on what you use the money for. If you take the money to live on, that is one thing. But if you take it to instigate a plot to blow something up or to throw sand in the wheels of the machine, then it is justified. He said this kid in Berkeley is interested in using money to buy materials to hatch a big plot. . . . The kid doesn't have time to work because he is working full time on the revolution. This government money will save him from having to get a job, and he can work full time on blowing up the system. I have a note in *Tyrannus Nix* that I would like to get on the record, page 82. It is a note about a line called "The poets and their sad likenesses":

Many American poets do in fact help the Government in sanctioning a *status quo* which is supported by and supports War as a legal form of murder: witness the number of avant-garde poets and Little Presses who have in recent years accepted U.S. grants directly from the National Foundation on the Arts or from its conduit, the Coordinating Council of Literary Magazines, making it clear that the avant-garde in the arts is not *necessarily* to be associated with the political Left. Cf. Marcuse's "repressive tolerance," i.e., the policy of tolerance and/or sponsorship as a self-protection against violence; or as Susan Sontag recently put it, "divesting unsettling or subversive ideas by ingesting them."

The state, whether capitalist or Communist, has an enormous capacity to ingest its most dissident elements.

DM In what sense does a poet help revolution, if at all . . . and what is the revolution?

LF It depends on which revolution you are talking about. I mean, the first thing a poet has to do is to live that type of life which doesn't compromise himself. It seems to me that taking government grants and living on them is compromising himself before he even starts writing.

JS I heard an answer to it while I was involved with the Unicorn Press and they were disputing the matter of taking government money. George Hitchcock presented a very realistic position for taking the money and using it in an almost anarchistic way. He stated that he wanted to be left alone and that this money would help insulate him against the system. He then brought up the point of hypocrisy in consumption. We live in America now and consume American goods and do, in fact, work and do our business in American cities. We are supporting the system in almost every way and to refuse free money seems almost silly. I mean, we are all buying goods that indirectly help support the war.

LF You can't breathe, you can't live in a country, walk down its streets, use a car, and certainly not operate a business or buy anything in a store without having to cooperate against your will. The point is what you have a choice to do and what you don't have a choice to do. You do have the choice of deciding whether or not you are ingested by the state voluntarily and thus becoming a functioning part of it—nourishing it symbiotically, so to speak. The carrot and the stick—*Waiting for Godot* still—Pozzo with Lucky the artist on a string. The next time Nixon runs for office, for instance, he can say he sponsored or supported you. So vote for him, baby. Let's not spoil the spoils system.

From another point of view: say you are running a press . . . I was never offered a grant personally, because I didn't apply for one. But I had some correspondence with Carolyn Kizer about people to recommend for these grants. I wasn't cooperating with her at all. I didn't wish to cooperate as the director of a press. It is doubly bad for a press to take government money. It is almost like a newspaper taking it.

JS What about independent grants like the Guggenheim and the Ford Foundation?

LF The radical would say that these large foundations are just as big murderers as the government is. Are they? I figure it is important to lead the kind of life where you don't have to take grants from any organization. You have to make it on your own without any help. At any point you can tell them to go fuck themselves. And not only can but do tell them. The real problem is to decide who's "them." . . . Well, you can say or print anything you want, according to the government foundations. The director of the program is obviously sincere in saying that there are no strings attached to the money. Grants are renewable the second year. Suppose during the first year you publish something that is really offensive politically or offensive to the sensibilities of those in Washington who hold the purse strings. If you say "Fuck you, Agnew," will you get your grant renewed the second year? Maybe yes.

Here is a part of Carolyn Kizer's reply to me:

> I see no reason why the government shouldn't subsidize attacks on itself. After all, this endowment gave $10,000 to Grace Paley whose activities in various Viet Nam and Peace movements are well known, and another $10,000 to Robert Duncan, who is not exactly friendly to our foreign policy. Why should you be? And what does that have to do with creative art? No, the attack will

come, and is coming, from Congress. One congressman has just sent for all the books written by people to whom we have given grants thus far. And it will continue when our anthologies from the best writings from literary magazines appear, because every literary magazine in the country has been asked to take part in this program. I am sorry that you don't wish to accept any aid from an organization that bears the Great Seal on its letterhead. I myself don't feel that this is the same as refusing an invitation to the White House. Neither does Lowell, for that matter, with whom I am in frequent consultation. . . .

Obviously, the government and congressmen scrutinize the presses who are given money, as she says they are doing in this letter.

Here she says,

Perhaps a similar plan would be feasible for independent small presses. Perhaps I should point out to you that some care and judgment involving considerations not wholly aesthetic will be imperative, particularly in the early stages of such a program. Work chosen for partial Federal subsidy will be subject to the closest scrutiny by persons anxious to attack the Federal Arts Program. Part of the responsibility for this program lies in the development of receptive audiences for the best works of art produced by society—irrespective of how they may offend taboos of specific groups. My own feeling is that shock treatment isn't suitable under such circumstances, but rather a slow and laborious process of increasing exposure to art in all its forms—not the least of which is books beautifully composed and beautifully produced.

Shock treatment isn't in order . . . but rather a slow easy careful development. That's it exactly—from a revolutionary viewpoint today, it *is* time when shock treatment is necessary! It sounds like the Old South when they say, "We can't have any fast changes . . . things have to develop slowly . . . you can't rush the desegregation . . . " and so forth. The blacks were fed up with that and started blowing things up. White radicals feel it is definitely time for shock treatment these days. And it seems to me that most of the poets, especially in San Francisco, are on the whole very quiet. They are certainly not engaging in any shock treatment. Neither for legalizing psychedelics or preventing eco-catastrophe or preventing world war.

DM There have been probably more benefit poetry readings this last year than there have ever been. One a week almost. All concerns: eco-logical concerns, against the war, draft benefits, People's Park . . . it seems like it has been easy to amass large groups of poets to read for nearly any benefit and cause. . . .

LF Who is reading books of poetry these days? The rock generation certainly isn't . . . say under the age of twenty-five. What books are they reading! If you went to the Fillmore and took a poll on how many people have read even Ginsberg, you would probably get about five percent. They just aren't reading books, it seems. The whole revo-lution of the sixties was psychedelic and visual and oral: the poster trip and the rock trip . . . the book wasn't it. Maybe now it is *Zap Com-ics*. The amount of *Zap Comics* we sell at the bookstore is enormous. The average dude who comes in and buys tickets to the Fillmore buys *Zap Comics*. They articulate his "community" for him. They articulate his "counterculture"—and City Lights Bookstore just got busted for selling *Zap*—we haven't been "ingested" yet.

JS What would he buy ten years ago if he came in?

LF Literature . . . Ginsberg. . . .

JS I am under twenty-five, I dig rock music, but I and a circle of friends that is relatively large have always been reading, hanging around book-stores. . . .

LF I was thinking of a group younger than you. Maybe it is splitting hairs about how young. . . .

JS I think a great deal of the movement is concerned with books. . . .

LF Reading books isn't the greatest thing in the world, maybe. We overdid it in my generation. Maybe it's not so all-important to be literate. This new book of mine that New Directions put out, *Tyrannus Nix,* they printed a lot of copies, but what is it going to change? It is not going to change anything, it seems to me. A good rock concert may change people's consciousness faster. That was the argument be-fore Altamont, anyway.

JS Let's trace one book. What about *Howl*? (Those early City Lights books

meant a lot to people in my high school.) Let's bring it down to the nitty-gritty. . . . Is *Howl* selling more than it did five or ten years ago?
LF Well, yes. It is selling more than it sold ten years ago and more than it sold five years ago, but this year the books on the list that sold most were the books by Brautigan. Brautigan's books outsold Ginsberg's, which is quite a surprise. Brautigan got identified with the hippie generation, though he was around long before hippies. He was around in the Beat days and the Beat nights—

There were a few new young poets in the Haight-Ashbury, but none of them ever got well known. It's as if you had to have a guitar to make it. Ginsberg, McClure, Snyder, these were all holdovers, bridge figures from the fifties. Not many others made that bridge. . . . And how did these poets from the fifties bridge the gap? Some used some kind of musical instrument to back up their voices. Like Ginsberg using finger cymbals and then the harmonium . . . and Michael McClure using the autoharp, and I use an autoharp. These were all attempts to bridge this gap. The single unaccompanied voice couldn't stand up to a rock group. I mean, it's murder to come on stage after a good rock group as a single unaccompanied voice. I did this down in Santa Barbara. They had a benefit last spring for Resist, part of Robert Bly's antiwar tour, and Rexroth was master of ceremonies. . . . I didn't get on until 1:00 a.m. I was part of an enormously long variety show program, and I had to follow Mad River. That was really murder. I did one long poem with a taped raga backing up my voice ("Assassination Raga").

I have been doing more with the autoharp lately. In fact, I have chanted some with Daniel Moore's Floating Lotus Magic Opera. Daniel's trip is a very definite part of revolution today. He pulls a lot of separate things together.
JS He is writing only for that now. He doesn't write any more poetry.
LF The libretto is his poetry. I mean it is very much like the poetry he published in *Dawn Visions*. Daniel Moore is really a musical and dramatic genius. Like you have been through the Living Theater, and you have been through Artaud, and here comes Daniel Moore out of all of that with a ceremonial ritual drama. Daniel's solution to the single voice. He started out with the single voice and then got the whole

Tibetan opera backing up his voice. One of the few poets who can make it on his own voice is Ginsberg.

After the blast of the rock scene—in '65 and '66—the San Francisco poets have been singularly silent. There have been a lot of poetry readings, but—for instance—the big reading we had at Norse Auditorium a couple of years ago . . . you know, an awful lot of awful poetry went down that night. Along with some great stuff.

2

LF There is a lot of talk about ecology, and yet they will have 5,000 people at Big Sur Hot Springs completely fouling up the landscape to attend an ecology seminar. Not to mention Altamont. There is really going to be an enormous ecological catastrophe, or ecocatastrophe, within the next ten years, unless something really drastic is done. Capitalism is an outrageously *extravagant* form of existence which is leading to an enormous ecological debacle, unless it is completely changed.

Theodore Roszak, in *The Making of a Counter-Culture*, makes a point that the young radicals are picking on capitalism when they could just as well pick on technocracy in a Communist country. It seems obvious to me that capitalism has got to go. The world ecologically cannot afford capitalism anymore. It's absolutely absurd. An unplanned economy, a laissez-faire economy, or a semi–laissez-faire economy, any kind of incentive capitalism, private incentive capitalism, these are luxuries the Earth cannot stand anymore. The resources won't stand it. The pollution of the atmosphere won't stand it.

There has to be absolute population control on a worldwide basis. Not euthanasia, not compulsory killing of old people. . . . We will have to have worldwide contraception beginning at age twelve. People are going to have to have permission to have children. This is going to be an absolute necessity. We are going to have to do away with these medieval nationalistic forms of government and have a form of central planning. The whole world has got to be run by a huge supranational nonpolitical central planning agency.

It's got to be a form of humanitarian socialism: not authoritarian but a nontotalitarian socialism. I'd like to think it could be a kind of Buddhist socialism. A planned socialist economy is the only way we can avoid the absolute devastation of Earth . . . the absolute pollution of Earth. It has got to happen. I mean, it is really coming up to the way it is laid out in *2001: A Space Odyssey,* where all directions are coming from a central control somewhere. It's a very pessimistic point of view, but some sort of totalitarian supranational state seems unavoidable. I think it is practically impossible to avoid this. This is the last thing anyone wants, but it seems inevitable—whether by cataclysmic war, which will end things up, with one strong central force in control, or by just plain ecocatastrophe. Capitalism just lays waste to too many resources. And the population jump that is going on now. . . . "One half of the people that ever lived are still alive." Think that one over.

I had a poem called "After the Cries of the Birds Have Stopped"—it saw the world of the future where all that was left were roving bands of mystics . . . like those that we call mutants today, would be the only ones left. Roving bands of long-haired mystics . . . the whole materialistic ideal of Western man in his business suit would go down the tube—

A lot of people think that practically any Oriental religion has more to say and has more answers today than Christianity does . . . especially for the youth in this country. It's not that they give an optimistic view of the world or of the future, it's just that they are more realistic. Who can imagine going to a Christian church these days? There are a few exceptions, like the things that have been going on at some far-out churches which are engaging the young on their own terms . . . like the Glide Memorial or the Free Church in Berkeley . . . that's where the Ho Chi Minh funeral parade ended up, at the Free Church in Berkeley. . . .

JS It is interesting that both of those churches you mentioned are in an Episcopalian framework. The church that most of us looked to a few years ago was the Unitarian one.

LF The new Unitarian center in San Francisco . . . the architecture inside is like a Japanese building or a building somewhere in the Far East. It is a beautiful center, and when Baba Ram Das (Richard Alpert) came back from India, that is where he spoke. He and other Jewish Buddhists, "Hindu Cantors," or rabbinic saddhus—

3

LF I am surprised to find that quite a few poets in San Francisco keep guns. I heard that Gary Snyder, Lew Welch, and James Koller held target practice now and then. I wrote Snyder about it and said I felt it was a sellout of his own values to keep guns. He wrote back and said, well, he grew up in the Northwest where things were different from where I grew up in New York City. In the great Northwest, people had guns like household utensils, and it was just an ordinary object that everyone had for survival purposes. He stated his position, which I recognize, but it still didn't alter the basic argument, as far as I was concerned. If you keep guns, then ultimately they are going to be used for the function they were built for. As long as there are guns, they will speak, telescopically. It looks like I'm stuck with the purist position again.

I met a wandering Japanese mystic here in the summer, Nanao Sasaki. He is a friend of Gary's. He is the one that founded that ashram on Suwanose Island. In fact, he is the one that told me about Gary's having the gun. After I wrote this letter to Gary, Nanao said to me: "I'm going to add a P.S.: We do not *have* to survive."

I think there are an awful lot of misguided poets in the West, in S.F. . . . I am not thinking of Gary Snyder now . . . there are plenty of other poets that believe in violence. From this you could explore violence on the left or violence among radicals who consider themselves on the left. I think this is one reason that *Ramparts* magazine finds itself on the rocks. *Ramparts is* a good example of the radical left which supported black power right down the line. . . . Eldridge Cleaver is one of its editors, which is good, because Eldridge Cleaver has about twice as much brains as all the other black radicals that I know. What I meant was, the radical left turns out to have been supporting large elements of the radical right. The most violent elements in the Black Panthers or in the black power movement are not strictly to be identified with Eldridge Cleaver. Naturally, I think Cleaver is great because he seems at least to realize the blacks don't have a monopoly on revolution these days—

"Right on" has become the motto of black power, shouted by many white radicals who never gave support to the word "right" before—

there are all kinds of rightist elements at work in radical circles these days, white and black. For instance, when you say if someone doesn't agree with you, you are going to use force on him, we are going to beat him up, we are going to pull out guns if you don't agree with us— that's also fascist. The assumption of adopting the ideas of Che Guevara, or the principles of guerrilla warfare, as something workable in this country, is absurd, because this is a completely different setup with an entrenched government so powerful it couldn't possibly be overturned by any band of guerrillas or revolutionaries blowing up power plants. Guerrilla theory is based on the assumption that in the early stages of insurrection the mass of the citizenry is going to rise up and support the guerrillas—and this just won't happen in the U.S.A., where the middle class is so well fed. Not until there is another Great Depression could it happen.

I took the plane from here to L.A. on the Friday afternoon commuter special. You are up there at 35,000 feet, sitting next to these executives. The one next to me had a plastic button that said, such and such a name, General Manager, Fairchild. These men ride along up there at 35,000 feet, and they really are the Roman emperors of the world. They have got this enormous technocracy which they control: the military-industrial complex. It's not just a myth. They are actually ruling the whole Earth, and it is so powerful that there is no possibility of this kind of entrenched establishment being overturned by any band of revolutionaries.

As, for instance, even in France it was possible for a student revolution to actually make the government fall, for the whole government to topple, and a new form of government to take its place.

DM There are those who would say that the student revolution, or the student-based anti-Vietnam movement, fought for in this country during the last five years, caused Johnson to resign.

LF I think that's true. People are always saying: what good does it do to march in peace parades? The snowballing peace movement, centered in peace parades in those days, actually did cause Johnson to decide not to run again. I mean, it seems obvious.

JS Well, that would seem to be an effective ploy against the military-industrial complex.

LF But that's as far as it can go. It can't overthrow the government itself and, as I said the other day, the only way it can happen in this country is if there is a great economic Depression again, like in the thirties. I think that will happen. Eventually there is going to be another great boom and bust, and then we will have economic conditions where it will be possible to have a real overthrow of the government. That Great Depression might very well arrive before this is printed—

Nationalism is a medieval form of government. The whole argument during the American Civil War was that the states wouldn't give up any of their states' rights until the federal government could work. Now nations still refuse to give up any sovereignty, or states' rights, in the UN. They refuse to give up their vetoes. And the U.S.A. is the first to refuse to give any of its states' rights. You will have a civil war on a world level so long as these countries won't give up their stupid nationalistic forms. It will be an absolute catastrophe unless they do.

Maybe everyone is getting hysterical on the subject of ecology these days. But it seems to me that things are moving very fast. Every day in the papers there is another ecological disaster. Today there was a story about "strange foreign birds" landing here and there. Or, the day before, there was a "strange epidemic that killed all the fish in the Berkeley estuary."

DM These things have been going on for a long time. The results via the media seem to be more interesting to the public than the process itself.

LF Someone said that the danger is people may well become bored with the word "ecology" before they really comprehend what it means. If we are fortunate, there will be a political revolution in this country which will allow a new ecological control of the world (which is a very doubtful possibility). Suppose you did arrive at a point where a planned economy was instituted. Then you could get down to what would happen to the individual. Is he going to be a mystic, or what is he going to do? Then the individual is free again to write poetry.

JS Would you try to institute a government more concerned with distribution of goods, more concerned with planning, with making sure that somebody is not building too many tract homes . . . ?

LF Right. That is why there needs to be an overall central planning.

JS Sure, and that kind of central planning is for distribution of goods. . . .
LF Of course, this is what the socialist countries are trying to do. This is what it was all about.

DM You start off working theoretically with equal distribution of goods and, all of a sudden, like in a matter of years, it winds up the same thing: somebody, a small nucleus of power, essentially more concerned with power than anything else. What is this peculiar continuity that takes place in revolution? Man reaches the point of overthrowing a so-called tyrannical government and, in turn, winds up propagating the same thing.

LF Man is by nature predatory. It's too bad we can't all be just "predators of sweetness and light."

4

DM One of the general questions we like to ask is, when do you recall your first responses to poetry, your first connection with it . . . ?
LF Up to now, if I had some biographical question to answer, I would always make something up.

Who's Who sent a questionnaire form, and for several years I wrote "Fuck you!" on the Who's Who questionnaire and sent it back to them. But they are very persistent people and they keep writing and they keep saying, "If you don't answer this, we will publish something about you which may not be correct—so you may as well correct this"—so you get involved correcting a column of type that they have written about you that they have scrounged from other sources. I make up a lot of things.

Was I probably born in 1919 or 1920 in either Paris or New York? Some days it's hard to tell. I really don't see the reason for giving a straight answer. For one thing, I enjoy putting on Who's Who. I have done this with a lot of different interviewers, since it is valid for a poet who considers himself a semi-surrealist poet.

If you are going to write in one manner and someone comes to you with some straight questions—why should you give them a straight answer?

For instance, there was a very serious French professor from the Sorbonne who did a long serious book on American poets, and he in-

terviewed me on tape. He asked me what my thesis was at the Sorbonne—
what my doctor's thesis was there. I told him that it was the history of
the pissoir in French literature. The interview was in French. And he
wrote it all down, and it came out in the book that my doctoral thesis at
the Sorbonne was called *The History of the Pissoir in French Literature*. He
is really pissed now. He found out. They'll have to change the index
cards in the Sorbonne where the damn thing is filed. Maybe the place
will be burnt down in the next revolution. That would help.

The way I happened to get into surrealism just now is that I've been
talking to Philip Lamantia, who has just come back into town. It's
really kind of exciting. He has a place in North Beach, a block from
City Lights. He is working with Steve Schwartz, who has started a sur-
realist magazine, *Anti-Narcissus*. Then there is Nanos Valaoritis, who is
an exiled Greek poet-professor at State College. He is more or less iden-
tified with French surrealism. He edited a magazine in Greece which
was a surrealist magazine. I am going to publish a book of their surre-
alist texts, I think. The whole thing comes together after all these years.
We talk and think about some word better than surrealism. At a time
when daily reality far exceeds "literary" surrealism, there really isn't
any better term. I mean, maybe there is, but no one has thought of it
yet. Superrealism? Hyperrealism? Unrealism?

Philip and I have had some funny surrealistic experiences since he
has returned here. We wrote a poem about one, one day. I wrote a
surrealist poem about the surrealist enigma of Ho Chi Minh's funeral
and how a girl we met in North Beach, whom we called Nadja, opened
the door of her womb to Philip Lamantia and inside was a light bulb.
Turn her on—

Anyway, I have been telling Philip that I don't see why he doesn't
consider me a surrealist, too. He says I am just writing fake surrealist
poems. Well, he didn't say "fake surrealist poems," but I had the feel-
ing he thought I was doctoring up my spontaneous visions and put-
ting "thought" in it—making it no longer a pure surrealistic product.
In fact, I *was* doctoring them up. Hyping them up, might be more
accurate.

DM It would be interesting to know your early sources, your early
teachers. . . .

LF The surrealist poets were some of my earliest sources. Especially poets like Apollinaire, who was not really a surrealist. He was more or less the con man of the movement, but I think I learned more from him than others.

JS You chose to go to France to school?

LF My mother was French. I was in France with her when I was a kid. . . . That's not true. [*laughter*] . . . Strike that. I was in France with one of my relatives, one of my French relatives . . . you can never tell whether these statements are true or not . . . I was kidnapped by . . . now this is absolutely true [*laughter*] . . . I was kidnapped by a man, a French cousin of my mother's, who took me to France in swaddling clothes and didn't bring me back to the U.S.A. until I was about six or seven years old.

So later I had some memory of speaking French, and it wasn't too hard to get back to it. It was a natural thing to go back to.

I went to Columbia and got an MA, but the idea of getting a Ph.D. at Columbia was so forbidding . . . the whole discipline and regime you had to go through to get an American Ph.D. . . . yet I wanted to use the GI Bill as much as I could. . . . So I went to Paris on it.

The whole thing about a doctorate at the University of Paris was that you were a free man. You just had to report to the director of your thesis like once every half-year. You could spend decades working on your thesis—some eternal students did just that—one on Rimbaud—they didn't care whether you ever came back. I remember going to the *soutenance*—the public defense of your thesis. It's like the orals they have in this country, but it is in one of those big renaissance lecture halls they have at the Sorbonne and is open to the public. You have a jury of professors up on the stage. You sit with your back to the audience, and the professors are up there in their robes, and they work your thesis over and ask you questions about it, in classical French, and you're supposed to reply in classical French. I guess that was one of the things French students revolted against about two years ago. I must say I made some classic mistakes. I defended translation mistakes by saying that a translation is like a woman—when she is faithful she is not beautiful—when she is beautiful she isn't faithful—

I was free, and this was ideal for someone who wanted to find time and bread to be a writer. To get my monthly GI check, all I had to do was sign a book once a month at the Sorbonne. I got five full years out of the GI Bill that way. And never went to class.

JS What was your thesis eventually on?

DM The pissoir?

LF What thesis? [*laughter*] This is absurd. In fact . . . it was on modern poetry: the *city* in modern poetry, in French and English poetry. In English there are things like Hart Crane's *Bridge* and Eliot's *The Waste Land*. All this fits into city poetry. Things like Francis Thompson's *City of Dreadful Night*. And in French, long poems like Verhaeren's *Tentacular City*—

DM When was this?

LF It could have been after the Second World War, centuries ago.

I didn't know any literary people at all when I was living in France in those days, and I didn't know any Americans who were there writing. Rexroth later told me: "Now I remember I met you in Paris, and you knew so-and-so and so-and-so . . . I'm sure I knew you. . . ." But I didn't know any of the people he says I met. Or it was another me. The first I heard of Rexroth was when I read his introduction to the *Selected Poems of D.H. Lawrence*—he really turned me on to Lawrence. I was living with a French family over in the workers' part of town, near Père Lachaise cemetery, on Place Voltaire. I lived with the family of an old Communist. An old man who looked like Beethoven and who was a music professor, a classical music teacher. I went to the Sorbonne once a month to sign this book, and otherwise I didn't have anything to do with any literary scene.

I got a place of my own in Montparnasse which cost me about $26 a year. It was a cellar with two rooms and a little tiny air-shaft kitchen with a sink hollowed out of solid stone, which must have been there since the Middle Ages, and a front room that had a French window on a courtyard. That was the only window in the two rooms. The middle room had no windows at all. It was very damp in there. And it was dark. There was only light from this front window.

I got the place by sneaking in one night. It was absolutely impossible to find any apartments in Paris. Even today you have to buy the key, and it costs an enormous amount.

I met a plumber in a bar, and he was tubercular, and his wife and children were tubercular. He had three children, and they were all living in this dank two-room apartment, and it was very damp, and the kids were coughing, and they were all sick—and he owed everyone in the neighborhood. We agreed that I would pay up all his debts in the neighborhood so he could leave, and he would move me in at night, and when the concierge came the next day, I would tell her that I was a friend of his and that he was away in the country. So the whole thing cost me $100 to pay off all his debts. It went on like that for three years. I had this place and kept telling the concierge that he was coming back. Maybe me and the concierge and the plumber were the original models for *Waiting for Godot*. Of course, the plumber never came back, and I finally sold the place the same way. Moved out in the middle of the night. That was the place where I wrote *Her*. It wasn't a novel, it wasn't supposed to be a novel. It was a surrealist notebook that I kept, a "black book." It is a book which New Directions calls a novel. They have to call it something. But it never got any reviews in this country. It came out in 1958 or 1959, right after *Coney Island of the Mind*, although I had written the first version of it in 1949 or '50. This book has never gotten any reviews in this country. I got some in France when it came out in French, because it fits into the French tradition of the novel. Like you can fit it in the Robbe-Grillet and Breton's *Nadja*.

Nadja was one of the books I stole from them. I also stole from Djuna Barnes's *Nightwood*. It's full of all kinds of stuff I stole from *Nightwood*—which I always thought was one of the great American expatriate novels. Really great prose. I once told Djuna Barnes that I thought her prose was man's prose, and she said that was the greatest compliment I could have paid her.

The speeches of Dr. Matthew O'Connor are absolutely great prose. They find him in bed dressed as a woman, and he talks of the Night. Watchman, what of the Night. He lays it out. . . .

In this country there is no tradition for a novel like *Her*. The critics don't know what to do with it; they don't have anywhere to place it. It doesn't fit in anywhere. The closest thing I can think of is the work of Anaïs Nin—Virginia Woolf underwater—though what she is saying and what she is preoccupied with is completely different. In fact, she wrote a book about the novel—*The Novel of the Future*—in which she listed *Her*. That is the only reference I have ever seen to *Her* in this country.

. . . .

LF Why is it that there has never been anyone really following *Finnegans Wake* in this country? What happened after that was a complete disintegration of the language and a dissociation of imagery which went into "cut-ups." This is the same surrealist dislocation of imagery which Bill Burroughs arrived at through the physical cutting up of texts. The French and Italian surrealists did cut-ups and collages many years before. Of course, what was new in Burroughs was what he did with it. In him, you have an artificial dislocation of imagery, which is one direction writing could go after *Finnegans Wake*. Joyce had done that as far as one could possibly do it, with his enormous brain, and his superlinguistic genius. The cut-up technique produces the same dissociation of imagery, the same dislocation of imagery, only it is arrived at by mechanical means. In Burroughs's case it didn't come out of the Joycean vision at all . . . it came out of the junkie vision. It was too hard on his own body to keep up the junkie vision. To arrive at a different type of reality dislocation, he cut up the words by cutting up the paper, which was easier on his own head and body. He put down drugs and picked up a pair of scissors. Anyone who can pick up a frying pan—

DM Is that what you could call native American surrealism: a strange, violent reaction to media, cutting it up and throwing it up . . . a sort of fragmenting?

LF Yes. McLuhan said it all, I guess. And we end up with no Joyceans.

DM I don't think so. What about Jack Hirschman?

LF Like in his book *Jah?*

DM Sure. That's like the American *Finnegans Wake*.

LF Hirschman doesn't have the utter brilliance of language and articulation of Joyce. Yet Hirschman has his own. . . .

DM I think it is there and will be known.

LF Henry Miller never did any experimentation with language in this sense.

DM But don't you think that those early books of Miller could act as a valuable contribution to native American surrealism?

LF *Air-Conditioned Nightmare*. . . .

DM Yes, and the *Tropics* and *Black Spring.* He was able to combine the lesson of Europe with the great Buffalo Bill American simplicity. Mickey Mouse faces 300 years of culture. . . .

LF You know, Miller was attracted to Kerouac, at one point. He discovered Kerouac quite late, evidently. I remember when *Dharma Bums* came out. Jack was out here, and he was going to go to Big Sur to stay in my cabin. That is when he wrote a book called *Big Sur.* His editors must have named it, because it had nothing to do with Big Sur. He never really got into the Sur at all, never got south of Bixby Canyon. Miller was turned on to the *Dharma Bums.* They were talking to each other on the phone. Jack was here in City Lights and Miller was in Big Sur. They were going to meet for dinner at Ephraim Donner's house in Carmel Highlands. Miller went to Donner's, and Jack was drinking in town here. The afternoon kept getting later and later. Kerouac kept saying, "We'll get there, we'll leave soon. . . ." It got later and later, and Jack kept telling them on the phone, "We're leaving now. We'll be there in three hours . . . two-and-a-half hours, we'll make it in two . . . Cassady will drive me . . . we'll be there in no time. See you at seven." At seven Kerouac is still in town drinking. Eight o'clock. Nine o'clock . . . Miller is sitting, waiting. Kerouac never got there. And I don't think they ever did meet. That was the end of it.

Dharma Bums had all the elements that would appeal to Miller. The on-the-road trip, the air-conditioned nightmare, the mountaintops, and that freedom . . . the whole idea of dharma bums.

I haven't seen Kerouac in a long time . . . but I imagine that Jack is probably sitting in front of his TV set, wearing a baseball cap, with a bottle of Skid Row tokay, watching the ball game on TV in central Florida. Something seemed to die in him early in the 1950s—the Hemingway parallel again. Killing himself. Yet, by age forty-seven, he's written more and better than the Great Hunter. . . .

5

LF The French intellectual is something that I put down lately. The whole French civilization has led to their having become very effete. Even many of the ones involved in the May revolution last year. The difference between the young radical out here on the West Coast and the French intellectual is enormous. The American can do things himself with his hands . . . he is into the whole survival thing. There's no such thing as the *Whole Earth Catalog* in France. Of course, there are utopian communes there, but you have no such thing as groups that are doing everything themselves, making everything themselves, like leather, clothes, books, tools, and so on. . . .

The intellectual in Europe is like the intellectual in South America, Latin America. He doesn't wash dishes, for instance. Still a woman's place to do all that crap. The intellectual in Latin America (this isn't so in France) may talk very revolutionary ideas, but he is usually very well dressed in a white shirt, necktie, and even cuff links. When Ginsberg and I went to South America in 1959, this surprised me. We met poets and writers and intellectuals and professors from all the South American countries at this conference in Concepción. Including a lot of Communists. And practically everyone was meticulously dressed. They didn't have drip-dry shirts in those days, either. In other words, there was a housekeeper, a *criada* back home, ironing those shirts and doing the laundry. No one questioned this, in public at least. . . .

The second big difference I found was there were no mystic trips going on in France. Naturally, there are older mystics, and there have always been writers. René Daumal—for instance, *Mount Analogue*—but in the young kids, the revolutionary-age groups, there's little mysticism . . . nothing like the Hare Krishna Society or Zen or Gurdjieff. The kids who are turned on to Gurdjieff in America, however, don't realize the European background for the movement. Claude Pelieu is a French poet and translator living in the States, and he enlightened me on the history of Gurdjieff in Europe. I don't know whether this is all true, but it seems that Gurdjieff was a White Russian refugee from the Revolution. He left Russia in 1917 or so, and made quite a few counterrevolutionary statements at that time. Then he traveled to the Near East and had some contact with the Sufis. It's in his book, *Conversations with Remarkable Men*. During the Second World War, according to Pelieu, Gurdjieff was living in the suburbs of Paris and received Hitler and several of Hitler's main henchmen. In London and Paris Gurdjieff's followers were rich dilettantes. Rich old ladies and members of the upper leisure class.

They have a big hang-up on money in the Gurdjieff groups. You have to pay quite a lot of bread to attend, in some groups at least. Over here, the kids don't realize the possibly neofascist tendencies. Of course, Gurdjieff shouldn't be held responsible for what various followers have done with his ideas in America.

I mentioned before the neofascist tendencies among radicals. And it is in things like Scientology, which is very full of neofascist ideas. I would class them all together as a sort of psychic authoritarianism.

JS A friend of mine did a study at UBC. His doctoral thesis was on the fascist approach of youth today and how it is like the German youth of the late twenties and early thirties. Then the kids about my age were going to the woods and reading Hermann Hesse. They were carrying backpacks and hitchhiking all over the country. Women were hitchhiking publicly, singly. My friend firmly believed that the movement today is turning toward a kind of neofascism, toward a kind of psychic or intellectual fascism. Very strange. You can probably document it. Especially in Berkeley now. If you are not a member of the team, you are an enemy. The only escape is to claim that you are a visionary incompetent. That's the only way I make it. I go and say that I am not going to march on your line, and I am not a black power advocate, etc., etc., because I have something working in my mind that makes it impossible for me to participate in your physical revolution. They all allow me, but they won't allow another person who is just a good middle-class liberal, just simpatico. Very strange. But they will allow visionary incompetents. In fact, they encourage them. They figure these people to be as harmless as any.

6

LF I came to S.F. in December of 1950. Rexroth was the center of the scene. Robert Duncan was here. There was also a scene around Duncan. Rexroth used to have Friday night open houses for all the poets who would go sit at his feet. I was very timid when I was living in France, and I would never dream of looking up a "literary figure." When Allen goes to France, he looks up everybody. He looked up Michaux or Céline. . . . I would never think of going out and meeting these people on my own.

When I came to S.F. I heard about Rexroth. I heard about him through Holly Bye, who was a friend of Kenneth Patchen's. Holly Bye was married to a printer named David Ruff, and they had a printing press. I met Patchen through Holly Bye.

The Patchens were living in North Beach. Patchen moved from the East Coast in about 1955, I think. I was living in an attic in Pacific Heights. I met Holly because she had gone to Swarthmore with Kirby, my wife. They were at Swarthmore together, and so she was the only person we knew here . . . the first person who had anything to do with any literary scene, and I think they took me over to Rexroth's house for the first time in about 1953. I was completely tongue-tied. I mean, he was a great man. I wasn't about to say anything! I went back for years before I even opened my mouth. I mean, even when he moved over to Scott Street, I was still the same way. I never said anything over there. I was too bashful to speak up. It was only in the late 1950s that I felt I could carry on a discussion with him.

DM Was Kenneth Patchen sick when you first met him?

LF He walked with a cane even then, but he was able to get around. He walked and shopped around North Beach. Shopping bag and cane. The Patchens lived on Green Street in North Beach, and he would come to the bookstore a lot. Except once. After we started publishing books, around 1955, it was Patchen's idea to have an autograph party for his book (*Poems of Humor and Protest*). We announced it and a crowd came, but he never showed up. That was the first and last time I ever gave an autograph party! His wife, Miriam, called up and said Patchen was feeling too bad to come.

Then his back got worse and worse. They moved to Palo Alto to be near the hospital, and they are still down there. It is in a sort of cul-de-sac off the freeway. And he just can't get out. He's just too sick. Painkillers all the time. It's a fucking tragedy. One of the great original American voices. And Stanford University has—so far as I know—never even recognized his presence. They should at least give him an honorary title of poet in residence. Even if they can't find a cent for him. It's disgraceful. Well, he doesn't need Stanford! I talked to him on the phone this week, for the first time in about a year. He said he had been a prisoner of his room for ten years. He sounds awful on the phone,

obviously in pain. . . .
DM Does the future look any brighter for him?
LF No. He's had so many operations on his back. The Patchens once sued the doctors for malpractice, which was a very bad thing to do, because the case was thrown out of court, and the real result was that no doctor would take his case. He would come up here and sit in the lobby of the hospital, and no doctor would touch him. He's been wanting to move away from this area, to go somewhere where he isn't blackballed by the medical profession.

The Patchens have investigated Florida and places like Tucson, where the climate is good, but he said on the phone last week: "There's one thing I can't tolerate still, and that is intolerance."
DM When did you first start publishing City Lights books?
LF We started the bookstore in June of 1953. There was Pete Martin, who was an instructor in sociology at State College, and he was also a film buff. Pete Martin put out a magazine which was sociologically oriented toward film. It was called *City Lights,* an early pop-culture publication. It had people like Pauline Kael writing in it, and Mickey Martin and the Farbers.

I don't know where I saw the magazine *City Lights.* There was a total of five or six issues and, for some reason, I sent them some of my translations of Jacques Prévert. I discovered North Beach around this time, about 1952. The Black Cat was the first place I ever went to and then the Iron Pot. I met Pete Martin around then. He said, "Oh, you sent me those Prévert translations!" He used them, and I think that was the first thing I ever got published.

The bookstore was started to pay the rent for the magazine at the same location, 261 Columbus. That little second floor was the magazine office. I didn't have anything to do with the magazine, but I started the bookstore downstairs with Pete Martin. The idea was that we would open it up a few hours a day. Pete Martin was full of great ideas. He now runs a bookstore in New York, called the New Yorker Bookstore. I've never been in it, but I'm sure it's one of the most original around, knowing Pete—

In those days there were no pocket bookstores in the country. There weren't any pocket books except Penguins and the cheap ones you found in drugstores. And there was no place to buy them except in places like drugstores. It's pretty hard to imagine no paperback bookstores, but this was in 1953. So Pete Martin's idea was to have this place that had nothing but the best pocket books and to have all the political magazines, from left to right, which you couldn't get anywhere else. As soon as we opened the place, we couldn't get the door closed. Right from the beginning it was open until midnight, seven days a week, since 1953.

Pete Martin had so many ideas that he'd take off on something else before he finished the first thing. He split for New York after our first year. Got married or divorced, and the bookstore just continued. We started publishing in 1955. Just poetry. . . .

JS The books were typically modeled after French books . . . ?

LF The little ones, the Pocket Poets series. The first ones we put out had a pasted-on label. I got this idea from Patchen's early edition of *An Astonished Eye Looks Out of the Air,* which had a pasted-on label window around the middle of it, with the title on it. The first one was done by hand. David Ruff and Holly Bye and Kirby and myself and Mimi Orr pasted on covers and gathered it by hand, like any other little press. The first printing was 1,000 copies. . . . [The first publication of the Pocket Poets series was *Pictures of the Gone World* by Ferlinghetti.]

Howl was the fourth book. The second was Rexroth's *Thirty Spanish Poems of Love and Exile,* and Patchen's *Poems of Humor and Protest* was the third book. And then came *Howl.* Now we are printing 20,000 at a crack on Ginsberg's books, on the reprints of all his books—*Planet News, Reality Sandwiches, Kaddish, Howl* . . . it's a lot of books of poetry. About once a year these books have to be reprinted. The first edition of *Howl* was only 1,500 copies.

We have over fifty books in print now. We were distributing a lot of other little presses up to this year, like Dave Haselwood, Four Seasons, Don Allen, Coyote, to fill out our list. It was an interesting thing to do. One bookstore where other bookstores could order all these little press books. We put them all together in one catalog and sent it across the country to libraries and book dealers. But it got to be too big, too much work. This year I decided I'd just have to slough off the little presses and just do our own books. . . . We were hung up in the city doing the dirty work on getting the books around the country, while half of the small-press editors were out in their communes turned on. I was also put off by the little presses taking government money. Most of them were taking grants from the National Foundation of the Arts, and I disagreed with doing that, and I didn't want to be caught up in cooperating in this.

I don't take any bread out of it now. I live on my royalties from New Directions. I used to work at the store like forty hours a week. Shig is the one that has always put in thousands of hours a week. The store couldn't have existed without him. He is the one that has really held it together all these years.

I haven't worked regularly at the bookstore in five or six years. In the fifties I worked there regularly, and that is what I lived on. I used to draw about $300 a month, at the most.

The bookstore really is unintentionally a nonprofit operation. Like in that old joke. For years the bookstore supported the publishing; now the publishing is better off than the bookstore. The bookstore keeps going, but there are more and more books, and there never is any cash left over after the fucking government gets paid! There are a lot of people living off it, though. We have six or eight people working. It's a good way to live, an interesting way to live—to say the least!

I have always believed in paying authors good royalties . . . as much as the New York publishers pay for paperback books. In fact, Allen Ginsberg gets more, because of the volume of his books. He gets more than paperback publishers normally pay. I don't know whether you would want to know how much royalties he got last year, but he got about $10,000 from City Lights. Which is a lot for a little press. The bottom dog on our list is Edward Dahlberg's *Bottom Dogs,* so far as copies sold each year go.

DM I guess you will be going on a reading tour now. . . .

LF Yes, I will be. It would be ideal when I go on a college reading tour to have something to back up my voice with. This is not to say that the voice can't make it on its own. It can make it on its own in a traditional reading, in a room with a lot of graduate students sitting there, the traditional type of poetry reading with a lot of polite mur-

muring and polite applause . . . but when you get into a mass scene where you have an enormous audience, not only do you have to have poems that have a good deal of "public surface" and might be considered performance poems, but it takes a very exceptional voice to make it with an enormous audience. Allen Ginsberg is one of the few that make it. He can be on the same program with a rock group because he has such a marvelously full voice. He could read the phone book and make it sound like a great poem.

For a person with a normal voice, like myself, it's great if you can use something like an autoharp. I can use an autoharp at home, but it is kind of cumbersome to carry around the country. . . . I can use it at home and turn on and get high chanting. But to do this at a big public reading . . . the idea is to come up with what you might call an American mantra.

One thing about the autoharp is that it is an indigenous American instrument. It's not like using the sitar or tamboura. And if you are using a guitar, you have to have a certain level of professional competence—unless you play it upside down in some cuckoo fashion and beat on it with a chopstick or play it with your teeth or something. Otherwise, I wouldn't get up on the stage with my guitar.

You can't take just any old poem and strum to it in the background. I am not talking about that. Nothing was worse than most of the poetry and jazz in the fifties. Most of it was awful. The poet ended up sounding like he was hawking fish from a street corner. All the musicians wanted to do was blow. Like, "Man, go ahead and read your poems, but we gotta blow."

Krishnamurti was here last winter and he was at a party. I asked him what he thought of chanting Hare Krishna, and he said, "Might as well chant Coca-Cola or Ave Maria." Kirby walked up and asked him for his autograph. And he refused. She really admired him. She had just finished reading one of his books and was very sincere about it. It was a faculty party after he'd given a lot of lectures in Berkeley. Mostly faculty people—everyone standing around in those cocktail dresses, suits; and he sort of away in a far end by himself. Kirby walks up with this book and pen and asks him to sign it. He would not sign it. He said: "Too much vanity." She felt really put down. It seemed to me that it is much more vain to refuse an autograph than to sign one.

I had a strange "conversation" with him, because he seemed very ill at ease at this party, like he didn't know whom to talk to. He didn't want to talk to all these people who looked like they were made of glass or plastic. He sort of looked like that, and I was the only guy in the room with a beard. This was before McClure and a whole contingent arrived. Anyway, Krishnamurti was standing around the punch bowl, but I couldn't get close enough to him to hear his voice. We were always about five feet apart. I would move up a little to hear his voice more clearly, and he moved back, as if he were afraid, as if I were going to break his bones or something. He was a very fragile-looking man. The conversation went something like this—he said: "I don't eat meat." I said: "Big deal! Neither do a lot of my friends." He said, "But I have never *tasted* it." I said: "OK, you win." That was about the sum total of my exchange with Krishnamurti. Brilliant.

Speaking of influence . . . Blaise Cendrars's *On the Trans-Siberian* was written maybe sixty years ago. Well, I read it and took the train in 1967. I took the Trans-Siberian from Moscow across Siberia—seven days and six nights—on the basis of having read this poem. I got pneumonia and was in a seamen's hospital near Vladivlostok in a town called Nakhodka, a workers' city. I damn near died! I could have died out there, and no one would have known for months and months. It was on the Sea of Japan, and there were no communications whatsoever with the outside world. None with Japan, and the only communication was back to Moscow. I don't know how we got started on that, except . . . except the power of the poem. I mean, that shows what literature can do in the way of changing the world. (I damn near died, thanks to Blaise Cendrars.)

Lawrence Ferlinghetti II (1999)

© Mary Calvert

September 7, 1999: I'm early and run into Ferlinghetti on Columbus Avenue. I tell him I need some coffee, so we head for Café Greco for a doppio-to-go and then walk back to his City Lights office. On the way to the store, he tells me of his Sephardic roots. Jim and Marina are there when we return, and so is a construction crew retrofitting the building against earthquake. Ferlinghetti is playful and shines with pink auras of exercise and the good life; he's achieved an admirable equilibrium, in contrast to too many of his fellow travelers. Like Jack Hirschman, he is often more at home in Europe than in the States.—DM

Lawrence Ferlinghetti (**LF**)
David Meltzer (**DM**)
James Brook (**JB**)
Marina Lazzara (**ML**)

DM [*testing the mike*] Say something.
LF Yeah, say something to see whether you're alive.
DM This is a coda to the interview that we did about thirty years ago.
LF Coda is "tail" in Italian.
DM Well, this is the tail of the tale then.
LF Let's wag the coda.

DM Coda goes into "cod" and "codpiece" and all of that. . . .

JB Maybe we should start with "Il Capo" and work our way down?

LF I always wondered about Cape Cod. Are there a lot of people out there wearing codpieces?

DM It's possible. Those Calvinists, you know, you turn your back. . . .

LF I know Provincetown is that way.

DM It's a strange place. Isn't H.P. Lovecraft from Provincetown?

LF Yeah. There's a lot of love craft going on there.

DM But seriously . . . I'd like to ask a relatively easy question: in the thirty years since *The San Francisco Poets* what has changed and what is the same?

LF Oh well, you know, there have been so many interviews about the Beats in the last ten years. It's such an old story now. You know, I think people ought to stop resurrecting this dead decade from thirty years ago. But what's different today? That's a valid question. Everything's different. In France you wouldn't know that 1968 ever happened. And here it's beginning to look that way, too. The Beats were Stone Age hippies. They articulated all the themes that became the major shibboleths of the hippie counterculture. The first articulations of an ecological consciousness. There were people like Gary Snyder and a big dissident antiwar stance, pacifist stance, turning toward Buddhism. . . .

DM But wasn't there a distinct difference in terms of the postwar generation coming out of the Second World War and the atomic bomb and the Holocaust, and the sixties generation coming to consciousness in the Vietnam War?

LF The sixties generation saw the Second World War as ancient history. That's the way the kids are today. If you mention the sixties, they think you're talking about some other civilization—the way we thought of the twenties, for instance.

DM But when one talked about the twenties, there was an aura of romance about a lot of that.

LF So now there's an aura of romance about the Beats.

DM That's right. And the further away you get from it, it seems, the more uncomplicated it all gets. It becomes simpler and simpler, like a fairy tale. . . .

LF It's more like a fish story that grows and grows. There's more on the scales every time.

DM What do you think of the persistent attraction of that particular era?

LF Not to sound like an oracle, but I would say this is what the world still needs today. It still needs the Beat message, more so than ever with the technological brainwash and general dumbing-down of America. . . .

[*Inside the bookstore, welders weld and drillers drill as they make repairs.*]

LF It's a technophiliac consciousness that seems to be sweeping the world. And more than that . . . it's that huge all-engulfing corporate monoculture that is sweeping around the world. It's the most boring culture imaginable. It makes everything looks the same. . . . Countries that were under dictatorships, like in Central Europe—the first thing they do when they get liberated is rush to adopt the worst features of American culture—like the automobile and the television. . . .

DM Fast food. . . .

LF Fast food and the whole schmear.

DM Why do you think that is?

LF We're in the middle of a revolution. It's just in its early stages—like the early stages of the Industrial Revolution. It's transforming everyone's consciousness. Ram Dass's "Be Here Now" was the slogan in the sixties, and it could have been the slogan for the Beats. Kerouac was very much "Be Here Now" before he got too drunk to be here anymore. Today with the cell phone, fax, television, computers, and e-mail, what they're saying is: "Be Somewhere Else Now." When you see a young guy obviously from Silicon Valley with his girlfriend in an expensive restaurant in North Beach, he's talking on his cell phone in the middle of dinner. Not only is it impolite but it's "Be Somewhere Else Now." You can say the Beats were a precursor of the sixties' youth revolt against all this.

DM Both were revolts against materialism.

LF Yeah, against materialism, militarism, against the technophiliac mentality, greed, Moloch.

DM But also the concept of power as being so overwhelming and in-surmountable, almost replacing the notion of Yahweh.

LF It was very noticeable in the fifties but not as glaringly obvious as today with the concentration of power, the rich getting richer and the poor getting poorer, the gap getting bigger. Warren Hinckle wrote me a note last week. He asked me to write a piece for the *Independent* against the sale of the *San Francisco Examiner,* against San Francisco becoming a one-newspaper town. I wrote back and said I can't really write occasional poems, but it's obvious that this whole incorporation and concentration is just a part of the worldwide concentration of power in fewer and fewer hands . . . the financial, the military, and every other kind of power in the hands of people like George Soros. The military-industrial complex, for instance—Rexroth used to rave about it—is still very much a reality today.

DM But now it's also disseminating to other countries, like India.

LF Or the bombing of Kosovo, for instance. Unfortunately, my friend Vaclav Havel wrote a piece in *The New York Times* claiming that the Kosovo war was the first altruistic war in this century. I wrote him a letter in which I said, I think you're totally wrong, I mean, the Americans weren't in there on altruistic grounds. They were in there to make the world a little safer for corporate capitalism.

DM Well, it's what they call globalization.

LF I remember ten years ago, Charles Schwab or another big firm downtown had a motto on their letterhead: "Go Global."

DM It's better than "Tomorrow the World"! In the face of all this, what's the function and role of art and poetry today?

LF Well, as Lenny Bruce used to say, "Art's been in the band a long time. I don't know what his function is exactly. I think he plays the sax and sweeps the place out at night." The function of art and poetry?

DM Does it have a function?

LF Well, yes, it certainly does. It has a function, but whether the function has any effect is another story. Poetry is mostly confined to very small journals. At best, a poet can get a poem into *Harper's,* for instance. If you're really, really lucky you get one in the op-ed page of *The New York Times,* which now has a policy against publishing poetry unless it's directly related to a current event. They published my "Populist Manifesto" years ago—though it was out of sync with what was happening in the world.

DM Has art itself become so marginalized?

LF It's become marginalized because . . . well, equate poetry with the left side of the political spectrum, just for the sake of argument, which it generally is, at least our kind of poetry . . . the left has no journals now, no major literary magazines. Journals like *Partisan Review* still exist, but City Lights sells maybe three copies a month. In the fifties and sixties, we sold thousands. There are no radio stations. And this is part of the corporate concentration again. The whole nationalization of KPFA and Pacifica is part of the same thing. They're closing down eccentric radio stations like KPFA. Stamping out the opposition. Up through the 1940s, say, the left was powered by the labor movement, but today it isn't. Today there is no motor on the left. The left and Soviet Communism—a corruption of Marxism—were discredited. But true socialism was never given a chance, except in the Scandinavian countries.

DM So there's the disintegration of the left—or a complete paving over it in terms of the information highway—is that what you're saying? That even to affiliate with the left is to affiliate with a kind of quixotic. . . .

LF Lost cause?

DM Which has a certain amount of pathos but absolutely no purpose.

LF I think that if we've accepted that it was a lost cause, we wouldn't be here today. I mean we can't accept that. . . .

DM That's what I'm getting at: does one just roll over as an artist, as a poet?

LF No, now I think you still have to hope for a revolution with a capital E. I think the only way you're going to have a revolution in this country these days is by going through another huge major depression like 1929. People are too well fed now. They don't give a shit.

DM They're numbed by abundance. This is a culture of unbelievable abundance. The Internet is a stupefyingly abundant domain. I know a lot of people who have Web sites and who are doing interesting work, and I know I can find any political subcultural radical or reactionary Web site. It's all out there, and that "all-out-there-ness" also boggles and further pacifies.

LF Web means, what, "spider web"? You get caught in it and you can't get out.

DM You can't get out.

LF That is, if you're a butterfly.

DM A butterfly or just a fly.

LF If you're an eagle, you can fly right through it, though.

DM OK, so where are the eagles?

LF We're looking for the eagles. There's one perched on the roof right now, but it won't come down.

DM I remember when we did the interview thirty years ago, you were talking about wanting to paint, that poetry was not cutting it.

LF Did you say we did this interview thirty years ago?

DM No, we did an interview thirty years ago, and . . .

LF Now we're doing the interview we should have done thirty years ago?

DM Possibly. I don't know. The beat goes on. . . .

LF Oh, no, let's leave that one out!

[*laughter*]

LF Without Allen Ginsberg there wouldn't be any Beat Generation. He articulated and created it out of whole cloth. Without him, there would be great writers in the landscape, but not called a "Beat" generation. He'd worked in journalism and could write a tight piece of prose. Very tight. Everything he ever published had that same compactness and attention to detail. He always said the concrete is the most poetic.

DM But what did Williams say about "No ideas but in things"?

LF Now there's a statement I always thought was really asinine. Things are inanimate objects, right? This produces a pretty deadly type of poetry. But, you know, "things" wasn't really what he meant. He should have said, "No ideas but in beings." This is what it really was.

DM So Allen was vanguardist and mother hen. . . .

LF Well, that's how he started out. He had this really great discipline for economy of prose and direct statement, but I feel he didn't de-velop beyond that. He wanted to be rock star, instead. Allen wanted to be more and more a performance poet with music on stage . . . per-forming with Bob Dylan, for instance, and hanging out with the Beatles. I think it did his poetry a lot of harm. I was his publisher up till the time Harper & Row stole him, ten years before he died. I thought there was a shocking deterioration in his poetry, especially in the pieces that were great performance pieces. Allen was a master performer on stage and could take one of those purposely doggerel rhymes and perform it alone with his harmonium or with a whole band behind him. It sounded great when he performed it. But on the printed page it didn't make it.

DM That brings up another interesting point of what happens when artists become celebrities. By becoming a star or perceived as one, you become further one-dimensionalized as an artist.

LF I know that's ruined my relationship with several women over the years! I find that even with semi-fame in a small puddle, fame is a disaster for the creative artist. It eats up all your time. Everyone's calling on you to do this and that. You have to do something with it, you have to answer it, you have to dream up some reason why you can't come, answer why you can't come. It takes time. There are a lot of things you feel you have to do. You have to fulfill your role, although you might not have done anything to get that role. It's thrust upon you. Like being poet laureate of San Francisco. I didn't even know it was going to happen. This past year being the poet laureate has been a disaster as far as creative work.

But I was critiquing Allen's poetry—which I had the nerve to do! I'll say this: Allen Ginsberg was never compromised. Even though he was in a Gap ad. At the bottom of the ad it said everything coming in would go to some charitable cause. As his publisher, I sent him royalty checks every year. I know that by the time the next year rolled around, Allen was broke—he'd given away every penny.

DM Isn't it true he created a kind of fund to help out artists and poets?

LF The fund was in his pocket. Just before he died he was calling people up and saying, "Do you need any money?" The night before he died.

ML So he was still taking care of them. . . .

LF People all over the world, people who had never met Allen, felt close to him. When we had the memorial at the synagogue in San Francisco; it was a beautiful event. We received so many wires and telegrams and e-mails from people who didn't know him personally but just felt close to him.

DM It's a success in the true sense of the word. It's not the tragedy of fame.

LF He was a genius. Another thing about Allen was, you can say that the "graph of consciousness school" of poetry was great when he did it or when another of the originators did it. Allen had a genius mind. He had a pack-rat mind. I remember when I went to Australia with him. He wrote down everything. We walked down the streets in Fiji, and he wrote everything down . . . the names of trees . . . he stopped and asked the natives what kind of worm was that crawling on the ground. And he would buy stuff. He started off in San Francisco. He went to the Army and Navy store where he bought a huge empty duffel bag about this long and this big and round. By the time we got to Australia, he had it full. You know, a medicine man's chopsticks, whatever, gourds and masks and things. A fascinating mind. But then when you have this same poetics practice by all these thousands of students who don't have the sensibility of the original creators of this style, this poetics, it makes for very boring poetry. I've seen the best minds of our generation destroyed by boredom at poetry readings.

DM Sometimes they're cruel and unusual punishment. Of course, like many poets, he had an ongoing curiosity. And he was a notebook person, and with so many of the poets we've been interviewing, the notebook is part of their practice. They're taking down everything, because sooner or later it's going to be used for something, and they don't want to forget the names. We are custodians of names, actually.

LF I got up at five this morning to write down a couple of lines before they escaped me.

DM What's to replace what's gradually vanishing of a particular movement and a particular consciousness and practice?

LF Does anything have to replace it?

DM I don't know. I'm asking you.

LF Maybe we don't have to exist. I really feel that this is the autumn of our civilization.

DM You do?

LF In so many ways. You might say that from the European point of view, the height of Western civilization was the Edwardian Age, ending just before the First World War. Think of the high Jewish culture in Vienna, for instance, or the culture in Berlin or London in the 1890s.

DM I'm interested in this recurrent interest in spiritual practices such as Buddhism, for instance, which has been important to most of the poets I've interviewed so far.

LF There's a turning inward in reaction to the materialist culture.

DM Does the turning inward lead to something that goes outward to . . . ?

LF Hopefully. To get back to Allen Ginsberg's poetry, I think Buddhist practice really harmed his poetry. It was a turning inward. In Zen you sit facing the wall for your meditation. I find there isn't the fresh observation, the freshly observed minute detail that's in his early poetry. The whole concept of "no mind" was an unfortunate motto in a lot of ways. No mind, no thinking? That's good?

DM Well, it's a particular kind of utopian ideal that suits many people. It's the ideal state. It's like a precursor of Alzheimer's. There's no past, there's no future. You're literally in the now.

LF Well, Allen needed Buddhism because he was by nature so aggressive. He was always out there, loved talking to people, and loved talking on the telephone.

DM It's interesting that the Buddhism he was first attracted to was Tibetan Buddhism. It's like Italian Catholicism, like Dante . . . it wasn't the Zen Buddhism that Gary's been practicing all these years.

LF Gary's sensibility is essentially Teutonic, it seems to me. Such a sensibility could be very opposed to Allen Ginsberg's poetics of ecstasy, for instance. Gary believes very strongly in the work ethic, which is the opposite of hanging out. That kind of thing.

DM Where's the "Teutonic"?

LF Gary's poetry isn't exactly ecstatic. Whereas Allen at one point was saying, "I'm only interested in moments of exstasis." But another influence on Gary would be Kenneth Rexroth—he's maybe the most important influence. I find that Gary's mountain poetry and love poetry, especially his mountain poetry, come right out of Rexroth. Rexroth was a great love poet and a great nature poet. It's really unforgivable that no one reads him these days. There was a certain *sublimity* to all his poetry.

DM Do you want to go into the future?

JB I thought we just wrote it off!

ML You told us we're in the autumn. Tell us about winter.

LF Well, no. I haven't written off the future at all! I mean there very well could be another revolution of consciousness in this country early in the coming century. In the sixties there was a revolution in consciousness. The political revolution was aborted. Maybe we don't see the big picture of what's coming. The ecosystem is such a huge, finely balanced system. It could crash like a computer before tomorrow morning. Take, for instance, the ozone hole and global warming. The ecosystem could reach critical mass just about anywhere. It could crash overnight. Of course, in the long run, it could happen anywhere where the fuels give out. Every city in the world is under attack from the automobile. Now we're gonna get really gloomy!

JB On a positive note, maybe we can talk about the destruction of San Francisco?

LF There is an interesting book that City Lights published a few years ago called *Resisting the Virtual Life,* resisting the technological and electronic onslaught. If you read the morning paper, about half of the stories describe some disaster, some crisis. Why are they cutting down the redwoods? Why are they cutting down the rain forest? Because they need more trees because there's more people. Why is the air polluted? Why more automobiles? Because more people demand more automobiles. You can have temporary solutions. Build another bridge across the bay. By the time you get it built, you'll need another one. You can get temporary solutions. The trouble is, in ecology every defeat is permanent and every victory is temporary. OK, so population control is the one thing that no politician in this country will dare propose.

Another aspect of the twenty-first century is that nations as we know them will no longer exist. Not right away, but within the century, because already pollution has no respect for boundaries. Multinational corporations have no respect for national boundaries. International finance has no respect for national boundaries. Nations around the world are having a harder time maintaining their borders, and there are huge immigration battles going on in all the Western democracies. In France, in England, in Italy, in Germany, in the United States. And this is only a hint of what's going to happen later in the century. The boundaries will be absolutely porous. They recognize this in Europe. I recently traveled from Italy to France without a passport. I couldn't get back in the United States without it, but . . .

DM So the nation-state concept is . . .

LF It's an antiquated concept that came out of the nineteenth century. Nations as we know them no will longer exist. Günter Grass told me when he came back from living in the slums of Calcutta for a year, about ten years ago, that he saw the twenty-first century with no more nations and the world swept by ethnic hordes in search of food and shelter.

DM So that's the future?

JB That's the good news!

[*laughter*]

DM Well, then should we . . .

ML Write poetry.

DM Write poetry?

JB Stock up on canned goods?

LF Stock up on poetry of light, of hope, of love. Stock up on ecology, humanitarian socialism, philosophical anarchism, pacifism, mushrooms, and pot cookies.

Jack Hirschman (1998)

Courtesy Jack Hirschman

December 30, 1998: I meet up with Jim and Marina in front of City Lights, and we walk into North Beach to a second-floor flat that Hirschman and his wife, artist/poet Agneta Falk, are house-sitting for some friends. It's a warm, lived-in place with paintings on the walls and bookcases jammed with emblems of booked time. The rite of "setting up" is performed: Aggie makes tea and coffee, and there are pastries on the table where we park our tape recorder. One of the most powerful poetry readers of his generation, Jack's voice is deep (further deepened by a return to cigarettes). We check the sound levels. Then begin.—DM

Jack Hirschman (**JH**)
David Meltzer (**DM**)
James Brook (**JB**)

JH I was born in New York, in the Bronx on December 13, 1933. My father was as a sort of nickel-and-dime insurance agent for Prudential with a big, fat book. His mother was born in the southern part of

Russia, in the Ukraine. She came here in 1899. My father was born in New York City, and so was my mother. I was born just when the Depression really got going. My mother worked as a secretary for most of her life—for another insurance company.

My father had an enormous influence on me. He was a man of great energy, a man of great willfulness. He was a New Dealer, and so was my mother. My mother felt that she was sort of a socialist because Eugene Debs had kissed her once. Though she was a New Dealer on the surface, she'd vote Socialist in the presidential elections. For forty-five years my father was the writer of a Pythian newsletter for a group of guys, mostly Jewish guys, that got together in the Knights of Pythias. The neighborhood was largely Jewish and Italian, so there were also Italians in that group.

My father was a man of great verbal energy. He fancied himself a man of the theater, was extremely handsome, looked a bit like Errol Flynn. Later on in life he played an extra in a film called *Supercop* in 1977. He was the neighborhood comedian, organizer of bar mitzvahs, weddings, and funerals. A funny man, but sometimes personally humiliating because he could make a joke about anything, including his family.

A big influence on my writing ability, he would make up words, like Joyce did in *Finnegans Wake*. I did my undergraduate dissertation on *Finnegans Wake,* somewhat precociously. I'd learned how to make words up from my father, who imitated Walter Winchell. He also had a great energy for sports, especially baseball. I kid a lot of young people by saying that when Lou Gehrig made his farewell speech, I was there. I *was* there. My father took me every week to Yankee Stadium. When the Giants were in town, we'd often go to Yankee Stadium and see the Black Yankees, because he also worked in Harlem, where he sold a lot of insurance. He had a touch with the black community, even though there was a lot of hypocrisy regarding blacks in Jewish communities. He took me to boxing matches, too. He had incredible street energy, had never graduated high school but was very well self-taught. He knew a great deal about opera, could write with both hands, had a great calligraphic hand. He was of that generation that learned on its own and learned a lot.

My mother related to the inward part of me. . . . One never knows the full dimension of one's mother or father because, even after they're dead—and both of my parents are dead—they still play a very deep part in one's life. My mother, I would say, was the one who would let things be. A very simple, beautiful woman whose favorite words were "live and let live" and "that's nice." When she saw something beautiful, she would say "that's beautiful." I remember seeing *Finnegans Wake* for the first time when she and I went to the Fordham Road library in the Bronx.

DM How old were you?

JH Thirteen, maybe fourteen.

I went to City College in New York. There I fancied people like Hemingway and then Joyce. Loving words and poetic language, I went to *Finnegans Wake,* and it reverberated when I thought about when I first saw that book. And at the same time I realized the influence of my father writing the Pythian paper and making up words. Well, I never wrote my own *Finnegans Wake,* but I did write 250 pages in the language of *Finnegans Wake.* Just as an exercise. I never really published any of that. I always felt close to making up puns or adding new words to the language.

DM You wrote a letter to Hemingway, and Hemingway answered you, right?

JH Hemingway's the reason that I'm here in California.

I started out as a reporter at the age of fifteen and a half for a weekly in the Bronx. *The Bronx Times* turned out to be a front for a wire service. Two guys were coming into the other room to the switchboard and giving out racing results. The cops closed down *The Bronx Times.* I didn't have to go to jail, but I was called before the Kefauver crime committee, along with my editor and the publisher. The deal was cut to shut down the newspaper and we wouldn't have to go before the federal court. I went to work for another newspaper on the other side of the Bronx, just on Sundays. I was about seventeen and going to college. Then I got a job working nights as a copy-boy for the Associated Press. I studied with a man, a terrific writer, who wrote a book called *God's Angry Man,* about John Brown. He played an early part in my political life.

DM Was that Erlich?

JH Leonard Erlich. A very sensitive, beautiful guy who had writer's block after *God's Angry Man*. Leonard was teaching Hemingway, and I sort of fell in love with Hemingway. I got hold of Hemingway's early poems and saw that he was the first poet—outside those we'd call Communists—who wrote antifascist poems about Italy. He was there. He saw it early. Before any of the others. He attacked Mussolini. I was very impressed with that and his writing on the Spanish Civil War. I wrote a couple of stories like Hemingway and sent them to him. Hemingway, lo and behold, wrote me back! I was really surprised and very pleased to receive that beautiful letter.

My first spiritual father was a man named Herb Barker, who was the night editor at the Associated Press. I'd pass his desk and put tissue paper on the spikes. Herb and I liked each other for literary reasons. I was young and a student and involved in literature. So I could sit and talk with Herb, unlike some of the other copy-boys. I showed him the letter, and he was very surprised. He said Hemingway was not known to write letters to young poets. Then when Hemingway nearly died in Africa, Herb came over to me one night and said, "Look, Jack, I don't mean to be cynical, but if Hemingway dies, could we use that letter on the A wire?" The A wire is the wire that goes immediately to all the newspapers in the country. I said sure.

Well, Hemingway didn't die, and I went off to student teach in Indiana, and then I went to Dartmouth in 1960. Then I got the job at UCLA. I had a wife and two kids, and I didn't have the money or a car to get across the country. I got a call around that time from the Lily Library back in Indiana, where I had been a student teacher for four years and had done my dissertation. . . .

DM What was the dissertation?

JH I did my master's on the Old English poem, "The Wanderer." My doctoral dissertation was called *The Orchestrated Novel*. The first section was on James Joyce, the second on *Nightwood* by Djuna Barnes, and the third on *The Death of Virgil* by Hermann Broch. Barnes and Broch were friends of Joyce.

To pick up the thread, I got a call from the Lily Library saying they heard I had a letter from Hemingway and were building up an American literature archive. Would I sell them the letter? I'm not sentimental about parchment. I'm sentimental about the words in the letter. I needed a car, so I sold that letter and a letter I'd gotten from Jung when I was back at City College. I had written Jung about *Finnegans Wake*. Some incestuous theme that I was talking about, involving Joyce and his daughter. . . . So those two letters paid my way across the country. The sad thing was that when I passed out of Yellowstone on the way over north of Idaho, I heard on the radio that Hemingway had killed himself. The first poem that I wrote in California was on the death of Ernest Hemingway.

DM How long was your teaching career?

JH I taught from 1955, when I began as a student teacher, to 1966, when I ended at UCLA. The Vietnam War had begun by then. The war—as well as a lot of personal things—had really shaken me up. But I did a lot with the students at UCLA, against the war.

DM Such as?

JH Using a David Smith sculpture as a drum on the campus to have antiwar poetry readings. Giving As to all the people who would possibly . . . well, they announced on TV that if you got an A you wouldn't be drafted. I gave a final examination in world literature where the students were to write about the relationship of the front page of *The Los Angeles Times* to what was really going on in the world. In those days, the paper put the Vietnam War stories on page 29. Meanwhile, you'd watch TV and see all these bombings, and then the paper would come out and bury the story.

DM Seems like a good way to start.

JH Between '61 and '66 in Los Angeles you saw the early shapings of a certain kind of culture. The gift of the work of art, the verbal-visual work that came out of influences like you and Wally Berman. That whole group of avant-garde artists would make collages, drawings, and poems, and give them away to friends and strangers.

DM Who else was in that scene?

JH George Herms . . . Dean Stockwell and Russ Tamblyn were both fine actors, people I knew behind that scene. I knew them as collagists and artists. Bob Alexander as well. This is part of the idea of the gift of the verbal-visual. A certain texture of Surrealism at the time that I would write about later in an essay called "Kabbala Surrealism." At the time, between '66 and '72, I was still within the aura of being actively, pacifically against the war. Ruth, my wife at the time, was working at KPFK. We did antiwar programs of poetry and music. There was a lot of activity like that.

We were living in Venice Beach. I wasn't teaching. I was writing, translating—translating on two levels: on the political level, and as you know, for your magazine *Tree*. For the kabbalistic span. Kabbalah is a dialectic of metaphysics, and then there is the other dialectic, of material relating to social struggles. I translated for another journal, edited by John McBride and Paul Vangelisti. I became influenced by their magazine and published a lot of translations and my own work in their *Invisible City*. That work was moving more toward, let's say, the Marxist dimension.

DM Who were some of the poets you were translating?

JH I translated Paul Eluard and Louis Aragon from the French, Sarah Kirsch from the German. I translated Rocco Scotellaro, Edmond Jabès (some of the very first poems of his published in this country, very political poems), Paul Celan, Neruda. In Venice I did the translation of René Depestre's *A Rainbow for the Christian West,* a long poem about the Voodoo gods invading the southern United States, the most racist arsenal centers. I regard that book as one of the great works in my generation. To think that I had the opportunity to translate at least two of this period's most important revolutionary works, Depestre's *A Rainbow for the Christian West,* from French, and Roque Dalton's *Clandestine Poems,* from Spanish, is very satisfying.

DM When did you leave Los Angeles?

JH In '73 I came up to San Francisco. I lived in a boarding house up on Leavenworth Street for six months and then in a hotel, the New Riviera in North Beach. Mind you, this was still during the Vietnam War. People were pretty crazy. The war had driven most everybody crazy to one degree or another. The situation in North Beach was mad, in the best way. Lots of drinking, lots of loving, lots of poetry. I didn't completely identify with the Beats, because I saw Beat, and I still do, as something whose ground is a toke of marijuana, and I had stopped smoking marijuana long before. I was looking for something more related to the social climate, social protest, social injustice.

Yet I had not really identified with the left in the sixties or early seventies except through the radio station, where we did antiwar stuff. I wasn't involved with the workers' movement at the time. Then I became more socially conscious of what was going on in relation to struggles bigger than a community of poets, became interested in getting involved in the mass movement.

That was when I started translating Russian poetry by picking up a Russian dictionary and simple Russian poets who were quite unknown. In those days, one heard only of Yevtushenko and Vosznesensky. Two years later, in 1976–77, I started to write poems in Russian. One of the great moments of my life was the day I started to write in Russian on the streets of San Francisco. I could write poems about anybody or anything in the same way I would write in American.

Between 1976 and 1987, I made 100,000 "agit-pop" posters. They were a sort of talking leaves, if I can use a Sequoian image, but they really go back to Mayakovsky and to the basic idea of the Russian Revolution, in which the verbal and the visual were equal. Indeed the Russian word *pisat* means "to write" and "to draw." I made these posters in seven gestures, including slogans. They were art propaganda work. "Amerus," a play on "amorous" and "America/Russia," and the word "Communist" (in Russian) were on every single poster. Yet there were no two posters alike. It was a verbo-visual manual experiment that was nourished as well by my life and work with the great San Francisco artist, Kristen Wetterhahn.

I became involved with the Communist movement, and in 1980, after a trip to Europe, I joined the Communist Labor Party, which had been founded in 1974. I remained with it until it dissolved—not for any fractious reasons, but politically and strategically dissolved—in 1992, working politically and culturally with many groups and comrades but especially with the poet and revolutionary, Sarah Menefee, with whom I lived for thirteen years. These days we work for the League of Revolutionaries for a New America, which is involved with an analysis based on the technological installation in modern life. We focus on the poorest, those who suffer most because of the inequities that result from technological, corporate tyranny. The poorest sectors of

society, the homeless, those who struggle to pay their bills. . . .
DM The range of your work is enormous, and it bifurcates at certain
junctions. I'm interested in hearing more about that split. There's the
poem as instrument and immediate intervention into the politics of
the time, the poem as agit-prop. And then there's this long work that
you've been writing for the past twenty-odd years called *The Arcanes*,
which is a rather extraordinary, if obscure, work in terms of the visibil-
ity most A-list poetry seems to inhabit. I'm interested in how you ex-
plain the split and what the purpose of these two kinds of poems are.
JH *The Arcanes* began in Los Angeles in 1972. They are my long po-
ems, process poems, by which I mean that I take influences from a lot
of the other arts and bring them to bear, rather than a concentrated
lyric that might occur out of the situation, like with "Human Inter-
lude." There is much more of a tension between the outer and my
inner world as well as between self and history. At the outset I called
this work *The Arcanes of Le Comte de St-Germain*, taking the image of
St. Germain, a mystical figure who was resurrected in every century. I
realized later on, when I got involved with the Communist move-
ment, that when, for example, Che Guevara gets killed and the next
day posters go up of Che, there's an immediate reincarnative dimen-
sion that takes place politically. I picked a mystic figure. But, in their
development, *The Arcanes* are transformations into political reality.
They go through strands involving the political reality that I've been
involved in, the political tensions and political struggles of the twen-
tieth century; for example, Holocaust imagery, Nazi imagery. Tech-
nology may be creating a new dimension that tames people. It's
repressing people even in the midst of the widest free choice that people
have the illusion of having. Their instinct to protest on a large
scale. . . . I was struck by the fact that the protest against the recent
bombing by Clinton of Iraq, in comparison to the '91 bombing, was
completely muted and tame on the part of the people. I feel it has to
do with technology. Technology has a role in taming protest, because
while we have access to technology to organize, at the same time,
something in the technological free play militates against that, causes
greater indifference. These are some of the things I'm trying to deal
with.

DM Do you think technology causes greater isolation, greater alienation?

JH In a paradoxical way. There's a greater cellularity. On one end, when you see someone with a cellular telephone walking down the street, that person is alone and hearing voices. These are some of the contradictions that I'm trying to deal with in *The Arcanes*. But I've written arcanes on many things. In fact, I wrote the *Baghdad–San Francisco Arcane* in response to the first Gulf War and read it at the event for Charles Olson in Wheeler Auditorium at UC Berkeley.

DM The involvement with the Kabbalah and Heidegger and the Street. How do you apply, reconcile these seeming contradictions?

JH Kabbalah is for me a dialectic of metaphysics. I think Kabbalah takes place in the metaphysical realm because it's involved with spirituality and, finally, light.

DM But that spirituality is applied in a political way, too, when it becomes the basis for messianic movements and reactionarism within. Mysticism aligns with this state.

JH I think you're absolutely correct. But don't take it monolithically. As a Jew, I know that Allen Ginsberg reflected certain elements of hasidic truth, and they were not reactionary. You're speaking of elements of orthodox reactionarism within any religious community.

DM But mystically authorized.

JH We know that there is a political dimension. The seventeenth-century Sabbatian Revolution wanted to overturn everything orthodox and make a kabbalistic revolution. That certainly was a political thing. This is something I feel close to because I see its manifestation in Sabbatai Tsvi as a prophet, in a sense. Since he ultimately took up the turban, he took up Islam. A Jew leading all the Jews back to Palestine, only to take the turban! I don't mean that Jews have to become Muslims or Muslims Jews, but that the two must live more deeply inside each other. I think they're going to have to. The modern economy and Marxism will help toward that goal. Otherwise, the Middle East will blow up, and other parts of the world will blow up, too.

DM So, then, let's go on to Heidegger.

JH Wait, I haven't finished with you. You were the one who really saved my life. You were the writer who engaged with me when I was in the most isolated part of my life. I'd left the university. I was living by the ocean in Venice, California, and you began a correspondence with me that engaged that dimension of the kabbalistic that I had been interested in. You showed me Kabbalah and the love of the word and the love of the letters as a real force. We became brothers in that work for many years. You recall that in the years when I went into the Communist Labor Party, even when I was doing my Russian posters, kabbalistic elements would come in. In fact, I have a whole book called *The Kabbalistic Soviet*. It's never been published, but it's a long text about those years in the seventies when I learned the Russian language. You and I have really been brothers in terms of this kabbalistic dimension. It has to do also with the Street, with poetry on the street level. If I can say it this way: it's not because one was a Jew and another one a black Jew, but I see a Street Generation rather than the Beat Generation. Poets like Bobby Kaufman and Jack Micheline are the ones that I identify with, rather than Allen. Ginsberg belonged to the supermarket world that he created toward the end of his life, which was a literary world, the literary Beat world. That was not where I was or where I am. When I became a Communist, I left that kind of Beat, too.

DM Because you've got a natural sense of rhythm. [*laughter*]

JH Very good, David. OK, Heidegger. His thing about the manifestation of being as at the same time its own concealment. There's this dialectic interplay between revealing and concealment. Now, it's not deception he's talking about. I don't think it's about his thing with Hannah Arendt and things like that. He's talking about the interplay between being and nothingness. And the concept of nothing plays a big part in this manifestation. Indeed, there are qualities in Heidegger that have elements of Kabbalah. I respect him for many things. He writes very beautifully about poetry and what poetry really is. But it's the fact that he refused the religious, that he refused the metaphysical, even though he might have to be interpreted metaphysically. At the same time, he refused the materialist. I am a materialist even as I am a poet. I believe in dialectical materialism, respect those who context the materialist position. But he also refutes the metaphysical, which is very strange. He therefore refuses the religious solution. Indeed, if you take the Kabbalah away from the Jews, take that dimension away from orthodox religion, you're nonetheless left with the texture of the poem that itself becomes religion. This is where Heidegger and Kabbalah meet. The art becomes "religion," and that's where we began as poets. In other words, we made the transfer—at least, I did— from any orthodox religious expression.

DM You vilify Pound's fascism, and yet you praise Heidegger. How do you reconcile that since both put their politics where their mouths were at one point or another in their lives?

JH No, no, no. Heidegger believed for a year and maybe even longer in National Socialism. And he did so in some kind of mystic—but that's not the right word—he believed in an ideal National Socialism. He has been accused of overlooking the Holocaust. But Heidegger never made speeches of such horrible, gutter-level anti-Semitism as Pound did. I suppose there was anti-Semitism in Heidegger. Here I do think it's a matter of language. You need only look at the language of Ezra Pound in those radio speeches.

JB I'm no defender of Pound. His radio speeches in Italy during the war were terrible. On the other hand, his situation was different than Heidegger's. Pound was an American poet in exile ranting on the radio, whereas Heidegger had an institutional position in Nazi Germany. What he said counted for something in Germany, but what Pound had to say counted for little or nothing in Italy. Those speeches count morally against Pound, but their political influence approached zero.

JH Well, obviously, from the point of view of Americans, you're probably right, since Pound is considered one of the great poets and taught in universities. He perpetuates finally a kind of political indifference. All I'm saying is that the Pound story has people saying either Pound was crazy or, oh, that was a particular period in his life where he went off his rocker. I believe, rather, that as a fascist using the language of anti-Semitism—the heart of Nazism—Pound was closer to Hitlerian fascism, linguistically, than was Heidegger.

DM In terms of the Kabbalah, specifically Luria and Abulafia, how do they inform your political work as a Communist? Are they antithetical or compatible?

JH [*laughter*] Abulafia, whom I regard as almost fundamental to all of the Kabbalah, was a poet. I think he was also a provocateur. I always loved that in a poet, in Allen, in Pasolini. I translated a lot of Pasolini's work because he was a provocateur. And I'm not talking about his lifestyle. Abulafia was the poet who changed the Tetragrammaton and put the name of a poet in. He identified with David the poet, and that's who God was to him, ultimately.

As for Luria, the older I get the more profound he appears to me. I translate him in secular terms. His idea of *tzimtzum*, of contraction, withdrawing, in order to manifest, is something like, when a guy talks too much [*laughter*], withdrawing in order that that what is before you unfolds. Which is the way I see women are often situated in the world. Because men are driven by much more social ego, up front. The allowing of things to be, which is at the root of compassion, also links up with things that I see in Heidegger because I think he's talking about an element of that. That is how Paul Celan became involved with Heidegger. I believe he tapped into a kabbalistic dimension in Heidegger. Luria lived only thirty-eight years, but he's had a profound influence.

But I think that everything is matter. That everything is in motion as matter. It's not about religion or spirituality as such, although one is also involved with spiritual life since, as a poet, I'm involved with energy.

DM So is there a difference?

JH Between the material and the spiritual? They're two aspects of the same thing. How could they not be? The spiritual dimension has to be informed by the material, and the material dimension has to be informed by spirituality, which is energy. But, of course, energy is matter. That's the problem. A poem is an energy transfer, as Charles Olson says, from the world outside through you onto the page. But that's also a very material process.

DM Your artwork is another extension of your political practice.

JH I come from the New York school of abstract expressionism. When I was in L.A. I had a couple of shows. I'd take woodblocks of Hebrew letters—I found them in London in 1965—dip them in ink, and smash them against canvases. During most of my life in San Francisco, I've preferred to give the artworks away. I truly believe that artwork should be given away, and in the best of all possible societies, books and art should be given as free exchange. There should be no price on them.

When I have a show it's only because I need to pay the rent. I have great difficulty getting readings in the United States, after publishing more than 100 books. I'm almost never asked to read at universities in this country, because I left the university system and took the Marxist-Leninist path.

JB I did want to ask a question about technology. Could you be more specific about the kinds of technology you're concerned about? Are you talking largely about communications technology?

JH Remember the Gulf War in '91 and the continual U.S. bombing of Iraq. I noticed that the response to the recent bombing was less than in '91. Now granted the '91 attack was built up over a period of time, while this was relatively quick. I take that into account. On the other hand, I do think people's access to technology, to pornography on it, for example, works against their manifesting more direct, mass motion. Don't misunderstand. I don't have a computer, and "pornopolis," as I've written in one of my arcanes, is everywhere. I'm suggesting that if eighty percent of computer profit is related to the pornographic domain, there is something there that militates against mass protest.

DM To interject one thing, besides being a site for "pornopolis" or monopoly or pornopoly and consumerism, the computer also links you up with as many radical organizations, left and right, as you like. I get your *People's Tribune* on line. I also get the White Aryan Nation information. I can find out about *Der Stürmer* on line as well as I can find out where Marx sat in the British Museum while he wrote *Das Kapital*.

JH So there are no secrets.

JB There are plenty of secrets, but there is also a lot more communication.

DM OK, enough about technology. Tell me about the realm of the erotic in your work—specifically in *The Arcanes*—how the erotic plays into the personal, not the political.

JH There has always been that element of the erotic in the longer poems. But I think, in the past decade, more. In the past three or four years, even more. The poems have been involved with erotic love poetry, and there's a certain quality . . . well, you tell *me* about the erotic. I almost can't see it objectively. *The Arcanes* are long works because they have to do with the receiving of voices that are not my own. On the other hand, I take responsibility for all the voices. I use certain withdrawing techniques, all poets do, when we receive voices. I enjoy the idea that I'm receiving other voices. This is also part of Eros. For me, Eros is a form of reception. The adventure of physicality, of sexuality, becomes also an adventure of receiving voices, images, etc. More recent arcanes, because of my new relationship with my wife, poet-painter Aggie Falk, reflect the political world intensely through our life together, since I'm also confronting certain things having to do with death and Eros, and also things kabbalistic and things political. All of these play parts in the texture of the work. Indeed, I would say that the last two or three arcanes have raised questions to me. It's not that they're off the Street, because I use Street language, and you know I came from a certain kind of hard-edged eroticism that comes out of L.A. in the thirties and forties. From my generation, as it were. But there are questions that are raised about the level. . . . When I wrote *The Satin Arcane* I realized then I was writing about something that's really not just me. It's everywhere. You, David, have had a lot of experience that way, so you know it's something that's just part of the texture of American life for the past generation or so.

DM One more question. This is the simple one. Have you thought about what poetry is and/or should be, and then conversely, dialectically, what it isn't and shouldn't be?

JH I don't know what poetry is.

DM Do you know what poetry should be doing? What's the job description?

JH I think everyone is a poet. But poetry is the art of concentrating language. Here I do mean it in relation to a musical scoring. Although one can concentrate language improvisationally in front of a microphone, I'm speaking of poetry on the page. The concentration of poetry tries to evoke the most resonant and possibly monumental part of human-beingness. It does that by focusing on the three things that underlie great poetry: birth, love, and death. And that's the primary content of all poems, in one way or another. The one distinguishing characteristic of poetry is the fire. The fire that feeds or makes the resonance manifest. And that I think comes from things like receiving most inwardly. Let me give you an example. One of my earliest voice inspirations was the Caedmon recording by Dylan Thomas. Dylan Thomas had a magic voice, a love of words that's extraordinary. He also had a certain fire that he breathes in his work. A fire I find missing in others. Here I'm speaking of presentation. But I also see that the presentation has to do with the page. That the page is a place where this black fire on white fire manifests. I think that's one of the things that moved me to Olson. I get a sense that there's really more fire going on out there on the page. I think sometimes that really happens with Charles. I like that. I think Allen has it. Amiri Baraka, of course.

Does that answer the question? I don't know what poetry is. This society that is so active, energetic, and at the same time so full of death, shit, cruelty, and indifference—this society doesn't have a silence like that in Paul Celan's work, for example, a silence that's really inward. I get the sense that American poetry is part of the entertainment scene. One thing for sure, poetry will come from the most vulnerable, wounded sections of society and one's own life. That's where real poetry comes from. That's where it's always come from. It doesn't come from anything institutionalized. That's not the real stuff.

Joanne Kyger (1998)

Courtesy Joanne Kyger

December 12, 1998: On an appropriately sunny Sunday afternoon, Steve Jones drives us to Bolinas in his friend's over-the-hill diesel Mercedes. Joanne Kyger's house is on the mesa, which she shares with artist/poet Donald Guravich. We set up our recording equipment in a studio/guest house, which is in its final stages of construction. As always, Joanne is a gracious and considerate hostess, wanting us to be comfortable before we begin. Teas are brewed, wood put in the fireplace, nibbles placed before us. Small talk and catching up before we begin.—DM

Joanne Kyger (**JK**)
David Meltzer (**DM**)
James Brook (**JB**)
Steve Jones (**SJ**)
Marina Lazzara (**ML**)

JK I was born in Vallejo, California, November 19, 1934. Six weeks later went to China, since my father was in the navy, a career officer. It was during the time when we wanted gunboat diplomacy. We took big iron ships over to China and parked them conspicuously to show what American naval force was about. We stayed there for two and a half years, and then I came back to Southern California with my family. We lived in Long Beach. I went to school there. Wrote my first poem.

DM How old were you?

JK Kindergarten or something like that.

DM Do you remember that experience?

JK Definitely. The teacher said: "Just tell me your poem and I'll write it down." There must have been a certain amount of visualization going on.

DM Do you have memories of writing your first poem?

JK No. I didn't write it. That was dictation. But it was printed in the school magazine, so I think being in print made an impression. My mother said, "Look, my daughter's in print." When I was in school, reading was a great escape for me. Also, writing in grade school and high school. I wrote a column for the high school newspaper in Santa Barbara. Leland Hickman and I were the feature editors. Went to the university there and studied with Hugh Kenner.

When writing your autobiography, you re-rehearse it. I go back to certain places in my life and re-remember them. There was a certain part in the seventies when you were supposed to "be here now." So I forgot everything. It's a matter of practicing one's autobiography, of re-finding it. Bring parts of your memory into focus.

I got to North Beach when I was twenty-three. A friend of mine, Nemi Frost, had a sister who had an apartment above La Rocca's bar. I got that. Fifty dollars a month. Went to work at Brentano's at the City of Paris department store. I found City Lights and read *Howl* and was monumentally excited by it. I had read Pound and Eliot. Yeats I really couldn't get. Psychoanalysis and philosophy was in the air. Wittgenstein and Jung and Joseph Campbell, who wrote *A Hero with a Thousand Faces*. I had a fairly open and supple background in terms of what's now considered "the New American Poetry." And I met David.

[*laughter*]

DM Do you recall writing your first poem?

JK I think I wrote out my first poems, at seventeen or eighteen or nineteen, out of psychological despair. In Santa Barbara, the public library had a workshop where everyone submitted their poems without signature. Someone read mine and said, "I certainly hope that's not your poem." Of course, it was. [*laughter*] So that kind of put a crimp in my style—I wasn't about to show this writing. But the writing was coming out of some energy of confusion and vowel sounds. It wasn't really formulated until I came to San Francisco and started to write some pieces.

DM I remember that in those early days you were self-effacing about showing the work.

JK When I went to that group that Joe Dunn introduced me to, the Spicer and Duncan group, I had a legitimate concern about reading my poems. I remember I showed you some things. You liked them. Trying to put these pieces together . . . I remember writing them and going over them . . . all my manuscripts of that time, which I still have, have these great splotches of red wine across them. I kept dragging them out and looking at them with friends. I used to type them up at Brentano's at City of Paris when I was supposed to be typing up their orders. I was trying to work on poetry. Yes, I suppose there was some way I wanted to present my thoughts and that energy that comes from poetry. I don't like to belabor writing too much. We write, and there's still that process of trying to get at some depth or warmth or spontaneity.

DM You wrote once that you wanted to control the line to enable your voice to emerge. Can you elaborate on that?

JK Well, the line was, of course, the line on the page. I started to think of that as a tapestry, an interweaving. How you rhythmically move your reader or yourself through the page is by the line, how you make your graph of syllables, your sounds . . . you score the page for your voice. William Carlos Williams, of course, made a great impression. The way he could treat the dynamics of the page. Also studying Charles Olson and his breath line. Kerouac's "Old Angel Midnight" was a little too giddy for me, but I remember being turned on by it. It was energy. . . .

DM In your first book, *The Tapestry and the Web*, the lines were long and tended to go across the page like a stepladder or stepping stones.

JK That was the idea. Of the warp and the weft. For me, it was very kinetic. Physical. I never did get too much personal instruction from, say, Spicer and Duncan. Like most things, you have to figure them out yourself.

DM What was the influence of Robert Duncan and Jack Spicer in formulating your own relationships to poetry at that point? Or afterward?

JK You know about that group. It could be very supportive. They were at least ten years older. If they were interested in your work, they responded to it. They were fussy about who they were interested in. It was very demanding. With Spicer, especially. A demanding but somewhat confusing sense of what was real in poetry; that is, whether you were bullshitting or not. I was never quite sure if I was. How can you tell whether you're bullshitting or not? [*laughter*] It was kind of a short tether. I think the activity of reading out loud was helpful. It was an informal group—it certainly wasn't academic. It involved going to the bar afterward and things like that.

DM Jack and Robert were opposites. One with his fierce economy and compression. The other with his spacious and endlessly weaving line and approach to the poem. We had the best of both possible worlds, and that could be confusing, too.

JK They also had their own kind of conflicts—you could see them. I always remember the time when Kerouac's "Old Angel Midnight" came out in Big Table. Robert said to Spicer, "This is a great show, shall we jump on the bandwagon, should we start publishing, should we get out there into these little magazines?" Spicer was holding on to some kind of local autonomy, and the Beat Generation was perceived as a self-aggrandizing, self-advertising, egotistical kind of phenomenon.

The Berkeley Renaissance was being translated into the San Francisco Renaissance. It all seems so much by the board right now. There was a certain sense of being true to yourself, your voice, staying close to your writing peers. White Rabbit published chapbooks. Selling them for twenty-five cents. Not advertising yourself. You shouldn't have a book out until you're thirty. Because you don't know what you're doing. So you don't want all this easy garbage out there yet. You're not really ready to do something like that because your voice is going to change, or maybe not. But true to the muse, the poem. And then there was going to Japan, where Gary was very antipublicity in terms of the Beat Generation. People coming to the door. He'd say, "No, I'm not interested in that, I'm into my studies and meditation." After that, coming to Bolinas, which doesn't want to be on the map, either.

DM Your involvement with Buddhism starts early on?

JK Yes, while I was in school. I was studying Wittgenstein and Western thought, and that led me to D.T. Suzuki. I had intellectual, metaphysical interests in Buddhism. I did think at one point that Zen Buddhism—there was a spark of notoriety that came with it in the late fifties—was a real answer. I thought, "I'll find out what the meaning of life is all about! Whew, thank goodness!" At that time, in the late fifties, there were maybe four books on Buddhism.

DM How did it become integral with the poetic practice?

JK What is Buddhist? This is what I still ask myself. I did a reading in Germany in the spring, and a woman said, "I think you have really assimilated your Buddhism in your work." It's beyond the dichotomy of "I" and "Thou." It's interrelatedness. . . .

Actually, the religion of Buddhism isn't very different from any other religion. It has teachers, and there's a temple; it has a daily practice. You bury the dead, you get married, whatever it is in terms of a larger construct that religion provides for people. The particular kind of Buddhism that caught the fancy of Americans in the fifties was meditation—Zen. It directed you to be aware of what goes on in the mind. As a practice, meditation showed this key to this enormous, buried energy, images. I think that's why it's still of interest. It's not so much the religious construct of it. We see religion as going to church and all the accoutrements of what religion helps you with through life. It's very easy to put this beatific face on Buddhism and say it's perfect and Christianity is really rotten and full of soldiers and slaughter. But I think all organized religions have always had their wars and disagreements and power structures. There were huge wars between different factions of Buddhism where they battled each other up one side of the mountain and down the other. Burned down each other's temples.

DM All in the name of compassion?

JK All in the name of who's going to own the land. Who's going to be the boss.

DM Many of the poets interviewed for this book were involved with the East/West House. Can you tell us something about it?

JK Well, the East/West House was started essentially as a place where people could study with Alan Watts and study Japanese in preparation for going to Japan. The culture of the late fifties was very much reveling—at least on this coast—in what Japan had to offer in the way of its cultural history: its gardening, tea ceremonies, beautiful folk craft, music, sense of nature—it was very culturally adaptable to this coast. Now it's something many people don't remember. What we think of Japan is its competition with the car industry, transistor radios, the computer chip, etc. Back then, Japanese culture was seen to be a way of being with nature.

ML How long were you in Japan?

JK For four years. I was married to Gary Snyder. I was twenty-five, and I was interested in having a household, and that presented some problems, too. I didn't want to be the wife of some kind of Zen mendicant. I said, "OK, you mean we can't have more than two cups? Well, what if I get more than two cups?" I'd fallen in love with Japanese cups. "What if I get more than two cups and put them away"? Things, it was things. What if I didn't want to wash the dishes right after dinner because I wanted to go and write or something? No, you can't. It was very much the way a Zen monastery was run. That kind of paying attention to details—finish something and go onto the next thing. So the sense of having a domestic life was also different.

DM Regarding the journal that you published many years ago about your journeys to Japan and India with Gary, Allen, and the rest, I always found it to be a very funny work as much as a kind of critique.

JK It was my particular refuge. They were the buddies. Would you guys like to read poems together? And they would say sure—but they would never ask me if I wanted to read. It was a very strong male bonding.

DM It does reflect the male dominance and privilege in the arts scene in the postwar period and the difficulties that women had in those male societies, especially where women were of equal stature creatively and intellectually. Does this attitude still prevail in literary culture?

JK Well, it prevails as long as a woman permits it. I don't think I have a really competitive sense. I remember giving my poems to Ginsberg on his way back from India. I was trying to get a manuscript together and I gave it to him, and he was just absolutely puzzled. He didn't have a clue. Philip Whalen was the person who has always been encouraging. He always says "just keep on writing." Someone like Allen is often "homophobic" about women. [*laughter*]

DM When did you move to Bolinas?

JK In 1969. I bought a house. That gives you a certain autonomy. When I bought this house it was $67 a month to pay the mortgage. I could always sort of come up with that. I didn't always have enough money to be able to leave town. So I stayed out here a lot. In the seventies I would go into the city. To New College, Intersection on Union Street, The Poetry Center at San Francisco State. Bolinas itself, in the early seventies, was back to the land. Everybody wanted to leave the city and go to the country, green out, smoke dope. It was very interesting to be here then.

DM How has San Francisco poetry scene changed?

JK Well, I don't go in that much. There's not a real center of poetry anymore, for various reasons. I think of the readings of the late sixties, where we had 500 to 1,000 people at a reading. Poetry was the news, the cultural news, and I don't think we've had this kind of energy, these kind of voices for a while—certainly, rock music took over a lot of social commentary. . . . The Language school I felt was a kind of an alienating intellectualization of the energies of poetry. It carried it away from the source. It may have been a housecleaning from confessional poetry, but I found it a sterilization of poetry. On the other hand, spoken word poetry is an identification with the voice energy.

DM There are two distinct operations: the writing and the performing of the poem.

JB Getting back to your practice, Joanne. We talked a little about your devotion to poetry and Buddhism and vice-versa. Is there a way that you approach poetry, your perspective on writing as an act—the way you sit down and decide or not decide to start or how things are to be arranged on the page?

JK Accepting that the mind is OK as it is. I don't have an official Buddhist teacher. I go through phases of practicing meditation on a daily scale and then not doing it for a long time and then going back to it. But you know it's not practice that's ultimately rejected—you just get out of the tempo of doing it. You find that when you finally sit or practice meditation everything about you slows down. Your "content" becomes more accessible and . . . it goes back to Trungpa's dictum, "first thought best thought." So what arises comes out. And then the next thing arises, and so you put that down. You trust that your mind is shapely and that existence has a flow of its own. It's not trying to restructure your thinking to come to conclusions. A hierarchical sense of where you are starts to fade away. In its simplest focus, that's how I see it.

DM Let's talk about your relationship with Philip Whalen's work and presence. How has he taught you—directly or indirectly—poetry and Buddhism? Or has he not? Has it been just reading his books and hanging out with him?

JK Phil would always just say just keep on writing. You have to get beyond the point where this is a good poem and that's a bad poem. Philip's playfulness showed the playfulness of the mind—he showed how different voices come in and they all have equal value and not just one voice is you. The equality of thought . . . there's a good deal of humor with Philip.

DM It's an interesting way of being serious. You often spin a poem with humor. . . .

JK So do you. . . .

DM I know. That's why I like reading your poetry. [*laughter*] I like the notion of the poem as a field of play; it's not necessarily some monumental Gothic cathedral you can't get off your head.

JK I think that *Just Space*, the book that Black Sparrow put out in the eighties, is essentially a kind of daybook, at times attempting to keep a longer narrative going, a story. It essentially is asking, "What does the day offer?"—in terms of the myriad sources of its particulars.

JB Could we step through the books now as markers in an autobiography?

JK OK. This was my first book. Don Allen published *The Tapestry and the Web* in 1965. I said that when I was in Japan I didn't have any real feeling where I was at in terms of writing. I came back to San Francisco, and Don wanted to publish a book. *The Tapestry and the Web* starts with the first poem that I felt was successful—written in 1958, when I was living in San Francisco and going to the Spicer/Duncan group. The early parts are San Francisco poems and poems written in Japan. It uses Homer's *Odyssey* as a structural outline, a trip into a life. I had read Joseph Campbell's *A Hero with a Thousand Faces.* You get an idea of narrative in terms of myth—Campbell expanded the idea of what myth was about into the currents of your own life. It's the oldest narrative that I could find on how to look at your life and how to look at this larger story. Homer was useful for me. Somebody asked me a few years ago, "Who are these gods and goddesses you talk about all the time?" I said they're around. But they were a lot more around in the late fifties and the sixties. It was a kind of concurrent mythology. Certainly, Robert Duncan used them a lot. It was part of a psychological family that belonged to poetry, and you could call upon them and turn them into voices, and they acted on the impulses and dramatics of your own life. And put you into the big story. Poetry wants to be inside the big story. Part of the voice of the big story. I don't hear too much about the gods and goddesses, anymore. Well, the goddesses are there with New Age religion. Demeter's around a lot. And Persephone. I don't hear a lot about Athena.

SJ Well, in pop culture there are those two TV series, *Hercules* and *Xena.*

JK Wow, I love that. In Robert Graves's *The Greek Myths* you begin to realize these myths are reinterpreted in a lot of different places—one person or god turns into another. What was the other book that came out at that time?

DM *The White Goddess?*

JK *The White Goddess,* right. Although since the White Goddess is a woman and the muse herself, she could never write poetry. Which I thought was a real cop out! [*laughter*]

DM The Spicer/Duncan group did place a heavy emphasis on muse and on certain forms of inspiration or reception. . . .

JK Lew Welch got so mad at them because they would always talk about "The Poem." "The Poem." Capital T, capital P.

DM And all Lew wanted was to have people in the bar understand his poetry, not Poetry.

JK Exactly.

DM "Inspirare" means "the in-breath," "to be breathed through." Something breathes through you, and you exhale it, and there's a poem on the page, and you say, hmm, what's this? These aren't my hands. That brings up an interesting question: who writes the poem? You were talking about how mind is writing a poem like in meditation, the mind's activity to project itself. But who's the mind? Is the mind you?

JK You've already inherited it. You've inherited paper. You've inherited a tradition. If you decide to enter into that tradition, that lineage, you already find yourself a part of it. You are already there. You are looking at the mind, or the mind is just looking. "Who" writes down what the mind says? I think the words have a mind of their own. You must discover that words want to put themselves down. I think after a while you're like a musician: you play your own tune. It's like a set piece. Without much effort. But it's dangerous. You could write the same poem over and over again. You find a form, an ear, a relationship of self to the world. You just have to keep yourself open because then this wonderful poem could come along and knock your socks off.

DM So it's not *The Invasion of the Body Snatchers*?

SJ Definitely not that!

DM *Joanne* was published by . . .

JK Angel Hair.

DM In terms of form, that book was very different from *The Tapestry and the Web*.

JK Right. I wrote it in 1970. In the early seventies there was a whole pared-down identity number that went on. *Joanne: A Novel from the Inside Out*—with the idea that the plot's so huge, all you have is this small space of notational nuggets. You're so busy living the novel that you don't have any time to write it down. So you just have little comments, hits in the middle of the day.

DM The footnotes to the novel.

JK It was just called *Joanne*. It didn't have any author name on it. As though it had written itself.

DM Just a black-and-white photograph of you on the cover. Could we talk about people like Berrigan and that younger group of poets associated with the East Coast?

JK The so-called second-generation New York School. I met them when I lived in New York City for nine months. That's when I met Anne Waldman and Lewis Warsh. I had published Lewis in *Wild Dog* when I was editor. That was a magazine Ed Dorn started in Idaho, and it came out to San Francisco. I called up Lewis and Anne when I arrived in New York City. In 1965 they and Ted had come out for the poetry conference in Berkeley. This was a major confluence of what was the New American poetry at that time. It was fraught with political and social excitement. I went to New York around 1967, and I met Anne, Michael Brownstein, and Lewis and Ted. I didn't like New York at all. I was too much a West Coast person.

DM I know some of the influences then, but who influences you today? Who do you read?

JK Well, I read my contemporaries still. I don't really curl up with a book of poetry. I love to read, and I read a lot. But I find that poetry is best read out loud for me. To catch the ear first. Some books of poetry are constructed so they are readable but I'm . . . well, often everything is lined up on the left-hand margin and the form looks the same all the time. I need a plot. I need to have something going on. So I can get in touch with the writer. I appreciate that. Philip Whalen I can read. Anne Waldman, Anselm Hollo, Ed Sanders, Alice Notley. I feel lonesome if I sit down all alone with a book of poetry. It makes me anxious. I read it a little while, and then I want to go write my own.

Philip Lamantia (1998)

© Harry Redl

November 14, 1998: Jim, Marina, and I march single file upstairs to Lamantia's North Beach apartment. Another poet's perch, cocooned by bookcases, art, artifacts, the significant clutter of the familiar and miraculous. Lamantia asks if he can smoke; he claims he smokes two or three cigarettes every day. (Which in metalingo means two or three packs, since he never stops smoking during the interview.) Lamantia crackles with immense intellectual energy and unpredictable amusement couched in rapid-fire asides. After the interview we walk with Philip for espressos at Café Greco on Columbus Avenue. Fueled by caffeine, we talk for another couple of hours.— DM

Philip Lamantia (**PL**)
David Meltzer (**DM**)
James Brook (**JB**)
Marina Lazzara (**ML**)

DM You were saying that you wanted to focus on what was happening in the Bay Area.

PL Yes—on what was later called "the San Francisco Renaissance," an expression Kenneth Rexroth first used in 1946. There were parallels to what was going on in New York at the same time. Here it was after-hours jazz in the Fillmore district and rhythm-and-blues at the Little Harlem off Folsom and Third Streets, both scenes celebrated by Kerouac in *On the Road*. Those of us, like Gerd Stern (he was "Jack Steen" in *The Subterraneans*), who knew Birdland and Fifty-Second Street in New York and Jackson's Nook here, were living these connections. For poetry, the main focus were the groups around Rexroth here and Robert Duncan in Berkeley.

DM I'm interested in your take on that history and how it affected you and your work and your path.

PL But then my *origins* are earlier, in Surrealism. That should be covered in order to make sense of my other experiences with the New York and San Francisco scenes. The latter were not unrelated to Surrealism, and yet for me there was a divergence by 1947. The origin of my interest in mysticism as well as a kind of religiously oriented anarchism was here, exemplified by the work of the Russian Orthodox philosopher Nikolai Berdyaev, which some of us were reading at the time, along with that of Dorothy Day and Ammon Hennacy of the Catholic Worker group in New York. In fact, I had an ongoing correspondence with Hennacy, who hadn't yet joined the Church. At that time he'd been living an extraordinary, nomadic life as a farm worker, and for years he'd been overtly refusing to pay income tax.

DM Your origins were in Surrealism, but you began writing here in San Francisco?

PL I began seriously to write while attending James Denman Junior High School in San Francisco in 1942. My roots were in Poe's poetry. The first six months I tried all the fixed forms—sonnets, odes, blank verse, and so on. I even did a complete imitation of Omar Khayyam's *Ruba'iyat*. My English teacher encouraged me greatly, so I read at least one poem a day to the class my first semester. Not long after, I was turned on to Surrealism through a great Dalí retrospective at the San Francisco Museum of Art (now SFMOMA), followed by an equally marvelous exhibition of Miró. Within weeks I had read everything available on Surrealism that I could get from the public library. There wasn't much: David Gascoyne, the premier British Surrealist poet— whose *Short Survey of Surrealism* was superb—Julien Levy's *Surrealism,* Georges Lemaître's *From Cubism to Surrealism in French Literature* (he was teaching at Stanford), and, finally, the discovery of the luxurious New York Surrealist review, *VVV*—two issues edited by Breton and friends—which I found in the tiny but ample no-loan library at the museum. In almost no time I had a dozen poems ready for publication and sent some to *View: A Magazine of the Arts,* which was edited, in New York, by the only important American poet who was plausibly Surrealist, Charles Henri Ford. In spring 1943 my poems were featured on one of *View's* large-format pages. On the cover was a photograph by Man Ray.

DM How old were you then?

PL Fifteen. It was just after this that I discovered *VVV's* whereabouts and sent other poems there to André Breton. He wrote, accepting three poems and requesting a letter from me "clarifying" my relation to Surrealism. Acceptance by the man I fervently believed the most important poet and mind of the century led to my decision to quit school and take off for New York. I arrived in April 1944 in Manhattan— which *View* magazine called on its masthead "the cultural center of the world." And so it was, the center for the painters of what was later called "abstract expressionism"—actually, a spin-off of Surrealist automatist techniques. Arshille Gorky, who in the mid-1930s shared a studio with Pollock, had already been hailed by Breton along with Gerome Kamrowski as one of the two American painters closest to Surrealism. True. Not so with Pollock, who was more distant. Breton wrote a famous catalog statement for a Gorky gallery show, and Gorky felt privileged that the poet gave titles to several of his paintings.

My milieu was mainly among the many English-speaking French and other European painters and intellectuals: Max Ernst, Duchamp, Yves Tanguy, Nicolas Calas, Kurt Seligmann, Pavel Tchelitchew, André Masson, the critic Leon Kochnitsky—and their American counterparts, the writers Harold Rosenberg, Lionel Abel, Parker Tyler, the painter William Baziotes, and Paul Bowles, who introduced me to world music. There were weekly gallery openings, jazz on Fifty-Second Street, endless parties, and almost daily invitations to lunch and dinner. Weekdays, I worked as an assistant editor at *View*, mostly rejecting the daily deluge of unsolicited manuscripts.

After the war ended in Europe, many of the key people I esteemed dispersed. Breton went back to Paris by way of Canada. I had a fight with Ford and resigned from *View*. It was all over for me, and so I came back to my native San Francisco. Since I had been expelled from high school for "intellectual delinquency," I had two years to make up in order to graduate.

DM What high school did you go to?

PL Balboa, a school rated, along with Mission High, at the bottom of the academic heap. Then and now, I believe. Someone just told me they mention my name in English classes at Balboa these days: "Well, look, we had a real poet who went here!" [*laughter*]

DM So you were back in San Francisco in 1945?

PL As it was, I'd met Kenneth Rexroth just before I left for New York. Once back here I saw a great deal of him for a couple of years. Above all, I was attracted by his inexhaustible and encyclopedic way of conversing. I visited with him at least once a week. We'd both stay up late, till four in the morning. I'd usually stay over because it was too late to take the bus home. Sometimes we'd talk a whole weekend. He'd cook dinners for me and his comrade-wife (she taught nursing by day). Weekdays, I went to a secular private school where in just one year I finished my last two years of high school.

But my real education came from and through the great Rexroth. He was so much a mentor I actually fell into mimicking him. It was like what John Keats wrote in a letter about the peculiarity of certain poets. To paraphrase: "I can walk into a room full of people and within half an hour I can take on the personality of anyone there."

JB This conjunction between you and Rexroth is interesting. You met him just before you met Breton, and you came back to San Francisco and there he was. Presumably, you were charged up about Surrealism—but it's well known that Rexroth was very critical of Surrealism.

PL Yeah, but he introduced me to everyone who was important in British and American poetry. He even "taught" me how to read contemporary Scottish poets, Hugh McDiarmid and Sorley McLean, in Gaelic transcriptions, as well as turning me on to Middle English poetry, Greek and Roman classical literature, modern philosophy, and, most significantly, sacred texts of the Western and Asian traditions.

DM So the involvement with hermeticism comes in. . . .

PL Surrealism is what brought me to what you call hermeticism. In New York I was carrying around two volumes of the works of Paracelsus translated by A.E. Waite in the 1890s. As a matter of fact, I loaned them to the then-fashionable Russian painter Pavel Tchelitchew, Charles Henri Ford's roommate of many years, who never gave the books back to me! I was fascinated by Al-Kemi, the alchemical tradition. I had long admired the superlative seventeenth-century color plates of the *Splendor Solis* I'd seen first in Manly Hall's library, where I'd been taken by my theosophic relatives who'd invited me to stay with them in Los Angeles in 1943.

JB So in the early forties, when you were meeting Breton . . .

PL Yes, it was during the Surrealist diaspora that Surrealism deepened what the manifestos of the 1920s initiated. The key for me was my weekly lunch with the painter-engraver Kurt Seligmann, who graciously allowed me to look at his many volumes of very early, amazing alchemical texts. This was an unforgettable experience. Though his oft-reprinted book *The Mirror of Magic* had an objective, detached, psychoanalytic critical surface, it was otherwise when talking with him. Kurt was a charming and rare person, the perfect cosmopolitan. This, by the way, is an example of the real meaning of "occultation." The occult should never be confused with the esoteric, which implies the inner meaning of any traditional teaching, whereas occult means what it says; that is, the "hidden," an example of which are the occult centers known in India as *chakras,* and, for those who can *read* clearly, chiseled on the walls of the Temples of Luxor and Karnak in Egypt, which I saw in 1989.

DM But getting back to the importance of the hermetic in terms of your own work and development . . .

PL Well, my continuing interest in that and a newly awakened relation to the sacred coincided with an extraordinary experience, at once erotic and mystical—true carnal love. Everything had to do with being in love and the woman I was in love with. I was eighteen years old when it began, and with it an abrupt change in the kind of poetry it provoked.

DM Were those poems published?

PL Yes, in my first book, *Erotic Poems*, in 1946. That's a title Rexroth suggested as I couldn't find one at the time.

So my poetry turned naturalistic, directly in opposition to Surrealism. It seems that what I've finally gotten to now is a synthesis of these two once-divergent directions. It's taken a long time, but I think it's clear enough in the whole fifty-year span contained in my latest selected poems, *Bed of Sphinxes*. But it's also there in the books just before it, *Meadowlark West* and *Becoming Visible*. But all my books could be considered initiatory stages of a quest at once poetic and spiritual, with parallel roots in revolutionary political theory and mystical expression—at first heretical and then increasingly oriented to more orthodox spiritual perspectives—and bracketed with an eruptive rebelliousness that marked my Beat period.

DM Let's get back to the comparison between the San Francisco postwar years and New York.

PL On the West Coast—Berkeley and San Francisco—there was an extraordinary convergence of poets, painters, ex–conscientious objectors, and radical anarchists—rebels of all stripes. Kenneth Rexroth was the central figure, with Robert Duncan and Bill Everson connecting the two generations. The common meeting ground was what we named the San Francisco Libertarian Circle. The regular structured meetings were announced weekly by postcards sent to about fifty individuals. I know, since it was my specific "organizational function" to type the announcements.

Actually, the focal point of the group was every aspect of anarchist thought, researched and discussed with passion and objectivity by a small minority; within the group there were various degrees of commitment. There were special lectures more or less monthly that set the orientation for a certain period. For example, I prepared one evening a presentation of Wilhelm Reich's theories, just being published for the first time in English. Rexroth spoke on Kropotkin. A first-generation Italian introduced the most important anarchist theoretician of the early twentieth century, Errico Malatesta, who had lived in exile in England. Some of these writings were reaching us from the British anarchist group, which also supplied us with their newspaper *Freedom*. *The Catholic Worker* arrived regularly in bundles from New York. There was even a connection with Albert Camus in Paris around his publication *Combat* and a small group around Paul Goodman in New York and the newspaper *Why?*

Robert Duncan was a participating member of the group; he had a few years back lived in a tiny anarchist rural commune in upstate New York around Holly Cantine and his companion, Dachine Rainer, who were publishers for several years of a high-grade anarchist quarterly, *Retort*.

As time went by, more and more people started to come to the meetings. Though we'd been meeting in at the dance studio of the soon-to-be cofounder of KPFA, Richard Moore, there wasn't enough space, so we rented a larger place from the Workers' Circle, an insurance-benefit society that owned an old three-story Victorian house in a central part of town. Over a hundred people used to come during the last years of these meetings, around 1948 or 1949.

Out of all this came the one-shot magazine *The Ark*, which I helped edit. That was in 1947. We published some of the poets in the group as well as work by W.C. Williams, Kenneth Patchen, Paul Goodman, and e.e. cummings. There was a cover drawing and paintings by Ronald Bladen, now known for his outdoor sculpture in various cities.

That whole postwar development was an exciting cultural environment. No doubt about it, it influenced a wider current that provided receptive readers for the City Lights Bookstore at its beginnings. Significantly, Ferlinghetti arrived on Kenneth Rexroth's doorstep a few months after the regular meetings ended, when Rexroth had begun his informal wine-and-cheese Friday evening open-house gatherings. These continued for years. They were still going on in the mid-fifties when Ginsberg (and later Kerouac) showed up on Rexroth's same doorstep with a letter of introduction from his friend W.C. Williams.

It was in this setting, at the early anarchist meetings, that I encountered the first hipster I ever met, Bill Keck. With him and his wife and a few of their friends, I formed—at Rexroth's suggestion—an anarchist youth group. These new friendships survived the crackup of the general discussion group. By 1948, Keck and his wife moved to New York, and so the first links were forged with the Greenwich Village scene, which was coming together then, and coming under Kerouac's scrutiny, providing models for Ginsberg's "Howl" and Kerouac's *The Subterraneans*. Allen revealed all the names and places in his exhaustive *Annotated Howl*. I was among those in the poem who were traveling back and forth between coasts, along with John Hoffmann and Christopher Maclaine, both originally from here, and Mason Hoffenberg, Anton Rosenberg, New Yorkers, and the original "link," Bill Keck. John Hoffmann, who died in Mexico at the age of twenty-five, was the poet whose poems I read at the Six Gallery Reading, and who was characterized by Carl Solomon in Ginsberg's quote from "The Myth of John Hoffmann." So there you have it.

DM How do you define "the hipster"?

PL John Hoffmann had a wonderful definition: "The hipster is a romantic idea." "Hipster" was a moniker for what a few of us saw ourselves as in the late forties and early fifties. Mailer wrote up his take on it in his pamphlet, *The White Negro*. For me, my life between 1948 and 1952 was a kind of descent into the underworld, marked by the necessity to buy marijuana and other illicit medicines from the actual criminal underworld.

Nevertheless, an abiding religious sense was always present among many of us—pot-oriented contemplative experiences, for the most part, and this is why Kerouac turned the meaning of "beat" into "beatific."

DM Kerouac strikes me as having a deep Catholic mystic bent that seems to permeate his work.

PL I didn't get to know Jack well until around 1956, when for the first time since my hostile rejection of the Church I became (surprising for anyone who knew me well) a fervently practicing Roman Catholic. But, indeed, I learned during the two weeks Jack stayed with me in the first floor "apartment" of my mother's San Francisco house that, although he had "lapsed" long ago, in his heart he had remained a Catholic, all right. He was also at that time—through an earlier meeting with Gary Snyder—very interested in Buddhism, hence *The Dharma Bums*.

DM Do you see a comparative relationship between Buddhism and Catholicism?

PL I see correspondences.

DM In what sense? Structurally? Or in essence? I'm curious because it seems everyone is becoming Buddhist. . . .

PL Absolutely not, not in essence. But there are many similarities in the two teachings. Most significant for me is what we call *caritas,* best defined as boundless and unconditional love similar to the Buddha's boundless compassion. While it's undeniable that Christianity and Buddhism are irreducible to each other, many Catholics who are into contemplative prayer have assimilated certain Buddhist meditation practices in order to pray better.

Also, for instance, on the spiritual/moral plane, one of the tenets in the Eightfold Path is the rejection of sexual misconduct, and Christ gave a similar teaching. And there's the concept of *harmatia,* which translates as "missing the mark," the real meaning of our word sin, and this resembles the Buddhist concept of right intention, right action. Unconditional love for others is the specifically Christic commandment, completing the Mosaic first commandment, and this parallels the Boddhisatva doctrine of forgoing even enlightenment and transcendent nirvana for the sake of helping other humans reach Buddhahood. There's a particular kind of Buddhism that seems very close to Catholic Christianity—I got that message from Koichiro Yamauchi, a young Japanese poet, a Nichiren Buddhist, who is translating my poetry. When he visited me recently, we found on certain levels almost identical teachings.

DM Would you say that poets are at the forefront of this fusion of spiritual practices?

PL When I first met the great Nicaraguan poet Ernesto Cardenal in 1961 on a retreat in the Cuernavaca Benedictine monastery, he was doing basic yoga exercises recommended by a French Dominican in *The Yogi of Christ.* Then, through Vatican II, an ecumenical opening was made to various Asian religious traditions—Thomas Merton had already found Zen Buddhism. Recently, I came across an interesting exchange between two priests, one Taoist and the other Catholic, in *The Tao of Jesus,* and the Dalai Lama's sympathetic reflections on Christianity have recently been published.

Then there are the spiritual . . . mystical . . . experiential connections.

Contemplation for us is analogous to Buddhist meditation. It tends to a perfectly centered, imageless state of awareness. This can inspire poetry.

ML So poetry is . . . ?

PL Ah! Poetry is the mean term between the physical basis for imagery and the metaphysical realm of being. This is what connects the affective to the cerebral, the heart to the sensual, and the mental vehicles of reception to the visible and invisible realms of being. In fact, poetry creates or recreates these mediations in the experience of those who are ready to receive it. In that sense, we are all poets. In the same way, one could say that all are potential suprabeings, beings to be "deified," as the Eastern Orthodox Church puts it.

DM The Spanish kabbalist, Abulafia, said that everyone is his own messiah.

PL Well, this I can understand within a hierarchic structure, which exists in both the eastern and the western wings of the Church, and which you can see in the fifth- or sixth-century writings of Pseudo-Dionysius. His *Mystical Theology* is the basis for the apophetic path. Saint Thomas Aquinas referred to this short treatise as the supreme authority for all that which surpasses the rational apprehension of reality.

DM Can the poem say the unsayable?

PL Isn't this what poets have always aspired to? Seemingly failing in the attempt but finally achieving a *miracle in words*.

DM As a poet, can you say what you don't know?

PL Not consciously, no, I don't believe so. And this is the big contribution of Surrealism. The Surrealists worked in what Freud called the unconscious. Of course, their practice did not entail the abandonment of the conscious—for poetry only rational control and preconceived aesthetic and moral determinations were ultimately rejected. This exploration was like a voyage in uncharted seas—and you could be shipwrecked along the way . . . in a psychological sense.

DM The poet as voyager. I know you traveled a lot. You lived in Mexico, didn't you?

PL Yes, I had an extensive life on the road. I first went to live in Mexico in '54. Mexico, a Catholic country, was for me, as for Kerouac, a multilayered inspiration. Some of the most beautiful parts of *On the Road* are about his Mexican experiences.

DM How long did you live there?

PL All together about eight years. Mexico City was wonderfully habitable in the 1950s. A great city, enormous, on a giant plateau stretching for miles in all directions. I walked a good part of it by day and by night. Rich with sights and smells, very unlike the United States in those days, and certainly not at all like Europe, though there were many baroque churches, many of them with subtle Indian interlacings.

DM Was there a Surrealist contingent in Mexico City at the time?

PL I met Leonora Carrington there, and saw a lot of her. I also spent a while with another great woman painter, Remedios Varo. But I wasn't in Mexico City all the time. I traveled and perched for long stretches in various regions—Oaxaca, Chiapas, and even remote places in the Sierra Madre mountain range in western central Mexico.

JB Was that with the Indians?

PL Yeah. With the Coras, though their name for themselves is Nayeri. Their culture and way of life is as remarkably preserved as probably exists in all the Americas. At least, it was so forty years ago. I heard recently it hasn't changed essentially—no cars or electricity—it's as close as you can get to pre-European contact. It was there that I began to return to the Church, to my own roots, inspired by their vision and ritual. That was my second contact with Indian ritual, the first being a night-to-dawn peyote ceremony of the Teepee Way that some Washo people held in the hills above Lake Tahoe in their original native environment. These primal nations seem to be keepers of essential and significant knowledge and practice.

JB Was it Artaud's writings that brought you to the Indians?

PL Partly. I had read Artaud's *Journey to the Land of the Tarahumaras* in 1948. And then I lived in one of Jaime de Angulo's houses for six months in the Berkeley hills in the early fifties, although Jaime was no longer alive. The house was a Maybeck-built beauty, and I remember it was there that I read Carl Lumholtz's *Unknown Mexico,* about the Nayeri, with whom Lumholtz had spent five years. They also had a peyote rite.

DM Let's talk about the nature of the ceremony or the ritual you went through. Can you describe the point of their ritual? What did the ritual lead to?

PL It was a sacramental celebration of *yahnah,* their black, juicy tobacco, not at all like the species we smoke. It's one of many subgenera originally cultivated in the Americas. The rite, though not in any way Christian, began in the one Jesuit mission church in the village at about ten o'clock in the evening. First, there was an elaborate ritual handling of a black wooden sculpture representing the elongated figure of a man, which they carried to their mobile, richly designed, and feathered wooden altar at the far end of the church, away from the Catholic altar. The "black man" was exquisitely carved. After about an hour we left, and they carried the sculpture in a black box along with the altar and other paraphernalia. The procession was guided by a single file of torch-bearing men up a hill to a place hidden from the view of the village below. We came to the stone-portaled entrance to their temple, on whose lintel the representation of a giant iguana had been carved. (I had already seen a living giant iguana basking on rocks near the river of the village whose Spanish name is Jesús María.)

Once inside the open temple, about forty men seated themselves, a third of them wearing stylized priestly garb of glimmering cloths. On one side of the circle I remember about five of them playing curious-looking bow-and-string instruments; others played flutes. And there was an enormous two-foot-high slab of wood, carefully honed, upon which the young men, one at a time, took turns dancing, providing resonant, percussive sounds in unison with the other instruments. This orchestra played some of the greatest music I have ever heard. This went on for about six hours, until dawn. Musically, I heard complements to Bach, Mozart, Balinese classical music, and Indian ragas! An amazing experience, communal and transcendent.

DM When you returned to San Francisco, after all of these travels, where did you relocate in a more permanent way?

PL Those eight years in Mexico were not successive. I traveled back and forth from Mexico to New York to San Francisco, spent half a year in Morocco, and lived a bit in Paris the period from 1950 to 1961. And then I was back in Spain, Morocco, Italy, and Greece, and then Spain again between 1963 and 1968, before I settled back in San Francisco.

JB So ten years or more have passed since your meeting with Breton in New York. Was there still a thread connecting you to Surrealism in some personal way or was that encounter a distant, if informative memory?

PL An interesting question. Except for a brief period, roughly the two years at Rexroth's "university of the mind" and two years attending classes at UC Berkeley, I began to inch my way back into a quasi-Surrealist interior. I remember reading for a small gathering at Kenneth's around 1951, and he remarked that the poetry had signs of "starting again" from the Surrealist origins. As Charles Henri Ford once put it, "Once a Surrealist, always a Surrealist." I more or less agree, insofar as a profound contact was made traveling into that zone "between waking and sleeping" and plunging into and going perhaps beyond Freud's notion of the preconscious. Didn't Baudelaire call it "finding the unknown"? Through Rexroth I did begin practicing in the area of his fundamental focus: *statement,* in his case philosophical. . . . I remember writing sort of "political" poems that made their way into rare anarchist publications.

DM You were a child during the Depression. Do you recall what San Francisco was like for you as a kid during that period?

PL I remember the 1934 General Strike. I was eight. My family were summer guests at my maternal uncle's rustic estate in the Santa Cruz mountains. We lived in a large two-story house, where on weekends as many as twenty other people would come for dinner and relaxation in a forest setting. For recreation my uncle had an ample boccie-ball court on the grounds. Most of the guests were, like my father, in the wholesale produce business. They were upset, for sure. The produce business was dependent on the teamsters who hauled, loaded, and unloaded the produce from the farms that stretched to San José and beyond. My uncle was one of twenty or so owners of the produce houses. For a few weeks, the talk about the strike was interminable. Most of the owners were Italian Americans, perhaps the greater part, as we, were Sicilians. Later, I read it was these commission merchants, as they preferred to be called, who hired the thugs to beat up the militant lumpers that were essential to the market, though the shipowners played a key role in repressing the striking stevedores.

I only heard about the General Strike in this way. Around that same time, the most shocking thing for me was seeing the photo of a child screaming in the midst of debris on a city street in the Spanish Civil War. That's a famous photo I've seen reproduced often, long after the event.

But my deeper awareness of politics came later when I was about thirteen, reading in the Communist bookstore on Market Street and getting around the city on my own.

JB San Francisco was a small town then.

PL I wasn't living in the center, I was living in the periphery. We lived in the Excelsior district, where there were still some farms. You can still see houses that had been farmhouses. It was also largely populated by Italian Americans—"little North Beach," it was called. No restaurants—just Italian delicatessens and bakeries. A family neighborhood.

DM There were marked differences between the West Coast, specifically San Francisco, and New York. Here there was strong political involvement and very compatible esoteric or mystical involvement as well, along with a sense of the natural community.

PL Yes, absolutely. San Francisco was more political, utopian, and environmentally aware. A more personalist or organic tendency here . . . the word "organic" was often used to speak of the kind of society we wanted and how to get it. "They can have City Hall!" was the attitude. I remember Rexroth's saying that one night at one of our meetings. This was part of his communitarian idea, which he wrote about later in *Communalism*. As he points out in his book, these communitarian ideas have their roots in the historic communes of the Middle Ages and further back in the first centuries of Catholic Christianity in the hermitages and lay communities of the Theban desert. Later, the only successful and long-lasting communalist society of the Americas flourished in the Jesuit-directed Paraguay of the seventeenth century.

DM It's interesting to see what there was to participate in during the San Francisco Renaissance. The Six Gallery was not the only event. There was also the Poet's Follies, for instance.

PL Before the Six Gallery reading, there was a big reading that Madeline Gleason put together with Bill Everson, Robert Duncan, me, and Rexroth at the San Francisco Museum of Art. That was many years earlier—in the late forties. And then a series of readings were given in various places, where twenty-five or thirty people could gather easily. Already this was the beginning of the poetry-reading scene here. The very first big reading attracted an audience of a hundred or more. This was a potential that Allen Ginsberg picked up on. He stayed with Kenneth, who naturally set the tone for all the things you could do, and Allen learned from him. Allen had many sides. When I first met him he was talking about how we should be ready to talk to Mao Tsetung—poet-to-poet.

DM I'd like to get back to what Jim mentioned about the East Coast—that the heavily mystical connection was not an aspect of the East Coast art scene. There seems to be a geographical tradition . . .

JB . . . that is peculiar to San Francisco and Northern California. Along with a century of environmentalism—as a kind of critical complement to a tradition of environmental destruction—and mysticism, we have imported and indigenous anarchism. San Francisco poets are critical of the very idea of the city. Whereas the New York poets are really poets of Manhattan, of urban spaces, urban times. New York School poetry is something like Apollinaire in Manhattan. You don't see nature at all.

DM All you see is that poetry reflects the external world, but doesn't bring the feeling of the interior life that seemingly so many of San Francisco and Northern California were involved in.

PL Except for the Transcendentalist movement . . . the forest was alive before it was cut down in the nineteenth century and paved over in the twentieth, and poets could write about it and write from it.

DM Emerson talks about seeing the steam engines going to the woods, and he's already aware of change.

PL But people did, even in marginal cultures, respond to nature. Until they started breaking away to the cities. It's here in the Far West that nature is still somehow with us, in spite of the devastation of the last three decades. *Meadowlark West* is a celebration of what's left in some still powerful natural places in Northern California. You can still get enough of it to inspire.

DM Well, when you talk about Apollinaire and the city, you're talking about modernism. When you talk about mysticism and nature, you're talking about a kind of antimodernism. And yet everyone in that particular group was affected by modernist poetry and poetics.

PL Ultimately, there shouldn't be any contradiction between the urban experience and what's left of nature—or revitalized nature, which remains a possibility. There is, in fact, an urban bioregional movement in U.S. towns and cities. There's a Green City movement in San Francisco, begun by Peter Berg and others. Nancy Peters and I went to some of their meetings—is it fifteen or more years ago?

JB Speaking of esoteric connections, there's your influence on the San Francisco punk scene in the late seventies, an influence that is never really talked about. But the evidence is there in Vale's publications, *Search & Destroy* and *Re/Search*.

PL Yeah, I never noticed it until you pointed it out. I had an interest in the punk scene. I went to Mabuhay Gardens a number of times. I find all that perfectly in line with most of my life, starting in the revolutionary heart of Surrealism and later in the Beat rebellion.

JB There's a tradition that comes through your research into the modern primitive—just about at the same time that a kind of disembodied modernism arrived in San Francisco with the Language poets. Their scene was almost anti–San Francisco.

PL Yeah, they're all floating above San Francisco.

JB Yes, floating over the New York–San Francisco axis. A different kind of poet. A different kind of person, in fact.

PL Well, to each his own. [*laughter*] I've read some interesting poems from that domain, but I can't see it as a direction, no. And it's been over as a movement for some time now.

DM Who are you reading now of the younger poets?

PL Ah, well, Will Alexander. He's not in his twenties or thirties—yes, Will Alexander. My favorite book of his is published by Sun & Moon Press, *Asia & Haiti*. I've known him for twenty-five years, met him when he came up from Los Angeles for the twenty-fifth anniversary party for City Lights. We also did a reading in 1998 at Beyond Baroque in Venice, California. Another admirable poet, a new friend of mine, is Andrew Joron, whose latest book *The Removes* I recommend highly. He's thirty-eight. Among the youngest, already a fabulous, great poet is Jeff Clark, whose first book *The Little Door Slides Back* was published in 1996 by Sun & Moon, when he was twenty-five. That book won the 1996 National Poetry Series prize. Another young poet friend, Garrett Caples, has just published in 1999 *The Garrett Caples Reader*, a wonderful book of prose and poetry. His erotic prose narrative "Metempsychosis" (in John Yau's anthology *Fetish*) had already won him a reputation in 1998. He's twenty-six. All three live in the Bay Area.

Somewhat older, in their forties, poets I've looked to are Adam Cornford and Jim Brook here, who has published his poetry in a number of fine chapbooks. And there's Sotère Torregian. I wrote an introductory note to an early book of his, *The Wounded Mattress*. He now lives on the Peninsula, in Redwood City. He's recently published *Always for the First Time*. He's been writing some amazing poetry lately and continues as a Surrealist.

DM Do you go to poetry the same way you go to other texts? Is poetry nourishing you in the same sense that it may have in a different time, or do you derive nourishment from other kinds of writings other than poetry?

PL I still look to poetry, of course. I do read poetry as much as I read anything else. Let's face it, I'm a polymath and my reading has always included sacred texts, the sciences, philosophy, history. . . .

DM I'm curious, because some poets stop reading poetry. Or just go back and read the classics to inform them and propel them, and sort of stay there and don't deal with the present.

PL I feel my orientation is more stable than ever in terms of my own going on with writing—I don't know if that answers your question. As far as other poetry goes, it too can spark poetry for me. I appreciate it for that. Yes, I feel that I'd like to read poetry, above all by the younger generation, for as long as I'm here. At this point, I'm winding down. . . . [*laughter*]

Michael McClure I (1969)

Fall 1969: Walked up a long wooden staircase into the light-filled living room, of the McClure's house in the Haight-Ashbury hills. We set up the clunky Sony reel-to-reel portable tape recorder on a coffee table in the living room, whose windows looked down into a backyard filled with trees. Paintings by Bruce Conner, Jean Conner, Jess, and McClure on the walls. Here's where memory mangles history: at least two other people were present, friends and/or visitors of McClure who shared his ecopoetic mission, but whose names and faces I can't recall. McClure's an archetypal Romantic in the full-blown heroic sense that Goethe was: naturalist, dramatist, poet, essayist, novelist. A serious, playful, complex trickster and sage; a smoothly amiable and disarming presence. After reassuring small talk and gossip, the machine's turned on, and the interview begins.—DM

Michael McClure (**MM**)
David Meltzer (**DM**)
Jack Shoemaker (**JS**)

1

MM I came to San Francisco for two reasons: (1) I was pursuing Joanna, and (2) I came here to take classes from Mark Rothko and Clifford Still. When I arrived I found out that they had left the year before.

The mystique of abstract expressionism fascinated me. I would have painted had I taken classes from them, but I never really thought of myself as a painter. It was that I was experiencing what the painters were experiencing at that time.

DM This was your fourth year of college?

MM Yes. I graduated from San Francisco State. The year before I spent at the University of Arizona. All that I took there that I can remember was German and the Short Story. Oh, I also took an advanced painting class and some advanced anthropology. Both classes were very interesting to me.

DM When did you discover the work of William Blake?

MM Very early. I was writing poems in the style of Blake when I was seventeen. After high school I finished writing the pictographic poems I told you about—although they became less and less pictographic and more and more formal vers libre. Then I discovered Blake.

I bought the collected poems of Blake and Donne because somebody had recommended Donne to me. I couldn't read Donne, but I discovered those unbelievable poems of Blake. In the process of that I also discovered Milton. And between Blake, Yeats, and Milton I felt challenged to teach myself metric, to teach myself stanzaic patterns and shapes of poetry, like the sonnet and the villanelle.

I wrote very little in college and not much of it did I care for. I suppose it was a hermetic period. It was like a very long silent meditation on forms.

I also idealized what Dylan Thomas was doing. And I was terrifically impressed with Roethke.

I was writing poems in the manner of Blake. A cross between Blake and Baudelaire, and at the same time learning forms like the Petrarchan sonnet, the ballad, the villanelle, the sestina.

It was very hard for me to write a sonnet. I might spend several weeks on a sonnet and then wait several weeks before I wrote another poem. I was very intent on having the meter correct, following the voice.

As for Blake, I used to dream I was Blake!

DM So there was Blake, Yeats, and Milton?

MM Yes, all about the same time.

DM What a rich panoply of teachers!

MM Yes. And I wasn't alone in this. There were five or six of us waiting, and we fed each other intellectively.

During the first couple of years of college, I ran with what were then called "beboppers," with jazz musicians, in the middle fifties.

DM Did you enjoy music?

MM No, I didn't. I got very little out of music. It wasn't until later that I was able to get it. I listened to a lot of classical music and enjoyed it. I like Beethoven and Mozart most.

I ran with the beboppers, going to all their jam sessions and night-club engagements, and not really hearing their music until I had been listening to it for more than a year. I was doing it for the drugs and excitement and because you stayed up all night and slept all day. Then, one day, somebody was playing a record by Thelonious Monk. And I heard that. Then I heard Bud Powell, and then I could hear it all. By that time, I was headed somewhere else.

DM What did you hear in Thelonious Monk?

MM A very exotic, highly structured, mysterious, emotional occasion. Elegance. Elegance of the intellect and the body moving in tune with the elements. Because you have to, you have to move. Move your hands around.

I found Monk and then, I think, I found Powell and then Gerry Mulligan—and who was the young trumpet player with Mulligan . . . ?

DM Chet Baker.

MM Chet Baker, Anita O'Day, Charlie Parker. I went through all of those: Gillespie, Parker, "Salt Peanuts," "A Night in Tunisia," "Ornithology," "How High the Moon" . . . and a whole host of people I've almost forgotten. I listened to the music for a year before touching it. Before it even got through my skin.

DM When did you get to San Francisco?

MM Nineteen fifty-four. I took Robert Duncan's poetry workshop, and I was handing in sonnets to Robert. Robert was astounded that a person who was so interested in poetry would hand in sonnets and villanelles. He kept trying to get me to write free verse, and I wasn't mature enough to explain to him that I had already been through it. Yet what I was doing interested him.

I think at first we were amazed with each other. I was amazed by his clarity of perception and his ability to express himself and to be concise. I had been through free verse, completely through free verse, and was experimenting with the very traditional forms like the sestina, the classical Petrarchan sonnet, and so on. Robert couldn't figure out why I was doing this, because he thought this kind of thing was a dead horse. For me, it was the final grounding in what I wanted to know before I split those forms completely.

We wrote poems every week, and Robert would be slightly dismayed at my sonnets. It was a very interesting confluence. Then I became personal friends with Robert and with Jess. They offered an opening to the possibilities that I was searching for.

DM Was he a good teacher?

MM Fantastic. It was one of the most brilliant things that ever happened in my life. To have Robert stand at the blackboard and speak for two or three hours about a line of poetry or a word or a poem or whatever came into his mind in relationship to his own work, or to the work that other people were bringing in. I believe in the cliché that poetry or painting can't be taught, but I was also present at the exception to the rule which makes the rule, which was Robert's class.

DM When did you start publishing?

MM The next thing that happened was that I met Jonathan Williams, and he offered to do my first book, *Passage*. It started out as a great stack of poems, but I kept editing them down. There was no size restriction. I imposed that restriction on myself.

I knew when I wrote those two villanelles for Roethke that meter and genre held no more interest for me. I had satisfied the desire to handle genre.

In looking at a sonnet you have to realize that you have an idea, a resolution of the idea, and a couplet to cap it. It makes you aware of the intellective process in writing the poem. Besides merely saying: I have a girl; it's spring; I got fucked; I didn't get fucked; the water is great; look, there's an animal . . . I mean, it makes you realize that you have relationships other than those, and you are forced to look at the structure of ideas behind a poem. A poem can't interest me very much unless it is both intellective and emotional.

All that was going through my head. It was like what was happening with the abstract expressionists at that time. They were learning to write their biographies in the movements of their body on a canvas. Whether this painting is looked at in 200 or 300 years was not of interest to me. What was of interest to me, although I couldn't formulate it until years later, was the fact that it was a spiritual occasion that I could believe in. And it was alive and brilliant while I looked at it. I was very much taken with that concept, and that's influenced me enormously. I still see things in those terms. I see rock and roll as a spiritual occasion. I saw the assemblage movement as being a spiritual occasion. I see the new earthwork sculpture as being a spiritual occasion. I saw Ginsberg as a spiritual occasion. The Beat Generation thing as being a spiritual occasion, the San Francisco Renaissance as being a spiritual occasion. I feel as if I am a string and these spiritual occasions are beads or pearls that pass over me in much the same way that a complex molecule, RNA, slides across the ribosome to create protein. It's as if I am a string that the pearls, or ribosomes, of events pass over and from this I form the protein of my being around it.

If we are, in a sense, genetically indestructible until we are brought to our termination, I think it's reasonable that, rather than starting with a predisposed philosophy or cosmology, we allow it to form itself around us. I also have the feeling that everything grows. My relationships to things grow. Oh, there are dead spaces. There are the knots on a necklace between the pearls. I also look forward to the knots.

I think a lot of us tend to exist in static situations—very much to our loss. Some can exist statically because of drugs. They can exist statically because of the situation dealt to them. By luck, you fall upon certain concepts. You can also form a feedback of intellectivity or emotionality or physical being and throw it out and bring back more with it.

DM Your many references to chemical procedures come from what revelation?

MM In the last year I read a book called *The Anatomy of the Cell,* by Björn Afzelius. He is a Swedish electromicroscopist. Although I had read quite a bit about genetic structure, it wasn't until I read this book that I totally changed my relationship to the material that we are made of—to our protoplasm. I realized that my picture of it was highly simplified. Even with a layman's understanding of contemporary microbiology, I still didn't have a picture of the complexity of the events that we are. I was still buying the idea we were given in high school that the cell is a kind of bag. I realized the complex structure within the bag, but I didn't realize that the structure within the bag *creates* the bag. Topologically, the inside of the cell is as complex a structure as we can conceive of. Any given cell. There are three trillion cells in each of us.

. . . .

MM I think your idea of, what did you say, rearranging the skin web is probably exactly where it's at.

DM I think that's what it is. It has to do with facing a series of crises of

self-image, self-perception, realizing the depth of the *selfless* forms.
MM It happened when I wrote *Fleas.*
DM Some of which were in *Caterpillar* 8/9?
MM Yes. Those were the first nine. There are 250 of them. They are
spontaneous and unrewritten. They're all in rhyme and average about
twenty lines each. They are childhood memories. They are an obses-
sion, like Billy the Kid and Jean Harlow were obsessions. The idea of
doing *Fleas* became an obsession, and when I finished them and re-
read them, I found that I had awakened many of the more complex
responses.

In other words, when I look at that chair I remember the chairs I've
seen in my childhood, which were out of mind before.

I became interested in the topology of how our mind works, and
about two-thirds of the way through writing, I discovered how infor-
mation is stored hologramistically in the brain. In other words, in
multitudinous sources, overlapping, instead of one, and it was pre-
cisely what was going on in me.

Everything overlaps everything else and lights it up. It isn't stored
according to our ideas of rationality. It's stored on an organic basis,
and everything overlaps everything, and as one memory is lit, it lights
the corner of another memory. If you light up another memory near
it, it will light up a memory that was unsuspected. Then that lights
the corner of another memory, and you light up another one near it,
and it lights up the one in between.

The new sciences of microbiology have a very small relationship to
the sciences that precede them. Boehme said that the universe we live
in is the result of the friction of the celestial-bliss universe rubbing against
the black fires—which I find as believable as atoms and molecules.

I think we have to believe everything that's reasonable to us.
Boehme's concept of our existence is as spiritually true, or truer, than
atoms and molecules.

In John Lilly's book, *The Mind of the Dolphin,* he goes to great length
about how little we know. And how much of mental health is accept-
ing the things that come from beyond limitations. Just accepting them.
I think that the more that happens to me that I can take per se, the
happier I am. When you're young and specters appear before you, you

learn very quickly either not to see specters anymore or to accept the fact that specters appear. I accept.

DM We often deny what we may be afraid of. The unknown is often a fearful connation and becomes an obstacle.... There are aspects of the unknown that provoke fear, and we can face fear a lot of times by rejecting it.

MM Byron was afraid he would never die.

DM So much of it is coming to accept whatever happens, being able to cope with it without much expectation.

MM I think the most exciting thing that's happened to me is the ability to think. When I say "think," it's nothing so heavy. It's just that I will imagine I'm at a Mexican temple in the year 1450 when it's being inaugurated. Forty thousand people are being sacrificed. Then I'll envision the scene, and I'll skip from there to another thought to another thought to another thought, so that I can't . . . it's very difficult for me to be bored anymore.

I saw Kerouac the day after he died.

DM You did?

MM Yes. I woke up in the morning, and he was flying through blackness, and it was great. And I yelled at him: "Hey, hey!"

DM And what did he say?

MM He didn't say anything. I wrote a poem in my mind. I didn't have my pen, but I wrote down what I could remember.

DM Kerouac was important to you, wasn't he?

MM Yes, absolutely. I think with Kerouac the most important thing was that I don't agree with Kerouac about very much. Yet I loved his writing. He is so graphic and concrete that I experience what he experienced—even though it is totally foreign to me. And it knocks me out to know what he felt and what he saw. So that, in a sense, he is like a real paragon. If there were 500 men like this that you could follow, you would really be in great shape. If you could see out of 500 sets of eyes besides your own and smell through 500 noses . . . I am willing to do it, if anybody will present it for me. I just read a book called *The Way of All Flesh*, by Samuel Butler. It was of equal importance to me as the book on microbiology. I mean, to see into Victorian society and to see into the interior of the cell are two really great sights.

2

DM When did you start writing plays?

MM Nineteen fifty-nine. I finished the first one then. The first one was called *The Raptors*. Then I did a play called *The Blossom*. *The Feast* was next, a play in beast language.

DM Could you explain the formulation of beast language?

MM There was no evolution. The idea of *The Feast* sprang into my head, went off light a light bulb over my head—like in the cartoons. Flash, flash, flash! And I saw the whole play, and I started to write it down in beast language with thirteen characters drinking black wine and eating loaves of French bread. Then I said, this is ridiculous! And I started writing what I imagined I should do. I wrote a great deal but had to throw it all away and go back to what I originally saw, what first flashed over my head. That was the only beast language I wrote until three or four years later when I felt a ball of silence within my-self—and inside of that ball was beast language. It was a source of pleasure, entertainment, and amusement and a great deal of concentration not to lose it. I knew there would be a hundred poems to write down as I heard them.

DM We were talking earlier about the form, the contour of your work.

MM I see what I'm doing as pulling out possibilities within myself. As a possibility opens itself, I create it. It isn't anything that wasn't already there. I can see the possibilities now.

DM All these events hinge upon a moment, the available perception, your disposal toward the moment. As a spectator to your work, as the audience, I can sense from your work a kind of pattern of development.

MM A lot of that has to do with my editing. A lot of it is self-acceptance. Like in *Hymns to St. Geryon*, I decided I should be what is represented there. In *The New Book/A Book of Torture*, I decided I should be what is represented there. Each one is like a very narrow vibration of what I am doing at a given time—what I felt was the most appropriate vibration.

There will be a lot of poems in my book that Grove is publishing right now, the book called *Star*, that are very much like the unpublished poems I was writing in 1955, 1956, and 1957, but I couldn't accept them then.

The Beat thing was over the horizon. American culture creates these great slots and pigeonholes.

JS And the San Francisco Renaissance was yours?

MM No.

JS I mean, it was the one they put you in.

MM Yes, I guess so. I highly disregard all that slot making. It looks like in the seventies all the slots are going to come down. I don't think we have to stand for the slots now. I think enough people have been slotted and pigeonholed. I think the audience can be depropagandized.

For one thing, everybody is going to be getting tired of the word "ecological," yet the ecological thrust is bringing people together. I recently wrote a poem beginning with two lines of a poem by Larry Eigner. I rediscovered Eigner's poems after not having paid close attention to him for a number of years. I got his *Another Time in Fragments* and began a poem with two lines of his and sent it to him along with my Rector poem. He responded with an article he had written on ecology and a three-page letter on thermal pollution.

JS Has ecology been a long-time concern with you, or does the vocabulary and concern come late?

MM I met Sterling Bunnell in 1957, and before that I thought in terms of biology or natural history or physiology or morphology. Sterling introduced the concept of ecology to me. So I would say it was a concern since 1957. Since then Sterling became and remained one of my best friends.

JS You were in a play of Duncan's in the early fifties?

MM Yes, I had one line.

JS It must have been a good one. What was the line?

MM I can't remember. The play was *Faust Foutu.*

JS Did that kind of predate your interest or begin your interest in drama?

MM Actually, the performance of Robert's play was a reading of it. The play should be performed because it is a very important play. As far as I know, it hasn't been given a public performance, and I would like to show it to John Lion of the Magic Theater to see if it is possible.

I found the beginnings of a play in a 1956 notebook. I was grasping for a play, but was only able to write dialogue. I wasn't able to carry the images of the persons in my head as I was writing. Only their voices. So it was unsuccessful.

It must have been about 1958 when Artaud's *The Theater and Its Double* came out. I was convinced by Artaud that texts were needed for the theater and that it would be the poets who would write these texts. I was inflamed with his idea of theater and the theater of cruelty. I've never been interested in absurdism, aside from the theatrical possibilities of it. But on reading Artaud, I looked at the poems that I was writing, and I thought that the poems were voice notations. (These would be many of the poems in *The New Book/A Book of Torture*.) I said, "Ah, this voice notation can be adapted to theater!" And then I wrote *The Blossom*, a play about Billy the Kid. Billy the Kid and the other participants in the Lincoln County War in New Mexico in eternity together, unaware of their death and former relationships. They speak as if they are mobile and motile sculptures in eternity.

JS Has it been performed?

MM Yes. It's been performed several times. It was first performed about a year or two after it was written. It was done at the Poets Theatre in New York by Diane di Prima and Alan Marlowe with sets by George Herms. I wasn't able to see it, but I saw a few minutes of film footage, and it looked beautiful. They did it together with an Artaud tape of *Let Us Be Done with the Judgment of God*, the tape of his voice done for Radiodiffusion Française. It had gotten into the hands of Ginsberg and myself. *The Blossom* was performed as a double bill with Artaud reading.

Then it was done at the University of Wisconsin by Robert Cordier. They brought me in to give a poetry reading and to see the performance. The department had OK'd the production of the play, but when I got there they said: '"No, no performance." They'd seen the rehearsals. "We won't allow this to run!" So two professors threatened to quit, and one performance of the play was allowed. The public couldn't be let in—just people who happened to be wandering by. However, the auditorium was packed. A lot of people had heard about it. Cordier owned a film company and flew in people to film it, and the university said: "If you film it, we will kick the students out for participating in the filming." And I said: "Stop. Forget it." The snow was four feet deep outside. So, I guess, that was my first taste of censorship.

The Blossom was done again at the Straight Theater in San Francisco about two years ago. It was coupled with a mime drama of Artaud's.

DM Did seeing one of your plays acted in any way affect the writing of the next play?

MM Absolutely. When *The Cherub* was done here by the Magic Theater . . . I wrote *The Cherub* after I got back from London. After fourteen or fifteen busts of *The Beard,* I said "fuck the theater," and I wrote a novel. When I got back from the London performances of *The Beard,* where I received massive rave reviews, I felt very joyful about the theater, and I wrote a couple of comic plays out of a feeling of happiness—and because the images were there within me to be developed. Actually, they just unfolded themselves from the start. John Lion asked me for a play to do at the Magic Theater, and we did *The Cherub.* And when I saw *The Cherub* I was very pleased to see this play in existence, and I wrote ten more plays in the same genre. And I called the plays, eleven plays, *Gargoyle Cartoons.* You saw them, didn't you?

JS Yes, I saw three of them.

MM Well, they are all alike, and they are all totally different.

JS Will they all be done eventually?

MM The idea is that they are like Noh drama. Noh dramas comprise several plays. The body of *Gargoyle Cartoons* is eleven plays. The director can choose three, four, or five plays depending on his temper, upon circumstances. He can string them together, like: *Wolf Tooth, A Piece of Jade,* and *A Piece of Thistle Down.* He can make a sculpture out of a theatrical event with any group of plays he chooses.

JS I saw things going on in the lobby prior to the beginning of the plays. Was that of your making also?

MM I believe in the total extension of mise-en-scène. Recently, I have written a play that totally breaks the stage space. I like to have the play set as meat on a shelf in space with lights and music so that they are sculptural. They actually have the three-dimensionality of meat presenting an image to you. For instance, *The Beard* is Billy the Kid and Jean Harlow in blue velvet. It's an image. Spider Rabbit is an image. The Two Meat Balls, the two balls of fur discussing the nature of reality, are image. The images are there and they unfold. The image is three-dimensional in my head. I can hear, see, smell, taste, touch it.

When I conceive of that image, it begins to unfold, and it unfolds as a gargoyle cartoon.

It's an image of meat. A meat-sculptural concept, which requires that I have it happen in my head. In 1955 or 1956, the only thing that was happening was literary. Voices in my head. The way you write a villanelle. You write a villanelle because there is a metrical voice in your head that you are pursuing. You demand it to rhyme in a certain pattern. But that's a voice, it's not dimensional.

Probably the very reason Robert was upset with traditional forms of poetry is that they are not dimensional. They can be, and it might be very interesting to make them dimensional again—as they were for Shelley or Keats. In contemporary terms, it's very hard to give any tactility to an inherited structured form. You want to get out there and stretch and push, and you want to give the imagery actuality, credibility, and vitality. You know, Olson brought in the idea that you do it with a thrust of energy onto a field. This is an interesting concept.

JS When we walked into the theater that night, there was a chick on a bed with a guy, and on another side there was a guy doing yoga in a glass case, and on the other was a chick playing harp . . .

MM And a guy in boxer trunks skipping rope?

JS Right. Were those pieces yours?

MM And it was full of fog? And somebody was barbecuing meat and serving it to a couple at a table. The idea was mine. As mise-en-scène extending into the theater and connecting with the plays.

JS I thought they were the fourth gargoyle cartoon.

MM No, they weren't. Although in a sense they were. It was all done by a girl named Evalyn Stanley. I told her what kind of feeling I wanted in the lobby, and everything that was there was hers. I may have said: "Somebody cooking meat." I didn't think of a boxer, I didn't think of a yogi in a glass case, but I said I wanted it full of fog and very bizarre happenings that were in context with the plays. So she arranged the whole thing. We were very fortunate in a costumer, also. Besides the director and the actors. The costumer and set designer were brilliant.

JS It was a great way to get into the play.

MM People became so hung up in the lobby that they would walk into one of the cartoons late 'cause they thought they were seeing the play.

JS I spoke to people who thought we were, in fact, in the play.

MM Yes. That's the way it should be. For instance, when we did *The Beard* here, on the opening night I had girls in strange costumes with whips and masks lead the audience to their seats. And there was a show of George Herms's pieces in the lobby. I was trying to extend the mise-en-scène as much as possible. There was a word on each seat that related directly to the play. When you took your seat there was a strip of paper on it printed in very, very large letters. It would say "silk" or "rock" or "boot" or "panty" or "blue" or "velvet" or "mark" or "tooth." The audience would sit holding that piece of paper they picked off their seat. Words that were repeated in the play. The mise-en-scène can feed back on the play.

In the play Billy the Kid would say: "There is nothing here but blue velvet." One person is holding "blue," and another person is holding "velvet."

I like the almost Paleolithic quality of having a stage, the very ancient idea of having a stage as a shelf. The ritual of contemporary psychological theater is that you walk in and confront the shelf. I prefer the shelf to be confronted as a pedestal. The total environment should be an entertainment—which also relieves the play of the burden of entertainment. The play obviously should entertain, but the play can also contain ideas. The mise-en-scène can also contain ideas.

JS The Living Theater has its own ideas about the show confronting you.

MM When the Living Theater breaks the stage space and comes down into the audience, I don't feel it is so much a Pirandellian extrusion of the stage toward me—I feel it's an actual extension of the stage up and down the aisles. For instance, in their *Antigone*, when the actors writhe up the aisles, I feel that they are carrying the stage with them. This is a matter of their presence more than anything else. I feel that the stage is putting out tentacles to engulf me. I don't feel that someone has come off the stage to break the reality of the rite.

I conceive of the play as being like a cell. It has its organelles, its ribosomes, and its DNA and RNA, and a good enactment of it is harmonically and biochemically in balance. You see this go wrong very easily when a director will allow an actor to take over a part for a laugh or a burst of applause.

Both actor and playwright have to create a living entity that gives rise and allows the spontaneous burst of applause, the laugh. So they are in balance with one another and create their universe around it. The sculptures of the persons within it are like the movements within a cell.

JS In that first play, the one with the little guy and the three pandas and the three naked girls and the giant frog . . .

MM That's called *The Pansy*.

JS . . . so much of that was involved with blocking . . . and with my experience in the theater, blocking was on the shoulders of the director, not the playwright. I am wondering how much of that blocking you were responsible for and how much the director was responsible for. There is not a great deal of dialogue. A great deal of it is involved with the dance.

MM John and I happened to be very much in agreement on many levels. I went to as many rehearsals as I could and approved of everything. I generally approve of what John does. I think *The Gargoyle Cartoons* are director's plays. Among other things, they allow extreme possibilities for the director. I think I can write a director's play because I'm sure enough of what is going on, on the stage. I think it will transmit itself with a great deal of accuracy to the director, and he will enjoy allowing it to manifest itself.

The other really interesting thing in drama is that it happens in your head in three dimensions—with real imagined meat doing it, and then when it's actually performed with a real flesh body, it's so different, and so much more real than when it happened in your head. It takes on so many complexities of the actor's temperament, of his stature, of his being, and that is when it really gets interesting. That's what stimulates you to go on in the theater.

JS Spider Rabbit is black. . . .

MM I had not intended Spider Rabbit to be black. As a matter of fact, I didn't want any racial overtones in the play. And I thought until the end that we were going to have Chris do it in whiteface. We tried it in whiteface and we said: "Oh, man, take it off!" I am not aware of any racial overtones in it. We are planning to do *The Beard* with a black Billy the Kid, probably Chris. This will be interesting. I'd like to see an all-black *The Beard*. I'd like to change them to Mae West and W.C. Fields or change them to Mata Hari and the Heap. I'd like to have them wear derbies with little halos on a stick over their heads. Rip Torn would like that.

DM Whatever happened with your confrontations with censorship in Los Angeles?

MM It's still being passed around the courts. Here is an interesting book. I have a new publisher . . . the State of California. This has almost a complete text of *The Beard*. The state illustrated it for me and added 200 pages of commentary to it.

JS Whose commentary?

MM State senators, finks, canaries, musk turtles, karmic debility cases.

DM I hope you are well protected by good lawyers and good vibrations. . . .

MM What's happening in L.A. is that I was convicted of disturbing the peace. I wasn't convicted of obscenity. I'm being sued for a half of a million dollars, and *The Beard* is being tried for fourteen arrests on, I think, eighteen counts. Something like that. They just arrested *The Beard* in Vancouver. Fortunately, the cast are being protected by the Canadian Civil Liberties Union. Again, it got very good reviews—as good as the reviews in London.

3

MM What I am most concerned with now is the river within ourselves. The biological energy of ourselves is extrusions or tentacles of the universe of meat. The universe of life covering the entire planet. Let's say life is four billion years old—it might be older—from the first complex particles of a certain type of material joined together in strings and then coiling and encapsuling themselves. The next biggest step for them is to become links, to form a coating about themselves. Traditionally, you think of a cell as being an enclosed substance, like a bag or a sac. It's actually not that. It's created from the inside outward, and it's highly complex topologically. From the first topological complexity becoming what we have come to call life until now—four billion years later.

If you could do as Spengler does. . . . He takes cultures and examines them side by side as if they were physical entities. If you can conceive of all life that has happened on this planet of which we are a highly complex extrusion, as a novelty of that body experience, and conceive of that body as unique, freed of time and space, and if you can conceive of it as a vast being . . . then you begin to conceive of yourself in relationship to the surge. It's not a systematic system. It is a systemless system, an expanding system, a system becoming complex as it stores rays of the Sun. The rays of the Sun furnish energy for this. It contains more and more of the energy, and it grows more and more. You begin to see your relationship to it, and you begin to see that there is a river, a surge, a source that is universal and that you partake of.

You are that thing, sensing and perceiving itself. You become dimly aware of the multiplicity of your sensations. You don't have five senses. Scientists say we have twenty-seven senses. You can't really conceive of this totality, because you don't have an infinitude of senses. But we have more senses than we know we have. We have deeper relations to this universe. I think, for the first time, an awareness of it is coming to us.

Take Camus. There he is confronted with horror, anguish, nausea, forlornness, etc., because he conceived the meaninglessness of a man's gestures in a telephone booth. He's a member of a very heavy Catholic society that has come to think in traditional-humanistic terms. You are partaking of the same culture—a planetary culture that is interlinked. You participate in various degrees of types of wealth or poverty it offers you. Camus sees this and says: "Oh, my God, look at the utter meaninglessness."

When a man sees this and can't relate to the universe—not only to the universe but the universe of beings—his reaction is like nausea or horror. I think now we are freed to recognize the possibility against that. Against a background of pollution, horror, and contamination, mass starvation, hallucination, and psychosis.

JS So the response then to four billion years of history is not nausea?

MM I think it could be very well like joy if we could deal with our inner beings. If we realize that we are not one intelligence but many intelligences, that we are not one cell but a congress of cells. If we can understand very clearly that we have developed two sets of emotions and psychology: the social emotions and the inner physiological emotions.

In a herd society (the traditional humanist herd society which really isn't humanitarian) we have developed a herd man, a lumpen man, whose motivations are exterior rather than inner-directed. It's possible for a man to blossom, yet very few men blossom.

DM Do you think that the inner river directs us in some way?

MM I think it's the important direction, but it's usually repressed by the social condition, by the snares and mazes and entrapments of the priest-centered society—as well as the graph of values that's made for you.

JS There are people that would say that we could acknowledge the flow as being your history of life, but that acknowledgment of it doesn't bring to us any direction at all.

MM Yes, but people always want solutions.

JS No, direction.

MM Let me skip from that for a minute, and maybe you will see. Everybody wants a solution instead of realizing that the universe is a frontier, that the universe is a messiah for this whole total . . . this beatific complex meat structure that you are a tentacle, an aura, an extrusion, an experiencing of. They say instead, we want a solution, we want a utopia, we want bliss, we want progress, we want revolution, we want this, we want that. These are all simplistic solutions. It's like we are all trapped in *solutionism*. As one solution fails, another solution is tried. Everybody wants a solution. When they realize the defeat of a solution they split as rapidly as they can to another solution to rid themselves of any anxiety.

It has to be seen very clearly that biological creatures do not exist with solutions. Biological creatures exist through motility and growth and the more complex constellations of memory, intuition, and perceptions of their sensorium. So you constantly destroy and re-create. You don't have a revolution to solve everything. Each creature is in a state of revolt, each intellective creature. Each creature that is able to feel with his meat . . . man or snake or wolf or rosebush . . . is in revolt, whether its revolt is its growth or whether the revolt is the deliberate making, the deliberate extrusion, the feedback loops to bring them what they want. To bring them what they want through manipulation of circumstances. But never technologically and not mechanistically.

JS Those would be our answers, though.

MM If the organism exists with problems, then the organism also exists with possibilities for solutions. All I am saying is we can grant recognition of that river within us which, in mixed vocabulary, could be the Hindu "we are all one," but it would seem that that doesn't lend any solution. "We are all one" is too easy. "I am many" is more where it's at. I am happy when my manys agree.

"I am many" is where it is at. I am a heart, I am three trillion cells, I am a lung, I am many neuronal centers; I am an obvious sensorium that sights, tastes, touches, smells, that I can verbalize and symbolize about—I am twenty-two other senses that are less easy to verbalize or symbolize about, several of which are totally unconscious and don't register on the part of the brain that I constantly recognize.

The manys of me must agree and must find what I call an intellectivity to commune with, free of desire for solutions or progress. We must look for mammalian betterment.

Our genes are one-and-a-half million years old. We spent one-and-a-half million years minus twenty thousand years developing at one thing and spent the last twenty thousand years selectively breeding to become something else . . . and developing a tradition that's not what the biological preparation was for. He evolved as a rare creature. We are no longer a rare creature. We evolved as a social animal, and we are becoming a herd animal, or gregarious as opposed to the social animal.

JS I'm wondering, with such an extreme and powerful overview, if you could draw it down to specifics that are meaningful within the deliberate confines of one's rational thought.

MM I don't think one man can do it—unless that one man is a great visionary. I don't think one man can do it. Man is a rare animal, but man is also a social animal. I don't think one man would find it. It's again like wanting a messiah, a leader. . . . It's going to have to be a pool of intellective, multiple intelligences, to conceive of creative betterment or find what we are "naturally" biologically and bring the possibilities of that into play.

We are very unhealthy. We were much healthier thirty thousand years ago. We were much more intelligent thirty thousand years ago. Thirty thousand years ago we had larger brains and more possibilities of constellative configurations. We probably were more perceptive thirty thousand years ago. There's been a great deal of selective breeding since the domestication of animals and cultivation of plants. We have developed a new type of man in a very brief time. We've done it the same way that you can develop new types of dogs. You can have a Chihuahua, you can have a Great Dane, you can have a malamute, from one stock. We have opted for one of the possibilities of our stock, and it seems to be highly unsatisfactory.

On the other hand, we can't romanticize the talk about Tarzan and Jane, or the noble savage, because that is a manifest absurdity. I mean, that's another kind of kitsch. No one man or individual or small group of individuals can conceive of the situation.

JS Let's say at the beginning of Western history, at the time of the Academy, one small group of men supposedly had a vision of . . .

MM Are you talking of Plato and Socrates?

JS Say that the Platonic Academy is an idea . . .

MM That was merely the development of the tradition that was already in existence.

JS It was more than that, it was the bringing together . . .

MM I love Plato. Not only do I enjoy reading him, but I consider *The Symposium* to be a truly great absurdist drama when it is performed— and not read. I don't think Plato could have been a playwright in that day when the Greek theater was so different from his ideas. What he did was to write closet comedies that are very beautiful.

JS The notion of the Academy that I meant was that it absorbed the countryside . . . they absorbed the folklore and history, and they wrung it through a kind of strainer, and out came Western civilization as we know it.

MM No. Look at what was happening at exactly the same time. Out of the East comes a mystery cult. From the population centers of the East, probably Egypt. . . .

JS Plato visited Egypt and was a disciple of Zoroaster, so he was in touch with the East. . . .

MM I'm thinking of the confluence. You are looking at the Academy as being the major origin of our humanist condition, but at this period there is a confluence. The mystery cults travel from the population centers of the East. The mystery cults are obviously a reaction to population density. They say you will be reborn, that you will be given rebirth within our community and that you will have immortality. The cult is evangelistic and these cults battle it out. Finally, you have Mithraism, which was the predominant mystery cult at the time of the conception of Christianity.

The Christians have destroyed practically all traces of Mithraism. We know very little about it. The Christians were the highly jealous winners of that battle of the cults. Christianity triumphed as a mystery cult. It was even more evangelistic than Mithraism. The whole society becomes a mystery cult, and the mystery becomes totally exoteric, totally at the service of the traditional humanism, and it conjoins with the traditional humanism to become a servant of it—bringing with it all the shit to support the worst hypocrisies, the natural bloodthirsty drives, as well as the kind human temperament. These ideas commingle, conjoin, confluence, and here we are.

This is apparently not only true of the West. A similar thing happened throughout the entire world. We are joined in a tightly locked total surface planet culture. This is only one possibility among many possibilities. It happens to be the one we have arrived at. I don't see any elements in any civilization that weren't a contribution to where we are at now. You can find the Mayans destroying Mexico. They did a pretty good damn beginning of it before the Spaniards got there.

JS When you mentioned that perhaps a group of men would have a vision powerful enough to use, I thought of the Platonic Academy. Things have been happening for the last four or five years where people have seemingly been calling for another Platonic Academy.

MM It will have to be a mammalian one. It would be right if we could get a few eagles and bears and dolphins in there, too, not to mention salmon, bison, and pandas.

I'd like to repeat something that's in *Meat Science Essays*, because you brought up Plato. One of the Greek mottoes that they liked to live by was: "Moderation is best." Moderation is highest. One of the catchphrases of our acculturated traditional humanistic societies is also "moderation." I discovered that what we now mean by moderation and what the Greeks meant by moderation are two entirely different things.

The Greeks went to extremes. You get drunk and have belladonna in your wine and have a feast and everyone talks euphorically all night long and then, in the morning, you take your baths and go to the agora and to the marketplace and then to exercise. You go from the extreme of drunkenness to meditation to the body athletic. It was the development of both the body and the mind, the ability to sing, the possibility of being drunk and the possibility of soberness, yet we hypocritically, and antibiologically, give lip service to a different kind of moderation. Our moderation of today is like the moderation of the relative confinement of your possible activities. To be in your car, to drive it to work, to do a job, to come home, to have a drink, to go to bed, to go to work the next day.

The individual in his own idealism, which is propaganda, is blocked in his possibilities, and the only possibilities that are open to him are the possibilities of checks and balances. Like, alcohol is OK—you can be excessive with alcohol because alcohol is traditionally inherent in this society. If you smoke grass then that gives you extra societal insights at this point. When grass becomes legal it will probably cease to do so. But at this time. it gives you extra societal insights, therefore it's a negative.

DM The idea of moderation, doesn't it also arise from perhaps an instinct for a kind of balance?

MM Yes, but the point I want to make is that the only balance you can achieve, that makes sense biologically, is to go not to the extreme of freezing yourself to death or burning yourself to death, but to find a center, a balance, a true moderation. You have to go to many extremes to form a center that is the true balance. From this balance center you have to have extensions to conceive of what the possible frontiers are.

You must know what you can do. You have to experience what you can do. And then you must choose your moderation from the possibilities. You create your moderation. Today, your moderation is handed to you.

Sexuality is highly orthodox, and it's rebelled against because of the intensity of the orthodoxy. The social unit is so orthodox that it seems inescapable. I mean, the family unit. The whole thing is not working. And won't work. It starts with a child. As a child learns to form what he sees into patterns, he's told specifically what the patterns are. He is propagandized as soon as he learns to organize sound.

A real biological moderation would be the result of a choice, i.e., I tried this and I tried that and I tried all of these other things, and I can do all of these other things, and I stand in relationship to all of these things.

Me, inner me, says I know what is happening. Nowadays, the inner me is smothered in favor of the social me. Social me is informed about the condition, and if social me isn't propagandized by word alone, he is propagandized by example and by the stress of overpopulation. Everyone conforms more and more as the swirl becomes more and more psychotic.

DM What are the alternatives for this society that you see as a poet?

MM I think Blake is an extraordinary example. Blake was a man in revolt; he was constantly in revolt. He developed a system that constantly expanded. It was very vigorous because he very seldom took the time for self-examination or denial. He accepted the changes as his perceptions, intuitions, visions, and sensorium absorbed more and more. He expanded. He expanded as a rose plant would expand or as any like creature in a natural habitat would expand, and, at the same time, he took a stand against all he didn't believe in. He didn't live in an ivory tower. That's what I'm saying. He didn't sit in a war field in Vietnam with a copy of *Walden* in his back pocket and a flamethrower in his hand saying, "I'm really not here because I really believe in Walden."

DM Blake had his treasure, he had his garden.

MM Every man has his treasure. It's inside him. It's called meat.

DM That's it.

MM Most men are propagandized and negated by a structure that has become so all-encompassing that only a man born in the fortune of circumstance with certain intelligences is able to see some crack in the structure.

JS The man who sees the cracks in the structure can still have his garden . . . can still have his inner peace.

MM No. I don't think so. Not now. If you take a populist view and look back thirty or forty years, you could find the man out in the farm with a sense of meaningfulness. But now farms are factory farms. Chickens are raised by the tens of thousands in conditions that are unbelievable. And I guess 80 or 90 percent of our population is in major metropolitan areas, so I don't think there is a possibility of it—except in the most extraordinary conditions.

JS Not in yours or my definition of the garden of serenity, but perhaps these people have different notions of it. . . .

MM There is no garden of serenity, there is no peace, saving that you insulate yourself and lock the doors. . . .

JS Or you watch TV.

MM That's not peace. That's a jitterbug thing. It's propaganda. It's a form of propaganda, a constant barrage of propaganda informing you of all the kitsch beliefs of the humanist tradition.

JS TV is perhaps another man's garden of serenity and meditation, a chapel of all the bullshit mysticism for the last ten thousand years. The warden at Lompoc Prison puts the TV on in the morning, and it stays on all day. He says if it weren't for TV, they would have more riots.

MM It's a baby-sitter.

JS It takes care of people. It's a garden of serenity.

DM How can you be serene when you can't see anything grow in your garden?

MM It's a narcosis.

JS Doesn't it take away the pain of life?

MM I don't think it takes away the pain. I would consider TV a pain-inflicting instrument. What actually happens psychologically when you watch TV is that you get into a state of self-induced autohypnosis. TV is a strong autohypnotic. You become fixated on that screen which is projecting itself at you. Nothing else registers on your reticular system, your neuronal screen. The neuronal screen, the screen of your being, is meant to experience the universe; instead, TV fills it with the projection of shit images. It whites out. I mean it whites your perceptions out. Sound comes at you loud. The visual thing comes at you very loud. As McLuhan points out, it appeals to your tactile sensorium as well. At least three areas of your sensorium are being hit at once. And it's all registering on that interior screen that's like a central source screen, or the central agency, for perception. All it does is white you out.

It fills you not with pleasurable influences but with painful influences: cowboys naked to the waist beating each other with chains. It's a mistake to equate the internalization of novelty with a desire for motility. Your body desires to move, your body desires activity, desires a frontier, so that your neuronal screen, actually your reticular system, the place where these images register, will be constantly active. You just lay there, and it fills the screen. That screen was developed for an entirely different recognition pattern and perception pattern.

JS I'm saying that the autohypnosis of TV is easily equated to meditation.

MM No, because it's not filling enough to be equated to meditation. Meditation works in an entirely different way.

JS Meditation is autohypnosis.

MM There are several kinds of meditation. Let me give you two. One is the kind that is done in Subud. You move your arms and legs randomly in a darkened room with your eyes closed. You shout or sing or chant rhythmically at the same time. Try to think while you are doing that! It's impossible. Your screen is blank. Totally blank. And your screen being totally blank, you are getting a feedback of your own sensations. Purely physiological sensations. Totally organic sensations of your body with absolute imagelessness feeding back to you. You realize you are the universe. Afterwards you feel high. You really feel good. An hour of that is fantastically rewarding!

The other kind of meditation is much more complex. You do it through a series of studies and rejections and acceptances. You learn to empty the reticular system or your neuronal screen. Either one works. What I am saying is that TV is not emptying your screen, it is only filling it up enough to white it out. You're not getting any feedback. When it gets blank you get feedback. After watching TV, notice that you feel exhausted. You have been through the meat wringer. After meditation, either Subud-type meditation or Hindu-Buddhist-type meditation, you feel invigorated. Sure those TV-watching people don't riot—they're too exhausted.

DM I was interested in your relationship to Wilhelm Reich. What effect did his work have on you and where did it lead you to?

MM Reich came like a bolt out of heaven for me. I found the muscular contractions and armoring he speaks of to be quite clearly within my own body. I tried to find a Reichian analyst. There wasn't one on the West Coast. I worked through experiments, exercising, automatic writing, and a lot of good friends and luck to find the armorings and to do what I could to eliminate them. I was in a state of extraordinary biological distress when I stumbled onto his work. I found it to be a great godsend, messiah-send—if the messiah is the universe.

Automatic writing is an extraordinarily helpful device if you just write what you want to write and know that nobody will ever see it.

DM I remember at that time that you were also very much interested in Yeats's book, *A Vision*.

MM I was very much taken up with his concept of gyres. In the sense of gyre that you have the helix of the DNA molecule—although the DNA molecule is a crumpled gyre. You can see that the gyre represents an ever-expanding systemless system.

DM The DNA molecule contains evidence of memory and history. . . .

MM The DNA molecule is the memory. It is the memory of the meat. Four billion years of memory telling you to be a mammal. Let me read you something here.

> But desire to know and feel are not eased!
> To feel the caves of body and the separate
> physical tug of each desire is insanity. The key
> is love
> and yearning. The cold sea beasts
> and mindless creatures are the holders of vastest
> Philosophy.
> We can never touch it.

We are blessed.

Praise to the surge of life that there is no answer
—and no question!

Genetics and memory

are the same

they are degrees of one

molecular unity.

Besides our body's being a genetic accretion of billions of years, it is
the actual accretion of our physical contacts with our environments,
our psychological contacts with our propaganda and our intuitions.
It's the actual meat on your bones, the constellation of the perception
and events, and, in addition, we have a storage center in which the
events that we can symbolize and verbalize about are activated. We
call it our cortex. There are other parts of the brain, too, like that small
part of the brain back there in the nasal area. In that area, they have
come to believe that memory is stored hologramistically. Memory isn't
stored in one place but stored constellatively in many places within
the mind. Memory multiplies and lights up the edges that the con-
stellation overlaps. The electrical and chemical activity that goes on—
several sources of it going simultaneously—are constantly interacting.
This universe of cells is in constant action.

If we empty this screen, then the experience is the universe. The
body of the universe manifested in our body. If we allow the screen to
be filled, then the screen is like the external reality vying with the
inner reality. Biologically, it's uncanny. If the existentialists were con-
fronted with this, they would have no answer—or they would want
no answer. "How can this be? Where's God, why are we here? What is
that man doing in the phone booth?"

Our bodies are like a multitude of fairy lands that all agreed to be-
come you.

There's no doubt that there's a very high alchemy that we haven't
touched yet. And that we have intuitions of in mudras and gestures. A

cell in the tip of your finger might be related to an atom in a star in another galaxy in a way we can't conceive of. The universe is an interweaving of such complexity that we are totally unable to conceive of it. You can imagine butterflies flying randomly through a shifting lattice. Can you imagine the multitudes of invisible presences surrounding it?

I think that what we've done is to choose the Faustian path in which we conceive of ourself as a tool or a mechanism. This choice is mirrored in technology. We conceive of our body as a tool or mechanism for the achievement of desires, rather than for the central being, the inner being, that creates and seeks in the outer and peers deeper into the inner. We think of manipulating exterior reality and ourselves as tools, as functions of something we can't touch because it isn't there. It's an abstraction. . . .

DM The mysteries. . . .

ANOTHER VOICE You're in the ninth sphere. . . .

Michael McClure II (1999)

December 3, 1999: McClure picks us up at the Rockridge BART station since neither Jim, Marina, nor I drive, and McClure's new house in the Oakland hills needs wheels to get to. It's being renovated. There's a crew of workers leaving as we arrive. We climb a steep driveway and are greeted by his McClure's wife, the sculptor and designer, Amy Evans McClure. She shows us her studio, which has some of her amazing works in process. Michael leads us up outside stairs into their living room, a sun-filled space with artworks by Amy, Jess (Collins), George Herms, Bruce Conner, and Wallace Berman, along with some Buddhist wall-hangings. He prepares tea. A cat fluffs about until finding a sunny spot on the carpet to settle into.—DM

Michael McClure (**MM**)
David Meltzer (**DM**)

DM It's thirty years or so after our last interview. . . .
MM We should do this more often!
DM I know, I know! Now the first question is, what happened in those thirty years? Give us an update.

MM Well, the big thing that happened was in 1986, when I met Amy Evans. We've lived together since and have been married for the last three years. She has sculptural greatness. I'm fortunate to be present around her work and have a companion who is an ardent artist. As I see her work grow, mine often reflects it, and sometimes hers reflects mine. Another person has also been important in my life, in my new life, in my *vita nuova*. Working with Doors keyboardist Ray Manzarek on stage, creating with a *compadre* who's a great composer and artist, is another ongoing achievement.

DM Amy got you sitting Zen.

MM Absolutely. That's been a major change. So to go back to 1972 . . . not too long after our first interview, a contingent of poets and intellectuals in the Bay Area went as protestors to the UN Environmental Conference in Stockholm. The group included Peter Berg, Sterling Bunnell, Stewart Brand, Joan McIntyre, and David Brower. That conference set many of our ideas about the environmental crisis and brought us closer on the issues. The next year I made a trip around the world with Sterling Bunnell, a visionary naturalist. The main purpose was to go to East Africa and Asia. This was the first of three trips I've made to Africa to take notes on the Pleistocene as it still exists. That trip was largely to look at birds and mammals. Later, there was more direct experience regarding the life of man. Many feelings about it were expressed in the essays in my *Scratching the Beat Surface*.

In 1970, I began extensive reading into new areas. In our earlier interview, I talked about coming across the idea that cells start from the inside and create themselves outward. In 1970–72 enormous amounts of information were coming out about the assemblage of the simplest levels of life and also about the symbiotic agreements that are made between simple organisms to make higher, eukaryotic organisms, organisms with nuclei. At the same time, I found the ideas of Lyn Margulis about the co-evolutionary origins of higher cells. Gary Snyder introduced me to Hwa Yen Buddhism in *The Buddhist Teaching of Totality* by Garma C.C. Chang. This book changed my idea of physics.

As I said in our earlier interview, science is beautiful, but I certainly didn't believe in atoms and molecules. In the thinking of the T'ang dynasty, Hwa Yen Buddhism that I was studying at that time, there is another system of physics—the nonphysics of nothingness. It is the sister discipline of Zen. I became involved in those ideas and laid out a deeper foundation for future actions in writing and thinking. I am not troubled by holding two ideas at the same time. There are atoms and molecules on this side of the fence, and on the other side you don't have them. I feel the richness of both systems. They are the two best that I know of.

I continued working in theater and wrote twenty-three musicals and plays. After writing the prose *Autobiography of Freewheelin' Frank*, about a Hell's Angel friend of mine, Frank and I began playing music together with George Montana. I followed my interest in music and wrote song lyrics. My plays continued to be produced by the Magic Theater, which did twelve productions of my work. American Conservatory Theater commissioned me to write *General Gorgeous,* and my plays were performed in New York, L.A., London, and Paris. Most of these plays were intensely comedic—visionary comedies that culminate in *Gorf,* which is about a flying cock and balls and a blind motorcycle dyke, and an alternative universe in ancient Greece, which had. . . .Wow, that's a hell of a question, asking me to catch up. I feel like I'm not on the right track.

DM No, you're doing fine. What changed for you, and what remained the same?

MM What remains the same is that in 1987 I began working with Ray Manzarek. I was performing with poet Michael C. Ford at McCabe's Guitar Shop & Music Club in Santa Monica. Mike Ford went on stage first, and while he was reading, a tall fellow came out and sat down at the piano and started playing accompaniment. Mike's a jazz poet, and this was jazz being played by an unknown but familiar-looking amazingly inventive musician. Then I realized it was Ray Manzarek, whom I had not seen since the Doors days. Ray heard my new poems when I read next, and we met afterward and decided to work together.

Soon afterward, we were asked to do a workshop at Brockport College in New York state. I had some notes on how to be a "lyric" poet, and Ray may have had some on being a musician. When we got to the college we looked at each other and said, "We're not going to do that, are we?" In the hotel there was a piano lounge. We went there to practice, and Ray played the piano and I read some poems. The music and poems went together, and we were *on*. The next day when we were announced, we stood up in front of a large auditorium and did poetry and piano together and received a standing ovation. Now that's wonderful!

DM It must have felt good.

MM It felt good. We said, wow, we've got to do this more—this could get better. Though I thought we were good when we first did it. This was a natural coming together. Ray comes from a profound interest in Beat poets. Although we're very different character-wise and personality-wise, we come from the same direction. We have Jim Morrison as a mutual friend; that's why we met each other in the first place, at the third recording session of the Doors. We've played 150 gigs since 1987. We play at colleges and music clubs, the Fillmore, Kerouac festivals, coffee houses, and outdoor music events. We've opened for bands and performed mostly in the U.S. but also performed in Japan, Mexico, and Canada.

Some of our repertoire is old. But the age of the poem does not matter at all. If it was significant to me and I wanted Ray to hear it, I'd send it to him on tape. He'd listen to it, and he'd feel to see if he had music for it. I was doing a lot of biological pieces like "Stanzas in Turmoil." As a matter of fact, that is the piece that Ray liked most. "Stanzas in Turmoil" incorporates a lot of Lyn Margulis's ideas about the symbiosis of higher beings and deep behavior and what spirit is. This was considered an arcane poem. Nobody understood it. But I discovered that when we did it together on stage, it was different.

We played the Bottom Line in New York—and in the audience were young men with long hair and Jim Morrison T-shirts and leather pants. They were yelling "Play 'Light My Fire,' man!" And Ray said "No, that's no what we do here." He asked the crowd, "How loud can you yell?" They yelled as loud as they could. He said, "OK, here's what we do." So we did "Stanzas in Turmoil," a poem that is seventeen minutes long in performance. At the end of that piece the kids stood with their thumbs up in the air and said, "That's visionary, man!" We were out there talking to people again. It was like the Six Gallery reading, when we got up on the stage on October 7, 1955, and found ourselves saying what was over the edge to people, we found there were people out there who were over the edge, and that we were speaking for them.

Ray and I are not going around to intellectual gatherings of people. We certainly weren't getting hired by college English departments. We were going to music clubs and to places where people did not know poetry, but they knew self-experience. We were doing poetry that was political and environmental—and, granted, a lot of it was for fun, too. We were doing what I started out doing at my first reading at the Six Gallery—only now it was more effective because I could not find anything so arcane that an audience couldn't understand it.

I thought about that for a long time. What I finally understood was that on one side of our brain there is a word center, and on the other side we have a pitch center. I'm not talking about left brain, right brain. When somebody is in an audience and they hear only poetry, it only works on one side of the brain. Just hearing the words. I'm only using part of myself. I'm listening to the words. I don't really under-stand the poem. I don't quite follow it. I'm not involved in the same way as if there were accompanying music. That's when the experience becomes entirely different. One experiences more of oneself in con-junction with the music; therefore, more is understood. That which was mysterious before is immediately understandable now. I don't want to exaggerate this. But I think one of the reasons Dylan Thomas was so popular when we were young was that he not only had the words, but he furnished his own music with that big Welsh singing voice of his. Everybody listened to Dylan Thomas.

We were performing at a blue-collar blues club in Flint, Michigan, and the working-class kids with long hair and beards were out there dancing, and I said, "Hey, you can't dance!" Then I realized that, oh yes, you can. There are many other moments I can look on that changed me completely regarding performance. I gradually came to feel perfectly normal and comfortable on stage. I started to have a good time while believing very much in what we were doing and tak-ing political and environmental messages to places that would not otherwise get that message as we were giving it to them. It was like at the Six Gallery reading when we looked out in the audience and thought, they're not scared of "Howl"—they *like* "Howl." When I read

"For the Death of a Hundred Whales," the audience is not offended. They like it. We're speaking for them.

The literary world hardly knows what Ray and I did. But on the other hand, there's a whole other world of young people out there—many of them came because they had their first spiritual experience with the Doors. Some of them came out of curiosity because I was being billed as a Beat poet with one of the Doors! Occasionally, some old friends of ours would come.

Oh, another thing happened in this period: I had an opportunity to write my fourth long poem. I had three long poems: "Dark Brown," "Rare Angel," "Dolphin Skull." I was going back to the first section of "Dolphin Skull," which is a series of stanzas taken from the unconscious, which is then followed by a single extremely long stanza, which is the portrait of one moment. Then I went to the first part of "Dolphin Skull," and I took from it lines that spoke to me and said "use me." I began new poems or new stanzas with them. I was taking lines that appealed to me at that moment from the deepest part of my unconscious that I'd been able to reach—one more long poem, "Crisis Blossom," came out of the intensity and crisis of that moment.

Finally, one summer Ray and I were through working, and Amy and I went to Bali. It was enormously beautiful and profoundly disturbing. The people are gentle and kind, and their art, as it stares at you from the walls, is formally raw. Living in a hotel room like a tree house, like Tarzan and Jane lived in when I was a kid. It was a troubling experience, listening to the river. . . .

DM What was terrible? The dark side?

MM The dark side hung on the walls, actually. The lintel in our bedroom had monsters carved on it, glaring at us as we slept. Or there's the dark side of the dances. And some of the temples that we visited. "Crisis Blossom" was going on through all of that. I felt more and more intense. There were moments it became so intense, I didn't have time to start with the section from the unconscious—I had to start with new words. But it was time to come home. We got on a Singapore Airlines plane, and over the China Sea the plane had a near crash. It dropped, and the oxygen masks dropped down from the ceiling. The woman behind us had a heart attack, and people were gasping. I thought it was the end of my life. I had no doubt. I just wanted to take Amy's hand and look in her eyes for the last time. Then the plane pulled out, and we landed in Singapore. We spent most of the night wandering around Singapore before going on to San Francisco.

Back in San Francisco, I was in much physical pain. I suffered from insomnia, and I had unwanted total-recall experiences from childhood. Finally, this led me to the hospital for the first time in my life. The first morning that I was out of the hospital, Amy said, "We're going to start sitting zazen." I said, "No, we're not. My back hurts." And she said, "Well, I'm going to." She sat, and it wasn't quite right, and I said "move your legs a little this way . . . your back should be a little straighter . . . straighten a little like this . . . put your leg like this. . . ." We sat every morning, and we became more deeply involved with the teachings of both Aitken Roshi and Suzuki Roshi because Amy was reading them to us each day. I was receiving advice from Phil Whalen and Gary Snyder.

I finished "Crisis Blossom," which I had started during my psychophysical meltdown. Then I began writing my first intentionally Zen poems, which came directly out of the sitting. There are ninety-nine of them, and they are called *Touching the Edge*. In those poems is a whole other part of my life that had been crowded out of my earlier poems. They say your consciousness is not what you see, hear, and touch, it's what comes into you and manifests itself.

DM They're certainly more direct and everyday.

MM They're meant to be ordinary. Zen is ordinary.

Then I had another extraordinary experience. After Amy read about as much from Aitken and Suzuki Roshi as we could possibly hear in one or two lifetimes, she started reading from Dogen, the thirteenth-century mystical, visionary Japanese founder of Soto Zen. Many times over the preceding decade I had tried to read Dogen. Dogen had been beautiful but impenetrable. But while sitting, I believed I was hearing him, and, to a large extent, understanding him. When I was fifteen or so, I discovered William Blake, and at sixty-five I discovered Dogen—or, more accurately, Dogen discovered me. So I had another main figure in my life.

You don't really expect to have a new figure in your life after a certain age—you think you've read everyone. The figures in your life are all lined up: Shelley, D.H. Lawrence, Lorca, Blake, Dickinson. . . . Then Dogen opened up the possibility for me to understand what I had already been doing. Something profoundly moving had happened, and I began my second book of Zen poems based largely on this inspiration. The book has long poems in it that are called "Dogen Sonatas." The book when published will be called *Plum Stones: Cartoons of No Heaven.*

DM Which of the Dogen books were you reading?

MM Amy was reading out loud to me from *Moon in the Dewdrop,* which was translated by Kazuaki Tanahashi with priests from the San Francisco Zen Center. These pieces felt like they were coming openly to me, after I had tried to read them five, ten, and twenty years before.

DM In the three decades since our last interview, there have been some notable absences: Robert Duncan, Allen Ginsberg, Wallace Berman . . . people who were important to your life.

MM I don't have anything to say, because I've said it. If I tried to sum it up, I'd say less. I do have a piece on Robert's death. I read my praise of Allen at his memorial. I summed up as much as I was able to at that time.

DM What you said at the memorial about Allen's impact politically and in various social struggles was valuable. Much of the testimony wasn't about that aspect.

MM Yeah, at the Six Gallery reading we discovered after Allen read "Howl" that we were all standing there with our toes on the line. "Howl" had drawn the line, and none of us felt like pulling back. I'm sure we thought it was dangerous. I still feel my foot on that line when I'm out there with Ray, when we're doing pieces on nature, biology, and politics at a music club. That may be one of Allen's first gifts to me, besides showing me the stanzas of *Mexico City Blues* that Jack was sending him in 1955.

Allen's other poetic gift would be in not making any separation between true poetry and true politics. Lots of times you fuck up and it's really politics you're doing. Shelley's a great example of that. I'm sure I've made a few examples of that. Allen sure has. But it doesn't matter—you have to have a practice. And you have to have a politics. I had my politics—I'm sure they were bourgeois anarchist politics. After "Howl" it was still anarchism, but it wasn't bourgeois anymore. "Howl" was of urgent importance to me. The same way it's urgent to find Blake, and urgent to find Dogen, and urgent to discover D.H. Lawrence.

One thing about contemporary poets that's troubling me is that they're all looking at each other. Just as we did. I looked at you, David, and you looked at me; we looked at Allen, we looked at Baraka, we looked at Diane di Prima, we looked at Joanne Kyger, we all looked at each other, we all competed with each other, we all helped each other, but at the same time we absorbed the major poets of the twentieth century preceding us. We read Mayakovsky, we read Apollinaire. We were also studying the poets of the nineteenth century, and we were going through poets of the T'ang and Sung dynasties. I know that so much that's going on today in poetry is young—and some who are not so young—people who are looking at each other and measuring themselves only against each other. It's not wise.

DM There's been an almost obsessive revival and revisioning of the so-called Beat project. What do you see as positive attributes, and what do you see as exploitative and diminishing aspects?

MM I'm sure they can be exploited and have been exploited. I don't know. I don't like the academic view of the Beat Generation—that it was three or four guys in New York City who sort of held hands and hugged each other and had deep and profound literary thoughts for their generation. There are other people who think that the Beat Generation is our first get-together at the Six Gallery reading. Because Jack Kerouac was there and heard Gary Snyder and my nature poems and Phil's Zen and mountain poems, the Beat occasion became centered around politics and nature in a different way. There are people today who enjoy writing that it all happened in New York and that it was a strictly urban phenomenon on Forty-Second Street and at Columbia University and in the Village. But that is not the case. Some truth is getting out. I know that the poetry of the Beats is the first literary wing of the environmental movement. Academic critics write books about what they can see, which is not much past Hoboken. That's exploitative as well as self-serving, and their picture is "cute" and useful to the media.

I spoke at Tom Marshall's class at the University of Santa Cruz where he had 300 students in his Beat literature class. He had 400, but they had to turn away 100 of them. He was teaching the literature as something closer to what it is because he is much more aware of what it is, and he's almost of an age to have been there. The students asked me what the times were like, so I told them what the fifties were. It was politics and environment, and it was fights among ourselves and supporting each other. It was a struggle. It was exciting.

DM In the crisis of the postwar reality of the atomic bomb and the Holocaust, many of the binding ethics and certainty were shattered and could no longer be put back together in the face of what the species had done.

MM You're absolutely right. Jung believed mankind could not recover from the propaganda excesses of World War II.

DM So it seemed obvious that existentialism and Zen would pop up as forms of deflection or of another path.

MM I see the Beat and San Francisco Renaissance phenomena as standing on many shoulders before ours. I had an admiration for existentialists such as Sartre and Camus, but what happened in the United States was deeper and more physical.

DM In that turning away from the void that had suddenly been opened up in Western Civ, the fifties became a lifestyle of uniformity and oppression, a political oppression.

MM That is what I tell people.

DM People have these notions, especially in trendy nouveau fifties schlock-shops on yuppifying Valencia Street, that the fifties were cool because of the objects. These are objects without any subject. These are objects that one accumulates as a way of retrieving some imaginary history. What do you think about the future in terms of the environment, spirituality, poetry? What are your thoughts as we enter the twenty-first century?

MM ¿Quién sabe?

DM You mean you don't have one of those little crystal poetry balls that you look into and get an instant vision?

MM No, I don't.

DM Tell me what you think of computers. Do you use them?

MM Yes.

DM What do they mean in your life? Do you still write by hand?

MM Yes.

DM Do you still keep notebooks?

MM Yes.

DM All the poets I've interviewed are notebook keepers.

MM I've kept notebooks for fifty years.

DM So the work starts in the notebooks?

MM Usually it does, but sometimes on the back of a laundry ticket.

DM Lawrence Ferlinghetti has a very dim view of the future.

MM I have no prognostications.

DM Even environmentally?

MM No. It's an intensely critical situation right now. I see it changing. . . .

DM For the better or for the worse?

MM The philosopher Alfred North Whitehead said, "It is the business of the future to be dangerous."

David Meltzer (1999)

© Frank Pedrick

January 3, 1999: It was Jim's idea to interview the interviewer; he also suggested our mutual friend and ally, Christopher Winks, to do the job. I first met Chris as a grad student in the New College poetics program. He was, as the parlance has it, "a returning student"; that is, a decade ahead of his twenty-something classmates. He has translated poetic and political texts from French, German, and Spanish, and he was a frequent contributor to Processed World *magazine. He helped me immensely in assembling my* Reading Jazz, *a critical anthology on jazz as a white invention. Jim, Marina (Chris's classmate), and this reluctant subject met at the Musical Offering Café, which faces the UC Berkeley campus. I may have been more upbeat than usual because it had been raining.—DM*

David Meltzer (**DM**)
Christopher Winks (**CW**)
James Brook (**JB**)
Marina Lazzara (**ML**)

CW I think the first place to start, of course, is in the core of the work and the life—namely, when did you first start writing poetry? When did poetry come to you?

DM I was eleven, in the sixth grade, and sat across from a girl who lived on my block. Her name was Carole Grossman, and she had beautiful blue eyes and shoulder-length curly hair. I was in love with her. There was an intercity contest where students in all the public schools were to write work celebrating Manhattan's bicentennial or centennial. I was good with words, but I had never thought about poetry. Mrs. Callahan said a poem would be more appropriate for the occasion, and I didn't want to admit that I didn't know what poetry was. I liked the idea that it didn't take up a whole page. That really appealed to me. I said I'd do it because Carole Grossman looked at me in a certain way indicating that I'd better do it or she wouldn't let me come over to her house around the corner and sit in the living room and do the things that we did. Very harmless things—I mean, reading Shakespeare out loud and playing the piano. Mrs. Callahan had said that poems didn't have to rhyme. And that felt good, too. It didn't have to fill up the page, didn't have to rhyme—it was getting better all the time! She said you could write "blank verse." And I went home and asked my father if he knew what blank verse was, and he said he really didn't know. He gave me an anthology edited by Louis Untermeyer called *Magic Casements*. I found a poem by Amy Lowell called "Patterns."

Poor Amy. She's now a footnote in the canon. Anyway, I was very impressed with the poem. It was the first poem, I think, I consciously read to find out how a poem worked. I had this portable typewriter, a Hermes Rocket. I decided to write a poem about the subway system. But I had no notion of what I was going to say. I sat down and rolled a piece of paper into this little portable on my lap and began typing. A remarkable experience. Suddenly, I was writing something that was coming through me. That's what it felt like. Intuitively, I understood the rhythms of the lines and line endings. I was amazed at how on one level I was conscious of so many things, the kinds of sounds words made and how some words didn't sound well with other words. All these things were converging in this wonderful experience I'd never had before—and I'd been writing all the time, writing stories, writing

The History of Everything, literally, that's what it was called. I kept on writing the poem about the subway—I think it was about four or five pages long—until it left me. I knew it had ended, it was over, and I was astonished at what had occurred. As I recall, the poem used the metaphor of the subway system as the interior of the city body—its pulse, veins, and all that. It got published in an intercity school newspaper. That was the first poem. And, yes, it was good for me.

CW It's interesting how you're covering Hart Crane's territory with the subway.

DM After I'd written the poem, I honestly (and naively) felt that I had invented poetry. And that was it. I didn't want to read anybody else's stuff. I didn't want to be damaged by any influence. I didn't want the anxiety. I was content within my hubris of all-knowingness. The poets who interested me were Carl Sandburg, Emily Dickinson. You must understand that even in P.S. 232 during the war years, there wasn't much concentration on poetry. I think the only poem we ever looked at—as I recall, in sixth grade—was Coleridge's "The Rime of the Ancient Mariner," which I'm sure is a wonderful poem, but when you have to memorize huge chunks of it and then recite it in class in these alien rhythms and sounds that don't come trippingly, especially for some of these kids in Brooklyn who had accents as thick as . . . well, it wasn't great. It was Sandburg's clarity that I liked. I still wasn't that much involved with reading poetry. To tell you the truth, the poets that influenced me most of all were not American. They were French modernist poets like Eluard and Cocteau.

CW So you were reading Eluard when you were . . .

DM Thirteen or fourteen. Thank God for New Directions! At that point, most of the available poetry translations were coming from New Directions. I read whatever New Directions published, and they published Eluard, Aragon, Supervielle (I loved his works because there was so much jungle in them). Lorca was another revelation. Wallace Fowlie had an anthology of twentieth-century French poetry, which I read with appropriate amazement. I was not interested in American or British poets until I was about fifteen or sixteen. It was the year the twelve-inch long-playing record came on the market, and I used to take LP records out of the public library, which was a godsend.

Wherever I lived in Brooklyn, there were great libraries. I checked out a Columbia recording called *Pleasure Dome,* an anthology of contemporary British and American poets reading their work. Hearing poets read their work was a revelation to me. Some of the oddest poets really knocked me out, like Ogden Nash, with the complexity of so-called "light verse," and I liked his Boston-ish accent. A kind of dry, flat tone, wonderfully intricate and wry. Marianne Moore reciting "In Distrust of Merits." Dylan Thomas knocked everybody out—this was like grand opera. I'd never heard anything like that before. And e.e. cummings and then T.S. Eliot, who kind of gave me the creeps but also intrigued me. Very contained, very controlled, very effective, because he had this kind of British-American accent. I loved listening to W.H. Auden. I became completely enchanted not by the poetry but by the poets' voices.

CW That's very interesting, because you've already said that sound is very important, that sound was the thing, and that you were talking about words as you were writing, that you knew how words sounded next to each other, which was always a preoccupation.

DM I came from a very musical family. My father had been a professional musician, a cellist, in the Rochester Philharmonic, even though at the time I got into poetry, he had changed careers and was writing for radio. We had lots of records at home. Seventy-eights all over the place. I was listening to them all the time: Piatigorsky playing the Dvořák "Cello Concerto," Gershwin's "Rhapsody in Blue," Albert Ammons's "Boogie Woogie Train," Mildred Bailey, Billie Holiday, Chaliapin, The Rhythm Boys, Casals playing Bach—it was all great to me. I didn't realize at that point that there would be distinctions, you know? I think that helped me. I still feel that way. I resent the ghettoizing or categorization of music for commercial ends. It creates fixed systems of belief consumers can inhabit without being aware of anything else,

CW You got exposed at an early age to bebop through your father, right?

DM Well, it started through me, but my father supported my habit. I spent a miserable summer in a camp. My grandfather was dying of cancer in my bedroom, so my family sent me off to camp so I wouldn't have to deal with it. But I wanted to deal with it. I felt miserable and homesick, grieving already for the loss of a wonderful man. When everyone was going down to the old swimming hole, I was like Kierkegaard up there in the camp reading something murky. Kitchen workers were setting up for lunch and dinner. One day, one of the workers, who were mostly African Americans, a lot of them World War II vets, plopped a Charlie Parker/Dizzy Gillespie 78 on the turntable and played it through the camp loudspeaker system, and, boy, that certainly woke me up! I went down to the cafeteria, and from that point on I'd hang out there and listen to the records during swim time. When I came home, I asked my father, "Have you heard this?" and he said, "Well, I don't know." He bought a twelve-inch 78 of Dizzy Gillespie doing "Salt Peanuts," where he scats. Then we started going to Birdland and the Royal Roost.

In New York, clubs served food, and even if you were under age, you could eat a sandwich and drink a soda or something. That was a real education. I strongly identified with the music. Everyone has their music. There's a certain encounter with the music that defines the moment and also defines the self. I loved the music. I loved everything about the musicians.

The hipsters I had not a clue about, but I'd seen people and liked the way they wore their clothes. That all fascinated me, so I got myself one of those cardigan jackets, a beret, weird-colored shirts and things, and started hanging out. Later on, when I was living with my father in a hotel on Forty-Eighth Street and Eighth Avenue, I would go down all the time to Bop City or Birdland. In my time, the really great musicians were shaping this moment through music—Bud Powell, Parker, Monk, young Miles. There were Monday jam sessions, and you'd hear all the guys who were in town. Singers, too, like Dinah Washington. Her boyfriend at the time was Paul Quinichette, a tenor saxophonist whom they called Vice Prez because he had a very Lester Young sound.

I didn't know at the time that while I was going into these places, Lester Young was in the Alvin Hotel, right across the street from Birdland, dying. Looking out his window at the street below, sometimes going to the clubs and listening to the music, and then going back up to the hotel room and drinking, and not eating. Kind of vanishing. There's this incredible photograph of him that was taken in the Alvin Hotel a few months before his death. Just scary. An empty saxophone case on the bed, the porkpie hat—he's completely shrunken into the drapes that he's wearing. His face is sunken and kind of fat-ter-looking, and he's got a perpetual cigarette in one hand and the sax in his lap. He was sitting on the chenille bedspread of this hotel star-ing out into space.

I had seen him—and heard him play, too. Saw Billie Holiday. In fact, one vivid memory of Billie Holiday was when she was with Norman Granz's "Jazz at the Philharmonic" at Carnegie Hall, and so much of the audience were these white college guys, no doubt stoked on booze, noisy. This was the last period of Billie Holiday's life; she was very frail at this point, like Lester Young. She started singing in a shaky voice, and guys would yell "Go! Go! Louder! We can't hear ya!" which was so painful. And Granz, to his credit, got down on the audi-ence and made it clear that this wasn't the drum duel and this wasn't the saxophone chase, not the honking martial music that enflames and engorges college beer studs into chewing up the chairs. And they quieted down. Intimacy is the nature of her music and is much better appreciated in the small club scene rather than this Christians vs. the Lions concert venue.

CW You said you were a young hipster. Did you try to speak to or develop any kind of rapport with any of the musicians you saw?

DM That was hard because I was so young. I mean, what was I going to do—go up to Bird and say, "Gee, I like your music"? I had no vo-cabulary to further a conversation with these people. I was just grate-ful for what they gave me. I had no way of repaying them other than listening attentively. I was listening to lots of other stuff, too, but this was the music that really claimed me.

ML Were you playing music?

DM Yeah, I was. I had a little career as a kid performer. I was on a radio show called *The Horn & Hardart Children's Hour*. I was a fairly regular performer there. What a scene! All these grotesque kids looking like voodoo-doll adults, you know, and their horrible stage parents and all that. I hated it. I sang, played guitar. I took piano lessons—but I didn't want to learn music, I wanted to make music. I started taking formal lessons in Los Angeles with Sylvia Tannenbaum, the wife of a famous studio string player. Her methodology was superb. She gave me Bach's *Notebook of Anna Maria Magdalena Bach* and Volume I of Bartok's *Mikrokosmos*. That's what I had to learn from, and it couldn't have been better. I worked with her for maybe a year or so. Even in L.A. I was also doing some performing on local TV talent shows.

CW Were you consciously bringing music into your poetry even at that time?

DM I was writing enormous poems. Even though I was learning from people like William Carlos Williams, for instance, who were very economical in their poetry, I still wanted to write *The History of Everything*. But then I got kind of cosmic and had a vision of writing a poem that started in the far reaches of space and gradually worked its way down to Earth and became more and more intricate in detail until finally there was one speck of dust, a little microbe. I worked at that a lot, and I started to write a lot of prose. I discovered Joyce, and I used to hang out in the Village and go to bookstores and see strange avant-garde publications, experimental prose and all that. I loved typographical adventurers like cummings. I remember reading his book *Eimi* and John Dos Passos's *USA*, and I thought, wow, this is great. *USA* knocked me out when I read it again. At sixteen or so, I was reading all of James T. Farrell.

I had a strategy: if I found a book that I liked by a certain author, then I would read everything by him. I would just start from the beginning and read until I couldn't take it anymore. Thomas Wolfe wore me down. But Dos Passos, that really knocked me out. Encountering Patchen's *The Journal of Albion Moonlight*—I didn't know what it was about, but I loved how it looked.

So then I started doing books like that. Huge manuscripts. I remember one was a book about the death of a homeless person I sort of knew in the neighborhood. I remember sending that to Houghton Mifflin. They had an award they gave to first published books. They didn't take it, but I had an interesting correspondence with the editor there. They were very impressed when they found out I was fifteen. They were very encouraging, but I still didn't get the money.

CW Some things never change.

DM It's important to realize that all this time I'm going to school in Brooklyn in an accelerated program for kids with monstrous IQs, and that's when IQ stood for something. The program covered a year in one semester, and by the time I was fifteen or sixteen, I was ready to go to college. The University of Chicago had given me a scholarship. At this point, my parents' marriage began to disintegrate, and we left Brooklyn. That was my mother's wish. She hated living there all those years because my father was making good money writing comedy for radio. He was putting all the money in accounts for all the kids for college, yet we were living in this funky working-class, very ethnic neighborhood that I loved.

That's where all my contradictions were first instilled in me. There was Orthodox Judaism, and then there was the Communist Party, and both of these things seemed very integral to me. I didn't understand the separation between church and state then. On Friday nights there would be synagogue services, and that would be when the CP storefront had its services, too, if you will. Living in that world of many languages: Yiddish, Italian, Polish . . . where you're close to the old world cultures and the new. My grandparents belonged to the Arbeiter Ring, a Socialist trade union.

There was much talk about politics and baseball—coming from a disadvantaged position and talking about such things as social justice. This was the time of the Rosenbergs and the beginning of the McCarthy era—left-wing culture and its play of ideas had to become covert and go underground. The Rosenbergs had a devastating impact on many levels. The end of World War II also had a devastating impact on me. In a sense, I think it still has to this day.

I was only about seven or eight when the war ended, and yet childhood in a strange and very subtle way ended, because I could not comprehend the death of the future. Especially as a kid, you're just starting out and suddenly your every day is numbered. It was also the beginning of an awareness of nuclear weaponry. I remember being both terrified and fascinated by those daytime atoll explosion photos you'd see in *National Geographic* magazine. Beautiful color photographs: bright sun, blue ocean, stuff rising up. I started reading a lot about the bomb at that point. Then there was the opening of the concentration camps. I'd go see the Abbott and Costello movies at the neighbor-hood theater, but newsreels cut through the joy of that anarchy. I guess I wasn't that much fun to be around.

CW You were very much a part of reconstituting this sense of commu-nity on the margins, first during the L.A. Renaissance and then the San Francisco Renaissance, thereafter called Beat. Could you talk first about the scene in L.A.? Nobody seems to know about it, because it's not as commodified as, say, what has been made out of the Beats.

DM When I came to Hollywood with my father, radio comedy was over. TV comedy had moved from New York. Television began to move to L.A. because it was becoming more like film rather than live video. My father also went through an acrimonious divorce and was having a harder and harder time finding work, because in a sense his skill was in radio, which is a different kind of writing. It's a writing that leaves a lot to the imagination, whereas television doesn't. Television is more physical and not as verbal as radio. He was seeing his work taken over by younger people who were more acclimatized to television.

I must have been sixteen when we got to Hollywood. I was immedi-ately depressed to be there. It was dull. I had all these ideas about Hol-lywood, you know. I remember walking from our hotel down Hollywood Boulevard to Vine Street. I had heard about Hollywood and Vine from radio days, and I thought, this is going to be it, the real deal. I got there and it was dreary. There was a Rexall's drugstore on one corner, a de-partment store on the other one. It looked like downtown Omaha. The only difference is that for about four square blocks there were all these movie houses, including some famous luxury ones. That's what I did for the first six months. I didn't go back to school. I went to movies and got a job in an open-air magazine stand on Western Avenue and Holly-wood Boulevard. I became involved in a whole culture of horse-race gamblers, gay hustlers, vegetarians, psychics, people who were after one thing after another. Without knowing it, I was finding teachers every-where by not going to school. I think my sabbatical from school lasted a year or more. Culturally, the place was dead, as far as I could tell. It closed down at ten o'clock—I mean *down*.

When I was about seventeen, I decided to go back to school and get my diploma so I could go to college, under the assumption that maybe college was better than high school. I went to Fairfax High School, which is on Fairfax Avenue. That was great because suddenly it was like being back in Brooklyn. There were Communists, folk singers, people in black stockings, old people talking Yiddish, so I felt great. But I was getting on in age, and still a sophomore in high school, with tons of writing, arguing about Kafka and reading *Finnegans Wake* for the second time. Imagine how I was at parties!

I also discovered more New Directions publications. Djuna Barnes's *Nightwood* and Henry Miller. I was reading Williams but not reading Pound; for some reason it took me a while to get interested in Pound. I had no program. I was still reading French translations, German translations, loved that Robert Motherwell book, *The Dada Painters and Poets*. I just couldn't get enough of that. Loved Surrealism as a surface, you know.

All of these things felt comfortable, familiar, and worth pilfering. As Robert Duncan said, poets are like magpies: they grab at anything bright, and they take it back to their nest, and they'll use it sooner or later. I used everything, everything that shone for me.

I went to hootenannies where everyone was singing "Take This Hammer," "This Land Is Your Land," "Everybody Loves Saturday Night." The Weavers with Pete Seeger would come into town. I started going to a movie theater called the Coronet Louvre, run by Raymond Rohauer, who became film curator at the MOMA. It was a repertory film house on La Cienega Boulevard, which was then and probably is now Art Gallery Central in L.A.

I was going with a girl named Peggy Halper, whose mother was a friend of James T. Farrell's sister. When Peggy and I were caught necking on the lawn of Fairfax High, there was a big scandal, and she wasn't going to be allowed to graduate. Of course, I wasn't going to graduate, anyway. I was still a sophomore. But this was her last year there, so I remember a woman coming in to tell me that we'd have to break up because I was compromising Peggy's academic career. But when I found out she was James T. Farrell's sister—I had read all of Farrell, including the Bernard Clare tetralogy—tons of volumes—that's all I wanted to talk about with her. That brought her down, you know, so it was a mission unaccomplished.

Peggy and I had to start meeting more covertly. When we went to the Coronet, we'd go across the street to a bookstore run by a man named Norman Rose. It was a very arty, avant-garde bookstore that had all the New Directions books and other publications, like the Wittenborn art books. I noticed that very interesting-looking people hung out there, including Wallace and Shirley Berman, who were very striking. I noticed that these wonderful, strange-looking people, who radiated a kind of gorgeous weirdness, would go behind a curtain into the back room and come out looking decidedly happier than when they went in. It still didn't connect with me—I was relatively naive about these things. It just made the aura of these people more interesting. When they came out of the room, they literally had a shine, eyes twinkling, a glazed look. That was my first encounter with the Bermans.

Peggy decided she wanted to be a sculptress. And we needed a place to meet, because it was getting very difficult to meet at her mother's apartment. Peggy found a narrow shed behind a fiberglass body shop; it cost $10 a month or so. It didn't have a bathroom. There was a mattress on the floor, a little table. She started doing things with clay. And after doing strange things with clay for about two or three months, she said, "I don't think I'm meant to be a sculptress, so I'll probably turn the studio over to someone else." The person who found it was Ed Kienholz.

Ed had just come in from the Northwest and looked incredibly Falstaffian, a big barrel-chested guy with plaid shirts and red hair and these great eyebrows. He took this narrow, funky, dusty, rotting place and within a week built a real studio from parts he scavenged in the neighborhood, the alleyways along Santa Monica Boulevard. He had really big hands and could build all these things—tables and benches. Ed's place became one of these places a lot of the artists would come to and hang out, because Ed was hugely convivial and would work regardless of who was there or what they were doing. He was working on very interesting constructions. It would be a while before he did the pieces that he's known for.

That's where I met so many of the artists and the acting subculture of L.A. I met George Herms. I met the Bermans there. Robert Alexander.

Dean Stockwell. Dennis Hopper. All these people were wandering in and turning on or drinking while Ed was painting and hammering away and drinking beer; it looked like he could inhale a six-pack and not even belch, you know. I started going over to the Bermans' place in Laurel Canyon and was introduced to pot as part of the ritual, the ambience of cool. Now I understood why everyone was so cool. It couldn't be otherwise. They were stoned out of their gourds. But—not to romanticize it—to smoke dope in those days was very serious and dangerous. You had to deal with and thus participate in a criminal culture. You had to know so-called criminals, career criminals, as part of this activity. They were also part of the scene. It was egalitarian by necessity.

ML This was in the mid-fifties?

DM Yeah, and this was also the beginning of another kind of emerging culture. Berman said his work was personal and not for sale, and was to be given away. So much of what he did, like the handmade journal *Semina* (literally, handsetting poems and printing photos and gluing them onto each page), was never sold. It was given away. The only time *Semina* was used as an exchangeable commodity was when the Bermans moved to San Francisco. Whenever Wally wanted some books from City Lights, he'd bring copies of *Semina* to Shig Murao, who would give him credit for books. In those days, the idea of what's now called "mail art" meant corresponding with each other. Everyone corresponded with whatever means they had. Berman would send collages and writings, drawings and messages, and David would send poetry and quirky drawings and postcards.

There was a cross-country network of people corresponding. There wasn't any sophisticated zappy print technology—mimeographs were an option. You had what was called a pixograph: that purple Jell-O stuff they print menus with in Chinese restaurants. If you were going to publish, you would have to either find a really cheap printer or you'd have to learn how to set type yourself. That tended to be restrictive. Books had a different meaning then: you're getting a book that somebody made by hand and put together, which takes a lot of time and effort. It has to do with the weight of it—both "weight" and "wait."

Wally was doing collages and constructions with interesting collisions of everyday images from newspapers and magazines—automobile accidents, sports images, girlie magazine babes, war images, and so forth, surrounded by esoteric symbols and by letters of the Hebrew alphabet. Above the triteness and everydayness of this image continuum was Aleph—the first letter of the Hebrew alphabet, which put everything into a strange tension, because on the one hand you'd see the normative images that newspapers and magazines use to increase circulation held at bay by this letter. The presence of Khurbn—the Holocaust—and the Jew in postwar U.S.A. Berman came from a sexual culture in which what was transgressive played into how you counterposed transgressive sexual images from that sexual history.

Each generation has a different relationship to pornography, the erotic—at that time, you couldn't just go on the Net and get pornographic images. Books and photographs and film circulated in subterranean ways, which had its effect on male culture. It was a male activity, a fantasy of power. Men always had been the major consumers of the pornographic necessity, not in terms of action but in terms of passive watching and then reaction. I've always been interested in writing the secret history of America's underculture of pornography, not the dominant culture. Manuscripts were sold that were carbon copies of sex books. There were so-called soft-porn girlie magazines, and there was an S&M subculture with fantastic images and texts.

At this time—and I was partially aware of it because I worked at an open-air newsstand—the gay rights and lesbian movements were getting started. You had the Mattachine Society's magazine—I think it was called *One*—and the Daughters of Bilitis were putting out theirs, and both groups were located in Los Angeles. These groups had to meet covertly because the Postal Service and the Feds were on their case. Gay hustlers were continually being entrapped by the LAPD. The cops'd go into a men's room in plainclothes and proposition them. The guy would say yes, and then they'd arrest him.

It's hard for people now to realize that to be sexually active with the same sex was fraught with all kinds of menace, and to be caught with two joints was. . . . A wonderful poet and filmmaker, Christopher Maclaine, who lived and died in North Beach, went to jail for something like three or four years for possession of just two joints. This was during the late fifties, early sixties, up here in the "city that knows how." But that transgressive charge was also part of the dissident culture's relationship to authority, although we never articulated it as such. When you get to the beatniks, the beatnik by definition was almost thoroughly apolitical. At least the ones they had in San Francisco. You never talked politics. That was uncool. Bob Kaufman was overtly political, invariably confronting the two policemen on the beat and antagonizing them to the point where they'd beat the shit out of him and take him to jail. Then he'd come back and do it again. I never saw anybody intercede or intervene—because that would have been uncool. There was also the same kind of hypocritical sex radicalism, male-privileged, no matter whether you were a beatnik or in Levittown. Same thing, just a different rationale.

CW You mention San Francisco and Bob Kaufman. You went up to San Francisco and took part in the scene before it was called Beat, right?

DM I came to San Francisco with Berman. He came for the weekend, and I came because I had a job working at a place called Paper Editions, a job I got through Norman Rose, who owned the bookstore where I first saw the Bermans. I don't know what year that was, but the first Pocket Poets books had come out. I remember reading Ferlinghetti at the open-air newsstand on Highland Avenue and Hollywood Boulevard. I thought, this is great; little books of poems. I remember that when *Howl* came out, that was a great opening up and out. . . .

CW What about Lawrence Lipton, Stuart Perkoff, people in the Venice scene?

DM I remember meeting Lipton. Jonathan Williams, the publisher of Jargon Society Books, had a van in those days and would fill it with books and drive across the country, going to art galleries and bookstores, selling his books, giving talks, and selling more books. He was selling Charles Olson, Robert Creeley, Stuart's first book (*The Suicide Room*), people like that. He came to the Ferus Gallery and hung out there because Ed was managing it at the time.

You must understand that Los Angeles was the great mañana capital of the world in those days. There were all these places you could go and hang out just to be with your own kind and to maybe get a little taste of something, anything from pot to Thunderbird. Thunderbird had just come out, and I would go with this wonderful artist, John Kelly Reed, over to Billy Al Bengston's studio in Silver Lake where we would sit and drink Thunderbird and watch Billy Al do all his stuff. No matter what was going on, he would be busy working and putting us poet-types to shame. John Altoon was another artist who had an open door for the marginals and was extremely generous. He'd just returned from Mallorca where he and Creeley were pals. John showed me carbon copies of poems Creeley had given him and issues of *The Black Mountain Review*.

But you asked about Lipton and the Venice scene. Some of us from the Ferus drove down to Venice in Williams's van for an audience with Lipton, who was an older guy who looked like any one of my Jewish uncles—balding, thick horn rims, cigar-chomping, and a spoken word evangelist before his time. He'd play reel-to-reel tapes of himself and other Venice poets declaiming their verse. Lipton's stuff was kind of corny to me, and the Venice scene seemed more like the Hollywood B-movie version of Beatsville. Perkoff was, hands down, the major poet there, and his work bears it out.

What I liked about San Francisco in those days was Chinatown—and North Beach, because there was still a European quality to it. Many of the landlords were first-generation Italians. The shops, like the wonderful Figone's hardware store, which is now gone—and what a tragic loss that was—typified what that neighborhood was like. The pastry shop, bakeries, Caffè Trieste. . . . Because it was European, it was friendly to artists. To the Italians, artists had a job and their job was doing art. It wasn't a perversion or an eccentricity or something you'd do for a hobby. At that moment it was very nice. Lots of very interesting people hung out; it was racially and sexually integrated in a way that L.A. wasn't.

What was interesting about L.A. in the war years were white alienated Jewish zoot-suiters like Robert Alexander and Berman hanging out on Central Avenue and very much involved with the musicians' culture—Dexter Gordon, Ben Webster, Parker when he made that infamous West Coast tour, a lot of others. Wardell Gray was a very good friend of Berman's, and, in fact, Wally did a very beautiful memorial collage when Wardell died in a mysterious, probably drug-related desert assassination. That's another aspect I touched on that gets buried under things—race relations and the impact of the Popular Front culture, and radio, during the war years. And jazz itself. Jazz was an integrated platform. Some deadline-driven drivel started happening. You had Ginsberg's *Howl*, the obscenity trials; you had Jack Kerouac and *On the Road*. This all became very quickly embraced by the media. The media then wasn't as massified as it is now, so it took a little longer to eviscerate the moment. It was kind of funny, you know. There would be beatniks and poets and artists doing the Grant Avenue circuit, and there would be Gray Line tour buses coming by with all these tourists looking through tinted windows at the scene. You had many professional beatniks who rose to the occasion—rent-a-beatniks. You had *Life* magazine coming in—"Life Goes to a Beatnik Party"— and *Look* magazine. It was all so weird. Naturally, entrepreneurship began. Suddenly, all these shops opened up, which changed the European rhythm or temporality: it became very frantic and crowded on the weekends. It was sheer hell. You know how it is. The dissidents are always the vanguardists for real estate. It happened to the Haight and other areas later on where rent was cheap and, in a sense, you could be left alone just to be weird.

CW But none of that process of recuperation really got hold of anybody but the East Coast people, because this was an East Coast Establishment–ridden thing. It never really englobed people like Duncan or Lamantia or you or Spicer. They more or less remained off the radar screen.

DM But not within their own axis. Basically, we all still hung out in North Beach because that's where there were bars that we liked going to. It was kind of a bar scene just like on the East Coast during the abstract expressionist days. Jack Spicer, of course, had it in for City Lights and had it in for Beat anything. He thought it was preposterous. Robert Duncan at the time had it in for Allen, but as a tribute to Robert's very fertile and fluid intellect, he resolved that and became a great advocate and friend of Allen's. But it was against Jack's nature to retract. Of course, Jack and Robert were great teachers for the poet, for this poet. I'd go to Saturday or Sunday salons at this lovely man's house, Joe Dunn, who was from Boston, I believe. He and his wife opened up their living room, and Robert and Jack would be the focal points, and young poets like me and Joanne Kyger, sometimes Michael McClure, Richard Brautigan, Ebbe Borregaard, George Stanley, and Harold Dull would go and await the two maestros. We would exchange work and talk about it as well.

It was interesting to be critiqued by two advocates of opposite poetics that for me then seemed very compatible, curiously enough. I thought you could use aspects of both, Spicer's vernacular economy and Robert's wonderful rhetorical mind. I learned from both of them. For me, it was much better than going to school—I'd found that out earlier. I had tried going to school again. I went to L.A. City College for a year and, outside of meeting Idell and Lee Romero there, it didn't stimulate me. Then I spent a semester at UCLA. I had only one teacher who did anything for me: Hans Meyerhoff, a German refugee who wrote a book about time and the novel and taught a course in literature and philosophy, modern literature, Kafka, Mann. He was a wonderful man and a very great teacher. There are two theories about how he died: the first is that he died accidentally, and the second is that he was killed in an automobile accident orchestrated by the FBI because of his involvement with the left. A very promising, talented man. But that was it. Two years of going to California's finest, and I was deeply uninterested.

JB Is it poetic injustice, then, that you have had a long career as a teacher?

DM It is. But at least I'm teaching in a place that theoretically is not your everyday institution.

JB You don't mean Vacaville State Prison?

DM I did indeed teach there. In some ways, it was more rewarding than other teaching jobs I've had over the years. But I've been teaching at New College for almost twenty years because it gives me the opportunity to create classes on subjects that I want to learn more about. I'm selfish that way. I'm interested in teaching subjects I want to learn. I learn a lot from New College graduate and undergrad students.

My first teaching job was with a high school in San Francisco, the Urban School. After teaching at Urban for a year, I went to Vacaville prison as a guest poet, at first. It was a very powerful experience for me. I really felt like I couldn't just go there and do the hit-and-run kind of thing, so I said I wanted to do a writing workshop. I got a grant from the California Arts Council—Jerry Brown's Arts Council. Gary Snyder and Peter Coyote were on the board at that time. I'd met Coyote years earlier when he was in the San Francisco Mime Troupe. Ferlinghetti and I were the intermission poets for a touring production of a short play by Ghelderode.

CW Could you talk about the sixties—beginning with *The Journal for the Protection of All Beings* and the scene around that, the end of the Beats, the so-called hippie movement, and alternative movements like the Diggers?

DM Well, at the beginning when *The Journal for the Protection of All Beings* came out—in '61 or '62—there wasn't a clearly defined entity called "hippies." But they came to be defined as quickly as the Beats in their day. The magazine was conceived by Michael McClure and me. We thought we'd ask Ferlinghetti if he wanted to publish it. If he wanted to, he could be one of the editors as well. Happily, he agreed. The three of us drew up lists of people we wanted to see in the journal. We wrote to a broad range of people asking them to write something inspiring about protecting human life, proposals for new ways of living—a very idealistic thing.

I remember writing to A.S. Neill (of Summerhill), and he said: "Well, I'm too old for this kind of stuff. You young guys, you can do it. It sounds wonderful, but count me out." We got a fascinating group of people, and we added a section that was an anthology of older key texts.

I was working in a small bookstore down the block from City Lights, the Discovery Bookstore, where I actually learned a trade. My mentor and Rabelaisian boss was Frederick Roscoe. It's the only trade I know, even though the nature of second-hand books, first editions, rarities, and books in general has radically changed now in terms of value and market.

I was also making music. My wife Tina and I performed. There was a big folk revival going on. I got out the old guitar, and Tina and I played with a wonderful friend named J.P. Pickens, who played banjo and was an ardent admirer of Lennie Tristano as well as Hank Williams. First, we formed some string bands because we were influenced not only by bluegrass but by that Harry Smith anthology on Folkways that was recently reissued on CD. Larry Fagin was living in a North Beach hotel at that time, and he brought the set up to our Jones Street flat and left it on our doorstep. We were living on Jones Street between Union and Filbert, perhaps the second-steepest hill in San Francisco. We worked in various combinations in San Francisco and Berkeley folk clubs. First we called ourselves, I think, The Snopes Family Singers, and then Better Than Nothing.

JB Were you writing songs?

DM No, we were basically doing covers of C&W, country, bluegrass material in the clubs and folk festivals. Then Tina and I began to perform, just the two of us. I'd play lead guitar, and she would play rhythm guitar, and we'd do a lot of two-part harmony. Tina had a rich beautiful voice, and I played unusual guitar solos that sometimes worked and other times didn't.

As I said, we worked a lot in the folk scene in Berkeley and San Francisco. On one of those occasions, Sam Charters, the great blues scholar, was producing for Vanguard Records, the Solomon brothers' outfit, as well as for Folkways, which were serving the last of that Popular Front kind of idealism, which Charters comes out of as well. Sam's initial work on his country blues, urban blues, and jazz anthologies was the beginning of what now has become a very flourishing and rich blues history, or available history, of this specific form of music. He heard us at the Coffee Gallery and knew my work as a poet. He was a poet as well. So he came over to our place on Jones Street, and we spent all night talking, drinking wine, and playing music together. He got us a record contract. Sam said: "I'm going to produce Country Joe and the Fish's first album. They're folkies, but they amplify. Maybe you should amplify, too. See what you can do." I forgot to mention that this was in the thick of the first wave of the San Francisco rock scene, and record companies were descending on the Bay Area signing up any weird-looking and psychedelic group trying to cash in.

At that time in San Francisco there were a lot of unamplified players who would eventually switch. David Crosby, in from the New York folk scene, was singing like an angel with a twelve-string. Janis Joplin had just come in from Port Arthur, Texas. She was twenty at the time and always worried about performing in these folk clubs and getting busted. She would get up on the small Coffee Gallery stage, and you wouldn't believe it was the same woman who became a symbol of white female angst, sexual power, and rage. Her hands would be clamped down to her sides—rigid. She'd have to get some guy to back her up. I remember being that guy a couple of times. She'd start singing, and this huge voice would come out of this statue.

It was a very rich and lively scene. Jim Gurley, who would become the lead guitarist for Big Brother and the Holding Company, and I were great pals, and we would play extremely spacey music on acoustic guitars at the Coffee Gallery. He already was a very spacey-looking person. His father had been a professional trick-car performer at fairs, and Jim burned most of his facial hairs off helping his father do a stunt like zooming through a ring of fire. Nick Gravenites played the Coffee Gallery, and some of the other Chicago musicians were playing around there, too. Jerry Garcia would come up from Palo Alto with his banjo. There was a lot of exchange and interaction, except that Jim and I and then Pickens, the banjo player, were always doing this free-jazz folk music. Outside stuff. But acoustic. And then Crosby went down south to L.A. and came back up and said: "Jesus, you know, man, you gotta go electric. I'm in this group, man (called something or other—it wasn't the Byrds then) and electricity is the way to go."

We signed the contract with Charters and then had to go electric and get ready to record in two or three months. We were to record in the same studio in Berkeley as Country Joe and the Fish. This was how Sam was cutting costs, you know—recording two groups at once. We got amplifiers, but we needed a bass player and rhythm guitar player, and we needed a drummer to be an official rock band. We were clueless. Well, Chris Brooks, an old friend of Tina's, put us in touch with these two guys—Denny Ellis and David Stenson—who had played with The Grass Roots. These guys were from Burlingame or someplace suburban like that. They'd been on the Ed Sullivan Show with The Grass Roots and then left the group. They were huge stoners—I mean, they were great and lovely, but they would take handfuls of acid and drive to the Avalon and catch two sets of the Dead and still be in Burlingame. They thought we were crazy. Tina and I were seven or eight years older. The drummer was poet Clark Coolidge. His initial discipline was music, and he wanted to be a jazz drummer. His father was a head of the Brown University music department. Arlin Coolidge was one of the witnesses on the Kefauver committee that investigated payola. Clark was living in Manhattan with Aram Saroyan, and both were part of the New York poetry scene. Clark came to San Francisco. Of course, the kids from The Grass Roots could hardly wait for the drummer because drumming is the deal. And when I told them Clark was six-foot-three or six-foot-four, they were like: "All right! He's got big hands! Oh boy!" We're rehearsing in the basement in Chris Brooks's house in some alley in North Beach, and Clark comes through this narrow doorway, this huge-looking figure with glasses carrying the standard jazz drum kit, and that's it. Well, these guys—their faces dropped. Suddenly, Clark realizes that he's a great jazz drummer, but he doesn't know anything about rock 'n' roll.

I wrote the songs quickly. Part of it was parodic of different forms I heard on the radio. The band was augmented by John Payne playing Farfisa, and J.P. Pickens on amplified banjo in the disk's longest track. The album was released—which is another too-long story—but Tina didn't like how she sounded.

We went to the Fillmore to perform with other bands as a promotional party for the Fish and Serpent Power, hosted by Vanguard, playing with Jefferson Airplane and Big Brother, all on one bill. We had never played at a place like that. We went up to the green room or whatever you call it, and there were our friends from the Holding Company, and, of course, everyone was sitting around smoking grass, this new stuff called Thai stick. So we sit there in this narrow room and start smoking Thai stick too, and wow!—and suddenly it's our turn to get on stage. We were drastically stoned—and to go on stage! By this time, Clark had expanded his drum kit somewhat, but there were no monitors, so he couldn't hear us well. At one point, he hit the ride cymbal with his stick so hard it cracked the shaft in half. Tina couldn't hear herself. She couldn't see anybody in the audience because it was unlit, and she hadn't smoked the stuff—she was always much more intelligent about things! Pickens, the banjo player, had his instrument amplified. Imagine having an amplified banjo in a psychedelic group! But he couldn't hear anything and kept turning it up louder. Payne's Farfisa was out of tune. It was a nightmare. Meanwhile, there was this other part of us that was so stoned we were standing back digging it all.

But for Tina it was an authentic nightmare—she liked intimate settings where she could see people's faces and communicate the song. When it was over there was tremendous applause coming out of the darkness. When we went backstage, people rushed up with "That was great, that was terrific!" And Tina said: "That's it, that's not what I heard, and that's not what I experienced—I'm out of here!" She left the band. So we lost the chick singer. And as for David, the bass player, and Denny, the rhythm guitar player—well, they'd done their gig and gone off to form or play in some Grateful Dead sort of band. So it's Clark and I and J.P. We've got a contract for a second record that's due in about six months or so. We put together another band, but this band was radically different than the first band.

Daniel Moore, a poet who was published by City Lights and who's now a Sufi, was playing things like shenai, the Chinese oboe, and conch shells and various bells, and he brought along a friend of his whose name was Christian. He never gave us a last name. Christian was learning how to play the alto saxophone. We had Bob Cuff playing rhythm guitar—Bob had been with a band called the Mystery Trend, which came out of the Art Institute. Jim Moscoso was learning how to play bass, Clark was on drums, and I was lead guitar and more or less the central vocalist.

We started working all over the place, and we did many strange instrumentals with the bells and saxophone and conch shell. Since I had a problem memorizing lyrics, I would start improvising lyrics. Which is what I did with jazz and poetry in the fifties at the Cellar. I figured that at least in the jazz clubs, one should improvise. These things would go on for twenty or thirty minutes. We played benefits.

We played the Straight Theater with Blue Cheer. They were the first real power trio, music of the amphetamine scene. These guys would play at a volume that was unbelievable. Killer. Your eardrums would be bleeding. If you had glasses, they'd shatter. It was so funny watching these guys. We performed with them at least twice. Once at an outdoor benefit and once inside the Straight. The lead singer of the trio—you couldn't hear him at all, he'd be screaming. The tendons of his neck sticking out like cable wire, his eyes popping out. You couldn't hear a word until there was a stop, and you'd hear this guy screaming. Then another high-decibel deluge would come, drowning him out. That was Blue Cheer. So there we were schlepping up with these weird instruments. We got pretty good at what we were doing, or so we thought. We enjoyed it. We were smoking lots of weed.

CW What's interesting to me is that you're improvising your lyrics. Nowadays, there's someone like Kurt Elling, for instance, who's trying to do the same thing. You were absolutely at the epicenter of all these things that later on become recognized as scenes, including the San Francisco scene, the Beat scene, and all that.

DM And maintaining a low profile. A little behind the beat. The story is that finally Sam Charters came to town and we said, "Look, we really want to do a live album." He came and heard us at the club and said, "Can't do this—this is not product, this is not getting anywhere." After all our work and all the excitement about cutting a live album, we suddenly realized Vanguard wasn't going to let us do what we were doing, and we all got demoralized. Clark at that time had fallen in love with Susan and got married shortly after. Jim wanted to get into funk. He joined a band called the Cleveland Wrecking Company. Bob vanished. I don't know what happened to him. I ran into him many years later when I was teaching at New College. He was managing one of those hotels on Valencia Street and was very secretive about why he had been out of the loop for such a long time.

Since Tina had been so disappointed with the first album, I thought that the new album would be built around her, more in an art-song mode. The second album was done with strings, and that was the first one that utilized poetry, too. It was called *Poet Song*. And then a guy who had been a lead guitarist with the Animals, Vic Briggs, was hired by Capitol to produce new and interesting records. He heard *Poet Song* and really liked it and said, "Let me buy your contract from Vanguard, and we'll put you on Capitol." And again I wrote a whole bunch of

songs and was flown down to the Hollywood studios to do the instru-
mental tracks. Some of the sidemen on the session were David Lindley,
Johnny Guerin the drummer, and Lyle Ritz on bass—he's the only guy
I know who recorded a jazz ukulele album. Kenneth Rexroth wrote
the liner notes. He liked what we were doing and was very supportive.
In the interim, I had done the *San Francisco Poets* book and gone down
to Santa Barbara to interview Kenneth for a wonderful weekend. He
was extremely generous.

CW He compares both you and Tina favorably to Leonard Cohen,
saying that you're much less distraught.

DM Also much poorer. As happens in the corporate world, new man-
agement came into Capitol just when the album-cover photograph
was taken, and they shelved all of Vic's projects. That was the end, my
friend. Superstardom was not to be. We were on welfare, and that's
when I started writing my agit-smut.

CW Would you talk about that? I know you're still doing that sort of
writing.

DM I'd love to, but no one wants to read my agit-smut because it's not
smutty enough. It's not doing what it's supposed to do. The work is
too distressing. I heard that you can't get off on it. I gather that means
I'm a lousy pornographer. . . .

CW What do you intend for agit-smut? What's it supposed to do?

DM I'm using it as a critique of pornography and as a deeper moral
and political critique. I declared that in the first group I wrote. I wrote
ten novels in about a year's time because it paid money, which we
needed. This was during the Vietnam period, and poetry for me was
not hacking it as a vehicle for doing hardball politics. A certain kind
of pornography was what I wanted to do as politics. (In fact, one of
the volumes was translated into French and published by Champ Libre
by Gérard Lebovici, who also published the Situationists. I didn't know
that at the time.) Those books had a certain circulation. Some of them
have been reissued recently.

JB Could you explain a little more about why you thought that poetry
wouldn't do the job you wanted it to do?

DM In many ways so much of the antiwar and protest poetry of the
sixties, like the poetry of the thirties, suffered from a kind of flatten-

ing of language, using telegraph slogans, headlines, screaming, and screeching—which was effective for demonstrations and so on, certainly utilitarian, but invariably, like all propaganda, empty on the page. One-dimensionalizing. How do you write poetry that doesn't compromise but can stir and activate? There's a tendency to supply people with conclusions, but you don't give them process. It seemed to me that process is much more important. Forget the conclusion— just allow the person to observe and think. I'm a firm advocate of the performative use of poetry as a political tool.

ML But even the role of poetry to do that was changing. It was also a sign of the times, in a way.

DM It was, indeed, and that's a good point, because so much of effective political poetry was in rock 'n' roll. Rock 'n' roll was loud with dissident voices. Of course, there was this great problem of dissident voices becoming instantly co-opted. You had Columbia Records exhorting, "Support the Revolution."

CW And admen saying, "The Man can't bust our music."

DM But the music existed and had great impact. So much music today, like hip-hop, is co-opted but still has a great effect. You could say the same about reggae, or any form of music from below. Even grunge and punk quickly dissipate as they become embraced. The paradox of that embrace, what is lost and what is gained. You cannot be pure. That's dopey like the romantic self is dopey. There are these great impure forms continually mutating out of the need to communicate. Expressivity, no matter what the shackles around it are, has this will-to-be. Built into that music from below is a great faith in the transformative power of statement, of music. An explicit faith in music and language. Poets have that kind of faith. I'm reading the book about Tupac Shakur by Armond White. Even there, power structures are put into place just as they're challenged. The emancipatory power of the art form. Is that bad? Is that good? Some will say: that's the way it is.

JB The audience for rock 'n' roll is, of course, vast, while the audience for poetry is minuscule.

DM Here, in the States.

JB And the audience for poetry is more and more an audience of poets. Who did you imagine as your public for the agit-smut?

DM Those books were published in North Hollywood by Brandon House. They hired Brian Kirby to be editor (Kirby had done a lot of work at the *L.A. Free Press*). Brian was in charge of the "quality" smut and wrote to authors he knew or interested him to write books. Once I started publishing, Maurice Girodias came over to the house and wanted me to write for Olympia Press, but when he told me what he wanted, the form and so forth, I refused. He would pay more, but he had a template he wanted. On the other hand, Brian wanted you to write what you wanted to write in that genre. Some other people he published in the series were Philip José Farmer, Charles Bukowski . . . Kirby Doyle's book was published by them, and poet Michael Perkins wrote for them. Perkins also wrote a book about that period called *The Secret Record,* a very good history and analysis of the erotic novels that were being published.

CW Didn't Jack Hirschman have something to do with them?

DM Jack was writing introductions because he had that Ph.D. which "legitimated" the books. (We started corresponding around that time, and his work and friendship have been generous and heroic.) I thought "the public" would be people at the bus stations and sex shops and all that. When I say "agit-smut," it was a way for me to vent my rage and politicize; it was a way of talking about power. In a sense, it was cleverly disguised Calvinistic writing. The subtext was very negative, because I saw everything in terms of power abuse and the inability to allow the individuality of anyone to enter into the abusive power that the fantasy is about, and the obsessive nature of it. Ultimately, it defused the function of the text. In other words, they were jerk-off books that people couldn't jerk off to. One printer, after reading one of my books as he was setting it on the linotype machine, quit his job. He said: "That's it! I've been printing this stuff for twenty-five years, and I'm not gonna type Meltzer's stuff!" I felt good about that.

CW Much of your poetry, which I think it would be good to discuss, deals with memory or recall or the triggering effects of music. You've described your work as sort of a "Bop Kabbalah." What can you tell us about the two terms, "Bop" and "Kabbalah"?

DM They blend together. They don't seem different. They're based on sonic and rhythmic practices and utilizing systems, musical or alphabetical, that have, if you so choose, profound dimensionality to them.

In other words, in Kabbalah you look at a text—let's say a sentence in Biblical Hebrew—and you see the first letter. You know it has four functions—phoneme, number, symbol (esoteric and exoteric), and letter—before you even get to where the letter converges into a word. This process of letter-to-letter-to-letter is continuous and mutating. Each letter of the Hebrew alphabet functions as a number. When you add numbers up, they permutate into other numbers that indicate other letters, other words. There you are, at the first word in the Book of Genesis which is "in-beginning." Not "in the beginning" but "in-beginning." The letters and numbers of that word alone—you could sit there and go on and in. It will take you, if you're really working hard, maybe twenty-five years to get through the first chapter, if you read it that way. Permutating, digging deeper, word after word into word into word. And still not get to the end of it. That's attention and submission and at the same time improvisation.

CW Something seems to run throughout your work. One of your earlier poems is about the Golem. To recall, to retell some of these older stories or tales or lore, if you will, not just from Hebraic or Central European tradition, but from all these other places.

DM To try to bring it into the present tense. I was trying to demythologize. I wanted to show that there's always the possibility of continuity even in the midst of advocating ruptures. It's in fact an even more mundane notion of everything having a potential of mystery attached to it. Anything. If you so choose. And I mean "mystery" in both senses: learning and unveiling. It's what Joyce was doing in *Ulysses*—remythologizing Homer in twentieth-century Dublin.

CW As a poet, your anthologies have always been a very important part of your work—*Birth* and *Death* and your two jazz anthologies as well, *Reading Jazz* and *Writing Jazz*. You're making a new work out of all those quotes.

DM True. I was inspired by Walter Benjamin's desire to "write" a book by gathering texts together that told the story he would discover in the collage. He wouldn't have to write anything; instead, he would let fragments cohere into a unified text. *Reading Jazz* used a polyvocal approach in a rigid, polemical way. There was no give or take there, no complexity. It's interesting how that book generated a more positive critical response than any other book I've written. Yet too often the central point about racism was never addressed. I was not being subtle. There was a certain kind of anger, I guess I'm a person who functions in a state of outrage. I sometimes feel like Rumplestiltskin.

Jack Micheline (1994)

Courtesy Vagabond Press

"I have to buy my own fuckin' book!" Jack Micheline announced with a grin as he slapped a copy of Skinny Dynamite *on the counter of Columbus Books in 1983. Nor did he hesitate to add that he'd just won the prize for "most valuable performance" at the Naropa Kerouac conference (1982).*

That grin stayed with me, but it was not until 1993 that I really got to know Jack while working at the Adobe Bookshop in the Mission. My familiarity with Chicago artist Eddie Balchowsky, one of Micheline's friends and mentors, created a bond between us, and Jack visited often.

The following short interview (March 1994) was one of what was going to be a series of interviews with Jack—all to be part of a grand collection of his work I was supposed to edit. Alas, the project fell through, only to be picked up by Matt Gonzalez, whose stupendous edition of Jack's Sixty-Seven Poems for Downtrodden Saints *(1997) remains the incomparable standard by which Micheline's work should be measured.*

A year after leaving Adobe, I ran into Jack for the last time in the bookshop. He scolded me for having just missed Carl Weissner, the German translator of his and Bukowski's work. He ran back to his hotel room and brought back

a photocopy of some of his poems translated into German for an under-
ground magazine with the endearing name of Cocksucker. *That evening he*
died on a BART train bound for Orinda and beyond.
  It was the big kid in Jack that we all loved. That grin of his sticks in my
memory with the last line of his poem "Bright Eyes":

Blow that horn, a long sweet sound. I'll kiss you forever.

—*ST*

Jack Micheline (**JM**)
Scott Thompson (**ST**)
Rebecca Peters (**RP**)

ST You told me before that you didn't set out consciously to be a poet.
You just found yourself as a poet?
JM "Found myself as a poet"?
ST Well, when did you first start writing?
JM I didn't know what a poem was! I still don't know what a poem is.
I wrote words on paper. Some people called it poetry. Some notes.
Well, let them call it what they want.
ST Where was your first poem published?
JM *Yugen* magazine, edited by LeRoi Jones. In 1955, 1956. I don't send
out to magazines anymore. I don't write poetry anymore. I paint! I'm
an artist!
ST What poets and artists have had the biggest influence on you and
your work?
JM There are many. Many influences. Walt Whitman, Carl Sandburg,
early influences, even Ginsberg's "Howl," Vachel Lindsay, García Lorca,
Apollinaire, Baudelaire, Mayakovsky—poetry influences. Writing in-
fluences: Sherwood Anderson influenced me—a very simple, very clear
writer. What other writers? A book called *Beyond Irony* by Maxwell
Bodenheim. Out of print. The biggest influence, that's a good ques-
tion. Langston Hughes was a friend of mine.
ST Was he living in Harlem then?
JM Yes, he was . . . influences . . . Mingus! Charles Mingus, when I won
the award.
ST Where'd you first meet Mingus?

JM At the Half-Note, a café on Hudson Street. I won the award. I said, "You give me twenty dollars' worth of jazz, Mingus records? And tell me I'm a great poet? I'm just beginning." He said, "Don't worry about it," and put his arm around me, "Don't worry about it." A wonderful man.

ST There's that photo of you reading with Mingus. Did you do that more than once?

JM I did it a few times. I mean, I ran away from New York and Mingus, and left him there alone to suffer. But I couldn't handle New York. I was too wild, I drank too much, too crazy. But I was recognized. Jack Kerouac wrote the introduction to my first book of poems. I got published by accident. I saw a sign on a door that said "Pocket Poets" on Cornelia Street, the street where I lived. I knocked on the door. The guy said he was going to publish some poetry, and I asked if I could submit something. I'd been fucking around for a couple of years. And then after he saw my manuscript, he said, "I'll publish you under two conditions: you change the shape of the poems. Instead of up and down, put 'em across the page. And find a famous man to write the introduction." So I had to listen to a lot of poets read their poems, 'cause I liked poetry, and I wrote Conrad Aiken a letter. Conrad Aiken said, "Why don't you ask the Beats? Your work is more 'Beat.'" I said, "But you write ballads, and I love your ballads."

ST Where did you meet Jack Kerouac?

JM He came to meet me. At Philip Lamantia's house when Lamantia and Howard Hart were living together. 242 West Tenth Street. Kerouac had seven Jesuit priests with him the night I met him. This was after *On the Road* was published. Seven Jesuit priests. And he cried when I read him "The Ballad of Benny Roads." I read him some of the earlier poems of mine. He thought I was a great poet. He was drunk. Of the thirteen times I met him, he was totally drunk twelve times. Totally drunk out of his mind. Well, that's the way it was. He was used, abused, and he abused himself. And he played Jesus Christ. He wanted to take the pain out of the world. No one can do that. He was a giant. Capote called him a typist. He broke Billy Rose's record, 120 words a minute on the typewriter. Can you imagine that?

RP There's a lot of the racetrack in your poetry. Could you say something about it?

JM Oh, I go out there occasionally. Not as much as I used to. I'm a plunger. That's why I stay away. A plunger puts $100 on a 30-to-1 shot to win.

RP But there's really something beautiful about the horses.

JM The way they move their asses. Hey, man, the way they move is beautiful. Man sucks compared to the horse. Men and women suck compared to a horse.

Anyway, my early beginnings were involvement with the left. I was a union organizer for a left-wing union in Chicago at the age of seventeen.

ST You were organizing for which union?

JM The warehouse workers. But then I was so good that I worked for Jimmy Hoffa in different places.

ST So you were working with the Teamsters for a while?

JM Let's say, lent out to them. I had a deep hatred of bosses. So they used my anger. They used my narrowness.

RP How did they use it?

JM By my working for them. Hey, I'm a true believer. If I do something, I'll do it right. If I lick a postage stamp, I lick it well. I do things in that kind of way. Passionately. If I lift someone's skirt, I lift it all the way, not halfway. I'm not known for my gentlemanly conduct.

Anyway, I've been influenced by a guy like James T. Farrell, who I read in a closet, 'cause I didn't want my mother to see me read it.

ST *Studs Lonigan,* you mean? Was that a banned book?

JM Well, there were parts, like when he made it at a party, you know, where he had his first experience with sex. We live in a puritan country. At that time, in the late thirties, early forties, I read the book in a closet, jerking off on the book. And when you're brought up in an uncultured family, where people worry about what other people think, especially if you're born in a poor neighborhood, in a low-class neighborhood, people worry, they become self-conscious very young. They worry about what people think and how they dress, and who judges you. So when you're born in this country, you're born with shackles on your brain and your heart. You're born with fear. You've read the story "In the Bronx"? Then you'll know about my childhood.

ST Was that story about the dog a true story?

JM Yeah, my mother gave it away. She was jealous because I gave my attention to the dog and not her. That's a human reaction. That I gave attention to the dog instead of my mother. So she was jealous of me having a fucking dog.

ST That influenced you a lot. It seems to have made a big impression on you.

JM Well, I got angry, man! Shit, when they take a dog away from you. I can't even have a fucking dog to love?! I gotta love my mother instead of the dog?

ST Did you ever have another dog?

JM No way! It's too small in an apartment.

ST You never had another dog in your life?

JM Never had another dog. But I paint cats now. I'm one of the best painters of cats in America. I'm gonna raise that money for a cat book in L.A., you watch. I'll get some actor to give me fifteen grand and put it out. I will. I don't paint 'em from life, I paint 'em from my mind.

ST How did the "melting pot" aspect of New York affect you as a kid?

JM When I was growing up, my mother used to buy meat in the Lower East Side, and you'd see Jews from different countries. Gypsies and Jews. And when I spent time in Chicago, it was a melting pot there. Polacks, Lithuanians, Greeks, Gypsies, Germans, Scandinavians, blacks, Chinese, a melting pot.

ST Was "Isaac," the story about the professor from Poland, based on a real person?

JM Sure.

ST How about "Cosmos"? That was based on a real Greek?

JM Yeah, he had the soup, the famous seaweed soup. These are real people.

ST When I read these stories, when I read "In the Bronx" and some of the stories from *Skinny Dynamite*, I'm reminded of *Street Scene* by Elmer Rice.

JM Hey, you know I met him! I met his son, and his son said he admired my work, my first book of poems. Elmer Rice wrote *The Adding Machine*. A wonderful man. He also was a Villager.

I got my education in Room 312 of the New York Public Library. I read a lot of books. Mostly radical books when I was a young man.

ST What kind of radical books?

JM Well, books about organizing in the South. Not *Das Kapital*. Mostly anarchist. All the speeches of the anarchists. During the Chicago trial. Haymarket. Somehow, I've been an anarchist most of my life.

RP How about the play *Winterset?*

JM That's Sherwood Anderson, right? I read it, and I saw it once. It was beautiful. You got that movie, too?

RP Yeah.

JM Wow, you got it, baby.

RP With the original cast.

JM Who is it, Franchot Tone?

RP Burgess Meredith and Margot.

JM Wow, you've got some real vintage stuff, sweetheart. I gotta keep in contact with you, man. I'll be sniffing around here to look at some of that great vintage stuff. You got any good gangster movies?

ST Do you like boxing movies?

JM Yeah, I saw *The Champion*. Hey, you know what one I wanna see? The one about Jake Lamata.

ST *Raging Bull?*

JM Yeah, I wanna see that one. You know, he beat me up as a young man. In a street fight. Cut my head with a fucking bottle.

ST Jack, there are lots of poor, lonely women in your stories. Are these the women who attract you?

JM I was attracted to . . . well, I can't call it ugliness. I'm a very rare guy, I'm attracted to people who are different. I never ran after chic women or beautiful women, women who are part of the Establishment—I always went after people like me. I was very self-conscious, I never felt that I fit in. I was born 2 lbs., 6 oz.; I was a premature child. So you know I didn't fit in when I came into the world. I always sought after sensitive, self-conscious girls. I used to find the fattest girl on the subway during rush hour and squeeze myself close to her body. And I always had an erotic sense. I still do. I look at the swinging . . . like a sculptor . . . movement of the rear end as it walks down the street. I'm still very erotic in the mind. My poetry is erotic in a sense. It must scare some of these fucking academics to death.

"Angel Baby" was taken from a confession at an AA meeting in Hollywood in 1969. Taken from a pure confession. You gotta get some material from real life. This was a confession from a woman at an AA meeting. I was in AA for a short time. Hubert Selby took me to it—you know, the guy who wrote *Last Exit from Brooklyn*. He was a friend of mine, ever since Brooklyn. I'm from New York, not San Francisco. If I was tough enough, I would've stayed in New York. I didn't want to stay there and become an anti-Semite.

ST Did you meet Selby in Brooklyn?

JM No, I met him in the Village. Before *Last Exit* came out. I helped publish that. I got Seymour Krim to read it.

As for my legal hassles, the guy who published *Open City* in L.A. in '69 . . .

ST John Bryan?

JM . . . was Bukowski's editor, who published this Sunday supplement of the newspaper. It wasn't bad, it's just that they put him in jail. They beat 'em up. He called me up—I was in New York when it happened—and I got all these famous writers to write letters, and they finally dropped the case, but he lost the newspaper. And finally A.D. Winans published the book of short stories. The only letter that was missing was Bukowski's letter.

ST Why did Ginsberg publish the letter that's in the front of *Skinny Dynamite?*

JM Because he wrote the best letter to Stanley Fleishman, the lawyer. He wasn't trying to promote me. You know, I didn't know that this was in *Skinny Dynamite*. Well, we didn't ask permission to use it. I don't ask anybody's permission. Let 'em say whatever they want. They have to ask permission to get published. I never ask permission. Now you know why I don't get published. Please, Mr. Ferlinghetti, publish my work, I'm a great poet. I don't have to. People know. The ordinary people know. Why do I have to ask permission? Why should I go to rich men and ask them when they don't know the American people? They're just looking at work. Maybe that's the way it should be done.

ST You're a fairly outspoken critic of the art establishment. . . .

JM Hey, man, the shit is in the museums. Most of the shit, the "art" crap is in the museums. Why is it there? Who knows why? Because the people who run the museums buy shit. They don't know what's good or bad. Or they're told what to buy. The guy with the biggest PR, you know what I mean? Outspoken critic of the literary establishment? I don't like what they do. I don't like what they publish, I don't like what they sell. Some work is good. Not all of it's bad. I don't know how the work is chosen. Either a man has a lot of money, politics, who knows. He owns an artist's work. . . . I don't know how it works, how a person's work gets shown. I went to the museum, I brought the guy my slides, and he didn't know how to put me in any category. Therefore, he wouldn't show the work. I don't know what to say. You say, "Your work has never been picked up by the larger presses" 'cause I haven't pushed it. I haven't written letters every week to Laughlin, "I'm great! Publish me!" I'm a shy guy.

ST In other words, you haven't been ambitious. . . .

JM All right, so I'm a lazy fuck. Hey, man, I never thought creativity had anything to do with publishers or art galleries! It's a private fucking thing. Between me and my muse. Between me and my spirit. What's it got to do with Ferlinghetti? Or any of these other cocksuckers? They don't love life. They don't love people. What do they have to do with life? They want to control what the fuck people see. They want to control life. That's what they're there for. They're not there to enrich mankind. To liberate man. That's what art should be used for. To liberate the sick and the wounded. To open up their fucking darkness inside their bodies. Art should be used as revolution. Like bullets. I'm dangerous, that's why they don't publish me! To use art to liberate man. To get man out of the dark ages. That's what fucking art's about. That's what I'm about, they know that.

ST Do you really think Lawrence Ferlinghetti is trying to control people?

JM What right does a man like that have, to have power, to control what people hear or not hear?

ST Jack, Eddie Balchowsky is an important character in your work. Where did you meet him?

JM I was sitting in an all-night café on North Avenue in Chicago about eleven-thirty at night when I first saw him. With his beard. He walks into the diner, and he's sitting there with his beard and his coffee, and he kept on insisting that he'd like to buy me a cup of coffee. We were talking, and it turns out that he was a veteran of the Lincoln Brigade of the Spanish Civil War. And he was an artist by profession. And a piano player with his one arm, and a man with a big heart. He had a sense of wonder about him. So it was a very great experience to meet such an energetic guy with one arm. A ball of fire, call him what you want. So you know, he loved the subway stations of Chicago, above ground, the El, where he did a lot of sketching. Lampposts and tracks of the El. Anyway, at this time he'd just gotten out of the Cook County jail. He was living above a Polish gangster bar. You know, on the near North Side they have an art show every spring? Well, he was getting ready to show his work. But not in the show, because they refused to let him show inside, because they didn't want no ex-cons showing their art. He got busted. He got busted with Lila Leeds and Robert Mitchum for marijuana. And it was in the headlines. All night I watched him do these paintings—with one arm!—and that morning he showed. He had a big sign, "My name is Ed Balchowsky. They refuse to let me show my work in the show, but I will show my work here, outside the show. Please enjoy my work and buy it." And he sold it all off.

Another story. He had a friend who lived across the way, Ken Crabbs. And Kenny was living with his brother and his mother and his brother Harry. They let me sleep in an apartment below them. About seven in the morning, I open my eyes, and there was a knife at my throat and a gun at my head. Two people I've never seen before in my life. I yelled out, "I'm not the guy!" The guy whose place it was wasn't there. Imagine that! Somehow, we got Eddie to come across the street to cool these guys off. "Hey, this ain't the guy you're looking for." The guy was out, had skipped town. So in a way, he saved my life.

Then Ken Crabbs moved to Denver. I mentioned Ken's name at the Kerouac conference [1982]. There were a lot of newspaper people— 'cause I won the award at the Kerouac conference—and they came and photographed Ken. A dear friend. Beautiful man. His niece, who goes to the University of Wisconsin—I send her art supplies and books. She has his same heart and soul. He was a great man, a great jazz collector, was part Indian, part German, and consequently a real American. We formed a threesome: me, Eddie Balchowsky, and Ken Crabbs. Of course, there was always Schiller, the photographer, who was around.

The famous photographer from Chicago, Schiller.

I say, I still say, till the day I die—the arts are controlled by a few people—they don't like the content of my work. They don't want to know there are poor people living on the earth.

ST What about an agent?

JM I had an agent. I had Gerry Nicosia's agent, and he couldn't get nothing published for me. I had 'em for two years. Now I can't even remember his fucking name. He'd send me the rejection slips. "We only publish mediocre stuff, we have to pay our rent." Anyway, Eddie was a great influence. I met him in Chicago, I met him in Denver, and I met him out here. He spent time in the Grand Piano on Haight Street, and he lived in San Francisco off and on—encouraging people all his life.

ST When did Eddie die?

JM In 1993. He jumped in front of a train. He would do that—die dramatically. He'd do something shocking. That's my story on Eddie Balchowsky. A dear friend, I own a lot of his paintings, a lot of his drawings. I actually sent Rosalie Sorrells one of his paintings. He had many friends. I wasn't as close a friend. But we loved each other. En-couraged each other in our own way. I knew him. Better than Kerouac. I even have a tape that I'll get around to giving to you—with Studs Terkel and all these people talking about him. You know what I say when someone dies? Don't do a book of testimonies, like they did for Bob Kaufman. Publish his work. Not the testimonies. They don't mean shit. Everybody gets a shot to say they knew this person? Publish his work! You understand what I mean.

As I've said about the art establishment, there are a lot of great art-ists that are better than the shit they show in museums. Who goes looking for great art? Who are the art critics? Where do they come from? What college did they get their degree from? What gives them the right to criticize other people? I'm not a critic of the establish-ment, I'm anti-establishment. There's a difference. I'm anti-Ginsberg. Ginsberg *is* the establishment.

ST What about intoxication? Did you ever use inebriates to write?

JM I drank a lot in the Village, but I never could handle my liquor. I was a lousy drunk. I puked up most of the shit. Couldn't hold my liquor. I mixed scotch and ginger ale, that's why I've got diabetes now. Did you ever go to a Chinese restaurant and eat sweet-and-sour pork? That's what scotch and ginger ale tasted like. I hear it's the national drink of Australia, so how far off was I?

ST What about smoking weed?

JM Well, I was born high. I was never into marijuana that much. My mother brought me up to be very conservative. I might've been wild, but. . . .

ST Did you ever trip during the heyday of the Haight?

JM Hey, man, I took two tabs of acid and kissed a cop in New York once! I'm out of it, anyway. That didn't really affect me. I was wild, anyway.

ST I see you have Adorno's *Prisms.* Culture or barbarism? What do you think of Adorno's claim that there can't be poetry after Auschwitz?

JM Oh, that's bullshit. It's just his point of view. What right does he have to say who should write poetry about what? Where does he get his fucking nerve? All poetry is dead?! It's like that famous guy who came from Italy, from Milan, he has a museum in Milan, a great art critic. He said, "I won't eat no fucking bird. Thanksgiving is an American holiday to commemorate the slaughter of the Indians." It's the same kind of mentality.

I was living in a $12.50-a-month apartment on Cornelius Street. Writing poetry and getting laid. Going to coffee houses at night. Going to studios with my friends. Getting drunk. Singing songs, getting laid. Writing poems and living in Greenwich Village as a bohemian. I lived at 18 Cornielius Street from 1955 to 1963. I left the country for a year and a half. Got married.

Kerouac made an ideal out of spontaneous composition. He was an innovator. So was Selby. Grove Press published Kerouac's writings on spontaneity. He experimented with the mind, the thought processes, breath counts. It was Ginsberg who brought up the famous essay by Whitman on the breath counts. Ginsberg picked up on Lorca's idea of the *duende,* the spirit, and I think it was Whitman or Ginsberg who talked about the breath counts. I have a short breath. My words are short. You notice how short my words are? It has to do with my breath.

ST When and where did you meet Charles Bukowski?

JM I wrote to him before I met him. It was in 1966. I still have a few letters from him. You've read one of them, right? He was living in a shack in Los Angeles. This was just when John Martin was beginning to pick him up. He was a wild guy. A horse player.

ST Did you ever go with him to the racetrack?

JM Yeah. A couple of times. We used to call him "Buk," "Hank," "Bullshit Hank," the guy who carried shit in paper bags. He was total memory. There were three people in the history of the world, James Joyce, Jack Kerouac, and Charles Bukowski—if you'd tell him a story, it'd appear a few days later in *Open City*. You tell 'em a story, and he takes it, uses it word for word.

Some of my best stories are my own experiences. I lived my poems. More than some of these intellectual bastards. They intellectualize their poems. I live it. That's why my work will live. Because I lived my poems. Does that make sense? Of course, it's how you write it, but it's what you put into it. There's some magic in my work. They cannot kill my work. They can't kill my poems. There's one thing they can't kill and that's a live poem. They can kill a poet, but they can't kill his poetry. Do you understand that? There's something that the shrinks and the doctors, the establishment can never figure out: why something lives after a person dies. The ingredient that creates that. And they can't figure it out because it's a rare gift, a muse, and it's connected to a higher spirit, don't you think? If it lives after a man dies?

Kenneth Rexroth (1969)

© Margo Moore; courtesy New Directions Pub. Corp.

Summer 1969: A young poet journeys to an old poet. I took a single-engine propeller-driven "hopper" flight from San Francisco to Santa Barbara—rows of single seats divided by a narrow aisle, claustrophobic enough to know if the pilot's deodorant was working. Carol Tinker, Rexroth's wife, picked me up, and we drove to their home in the hills of Isla Vista. Besides my backpack, I was lugging a Sony portable reel-to-reel recorder that weighed anywhere from twenty to fifty pounds, depending on my stamina. Their house was spare but elegant (unlike Rexroth's old apartment on Scott Street in San Francisco, which was overwhelmed with books and art). The kitchen was like those drooling glimpses you get in gourmet magazines and PBS haute cuisine shows. Wine was opened, and Kenneth took me into the tree-shaded backyard to a table, where I set up the machine. He was uncomfortable about his distended belly and told me it was the result of some kind of hernia. I turned the tape recorder on and put the clunky microphone between us. After preliminary banter, Kenneth began talking, and I was instantly enthralled and deeply honored to be in his presence. You must understand that Rexroth was the bane of many poet-peers of my generation in the Bay Area in the fifties. His Sunday KPFA hour was often listened to for snotty laughs and eye-rolling groans (as well as envy and desire). We younger poets had different histories, mentors, loyalties, prospects. There was something unintentionally comic about his voice: a droning patrician W.C. Fields bluster and mashed-potato hauteur spouting off on dazzling variety of subjects addressed with irreversible finality. Robert Duncan said that the "voice" Rexroth constructed through time bore little resemblance to the voice he brought to California from the Midwest. Carol created a chez Rexroth dinner for us, with considered wines to match the cuisine, which opened up off-the-record convivial chatter and ferment.

The next day we sat in another room of the house to continue our conversation. Rexroth's stint at UC Santa Barbara was his first "official" teaching gig. He relished it, giving immense support and encouragement to his students; he made it clear that he was still un-squarably hip and tuned into poetics, politics, and the subversive potential of sixties pop music. I was surprised that the catholic Rexroth was also very Catholic (in the Jesuitical mode) while, at the same time, deeply enmeshed in Japanese and Chinese thought and art. I sensed that he felt, as an elder, not venerated but displaced by the younger poets he considered his protégés. An exhilarating encounter further enhanced by Kenneth and Carol's immensely generous hospitality. Rexroth died in 1982. He is greatly missed.—DM

Kenneth Rexroth (**KR**)
David Meltzer (**DM**)

1

KR I came to California in 1927 to live. The day I got into town, San Francisco's leading poet, California's leading poet, killed himself. George Sterling. He pretty well represented the California scene in those days, which lived on its past. The San Francisco literary world was dominated by people to whom the native-son-and-daughter thing was all important, although most of them were not native sons and daughters. I don't think Gertrude Atherton, George Sterling, any of these people, were born in California.

It's hard to believe now, with all the tremendous activity that has been in San Francisco, that San Francisco, when we came there to live, was very much of a backwater town and there just wasn't anything happening. There was this myth of Carmel. which is just like it is now . . . like the myth of Big Sur . . . and a lot of those people are still alive down there . . . they stagger, run around juiced, and bellow out folk songs.

That's really the reason we stayed here, as it was a long way from the literary marketplace. We didn't know anybody who wasted his time talking about what Horace Gregory thought of Oscar Williams. We met people who would say to you, "Who do you think is California's leading writer?" And you would say, "Gertrude Stein." They would say, "Who is that?" And then they would say, "Oh, yes!" They knew her, you see, her brother was in society on the Peninsula, but they didn't know she wrote. It was a very strange scene. It's like Santa Barbara now. It was a little time pocket.

DM What was Robinson Jeffers' effect on the California scene at that time?

KR Jeffers wasn't very well known in California then. He was just beginning to acquire a reputation among a very limited number of people. The people who dominated the literary scene in California looked down on him. They viewed him as being terribly modernistic.

We just didn't have any competition. It was like Picasso dropping back into the world of Trollope. The leading painter in town, Maynard Dixon, came over to see me and looked at my paintings on the wall and said, "Hmmmm, I see you have been experimentin' with abstract form, like Matissy and Picassio!" So it was a great place, you know, because there wasn't any sweat. That's why we came to San Francisco.

DM Was it in the thirties that the California poets and artists became more involved with the world and with each other's works?

KR I don't think there were very many people in the thirties. There were people in San Francisco who were writing and not publishing anything when I came. Most of those people became involved in red San Francisco. The interesting thing is that most of them became practical labor organizers, rather than bohemians sitting around in Union Square arguing about proletarian literature.

There was a real pattern there, due to the fact that there were all sorts of things wrong with red literature in the thirties in New York. But when the Communist artist and writer's groups were formed, the John Reed Club . . . the one in San Francisco, they put up some pretty stiff qualifications. The members were actually artists and writers. They stayed around.

What happened in New York was that the clubs became dominated by bohemians who didn't do anything except argue about Marx, whom they had never read, and they would avoid the artists and writers. It's very hard to convey to the present generation what that was like. People talked about Communism in those days the way people talk about acid or smack. I mean, they bored you to death, and they didn't know anything about it.

I was sort of the outdoor organizer for the John Reed Club. I was organizer of everything in the West, and, of course, the New York apparatus thought the West started at Hoboken, and that is one reason the Chicago organization was better—the reason it had people like Dick Wright and Farrell and people like that. Outside of New York, we tried to confine the thing to bona fide artists and writers. In San Francisco, our people were actually involved in the real labor movement. You have to understand that there was an enormous amount of bullshit. People were running around talking about "the masses" and there wasn't really any contact with the masses. But hell, I mean, I wrote the *Waterfront Worker* . . . all of the goddamn thing, week after week after week. A mimeographed thing we used to hand out on the waterfront long before the strike. All of us were actually involved. We were involved in the Agricultural Workers Industrial Union. I had somebody ask me one time at an anarchist meeting in Italy, "Is *The Grapes of Wrath* true?" One-eighth is true. In the novel, one guy gets killed. In a Bakersfield cotton strike, to which I took Steinbeck, eight guys get killed.

You see, all of us were very actively involved, and this makes all the difference in the world. Another thing, very few of these people were orthodox Commies, because the basic tradition on the West Coast was IWW. The attitude was really an anarchistic attitude, and for many years I treasured—to flaunt in the face of the FBI, if they ever bothered me—an application to the Communist Party that had written across it, "Comrade Rexroth is a very valuable comrade, but he is entirely too much of an anarchist to be good party material." It was signed by Earl Browder, the general secretary of the party. This movement stretched all the way from Seattle, where the IWW dominated the intellectual and bohemian world in the years around the First World War and well into the twenties. People like Gary Snyder, over a generation later than myself, and I grew up in very similar worlds.

The first time I met Gary Snyder, he hitchhiked down and stayed at the house. He was on his way from Reed College, and I said, "Gee, you're tan, what have you been doing?" And he said, "I have been working on a lookout outside of Marble Mount on the Sagit River in the Mount Baker forest." And I said, "I used to work up there. I was a patrolman before they had lookouts. . . . The guy I worked for just got the job. He was a wonderful district ranger, his name was Tommy Thompson." And Gary gave me a kind of funny look and he said, "Well, that's who I was working for this year. It is his last year and he is retiring."

Of course, there is another thing: people on the West Coast work. Ginsberg when he came out here, as he said in interviews, was working as a market researcher, which is just a shit job. It's like being a floorwalker in a dime store. I said, "Why don't you work? How much are you making? Forty-five dollars? You can't live on forty-five dollars in San Francisco. That's not money. Why don't you go to work, get a job?" Ginsberg said, "What do you mean?" And I said, "Ship out. Do you realize that when they go into the Bering Sea, you are in hot water? And you know what that means? That means double pay. You come back with more bread than you know what to do with!" I don't know how many trips Allen made in the next couple of years. In the East people don't think like that. We were talking earlier about Hart Crane. He spent all his time fretting about his economic problems, but if he had been a Westerner, he would have gone out and gotten a job in the woods or at sea or something like that, and he would have made a lot of bread. A hell of a lot more bread than he ever did writing advertising copy for candy.

There's another thing that I would like to point out, and that is that there has been right along in San Francisco a pretty consistent, relentless organizational activity. At the time of the Moscow trials and the general bankruptcy of orthodox Bolshevism, relatively few people in San Francisco became Trotskyites. The people who did were pumped in from New York and were connected with the Sailors Union of the Pacific. Most people just backed away and went back to what they were before. All during those years we always had poetry readings and discussions, and then during the war we set up a thing called the Randolph Bourne Council in which we gathered up the radical intellectuals in town that were not Stalinist. We tried to gather the Trotskyites, which was hopeless. Immediately after the war we simply organized an open and aboveboard Anarchist Circle. We used to have bigger meetings than any other radical group. All of these people, my generation and slightly younger, were involved in it, they all came . . . Bob Stock and a couple of other people who were in the group had poetry readings too on another day in the week . . . all closely tied with the Libertarian Circle. The whole purpose of the Libertarian Circle was to reevaluate and refound the movement. You have no idea of the degree to which orthodox Bolshevism had completely conditioned the minds of the generality of intellectuals in those days. We used to shock people because we used to say, "We don't proselytize, we don't have any agenda, we don't have any chairman." There were 200 people, and there was no chairman, and it was all very orderly. It was necessary to work out these techniques of group relationships, techniques of discussion which you might call a new kind of dialectic, and then information . . . week after week after week people led discussions, people would volunteer to speak about libertarian literature, education, agriculture, everything under the sun. It was a long process of education for the whole generation of people. These people are now between forty and fifty. We had all kinds of college students . . . all of the San Francisco poets of that period, lots of writers . . . people who became psychiatrists, people who became college professors, people who became engineers, they are all still around.

Out of the group came KPFA. Lou Hill was a member of our group as well as most of the people who were the original KPFA staff. The station was devoted to the reeducation of its audience on what you might call libertarian principles. There was a constant dose of poetry, for instance.

Later they all began fighting with one another and became impoverished. They cannibalized an immense library of tapes. The first tapes Dylan Thomas ever made . . . I was in England immediately after the war and taped readings and interviews and sent them back to San Francisco. These things were priceless. David Gascoyne, Dylan, Henry Treece, Alex Comfort, Herbert Read, and George Woodcock . . . discussions with the whole English anarchist circle.

We kept pumping in stuff from all over, in German, in English, in French. . . . I sat up night after night after night writing letters abroad, and this material just flooded in, and it didn't go to New York. I was corresponding with Simone Weil, Camus, before the *Partisan Review* ever heard of them! Later they were turned up for New York by Dwight and Nancy MacDonald. The person in New York who dug this thing at all was Dwight MacDonald, with his magazine *Politics* . . . to which none of us would contribute. This annoyed Dwight very much!

We set up a thing in San Francisco in the thirties called the Artists' and Writers' Union, which generated a strong tradition. People who are that old remember it with great fondness. The members were all highly qualified artists and writers. Then the WPA came along. We had certain contacts in Washington, and we knew this was going to happen, so we were ready to capitalize on it. Before they ever set up the WPA, when Roosevelt first came in, they started shoveling out money to relieve the crisis. They set up a thing called the Public Works of Art Projects, and I got a telephone call in the middle of the night from Washington, and I was told that they were going to set it up. So when the director of the De Young Museum and a rich patron and our big rich commercial artist met for their preliminary meeting, there were about 250 people in the court of the De Young Museum, notified overnight! And they were all bona fide artists. We just took over.

We decorated Coit Tower. It looks like the Diego Rivera funny papers, but it was a very great achievement. Nobody else in the country did a goddamn thing except take government checks. An awful lot of stuff was definitely accomplished. No other WPA program later put out anything like those magazines we put out . . . and we were responsible for a book, *American Stuff*. We got creative projects set up. There were all kinds of people who we told, "Here is your check, go home and write." Eventually, we got people on creative writing projects all around the country. People wrote books of poems, novels, and some got themselves Ph.D.s, but of course all of this had to be done quietly because of congressional criticism. But a tremendous amount was accomplished. Between 1950 and 1955, the necessity for organization began to die out because other people could become activist. It was no longer necessary to educate somebody to make an anarchist poet out of him. He had a milieu in which he could naturally become such a thing. But for years, it was a slow process of breaking down rigid ideologies and then creating a different thing.

2

KR The Vietnam War was a disaster because until the Vietnam War got hot, the dominant tendency in the movement in America was anarchist-pacifist . . . and religious in various ways. What happened with Vietnam, and the Russian-Chinese split, was that the movement again fell into the hands of people who were representing other people's foreign offices. American radicals are placed in the ridiculous position of supporting the foreign policies of Ho Chi Minh or Chairman Mao or Fidel Castro or Tito or Israel. That may be better than Stalin, but it is still an army, it is still a foreign office, it is still a state, and I think that were we let alone and the Vietnam War ended, this would die out. You see, the Vietnam War gives . . . in the strict sense of the word . . . a political complexion to the movement which it had almost got rid of.

Today, so much in the movement is dominated by state-ism. What is Israel? Israel is another bourgeois state. Not only that, but it is a theocracy. You walk up and down the streets of Tel Aviv publicly eating a pork chop sandwich and find out what happens to you. You know! Here's a Negro in San Francisco, and he is running around in African clothes, and he's talking about the glories of the Congo or Nigeria or Ghana or whatever side he has taken. Why? What for? It is just another state. It is the same old shit come back, as Marx said. This doesn't mean that I am supporting the Vietnam War or that I am proimperialist, pro-Arab . . . but with all this national tension there has been a recrudescence of state-ism in the American movement, but it is only the leadership. Students don't have this attitude. For students it's all a lot of crap, except for a few blacks who just discovered it—who just read Fanon.

The students participate in issues that involve them. They participate in an anti-Vietnam demonstration because they are going to be asked to murder and they are going to be murdered. They participate in actions against the deadly system of the university which is designed to turn them into murderers. The objection to the Vietnam War on the part of students is an organic objection. I have never been able to understand why anybody went to war. I look at a guy marching down the street in uniform, and I can't understand it. I can't understand anybody doing that. Somebody comes around to me and says, "I could never face my mother, my family, the social pressures. . . ."

I once spent the day with a leading Comintern representative in Hollywood, a wealthy movie actor, and a couple of sophisticated top Communists in the movie star's yacht arguing with Eisenstein, trying to persuade him to stay in America. Any movie company would have given him anything, anything! I'll never forget it. We all got sunburned as hell, and the argument was just hopeless.

He said, "No." The Russians told him that if he defected, they would expose him as a homosexual. And somebody on the yacht said, "Well, so what?" And Eisenstein said, "It would kill my mother." So he went back to Russia, and Stalin destroyed him . . . artistically. I never really understand people who yield to pressures like that.

I don't understand anybody who goes into the army. Who in the hell wants to go into the army and shoot anybody? I just can't conceive of it, for any reason. I mean, any prison is better than the army . . . any prison. So when a movement objects to a war, the rank and file, whatever their leaders represent, the rank and file have a perfectly natural organic objection.

The university is set up today, and is set up for no other purpose, to provide bureaucrats for the military-industrial complex and to hold bodies in cold storage—off the labor market. It is set up for nothing else.

The students object to this because it is soul-destroying. The human relationships in a university today are soul-destroying. The fabric is soul-destroying. The way the classroom is set up with that one-armed crippled furniture, like an old-time cafeteria . . . the way you can't turn around to look at somebody; the way you have to face the boss on a podium. When I go into one of my seminars, I break this up completely. We sit on the floor. We get a room where we can move the furniture out of the way. I sit in the back amongst the people. Or we sit in a circle. The university is not unique: there is built into all society today actual physical soul-destroying structures. Did you ever take a chick into a motel in Southern California? It has a fucking machine in it. The bed fucks. You put a quarter in it and the bed fucks. You don't have to do any work. Right here in Santa Barbara, within walking distance, is a motel, and every bed has a fucking machine in it. This is not a joke, this is true. They say it is a Relaxicisor, a Jacuzzi, or something . . . but that's what it's for.

The whole civilization is like this, so that the revolt of the movement, young and old, is against the destruction of the human race. All these people come around, yellow, black, and Latin American, and say, "Oh, man, all you have to do is just to follow our boss and do what the state tells you to do. Go to Israel and live in a kibbutz, and all your problems will be solved." That's a lot of crap. They're not solved at all, as is self-evident from Czechoslovakia or the relation between Russia and China. . . .

I have complete sympathy with the movement, but I no longer belong to anything. (I guess I belong to Resist. I think I signed something and sent them some money, because its purpose is the oldies to help the youngies. And the leadership . . . people like Chomsky, Reisman, and Fromm . . . I look on these people as considerably to the right of myself . . . of course, Chomsky is changing.) I think it's a disaster that this new wave of revolutionary nationalism has become reflected in the American movement, with which it has nothing to do.

DM In a sense, though, this is a reflection of the powers that they are in resistance to. This happens often, don't you think so?

KR Sure. What do you think would happen to you if you marched down the streets of Peking with a banner saying: "Free Grass, Free Huey, Free Love"? . . . Oh shit! [*laughter*] All these regimes are extremely puritanical, and their art is . . . did you ever read *Chinese Literature,* the magazine they put out? It's just appalling.

DM As bad as reading *Soviet Literature?*

KR That's Gertrude Stein and James Joyce compared with the stuff that comes from China.

DM What about the radical art of today? Do you see anything beyond propaganda in the poetry and in the fiction?

KR Fiction, you know, is like painting. It's become so commercialized that it destroys the people who create it. Mitch Goodman, in a number of *Liberation,* talks about Mailer. He says what everybody knows about Mailer. He criticizes Mailer for the long attack on Paul Goodman, which I thought was simply scandalous. The reason that a guy like Mailer comes into existence is that there was this young radical kid running around Okinawa or Guadalcanal or some place jumping from foxhole to foxhole, and jumping beyond him is a publisher's scout or an agent with a checkbook and a contract. Look, the first American antiwar novel was John Dos Passos's *Three Soldiers.* It came out in the middle twenties. These other guys were brought up right away to give them something really antiwar . . . but they got all the gold when they were twenty years old and haven't been a damn bit of good since. The same is true of painting. Painting has become incredibly commercialized. If a Buick agency was run with the ruthless commercialism of a modern art gallery, it would go out of business. It would be just too commercial. You have to be just a little human to sell Buicks.

And poetry . . . book poetry in bulk has come to be dominated by the professor-poet. Publishing a book of poetry is part of the publish-or-perish setup. You go to any university today and you are up to your ass in poets.

I get this stuff that comes to me for review. People say, "Why don't you review it?" I can't read through any of it because it is toilet-paper poetry. Every sheet looks just like every other sheet. It's fantastic.

In the McCarthy period when the only expression of any kind of radicalism was confined to science fiction, I used to review science fiction for KPFA. I sat around one night making a tape for them. I had a bunch of science-fiction books stacked up before me . . . you read them, you know, zip! Just like that! I'd put the unread ones in one pile and read them and put them in another pile, and I went to take a piss

and returned and picked up a new book, read it, and Christ! I get fifty
pages into it and realized, gee, have I started on the wrong pile? I have
already read that!

Well, the poetry is the same way. You know where the poetry is. The
poetry is in song. The poetry is in direct relationship. The poetry is
the kind of thing existing in San Francisco, that continuous human
contact. At one time just the Libertarian Circle and Bob Stock's base-
ment and now . . . God knows how many . . . there must be a hundred
poetry readings a night in the damn city, in crash pads, in coffee shops,
everyplace under the sun.

A person like Leonard Cohen, for instance, was getting nowhere
with the literary establishment. You had to go to Canada to even hear
of Leonard Cohen. But the minute Leonard started singing, he went
like wildfire all over the U.S.A. He can't sing. So much the better. (This
is something you run into all the time. People are always saying, for
instance, Dylan is terrible, he can't sing. . . .) Leonard Cohen can't
sing, but that's part of the thing, and they don't understand this. The
thing that makes Leonard Cohen what he is, is that he doesn't give a
fuck whether he sings or not. I mean, he is communicating . . . he's in
direct communication with people, which is one of the reasons, of
course, that he opts out of show business.

You know what happened last year . . . he had a tour set up, and he
started out on it and soon he said, "To hell with it, I'm going back to
the Greek isles." He had lost human contact. This is where poetry is.
The poetry here is in the same place that it is in France. The greatest
postwar French poet is Georges Brassens . . . the poet-singer. It sure as
hell isn't Yves Bonnefoy, who is a kind of bad combination of Yvor
Winters and H.D. Jesus Christ, what good was 2,000 years of civiliza-
tion to produce that!

Now there are hundreds of people, and they are all over the map.
There are a few great ones. People like Anne Sylvestre . . . incidentally,
all the young singers and poets are anarchist. Listen to their records,
they make all sorts of sly digs at Leo Ferré, Louis Aragon, and the old
guard. From the days of Apollinaire to the present, the leading French
poets worth their salt all wrote for direct presentation; the modern
tradition goes back to the nineteenth century, to Charles Cros and

Aristide Bruant, and continues to the Middle Ages. That is why I am so interested in the stuff that you do, because you are the only one of the San Francisco group who has really made a very professional thing out of this, nobody else has. I would if I had the time, but I am getting old and have just so much time to do what I have to do.

Back in the days of poetry and jazz, Ferlinghetti, Patchen, and myself all were well aware of this. The essence of the thing was in the direct speech of one person to another. Since none of us were singers, we read. Also there were other reasons for that. It gave a jazz musician much greater freedom. And poets were a hell of a lot easier to get along with! Just talk to a jazz musician and ask him what he thinks of a singer.

DM Would it be possible to talk about the poetry and jazz? For instance, when did you actually begin experimenting with it?

KR When I was a young kid in my teens. I ran a place in Chicago, with a couple of girls, called the Green Mask. We used to have poetry readings there all the time. The girls were a couple of carny and show-business women, and the Green Mask was a hangout for show-business people. One of those old-time places where everybody goes after the show, where people get up and sing. Maxwell Bodenheim (who couldn't write for sour owlshit) and Langston Hughes and myself used to do poetry and jazz with a Chicago group, the Austin High Gang.

Dave Tough was the youngest member of the group and was himself a poet. Dave Tough was just about the first hipster. He was a head, and most of the time lived with gay women, and he wrote poetry—real far-out poetry. There was another drummer, whose name I forget, who lives in Florida now, who has Dave's poetry. I have tried to get at it. I turned Barney Rosset on to it, but I don't know what happened. It wasn't amateur illiterate stuff. Dave Tough was, of course, the greatest organic drummer . . . the only musician, except Mary Lou Williams, who went from the old-time jazz to the new-time jazz. Nobody else did.

DM I remember hearing Pee Wee Russell playing "Blue Monk" recently. . . .

KR Yeah, but played in that strange Pee Wee way. I mean, the thing about Dave Tough is that he moved from Chicago jazz into modern jazz. He was in the first Herd with Woody Herman, for instance, and through it all became a thoroughly modern drummer. He was certainly as interesting as Roach or even Elvin Jones.

Later, in the John Reed Club we used to do a certain amount of revolutionary verse. I did a thing with Louis Aragon's "Red Front" . . . and then it all sorta died. Jazz died. There was very little action in jazz for years.

See, the great problem, is that to do a thing really well in the first place, the poet has to know a great deal about music, either play an instrument or be able to write music or both. He should have some idea about what is happening. Then the band has to rehearse. You don't just get up and blow. And if you lived in San Francisco, the better bands were not available, because they were on tour. The musicians were moving around all the time. That's why we started in The Cellar, because the owners were the band. The piano player (Bill Weisjahn) and the drummer (Sonny Wayne) were the owners. And Bruce Lippincott on tenor . . . they were the house band. Other musicians came and went and played with the band. (Mingus and I did something a long time ago in The Black Cat during the war, just for fun one night.) As soon as Ferlinghetti did it, then Patchen brought out his record with a highly trained group. Mingus and Langston Hughes played the Five Spot in New York after I did, and I understand it was very successful.

Two things happened during the Beat Generation time. The hucksters couldn't understand it at all. I remember having a conference with a record company, with Laughlin and the New Directions people, about marketing Patchen's record. The executives of the company didn't know what they had at all. They didn't know how to sell it. The only thing that was selling at all was this Ken Nordine record . . . which was to us what Rod McKuen is to Ginsberg. A strictly commercial scene.

Steve Allen got that same idea. I don't know how he formed his friendship with Kerouac. I was booked into the Village Vanguard, and Kerouac recruited the gig. They throw you out of the Musicians' Union for doing something like that, but he went to Max Gordon and recruited the gig. He said it would help build up my show. Well, he was pissy-ass drunk every night, vomited on the piano, and made a general ass of himself, and Max said to me, "Look, I'll buy your contract."

Steve was very upset. I said no to Max. (Max started out in life as an anarchist poet; very few people know that.) Well, this started a thing so that in every Greenwich Village coffee shop and bar for about two years, all kinds of bums with pawnshop saxophones put together with scotch tape, and some other guy with something called poetry, were, like, you know, blowing poetry, man, dig? And it was absolutely unmitigated crap. It killed the whole thing. It had a terribly bad effect. There wasn't anything like it in San Francisco, because we had done the thing in San Francisco. . . . People knew it, people knew all about it, even though there was an awful lot of trash at the Coffee Gallery, but by and large the music was better, and the poetry was better, too. But the stuff in New York was ridiculous; and, of course, it's that whole New York commercial scene. That was all it was for. To make the tourist go to Greenwich Village. You went down there where the first miniskirts were worn, and the miniskirted chicks were waitresses, and you got yourself a free grope, and you listened to free jazz and poetry done by a couple of stumblebums who weren't being paid anything, and it killed the whole thing. Then Lipton in Southern California staged the first big show. It was very successful, Shorty Rogers heading one group with me and Freddy Katz heading the other. Lipton, Stu Perkoff, and some others. This was quite a show. And it ran for weeks and drew all kinds of people and made all kinds of bread. The musicians were top musicians.

I was always luckier than anybody else because I knew more about what I was doing. I got top musicians. The people I had working with me at the Five Spot were part of the Blakey organization: Bobby Timmons, Doug Watkins, and the star of those days, Donald Byrd, and Elvin Jones on drums, and then Pepper Adams on baritone. The same in Chicago. The band I worked with up and down the coast was built around Brew Moore, who was a Lester Young–type tenor. He was very good for Kansas City soul. An awful lot of work went into this, long rehearsals. I always worked with head arrangements. Patchen worked with stuff that was all written down.

But you discover that jazz audiences don't know shit from wild honey . . . and that includes a lot of the musicians. One of the things that I did, and still do, is done against Eric Satie's "Gymnopédie No.

1." It is called "This Night Only." People always think it is a George Shearing number. I used to do a thing with a Neruda poem to a 12/8 samba rhythm. I remember sitting down with two of the leading New York critics who were supposed to know something about music, who write about pop culture, jazz, and stuff like that . . . and they said, "Kenneth, why you know, that boogie-woogie number you did was very good."

The interesting thing was that they didn't know what 12/8 was, but they dug the 12/8 which was the essence of Jimmy Yancey, of boogie-woogie. Yet they didn't knew it was Latin music. Dig? They were jazz habitués. In the Five Spot at least one night a week. That's one of the things that's heartbreaking about jazz.

Today, you have a highly trained audience which has grown up listening to, you name it, Judy Collins, Joan Baez, Pete Seeger. They have good taste in rock, which is why they put down most rock now because it has been debauched. You have a trained audience, which you did not have in the day of bop.

People still say the most absurd things. "You know, that Charlie Parker is polyrhythmic and atonal." Oh, my ass! I mean, there isn't anything in Charlie Parker that isn't in Beethoven!

DM They have reissued tapes of Parker playing in nightclubs, and often the audience chattering is louder than the music. . . .

KR Of course, that's another thing. You play in New York and you discover what hard bop really is. Hard bop is music for people who don't listen. I would never put up with it. In the first place, I have a lot of projection, and I won't permit any nonsense. I'll just stop in the middle of a poem . . . but the minute I got off the stage and the band took over, everybody would start talking again. It was scandalous! Beautiful musicians like Watkins and Timmons, you know, young guys . . . no wonder they never got anyplace. Well, shit, I can see why. Bobby would play a solo piano number, and these motherfuckers would be talking at the top of their lungs. Cash register banging, waitress clinking around . . . that's what I always loved about John Lewis. "The waitresses don't hustle drinks during the set, the phone doesn't ring, and take the bell off the cash register." Boy, that's really twisting the arm of the owner! But Lewis and Mingus are the only people . . . Lewis, of course, was polite whereas Mingus was rough. But John is the only person who has been able to get away with demands like that when his group performs at clubs.

DM I get the feeling that jazz today is even more neglected than at that time. . . .

KR Neglect? It's lost connection, partly because it's so blatantly low-brow and partly because it's so crazy racist. And its racism really doesn't have anything to do with black or white, it's just that there are too many pigs at the trough. . . .

The black dominance of jazz is due to the fact that there just aren't enough gigs to go around. Blacks have got their leverage, and they levered other people out. This is all tied in with bohemian black negritude, which has divorced them from their sources. Folks don't buy this. This whole Ayler, LeRoi Jones scene cuts them off from folks, from black people, so that they lose their roots. Their white audience will only take so much of it, and then they get bored. People get tired of being told musically, "You motherfucker, you kept me in slavery for 300 years." The average guy in the audience didn't, he came over here to escape Hitler or Pilsudski. Then they discover that and they say, "You dirty Jew!" The audience gets tired of this after a while. Masochism is only fun for a little while. That's been a big factor.

Also the fact that they won't get away from these songs which provide them with certain kinds of changes which they can work on, but the lyrics of which are absurd. Look at all the jazz standards, and then think of the words to them. There has been a demand, you see, for lyrics of a counterculture. I mean, jazz really wasn't enough of a counterculture, because jazz really isn't . . . jazz was, after all, music played for dance halls and cabarets, and anybody who says it isn't is crazy. It's not the voice of a counterculture that most radical rock is.

I mean, you couldn't get out of the Sunset Café for less than $30. It cost you more than that to go to the Cotton Club. Langston Hughes said a wonderful thing about the Cotton Club. "You know, they didn't let in common niggers like me. It was for people like Bojangles Robinson." That isn't quite true, because I went to the Cotton Club with Langston . . . but it is roughly true. Above it all, like God in his heaven, was Duke. It was disgraceful, you know. The show would just make you vomit. Talk about Tom minstrel shows . . . these spade chicks walking around pretending to be cannibals . . . it was just terrible! No wonder Duke is so imperturbable. He would die of shame, otherwise— not for himself, because his music is magnificent, but the whole atmosphere of the Cotton Club was horrible.

The thing in music that has happened in the last ten years is not as assimilable.

There's a lot of stuff that's assimilable, and the square can't tell the difference. *Time* magazine is always discovering some new rock group offering wonderful lyrics about I-love-America, sung by people that look like Norman Rockwell Coca-Cola ads—but it doesn't go. Neither does the phony acid rock go. The audience won't take it.

I went to the Both/And Club one day to hear Philly Joe Jones. Philly Joe Jones is a great drummer. He's another organic drummer like Dave Tough. It's like a heartbeat, you know. It doesn't have to be loud. I mean, he could make a great thing with just one brush. And everybody in the audience was gray-haired. It was very funny. I said to the owners, "God, it's old home week!" And the owners said, "Yeah, it sure is. I don't know. Changes have been taking place, you know. I feel like we are booking Bix Beiderbecke."

Students of mine, even Negro students who really dig jazz, stop with Ornette and Mingus and maybe three or four other musicians. This savage hard bop, I mean postbop, that has come up in the last couple of years in New York . . . civilization is breaking down. Don't forget that jazz musicians work for a living; they have to work in clubs and they are not living off in communes. If you play a guitar you can say, fuck it, and walk out under a redwood tree. But jazz musicians are tied into a very fierce and ugly scene which is controlled by the Mafia. . . . What kind of a world is this to work in? A modern folk singer or a modern rock musician doesn't have to do that at all . . . he is not tied into the gangster world. . . .

3

DM There is a seemingly different response to spiritual matters in the West Coast, a type of lifestyle and response more basically rooted to

Oriental and preinstitutionalized Judeo-Christian concepts. . . .
KR One reason is simply that oceans, like the steppes, unite as well as
separate. The West Coast is close to the Orient. It's the next thing out
there. There are a large number of Orientals living on the West Coast.
San Francisco is an international city, and it has living contact with
the Orient. It also has an internal Oriental life. Once a week you can
go to see a Buddhist basketball game, if you want to. There are Bud-
dhist temples all over the place. To a New Yorker this is all ridicu-
lous—the Orient means dime-store incense burners. It is very unreal.

For years, I noticed in Pound's *Cantos* two ideograms that were up-
side down. I used to pester Laughlin about this. I used to make fun of it.
Ezra by this time had gotten very dim-witted, so he didn't notice it.
This was after the war. . . . Laughlin said something to Eliot about it,
and Eliot burst out laughing and thought it was a great joke. Not that
they were upside down, but that it would worry me. He said, "But, you
know, no one pays any attention at all to that sort of stuff. You know,
that Chinese thing. Nobody reads Chinese, anyway." Eliot's attitude
toward Ezra's interest in the Orient was that it was a great deal more
ridiculous than his interest in Social Credit or his other crackpot ideas.

Large numbers of people have gone to the Northwest and to Cali-
fornia to get away from the extreme pressures of a commercial civili-
zation. On the West Coast it is possible to beat the system. It's possible
to be a fly alive on the flywheel, which it isn't in New York. I would
have been an utterly different human being if I had gone back to New
York. That's why I stayed on the West Coast. Of course, there is an-
other aspect to the whole California business: religious communities
and new religions and swamis; you know, maybe that's just because of
a large number of middle-aged women. You know what they call those
swamis in old-time show business? They called them "rag heads on
the menopause circuit." But, at the same time, a guy like Krishnamurti,
who certainly plays the menopause circuit, not out of his own
wishes . . . I mean he doesn't ask for it, they come to
him . . . Krishnamurti is a very impressive guy. His stuff is very intelli-
gent. He is no Kahlil Gibran. He has wonderful answers to give.

This is all part of the wartime thing, too. Allen Hunter at the Holly-
wood Congregational Church is the guy who turned on people like

Auden, Aldous Huxley, Pravananda, Gerald Heard, and, of course, Isherwood, who is still around. All of these people were extremely influential on the pacifist and anarchist movements. This was another focus. And it all fed into the thing that made the San Francisco scene. People would come down from the CO [conscientious objector] camps to us in San Francisco, but they would also go down to see Isherwood or Aldous Huxley or somebody like that. Something definitely was being built up.

The big influences in the Northwest were Mark Tobey, who was a Bahai, and Morris Graves, who was a Vedantist. They were both very serious about it. Mark Tobey is a big wheel in the Bahai movement, in so far as they have big wheels. And Morris Graves is very serious. A lot of western migration was in the first place to get away from the destructiveness of the big metropoles and then to find new spiritual roots. That's true of all classes of people, not just intellectuals.

I think it's a great mistake to put down the thought of an old retired couple in Moline, Illinois, who decide to get themselves a little house in the rose-colored slums of Southern California after going to a Vedanta meeting. There's nothing wrong with that. The guy comes home and says, "Ma, I think I am going to sell the secondhand car business. I think it is a rotten thing. I think we got enough money and we will go to California. I was sure impressed by that Indian fella we heard at that lecture, and I think we'll go out to Glendale. . . ." What's wrong with this? Is it any different than Allen Ginsberg?

I have always said that the greatest shock Kerouac ever got in his life was when he walked into my house, sat down in a kind of stiff-legged imitation of a lotus posture, and announced he was a Zen Buddhist . . . and then discovered everyone in the room knew at least one Oriental language.

You have to realize, too, that KPFA fed us an awful lot of this stuff. For years and years, Alan Watts and I were back-to-back on Sunday. Alan was handing out the Sunday sermon. This was all very influential. The very name, "Pacifica Views," Jimmy Broughton's brother was, I think, the financier of it. There are lots of connections here that go back to the war years.

Then, too, consider the large numbers of conscientious objectors who made up the movement in San Francisco. Most of them were real young kids who just didn't know any better, and they went on doing what their Sunday school superintendent told them to do after he stopped telling them what to do. They found themselves out here in concentration camps. They had no roots, no background at all. They didn't really understand what had happened to them. And they began to put together a thing. Look at the tremendous Catholic, pacifist, anarchist movement that exists today. Well, Christ, the San Francisco Fellowship of Reconciliation assumed the responsibility of feeding the Catholics in CO camps. It was impossible to do it. They damn near starved to death. I can remember when the Catholic Worker group numbered in the whole U.S.A. about two hundred people. Lots of those people came to the Bay Area and settled here. Today, it's an enormous movement all over the world. It's now universal. Civilization is in a state of total collapse. We live in a corpse, and more and more people know this and seek for a way out. . . .

An awful lot of these people stopped writing or write very little. There was a whole group of people around Berkeley those days who were not part of Bob's Berkeley Renaissance and were members of the San Francisco circle. They are still around but most of them are not writing. One, of course, who is still writing is Philip Lamantia.

He has an incomparable European reputation but is not well known in America. Of course, the thing about Philip is that he doesn't promote himself at all. I mean, not at all. And he is always away. You know, he is off someplace. He is in Mexico, or he is in Tangiers, or he is in Spain, Paris, and he is ignored by the American avant-garde establishment. Yet everybody knows . . . you ask Ferlinghetti or Duncan or somebody like that, and they all acknowledge Lamantia's importance—but he is not around when the prizes are awarded. And, of course, Philip represents as all of us represent something that for many years has been an absolute obsession with me—and that is the returning of American poetry to the mainstream of international literature.

I have said on lectures that the source of infection in Czechoslovakia was the Viola, the nightclub. They used to read Ferlinghetti and Ginsberg to records by Thelonious Monk. They originally wanted to call the club The Cellar. But then somebody had a chick named Viola, so they called it Viola. But, believe me, there never was a club between wars in Prague called the Swanee River where they could read Allen Tate to Stephen Foster. That didn't occur! Today, we are all a part of the world literature, and we have a profound effect on world literature.

You get off a plane, and a guy picks you up from the Society of Cultural Relations in Germany. He says, "I understand you live just a little ways from the commune of The Mothers," or, "I understand John Handy is a friend of yours. . . ." Now he'd say—and don't think he wouldn't—"Have you heard Dave Meltzer's latest record?" The San Francisco scene dominates world culture.

Between the wars, an extraordinary combination of Ku Kluxers and bankrupt Trotskyites in New York dominated American literature, and made it totally provincial. American literature was back where it was before the Revolutionary War. It was a provincial imitation of English baroque literature . . . Anne Bradstreet. It had no connection.

You talk to these people about contemporary literature, and they don't know who you are talking about. Allen Tate, for instance, is a good friend of mine, but Allen Tate goes over to Europe, and you discover that he lives entirely within the world of Paris-America . . . he doesn't know anybody . . . they are shut away from the whole . . . you see, the world economic crisis obliterated the whole Paris-America scene. A person like Eugene Jolas and a magazine like *transition* became inconceivable . . . and this all led to the provincialization of American literature.

DM It lasted quite a while, didn't it?

KR Oh, Christ! Since most of the people, except the Southern Agrarians, had been one-time Stalinists, they just took over all the techniques of Stalinism . . . you know, hatchet reviews and logrolling and wire-pulling and controls of foundations and academic jobs and so forth . . . they had the thing absolutely by the balls, just like the Commies had had it just before them. If you got in the *Partisan Review* you could put up your little pattie and get a job on any English faculty in the U.S.A.

We fought these people continuously . . . a lot of them had been taking exercises so that they could keep fit when they were put in the prisons during the coming war, the Imperialist War, and what happened? They were all in the OSS and now the CIA. They all were! Every single motherfucking one of them was! Name anyone that wasn't! I know all of these people. They were all chairborne on a gravy train of human blood. And don't think that we didn't say so. We said so continuously. I mean, we never stopped! Once I pinned the name "Pillowcase Head Press School of Literature" on Red Warren and Allen Tate and John Crowe Ransom, it stuck! You have no idea the domination of these people. They are afraid of me, because they have never dominated me.

You go back to New York, immediately after the war, you know, and Phil Rahv takes you out to dinner and with tears in his eyes says, "Why don't you contribute to the magazine? Why, we publish Zukofsky!" But don't forget, all these people were forgotten: Zukofsky, Walter Lowenfels . . . all these people were as though they had never been. And if you mentioned them, Rahv looked embarrassed, like you had just farted.

I was at this big poetry powwow that *The Groves of Academe* was written about. They were having this long discussion on the History of American Poetry, and I said, "You have left out the whole populist period!" And they said, "Who's that?" And I said, "William Vaughn Moody, Carl Sandburg, James Oppenheim, Lola Ridge, Vachel Lindsay." (Most of whom were Socialist.) With an expression of utmost contempt on his face, "Cal" Lowell said, "Well, of course, in the West, Rexroth, you haven't learned that those poor people aren't poets at all."

I don't think they were very good, but it was a question of history . . . it wasn't a question of fashion. . . .

The poems in Sandburg's first two books, before he supported the First War, are really terrific. I mean, all that stuff about dynamiters and prostitutes and so on . . . it's terrific.

We finally broke it. Nobody else broke it. We broke it. And we had damn few outlets. Most of these people are not acceptable today. A few years after the war I was asked to do a survey of modern poetry and an anthology for the *New Republic* . . . and I had Olson and Creeley and Denise Levertov and Duncan and Lamantia. I wrote an article and gathered their poems and sent the material in to the *New Repub-*

lic. I didn't hear anything, but they paid me. I said, "When are you going to print it?" Finally, I got an abusive letter saying: "Rexroth, you and your provincial poetaster friends . . . what are you trying to do? Trying to foist something off on us?" This is the way it was. But we broke it.

Bly has done wonders. When I first met Bob, he was a real young guy, and we used to talk about this domination. The young people coming up need to be reconnected with the avant-garde tradition of the world. This was something that he agreed with. This is the reason for his publishing Vallejo, Trakl, Neruda, and other world poets. All you have to do is go to the university, and anybody with gray hair is still teaching the seventy-seven types of ambiguity in the poetry of John Donne. Its interesting that these cats are all juicers, too. They will come around here in Santa Barbara and say to me, "Say, remember that party in Berkeley when Roberta pissed out the window?" They are the greatest argument for grass that you ever saw in your life! And they are still teaching this shit. I.A. Richards, T.S. Eliot, I mean, those critical methods.

On the other hand, the people that came up after the war are now also locked into the establishment. Like LeRoi Jones. What is LeRoi Jones? Is he a genuine motherfucker? He is a college professor! How does he make his living? He has never been anything else but a college professor. If he isn't working now as a college professor, it is because he is a pie-card artist. He is a professional bureaucrat. Roi's a college professor. He has never in his life been anything else.

They can't understand that they are now the establishment. Ginsberg does. Of course, Allen has ten times the brains of the rest of them. He has sense. He has a sense of what happened to him and where he is. He has insight, and, of course, he has connections with the younger people. He's like Dave Tough. After all, Allen is the only beatnik who is still alive. The rest of them are dead. I mean mentally. . . . Allen is never uptight. He is always available. I would go nuts if I was as available as he is. Christ, I would go out of my mind! He is always available, and he is always connected with people. Gary Snyder is the same way, except it is more systematized. He's the old type, really.

You go around to the universities and you meet guys that are emeritus. I had dinner once at the University of Pennsylvania with a lot of cats who remembered Ezra Pound, and they were all swingers. White-haired old men . . . seventy-five years old . . . but they were real swingers and real scholars. They knew Provençal and they knew Latin or English literature or whatever . . . and these other people don't know anything. They write a doctor's thesis on T.S. Eliot, and it puts them on a step of the escalator and there they stay. Eliot! Shit! They write a doctor's thesis on Elizabeth Goudge and Ruth Suckow. You have no idea!

DM What changes do you advocate in the university? What changes do you offer as a teacher?

KR I don't believe in universities at all! I believe the university should be totally dissolved. I think there should be more colleges than high schools. At least as many as grammar schools. They should be in the neighborhoods. In a climate like California, most of the activity should be outside. And the teachers should be beautiful people with long white whiskers and white robes sitting under oak trees and answering questions like Krishnamurti does. Leave all this superstructure and infrastructure to the engineers, the slipstick boys. Leave the buildings to them. But the humanities, I think, should be human education, dissolved into the neighborhoods and available to anybody. Everybody, young and old, should be able to come on in and sit down. This is what we were talking about. I am no advocate of Krishnamurti—he means little to me—but his way is the way to educate people.

I point out all the time: you can't teach creativity in the university system. The creative personality survives in spite of it, by living contact. Creative education, development, liberation, occurs more often in coffee shops off campus than on the campus. If you really want to do something about creative people, move the coffee shop into the curriculum.

That's like this class of mine: we come in and we kiss one another. We play a track off the new Airplane album, or something like that, and dance. The Esalen technique applies it from the outside like a mustard plaster. I had this student who goes to Esalen all the time, and I said, "You've got to realize that unless this stuff is done in context, it is unreal . . . it is like carrying a party card in the Association for the Advancement of Cunnilingus. Like, who needs it? Who needs it?" I said, "You evolve things in the activity, the doing. . . ." This was a revelation to her. She said just by being confronted by that problem, she learned more than she learned from seminar after seminar at Esalen, which cost all kinds of money. More than she learned in all the group gropes she had gone to. She learned she really didn't know how to evolve this communion out of a given context, and since she didn't know, she was fundamentally a square. Because who needs to be taught to grope? The answer is most of America. I am not putting down Esalen and its poor benighted uptights.

It takes a whole year. It's only in the spring semester that you begin to get a real interaction from your students. Everyone is relaxed, and they all know one another by that time.

There's a guy on the faculty who said to me, "I don't understand what principle you are using to do this. They tell me you let your students get away with murder. How do you discipline them?" And I said, "I don't. It is all self-discipline." He said, "Well, who is the authority?" I said, "There isn't any authority." He said, "Who is responsible?" I said, "We are all responsible together." "Yes, but on what principle do you keep the thing going?" And I said, "Well, I guess you'd call it agape."

Now this man is a Ph.D., fifty years old, and he looks at me with his mouth open, muttering: "Agape? What . . . what . . . ?" And I say: "Comradely love. Agape, it's a Greek word. The class is like an underground Mass." And he mutters.

Then we talk some more and I realize what this idiot thinks I mean. A Black Mass! This shows how totally isolated he is. I mean, this is a guy who has spent his life at the bottom of a disused missile silo. I mean, he doesn't know about anything! In the first place, he had so little idea about how the universe, the world, people were put together that he could think I could get away with a Black Mass. If I wanted to. . . . He hadn't read the newspapers, he had never heard of an underground Mass. He didn't know anything about changes in the Catholic Church. I told my students about the discussion and said, "We might as well be hung for wolves as dogs." A girl said, "I'll get up on a table and take off my clothes." And another one of my students said, "I'll swing the incense pot." If a guy like George Leonard knows . . . George wrote that book, *Education and Ecstasy.* Did you ever read it? It is kind of corny . . . he belongs to that world of Howard Gossage, Jerry Et-Hopkins, and Herb Caen, the Squirt Set, the junior jet set. He can't help it. But his ideas are right.

I would like to talk about music and poetry as the real pivots, the top and bottom pivots of the door into the counterculture, into the alternative society.

The stuff that isn't a part of that, in my opinion, just doesn't count. This is not a question of fashion. But I'm inclined to think that it's not going to win. Within a fairly short time, the suppression is going to be unbelievable.

See, Americans think that there are such large numbers involved in various things that nothing can happen to them, that they are protected. For years, blacks have been saying, "We got ten percent of the population." But Hitler exterminated six million Jews and six million other people in a population of sixty million. And they weren't as conspicuous, they didn't have black skin. So what is it? Twenty million blacks . . . that's nothing. They can make them into Gold Dust Twins soap and sell it at a premium in Orange County supermarkets and never miss them.

I said this long before . . . I think that if this thing isn't stopped . . . anybody who stands out, like black people or anyone else, just doesn't stand a chance anymore. They will be eliminated. I think the same is true for the counterculture. They are just not enough people, really. This is why, again, poetry and music are so important. Because all these politicos, all these guys representing somebody else's foreign office, they believe in marshaling people around like troops. Confrontations . . . horrible as the People's Park episode was, let's hope some people learned their lesson. I mean, what's this one whirligig about a can of poison gas? Shit! That was the end of it. And here these people marching . . . thousands of people . . . up and down Telegraph Avenue, like the troops of Frederick the Great. And one little heap of junk can fly over them and scatter some dust and the thing is gone, destroyed. It's all right to say that power comes out of a gun, but, shit, man, their power comes out of the hydrogen bomb, and when push comes to shove, they have Teller's doomsday machine in Livermore . . . and it's good-bye. To everything!

The techniques of massive paramilitary confrontations are, in my opinion, absurd. The Sunflower Sutra has more effect than a Columbia University takeover. It does. It's just a fact. Because all you have to do is co-opt most of these people. They found it out with the blacks. All you have to do is to pick a government office at random . . . take the Yellow Pages and look up the United States government and shut your eyes and put your finger down, read the address, and go to the office. Walk into the guy and say: "You motherfucker, I am going to cut your gizzard out," and he says, "Here is a twenty-thousand-a-year job!" It's a fact!

The head of the Poverty Program in the Fillmore was a notorious three-time loser, an extortionist, somebody that no Negro would touch with a ten-foot pole with a six-inch extension. He'd been thrown out of the Muslims, been thrown out of the Panthers, been thrown out of everything . . . and here he was, the boss man. All you have to do is co-opt people like that. And if you can't co-opt them, then you destroy them.

Whereas the counterculture as a culture, as a way of life . . . you can't catch up with it, it's in the bloodstream of society. You can't pin it down. Its effect is continuously corrosive. It's these capsules they stick in people that keep feeding medicine into their bloodstream for twenty years. The more the poetry of music is massive confrontation, the less effective it is. It may be effective in a very limited range, but the other thing is effective over a long term. This is true of the whole protest-rock and protest-folk bit. Young people are wise to the fact that Donovan is more revolutionary than Dylan. The whole thing that has grown up around Leonard Cohen is more subversive than Country Joe and the Fish. And as the years go by, it becomes completely phony. Play Pete Seeger singing "I Dreamed I Saw Joe Hill Last Night" . . . it would make you throw up. . . .

DM To my mind, Pete Seeger has always been a singer of the radical movement. . . .

KR Seeger was brought out in café society downtown. Christ, that goes back a long time. It's cooked, you know. A lot of Pete's stuff is cooked. Woody was much better because he was less a part of the apparatus and more uncontrollable, more of a natural.

You used to hear cats singing in the International Labor Defense Organization, you know, records can still be found, "Swing Low Sweet ILD," supposed to be a Kentucky miners' song. Horseshit! That's artificial . . . that's the cooked thing! Seeger just can't get away from it, except in some individual songs.

And people like Joan Baez, people like that, are too innocent, and they don't believe in being hypercritical. I don't know a single song of Joan's, either on record or in concert, that is that kind of cooked party-line stuff—whether it is anarchist or Communist. She doesn't do things like that. That's her instinctive taste. If you were to talk to Joan about things like this, she would be offended. She thinks I am a baddie. She doesn't like me at all because I am a man of violence.

Look at the effect she has had. Her effect is radically subversive. There's a wonderful story about Joan Baez. She was responsible for the big Wolf Bierman bust in East Berlin. They had a Vietnam thing in East Berlin, and Joan gets up after Bierman has sung and says, "I am going to sing a song dedicated to my good comrade Wolf Bierman. The song is called 'Freiheit.'" Joan sings the song in German. The next day they called Bierman down and said, "What does she mean 'comrade'?" He said, "She isn't my responsibility, I didn't have anything to do with it. . . ." They told him to give in his work permit and his travel permit . . . they busted him for a year.

Joan gets very few dates in the hard Iron Curtain countries like Bulgaria, East Germany, and Russia. She has been to Czechoslovakia, Yugoslavia, and, I guess, Romania. She may have gone to Poland during the thaw. But they all know. When she gets up and sings "Barbara Allen," it is subversive.

The real thing about your stuff, or Joni Mitchell's stuff, for all kinds of people like this, and all kinds of people that are not getting recorded and booked, is that it involves and presents a pattern of human relationships which is unassimilable by the society. What the songs speak of cannot be assimilated. I mean, here is a love song . . . but the kind of love it sings of can't exist in this society. The song gets out like a bit of radioactive cobalt. It just foments subversion around itself as long as it is available. I think this is much more important. Because everything else can be crushed.

I mean, you can have wonderful communes in New Mexico, or sleep under a tree, or sleep in a canyon, but you never heard of a latrine there, and the food is always burned, and the kids get ringworm . . . in New Mexico they play with the Spanish kids and get lice, and pretty soon the thing falls apart because they don't know how to live, and all the Gary Snyders in the world aren't going to teach them. I mean he can't go on handing out merit badges in Woods Communes forever. It ain't going to do them a fucking bit of good. He is going to get tired of saying, "A real Zen master says, 'Don't shit on the ground, especially alongside the sleeping bag.'" It's not going to have any effect. These people are all vulnerable, and they are still living on money from papa and mama. And they are all rich. When those people hit New Mexico, it was amazing how those people went and bought up land. And they are still buying it up. And the land has tripled in price!

DM It seems clear that so much of the revolution is middle-class consumer oriented. The middle class consumes revolution, makes it into stuff, goods, and takes the life out of it.

KR Yes, of course . . . that's why the spades hate it. You know Hannibal Williams? He's a guy that has been fighting relocation in the Western Addition's Citizens' Organization. Hannibal is a very nice guy, and I remember having a discussion in the coffee shop in the Howard Church. I had just come back from Europe and the flower children had decayed, and it was obvious that the Mafia had taken over the neighborhood. This conference was all about the relation of the hippie community to the Haight-Ashbury resident community, primarily black. And, of course, the reason the Haight-Ashbury developed was that it was red San Francisco. It was full of retired longshore organizers whose kids now smoke pot and sing Pete Seeger . . . and blacks . . . it's a genuinely integrated neighborhood. That's how the people got in. They wouldn't have gotten to first base if they had gone to the Sunset or Richmond District.

Anyway, some guy got up and said he had just hitchhiked from a very rich suburb, and he was stoned and dirty and he was fat and had a lot of beads, and the hippie stuff he wore was all new . . . and he said something about the relation between the hip community and the straight community. I was going to say something, but Hannibal jumped up and said, "You got it right, man, but you got it ass backwards! You are the straight community, and the community you are invading is the hip community! You come into this neighborhood and you imitate my clothes. I wear blue jeans because I go to work! You even smear paint and plaster on them . . . yet you wouldn't know which end of a paint brush to hold! And you take over my house or my flat and you play my music on your fucking $2,000 hi-fi sets, which you turn up so loud you keep my children awake all night!"

When he got through, the people reeled . . . but then it reeled right off of them. . . .

Allen Cohen, who was editing and putting out the *Oracle* at that time, attacked me. And I said, "Look here, it's true. You are all engaged in a bourgeois enterprise. Don't shit me, man! You are a businessman! You are engaged in a bourgeois enterprise! Face the fact that you are middle class. . . ."

On the Great Grass Road, you know, you find a chick dead in a ditch fifty miles out of Kabul, barefoot, clothed only in a blanket with a hole in the middle of it and a rope around her waist, and she's got a bindle, a bag, and in it is a diary about all the Arab truck drivers she's sucked off and been cornholed by, and strapped to one leg she has two hypodermics and some medicine . . . and strapped to the other leg, $10,000 in travelers checks! That's an actual case. There are thousands of them . . . all you have to do is just make the Great Grass Road . . . go from one of those places to another, from Casablanca on . . . you can't pass Burma . . . to Calcutta. These people are all rich. I mean, rich, not just middle class!

The real far-out hippie is the person who is actually engaged in a personal revolt against the very evil family, a corrupt society, and so forth. It is not a massive social phenomenon, except it is a social phenomenon reflecting the collapse of this society. People are crazy enough to think it's the revolution. I mean, this is ridiculous. It is as ridiculous as believing that the circle of princesses around Rasputin was the revolution. Because it is the same thing. Exactly the same thing. There's not the slightest bit of difference between Rasputin's circle and upper-middle-class hippie life.

DM A majority of the new consumers consider themselves to be the revolution because they are consuming the cultural ideas of what is relevant: the records, the books, stuff like that. . . .

KR You see, you have to draw a line. A lot of these people just don't know anything at all. All they are interested in is cunt or cock and dope . . . and preferably spade meat. . . .

Down the street from me in San Francisco is a so-called shoeshine parlor. I don't know why they don't call it an athletic club. The only thing they use the shoeshine stand for . . . I pass by sometimes, and the door is open and some chick is balling some guy . . . these old cats in bib overalls: asphalt spreaders and ditch-diggers and one thing and another . . . middle-aged blacks, most of them juiced all the time. These chicks . . . will fly to San Francisco from Sweet Briar, and they take a cab from the airport to the Haight-Ashbury. They go to a Salvation Army and get some old rags and real hip threads, and they buy some beads at the Psychedelic Shop, and they head down Haight Street. And they come to the shoeshine parlor, and there will be a big old black grandpa leaning up against the window, chewing snuff and juiced out of his mind and dirt all over his bib overalls. and a chick will walk up to him and say, "Sir, would you care to enjoy my body?" This scares the shit out of these guys when it first happens! And they will come to me and say, "Mr. Ken, what is this? Are these chicks crazy?" And the young chicks go back to Sweet Briar and they say: "Girls, do you want to come up to my room? I had a lover in San Francisco . . . an authentic Negro. And I have the most interesting little parasites. They are the same kind that Negroes have. They are called crabs, and I want to show them to you."

Like the cat Hannibal had the rap with—I said to him, "When do you think 'Howl' was written?" He said, "Huh, man?" I said, "You know, 'Howl,' Ginsberg . . . the Ginsberg that runs the secondhand clothing store at Fillmore and Haight . . . " (there isn't any such place). He said, "Oh, yeah, man, I get all my threads there. . . ." I told Hannibal that I didn't invent this guy, God sent him to me.

The reading that we gave for the Planning and Conservation League (June 30, 1969, Norse Auditorium) was very significant. Because in the first place, nobody really knew who they were. I'm supposed to know all this stuff, and I didn't know anything about it. But everybody responded immediately to what it was, and the people came out. And the people who came out were very interesting. The last benefit that I had read at was for the Free Medical Clinic at the Straight Theater. There was all the difference in the world. Because that Norse Auditorium conservation thing was full of flower children. It was full of people like the people were five years ago. They were serious people . . . they weren't meth heads . . . they were an entirely different kind of people than those who would be brought out for something in the heart of Haight Street. They knew, they were well informed. They knew who the poets were at the reading, and they had also come out for this ecological bit. We forget that this thing is going on under all the noise.

On the other hand, there is this thing which is strictly controlled by the Mafia. The world of the zombies in the Haight-Ashbury. They are not interested in all that psychedelic baloney that everybody was talking about before. They don't want that. They want massive destruction right away. They don't want any LSD . . . they are not interested in that . . . or an expanding consciousness . . . they want to get stoned. They want to stay stoned. Like hit on the head with a half-ton stone.

You remember the cat they arrested? They took him to the Park station because he had been going around the neighborhood, up and down the street, telling people that he had a peace pill to sell. He said that he had a friend that worked in the chemical warfare laboratory and that he stole this stuff and pressed it into pills . . . and he told his customers that it was a fifty-fifty chance that the pill would either give you the greatest high you ever had, stone you out of your mind for four days, or it would kill you. A fifty-fifty chance. And all it would cost would be $10. The cops busted him, and they were going to beat the shit out of him . . . but he said, "Look, man, it is just an aspirin." So the cops let him go. But it shows . . . he was making all kinds of money selling aspirin tablets that might kill you. It is so easy to confuse the two things.

These rabid apologists for the dope culture, like Burroughs, they confuse the issue. Of course, Allen to a certain extent did that for a while. All this stuff of Alan Watts's. . . . I think the two things are quite different, and I think you lose sight of the lost dogs that are running around, of what is really going on underneath. These people may dress the same, but actually with a sharp eye you can distinguish the differences.

Here is a chick in a poncho and tights and beads made out of chicken vertebrae around her neck. And here is another chick, and she seems to be dressed just the same, but you can tell the difference . . . it's a subtle thing. Yet neither one of them comes from the working class . . . they are upper middle class. They are people who are opting out of the military-industrial society. They wouldn't have the option if they weren't up at the top of it. You can't get any options, otherwise.

5

KR For those people that we fought as they grew up, poetry is an important experience. Poetry is life affirmation, they really dig all this Gary Snyder bear-shit-on-the-trail poetry, they have contact with nature, and, of course, as you know, the genuine ecological revolution's rolling now and involving thousands.

If Diane di Prima had stayed making the scene around Tompkins Square, she would never be writing for an ecological crisis news sheet. And don't forget KPFA's connection with all of this. KPFA has given hundreds of programs, thousands of programs, in the past twenty years on the ecological crisis. And I, on my own program, have never let up on it. There has never been a book, even a bad book, on ecology and on the environmental problem that I haven't reviewed and used the book as a peg to hang a long ecology speech on. KPFA has had countless people of importance talking about Famine II and Famine III and Famine IV. And all this DDT uproar that has now hit the paper. The DDT thing has been about on KPFA for over ten years, since the first evidence began to come in.

The use of the power structure, the subversive use of their techniques by Dave Brower, was decried immediately by his old rock-climbing comrades—who are now corporation lawyers and other shits of that sort. I mean, fuck, these people who are corporation lawyers, they know perfectly well that the success of a business is measured by its indebtedness! I mean, that's the way you measure a business. A successful business owes five million bucks, and an unsuccessful one owes nothing. They accused Dave Brower of running up enormous debts for the Sierra Club. Yet he was using the techniques, the basic techniques: utilizing the bourgeois publishing scene, Madison Avenue, lobbies, everything his detractors' clients used all the time. This is what happened in the Sierra Club. They objected to Dave Brower because he was fundamentally subversive. They made the most shameful appeals! "How we used to have a good ole hiking club and used to go out and eat peanut butter soup and put raspberry jam on the snow in the passes . . . " and all this kind of crap. Well, the "good old days" are gone. Very few people in Berkeley know this, but there is a native-son-and-daughter Berkeley establishment that really runs the university. They are also the people that run the Sierra Club, and, of course, they think they are the most liberal souls on earth. But the ecological crisis is of such a grievous nature that it is only by the most massive action that anything will happen at all . . . and probably what should happen is not going to happen. You know, there is no way of extrapolating into the future that will be effective. The only people who know this as a mass, all of a sudden, are the counterculture who latched onto it because it explains what is happening.

All this struggle against papas and mammas, in which idiots lead mass demonstrations in Berkeley and think they have the offensive, they don't have the offensive at all, they have the defensive. I mean, it is the papas and mammas that have the offensive. This is why it has such a family character, because it is a fundamentally . . . it is a phenomenon of species death due to the breakdown of the biota of the ecological relationship.

A few years ago, they were saying the reason the dinosaurs became extinct was because the vulcanism of the Jurassic filled the sky with dust and cooled the climate, and the marshes got too cold for the dinosaurs' balls, and so they became infertile. Well, the dinosaurs didn't become extinct because they had cold balls. They ate all their eggs. Say this and people who are listening dig it. It's like being converted to Methodism. The whole thing clears up. They can understand what it is all about. And this is why the whole ecological thing that Gary's been preaching—you know, he has made himself the leader of it—is so important. It is the key.

Charismatic, you see, everybody says Bolshevism broke down, that other things were never tried because they could not envisage a real alternative that would work or, to use correctly the misused slang, a "viable alternative," something that wouldn't be stillborn. An ecological revolution can scientifically extrapolate into the future certain essential conditions. It can say this and this must occur. There must be so many people to so many acres. There must be so many people to so many square feet. There must be certain kinds of relationships, certain kinds of agriculture: there are all kinds of things that must be, and this necessitates certain methods of production and distribution, etc. You create, as they say in science or math, a model and it is a clear model. The Bolsheviks had no model. They had no model at all.

It is just like the blacks. They have stopped doing this, but whites used to say: "What do you Negroes want?" And people like Roi would say, "That's your problem, motherfucker." Well, they don't say it anymore, because you can't do anything with that. After a while you get your head beat in, you get shot. "That's your problem, motherfucker," is not a sufficient prescription for the future. You don't want to go out and get yourself killed for that.

The ecologic crisis provides—the way that Marxism with all its bullshit about scientific socialism never did—a scientific model for a just society. The interesting thing is that this resembles far more the thing that Marx and Engels attacked: utopian socialism.

You want to know what the future should be like? It should be like William Morris's *News from Nowhere*. He was more right than Marx. He talks about an idyllic underpopulated England with the old type of Japanese gardening and pre-Raphaelite costumes. And he is right and Marx is wrong. Until recently, Doxiadis was talking about a world of 200 billion people, all kinds of shit like that, and then suddenly he woke up. I used to argue this with him. Then I met him in Athens recently and he had awakened. He has become obsessed now because it had come to face him: the famous honey of Hymettus, the long mountain above Athens, is no longer available. The bees are gone. They have gone over to the other side of the mountain. Athens is like San Francisco. It is a wind-swept city, but the smog has driven the bees off the slopes of Hymettus . . . so Doxiadis doesn't talk about 200 billion people living on the Earth anymore.

Look inside the Iron Curtain countries. Part of the revolt against Moscow has been that formerly orthodox Marxists have said, "Look, man, we are up to our asses in steel mills. We need uniformly planned development for a stable population, and we don't want to be a bread-basket for Moscow." The thing that has really turned me against Communism, I mean, orthodox Bolshevism, long, long ago, was not the Moscow trials or the expulsion of Trotsky or the right wing, or the trials of the engineers, or anything like that at all. I expected most of that, even as a kid. It was this.

The Russians used to put out a magazine called the *Economic Review of the Soviet Union.* I had a job for *The Nation,* or some fellow-traveler periodical; I was asked to write an article on the Soviet lumber industry. So I did. Out of the *Economic Review of the Soviet Union,* which had various references, I got information and did a tremendous lot of research. They brief all this stuff in English. They put out scholarly publications in agriculture in the days before Stalin killed them. They would have briefs in the back of the trade papers in French or English. Knowing a little about lumbering, I discovered that the Russians were doing the most ruthless and destructive lumbering in the world. And, furthermore, it was being done by slave labor. That Weyerhaeuser was the Sierra Club in comparison to what they were doing in the mountains of Georgia or the forests at the edge of the tundra. I became more interested, and I discovered that there wasn't any difference. It is all, East and West, production for production's sake. No human values are involved.

The Chinese know this, but the Chinese can't deal with the problem because they have an enormous reforestation difficulty. They plant twenty trees here, yet they have to cut down 200 there because of population pressure. The two different agencies in the country work at cross-purposes.

You see, this involves an important matter: human relationships. Human relationships that are expressed in the lyrics of the best modern songs. Human relationships in song that is unassimilable. These are ecologically sound relationships. They imply a society which is quite different, and the difference is an ecological difference. Everything ties into it.

Right now there is a Moholy-Nagy show here. I knew Moholy. . . .
We went with a student of mine, a girl, and she thought it was great. She was very excited, but my ex-wife, Marie, and Carole and I—we were very depressed. In each one of those little pictures and circles and squares and lines, Moholy thought he had something that would reform the world . . . it would go out from the painting and create a new society. He thought that it would do this by using the production methods of capitalism. He was wrong and failed. He was absorbed as a design consultant. There are Moholy-Nagys all over typography ever since. The whole Bauhaus scene . . . that's what it all meant. And, of course, that doesn't mean much to people anymore, now. Who takes Bauhaus art–style classes in modern art anymore? The professors don't explain this to anybody, and they don't understand that this is what it was all about. It is all so tragic to see those beautiful pictures and to think they are all essentially failures because they didn't do what they were intended to do.

The whole problem is to find works of art which remain permanently unassimilable and permanently corruptive. This means that they don't really differ very much from anybody else's work of art. The songs of Shakespeare are permanently indigestible and permanently subversive.

I think we have talked long enough.

Remembering Rexroth (1999)

July 31, 1999: That morning, I first meet with Christian Parenti, Gloria Frym, and Sheila Tully, New College colleagues, at the entrance to UC Berkeley, to get our signs and banners to march with hundreds of others to KPFA—a radio station that Kenneth Rexroth helped found fifty years ago—in protest against Pacifica's restrictive sell-out management policies of one of the last progressive FM stations left in the U.S. After a few hours marching and rallying, I walk back to The Musical Offering Café on Bancroft, where I had started. Jim is already there with his friend and comrade, Ken Knabb, along with Morgan Gibson, on a rare visit to the U.S. The café is split in half: its front section is a combination coffee shop, elegant fast-food eatery, and nighttime haute cuisine restaurant, while the back section is a choice classical music store. Hence, much early and Baroque background music accompanies our tapes.—DM

Morgan Gibson (**MG**)
Ken Knabb (**KK**)
David Meltzer (**DM**)
James Brook (**JB**)

DM Ken, you knew Rexroth in the sixties?
KK Yes. Not very well, but I got to talk with him quite a few times. Morgan actually knew him a lot better.
DM You also met him quite a bit earlier, Morgan?
MG Yes, I was in touch with him in the fifties. I saw him extensively in the sixties and got to know him even better during his visits to Japan toward the end of his life.
DM Ken, what made you write *The Relevance of Rexroth*?
KK I think the answer is connected with the question Jim posed as a theme for this discussion: why are the Beats still considered such a big deal while Rexroth has been so strangely neglected? In part, it's a generation thing. There were the classic modernists, Pound and Williams and so on, and then the Beats—and, in between, there was a wasteland generation, and that was Rexroth's generation. The sort of an-

thology that Rexroth would normally appear in doesn't exist because nobody puts out a book called *Poets of the Post-Classic-Modernist Pre-Beat Era*. You couldn't even come up with a good title. Rexroth and his few peers did not really form a movement. In retrospect, you go back and say, "Well, there was also Henry Miller, or Patchen, or this or that other poet." But at the time these were just a few isolated voices crying in the wilderness; they were drowned out by all the New Critics and Stalinists and so on. It wasn't until the fifties that you could look back and see that something had been building up. And then you see how much Rexroth had contributed to what was to come later. But until then he's kind of out of it, there's no pigeonhole for him.

DM Many of the authors we interviewed acknowledge him as a forebear.

KK It's good that they acknowledge him, but it's not enough. There's something big missing there, and what I think is missing is . . . I don't know if you're familiar with the Situationists?

DM I consider your *Situationist International Anthology* an essential reference.

KK Well, as it happens, the Situationists were pretty much contemporary with the Beats and hippies (if you can consider the latter as two phases of a single movement). The Situationists looked back at different aesthetic movements from the Romantics on—Impressionists, Symbolists, Naturalists, Futurists, Dadaists, Surrealists, and so on—and they saw these as successive stages of a kind of self-superseding of art. In each case, you could say it was a movement toward greater closeness to life, or relevance to life, or criticality of the medium, or criticality of the society they found themselves in. And in the fifties the Situationists contended that this development was at an end—that it had gone so far that no further possibility remained for art. To go further you had to go beyond art, you had to supersede art, bring creativity into subverting everyday life, into revolution. The idea of just writing a different kind of poem had become meaningless.

While they were saying this in Europe, the Beats and hippies in America were pretty much oblivious of these considerations. But they inherited the same situation. In a somewhat confused, half-conscious way they were expressions of this same historical development that was merging art into everyday life. You might still write poems or songs, but there was a sense that this was simply part of your adventure, part of your life.

DM It wasn't a specialized calling.

KK Right. So the Situationists are basically making the diagnosis that this can't go further without bursting out of the aesthetic boundaries. And if you think about it, there has been nothing since then that we can qualify seriously as an aesthetic movement. There have been movements like punk, but they've been more a matter of lifestyle than of art—there's been no real aesthetic innovation comparable to Surrealism or Symbolism or Romanticism. The Beats are the last artistic movement of any apparent significance. And even in their case, if you look at what gives them their continued notoriety, it's more a matter of their lives than of their art. People are intrigued by Gary Snyder not because he writes good poems, even though he does, but because this is the guy who was a fire lookout and then went to Japan and learned about Zen. Or Ginsberg is the guy who took his clothes off in the middle of a public reading.

This is what I meant in saying that those poets' acknowledgment of Rexroth is not enough. I don't think Rexroth's primary importance is as a poet, not even as a poet who had a political side. His vision implies going beyond poetry and politics, even if he himself wasn't totally clear about all the ramifications of this. It's ridiculous if he's only thought of as a guy who wrote some very fine poems, and even more ridiculous if he's only remembered as a guy who paved the way for a few later poets who are actually far less significant than he was. He's a figure of historic stature, worthy of standing beside the greatest thinkers and visionaries of the past. He straddles East and West, nature and civilization, mysticism and skepticism, radicality and magnanimity. This is why I wrote that book. By going through Rexroth I was able to deal with all sorts of tricky issues—how can this thing be reconciled with that thing? I couldn't have picked out any other writer, classic or modern, who would have enabled me to address so many of my own concerns simply by quoting him and then making a few criticisms in the rare cases where I thought he didn't get it quite right. He covered everything. No one else did.

MG He could have identified himself as a Beat, but he chose not to, out of integrity. I see him disagreeing with the Beats. I'm not saying all of this because I worship Rexroth. I think there are many flaws and contradictions in Rexroth's work, but I think he's quite distinct from the Beats in several ways. One is aesthetically, in that he is really a traditional, classical writer in many ways. He advocates anarchist action and revolution, but in his own personality, his attitude, his way of writing he is highly disciplined. His aesthetic is cubist, not surrealist. Conscious construction rather than the "free expression" that Ginsberg and Kerouac advocated. And he had a much better sense of the Western and Asian traditions, bringing that into the present work, the present writing, whatever he was doing. The Beats had a rather spotty sense of the background.

While we were driving over here I was ticking off the answers to that question of why he's not very popular. First, he is a countercultural figure, but he's really apart from the counterculture, since he's such an elitist, an arrogant elitist. And most people saw him that way. I mean, they might admire him or agree with his anarchism, but they saw him as an elitist who's got the final answer. If you didn't agree with his anarchism, he made sure you were humiliated. And then, how could most young people identify with a guy who seemed so old-fashioned in some ways? They might say, OK, in another age or another part of America, he might support us, but they couldn't identify with such a traditionalist. Their radicalism was impulsive. It didn't require theoretical knowledge. You didn't have to know history to be a sixties radical. Some did, but you could be out on the streets doing your thing and not know anything about Kropotkin or Marx, whereas Rexroth insisted you had to know all of that before you formed your own position, and act accordingly. Another reason he was far apart from the general culture, though he spoke a great deal about revolution, was that when I knew him he was not really an activist. He told me in the mid-sixties that he wasn't invited to antiwar demonstrations. They felt that he was above it all, and he did tend to pooh-pooh the politics of the times.

DM Yes, he had that unfortunate attitude, which was off-putting. I remember as a young poet listening to his radio show on KPFA with other poets, and we used to listen to it at times just for laughs—this windbag just going on and on, all these proclamations, this is so and that's so. But again, that was our own youth and our own historical turpitude.

MG I'm glad you said turpitude, because I think there's an ethical difference. There's a kind of amoral, hedonistic quality in the counterculture—there is also a heavy moralistic political aspect to the counterculture—but Rexroth's morality is more complex. It is not the Weatherman or Maoist kind of dogmatism. On the other hand, it's not pure hedonism. His ethics are philosophical and religious. His longer poetry and plays dramatize philosophical dilemmas. And he seems to swing between Buddhism and Western anarchism—and Catholicism. Do you know Father Huerta, his confessor, a Jesuit? A wonderful man. Sort of a worker-priest in the streets. He and Rexroth were very close the last couple of years. My background was anything but Catholic; I always had trouble identifying with that. But I think it enriched his idea of love. And love permeates all of his thought—the revolutionary ideas as well as the mysticism, the social philosophy, everything is permeated by love, a kind of Christian love. I think it's the body of Jesus, the body of Christ that we are all supposed to be part of. I think it's very much part of his mysticism, though he didn't talk about it much, but it entered some of the poems—*The Heart's Garden, The Garden's Heart,* for example. It's in all his other Buddhist poems, too. He found Buddhism compatible with Catholicism. He saw Buddhism as a thing you do, a meditation practice, a contemplative attitude. It's not a set of beliefs or a dogma.

JB Rexroth talked and wrote a lot about San Francisco and the Bay Area of the time; that is, the late sixties, early seventies. And he would often refer back to the earlier era of red San Francisco and the longshoremen and labor organizing. Haight-Ashbury was a working-class neighborhood, which is one reason things could happen as they did in the sixties. People did not move into the Richmond or the Sunset. They moved into the Haight. San Francisco is now a very different place, almost a kind of theme park of itself. Shouldn't we talk about then and now, and why the scene is so different? The city started changing quickly in Rexroth's last years, with the culture congealing into Reaganism at the end of his life.

MG He used to say that San Francisco was on the verge of being the

Paris Commune of America. I mean, he really thought that this was the beginning of utopia. He said it was the most radical city in the world. He just idolized it. And then when he moved to Santa Barbara in 1968, he said it's all going into the sea. He thought the Haight-Ashbury hippie scene was the utter collapse of civilization. I think he identified the whole fate of the world with San Francisco. He admitted defeat. As early as '65 he said, well, we've had it. This is it. We're not going to make a utopia. Even the early poems sometimes say that, you know. "We had this dream. It's gone. We were the happiest men of our time. But it's over."

KK It's not just San Francisco, it's the whole society. A generation has grown up with the spectacle, as Debord says. Younger people have grown up in a world that's almost totally dominated by the spectacle, they have no conception of what was around in the past, not even half a century ago.

DM Yes, there's been this continuous pacification and almost stupefaction from the tyranny of abundance that really seems to be short-circuiting any kind of political movement. . . . In the last period of his life Rexroth wrote some very interesting books, like *Communalism,* the *Classics Revisited* essays he originally wrote for the *Saturday Review,* translations from the Japanese, French, Chinese—a wonderful range and acuity and also stylistic availability.

KK *Classics Revisited* is not only the best book about the classics, but if I was confronted by someone from Mars and they asked, "What is humanity about?" I would say that if you take that one book, you've got everything—all the potentials, all the tragedies, all the beauties, all the absurdities, all the different ways of looking at life, all the different stages where people have made a breakthrough in the sense of self, or community, or relation with nature, or what have you. It's all there, in those little essays of three or four pages.

JB That still slips past the question about how Rexroth drops out of the picture. You present an image of a fellow who's written all these essays and popular articles for newspapers and magazines, who's written poetry, who's a very public intellectual . . . it seems like everything's going for him—and then something doesn't happen. Why isn't it now available or interesting to people?

KK I think he had some blind spots that prevented him from going a step farther and following up the implications of all these insights that he had. It would have pulled the rug out from under his aesthetic orientation. He had this notion that the poem was going to subvert people little by little. That it was more effective to be subtle and not just use crude propaganda. He clung to the idea that artistic creativity was the thing that would hold things together even if society went insane all around it. I think the Situationists were right in questioning such an idea. This is not necessarily to say, as they did, that art is totally dead, but it's not on the cutting edge anymore. The cutting edge is more like what the Situationists were doing. Rexroth didn't make that leap. Had he done so, you would find people interested in him just like people continue to be interested in Guy Debord. Rexroth is in some ways much wiser than Debord, but he falls short in this matter of not really seeing beyond art, not having a clear critique of the spectacle.

JB I think that's probably true about the limitations of Rexroth, the outer limits of his thought and practice, but then you have people who are much more limited like Gregory Corso or Jack Kerouac, and they have maintained their popularity.

KK People like Corso and Kerouac are easier to assimilate; they're very consumable. You know where they're at. But Rexroth—nobody knew where he was coming from. You could not say this guy's a beatnik, even though he's very hip. You could not say he's an academic, even though he's incredibly learned. He's sort of classicist, but he's also a revolutionary. . . . People don't know what to think about somebody like that.

JB So you're saying that if Rexroth had been more than he was, he would have gone beyond the available categories and become more interesting to the public at large. Or if he had been less than he was, he would've been more easily consumable.

KK Precisely.

DM Morgan, what was your motive for writing your book on Rexroth?

MG In *Revolutionary Rexroth: Poet of East-West Wisdom* I tried to draw together the diverse directions of his work—anarchism, mysticism, and erotic love. I thought there would be a kind of unity to his worldview or at least a coherent set of ideas or values, and I tried to argue for that in the book. But recently in rereading his work, I think his ideas are much more diverse and cannot be explained in terms of a coherent theory or philosophy. Very well, he contradicted himself. As Ken said, Rexroth probably did not want to be labeled.

DM I'm thinking of his introduction to the alchemical works of Thomas Vaughan and that Waite book on Kabbalah—a whole branch of the Western hermetic tradition he endorsed in a sense by writing those introductions. How does that relate to contemplative Buddhist practice?

MG That's a big one. I don't know as much about Western mysticism as I know about Buddhism, so I hardly know how to make that comparison. He was very much interested in Indian Vedanta as well as Buddhism; that is, the non-Buddhist tradition of India. But I don't know enough about Saint John of the Cross or the other Western mystics to say anything very helpful. He had a number of holistic metaphysical experiences, he claimed, going back to childhood, where he sensed the harmony of the entire universe or all reality, universe and supernatural combined. He seemed to think that these intuitions were quite profound, and they convinced him of a kind of spirit of love throughout the universe. Then the different mystical writers he read, whether Asian or Western, seemed to confirm that for him, or express it in different terms. But he didn't need them to convince him. In other words, he didn't read mysticism in order to have mystical experiences.

KK I think he's seeing all these things not so much in contradiction, like whether they're orthodox or not, but as different perspectives on a fundamental reality. There's a reality that is just part of being a human. It's embedded in the brain or the psyche. It underlies all these visions and powers and conflicts and possible transcendences. He's experienced it. Other people have. And they have communicated it in different ways. In that communication, somebody like Boehme or other hermeticists might be particularly vivid cartographers of these things. Other more orthodox mystics might be less imaginative cartographers, but then some of the orthodox people might express it well, too. Rexroth would try to point out how you have some Christian mystic doing this and some Japanese Buddhist doing that, and then you have some atheist experiencing a similar thing over here—so you get a sense of the whole world or worlds in there or out there, or both at once, and that you can draw on any of it. It was as if you're visiting Europe. He'd say, "Here's a map of Paris. Check these things out."

DM I think that's a good way of looking at it. So in a sense, then, it isn't contradictory in the larger picture.

MG I wanted to add, I don't think he ever was seeking enlightened experience, like satori. He was quite unlike Kerouac and Ginsberg in that sense, who were running around trying to find satori, the secret, the wisdom. In his view it had already come. It had come to him. He had a number of these experiences that he thought were genuine, and he was perfectly content with them. He didn't need to induce an experience by drugs or by reading certain texts. In a sense, he felt he already had it, whether rightly or wrongly. And he didn't need external stimuli. I think that's a very basic difference with other poets who might be mystical or visionary.

KK He did go out into nature periodically. I think it was partly to reconnect with that. I don't think he went out there and came back from the Sierras and said, "I've seen a new vision." It's more like going back—he's been through a bunch of turmoil in the city, so it's time to go back to this place that's always there. It's in here, within you, but it's a little easier to connect with it when you're in the mountains.

DM Also, of course, he's a very underrated poet of that wilderness, that nature.

KK An awful lot of his poems are about nothing but that. They look like they're about nature, but really they're about the transcendent experience—the unspoken thing—like Japanese and Chinese classic poems often are. The poem talks about the moon, the trees, there's no mention of "me," but there's an implicit hint.

MG There's considerable interest in Rexroth in Japan because of his presence there. A lot of instructors teach Rexroth, proportionately more than in America. A lot of people met him and passed on the word to their friends. I can go to a university in Japan and someone will know his work or at least have heard of him.

KK There does seem to be a revival of interest developing. Several volumes of his writings have recently been published in French, other people are translating him into Spanish, and the Rexroth material at my Web site (www.bopsecrets.org) has been generating enthusiastic responses from all over the world.

MG I think we're mixing two questions about poetry. One is why certain poets remain fashionable, popular, and commercial, which the Beats are, regardless of literary quality. Why are they published and popular and making money and so forth—as opposed to what keeps a poet's work alive for centuries? I don't know what makes fashions. Perhaps the Beats in five years will mean nothing to people. I just reread all of Ginsberg, whom I admired for years and years. Now I can't imagine wanting to read him again. Whereas I also just reread all of Snyder, and I want to reread him next year.

Where is the serious interest in the great literary and philosophical traditions of the world—Chinese, Western, whatever? That has died, and in the face of that collapse, Rexroth speaks wisely to us. I think people appreciate Rexroth seriously because he connected the plight of our world with the traditions. If you're not conscious of the traditions and you're not thinking that they might still be alive, you don't grasp what Rexroth is talking about. When I read Rexroth's poetry, for that matter when I read Pound's or Eliot's poetry, I started reading the poetry of the world. What readers do that today? How many people are aware of the world before their own lifetime?

Gary Snyder (1999)

© Raku Mayers

February 1999: Marina, Victoria Shoemaker, and I meet one afternoon with Snyder in his exclamation-point narrow office at the University of California in Davis. Metal bookshelves hold a diverse spread of titles of poetry books by his contemporaries—Lew Welch, Philip Whalen, McClure—and peers—Allen Ginsberg, William Burroughs, Kenneth Rexroth—as well as Loeb Library volumes of Greek classic lit translations, and Buddhist tomes, including the quintessential R.H. Blyth four-volume compilation of Japanese haiku. Immensely gracious, attentive, amiable, and sharp-eyed, Gary offers us a hit of sherry at the midpoint of our conversation.—DM

Gary Snyder (**GS**)
David Meltzer (**DM**)
Marina Lazzara (**ML**)

DM Could you begin with the biographical: family, background, ancestry?

GS Born San Francisco, May 8, 1930. Father, Harold Snyder. Mother, Lois Wilkey. Moved to Seattle, Washington, at age two. Settled north of Seattle on logged-over rural countryside land with small tarpaper shack on it. The Depression under way. No jobs. My father fixed up the little house and made it better and bigger. Fenced some land and we got cows and chickens. Split cedar shakes to sell and became semi-self-sufficient out in the countryside. At six, I started going to the local grade school, Lake City it was called, a rural area then. Went through that grade school up till World War II. Jobs started turning up all over, and my father got a job that took him to Portland, Oregon. So we all moved down to Portland, where he worked for the Veterans Administration. I went through high school there in Portland, which is where I also started back-country skiing and mountaineering. I had a crew of enthusiastic mountaineering friends. And then directly went to Reed College, also in Portland, and finished four years there.

DM What was your major?

GS Interdivisional Anthropology and Literature. Supported myself working for the Forest Service some summers or in logging. And then went on and logged the ponderosa pine timber, scaling the first season out of Reed. I went to graduate school at Indiana University in Linguistics and Folklore for just a short while. Came back to the West Coast and went back down to the Bay Area, where my father was living. Entered the Graduate School of East Asian Languages at UC Berkeley. Continued to support myself by working summers in the Northwest on fire lookout. I trail-crewed one season in Yosemite National park. And then in 1956 departed for Japan, where I lived for twelve years. Is that enough?

DM Why did you choose Literature and Anthropology as twin or interdisciplinary studies?

GS Naturally interested in literature but then I was drawn to curiosity about Native American oral literature, and to do that you have to get some sense of Americanist linguistics. I was drawn to all of those at the same time, thinking there were some connections that I might find that would throw light on contemporary poetics. I was a close reader of Pound at that time, and I already had an interest in Chinese and Japanese poetry. Through Pound's and then Waley's translations.

DM Let's go further back. When did you discover literature and poetry?

GS As early as I can remember. I was reading voraciously as a kid from seven or eight on. I really read fast and widely. We had almost no books in the house except the Bible and Robert Browning. [*laughter*] But we got books from the Seattle Public Library regularly. I can hardly keep track of what I read. Except I know I read a lot of Native American stuff, a lot of short stories and fiction on the West, and a lot of novels about imperialism and colonialism and a lot of history. This was from ten years old to fifteen.

DM What provoked your interest in subjects like Native American, colonialism, imperialism?

GS Well, the Native American interest was partly because I was curious about where I lived. I got the idea that the local folks knew something that the white folks didn't know. I also got that from hanging out at the University of Washington Anthropology Museum, a fascinating place in those days. Full of baskets, canoes, carvings. There was a whole culture there right before our eyes. In the thirties, you could still see those people paddling their canoes over to Seattle and selling huckleberries. And my parents were political radicals—socialists—who talked a lot about exploitation and imperialism.

DM "Socialists" as defined by what exact affiliation?

GS You know, in the thirties we said "socialist" so we didn't have to say "Communist."

DM Because there is a strong socialist tradition in American history.

GS My grandfather was IWW—Industrial Workers of the World. My father and mother were sort of on the edge of the party but not really members of it. They were involved in different left-wing front organizations at various times. My father was doing labor organizing on the Grand Coulee Dam project.

DM So that was just part of the culture of the household?

GS Yeah, and the culture of quite a few people. Thirties Pacific Northwest, labor movement, left-wing. It was all over the place.

DM So much of the art and literature that you're identified with marks a period where there's a retreat and a recoil from that enthusiasm or desire for social change.

GS Well, I got a perspective on Stalinism very early and never identified with Soviet-style Communism. I never made that an issue for myself. In fact, that was a source of contention between some fellow students and me when I was in college. There was a strong pro-Soviet left-wing student group there.

DM Because of the war?

GS No, this was after the war. I identified with the non-Stalinist left. It wasn't like I had to convert and then be disillusioned, because I never identified with the Stalinist left. When I came to the Bay Area and met Kenneth Rexroth, I was happy to find a poet who was thinking in the non-Stalinist terms of the left and anarchism.

DM Didn't he call this tendency "libertarian"?

GS He used "libertarian" before the right wing was able to seize it. It used to be an alternative word for "left anarchist."

DM What was the watershed encounter that made poetry as a practice or vocation clear?

GS There were several things that happened with me in terms of poetry. I started writing poetry as a youth, at six or seven, because I read poetry and my mother read some poetry to me a lot when I was very little. And so it was something to do. When I started mountaineering at fourteen or fifteen, that so moved me that I started writing poems to try and express mountaineering feelings in free verse. I wrote a bunch like that. Then I ran into D.H. Lawrence's *Birds, Beasts, and Flowers*, and I was very taken with it. Started reading more contemporary poetry. I read enough in college and hung out enough with people who were talking contemporary poetry, met Phil Whalen and Lew Welch. I became very embarrassed by my earlier poems. Put them away and hid them. So that was watershed number one—that is when I discovered contemporary poetry. I hid my mountain-climbing youth poems—and some love poems. Mountains and girls. So next, I wrote under the spell of Pound, Stevens, Yeats, and Eliot.

Then I got out of college, went back to work in various jobs, knocked around the country some. Went from coast to coast. I concluded that those modernist poems weren't worth anything, either. So I put those away. Then in the summer of 1955, at twenty-five, I worked on a trail crew up in Yosemite, in the high country. I was in isolation with just a few fellow workers up there for two and a half months. I was way back in the north part of Yosemite Park. In those days, nobody came in there. You didn't see a backpacker all summer. I started writing again, poems that were reflecting influences from my Chinese language studies.

DM When did you begin Chinese language studies and why?

GS Oh, that was so I could understand Zen texts.

DM How did you come upon Zen?

GS Through anthropology. Through art and art history. Through personal spiritual questing. They all kind of converged about the time I was twenty.

DM That was about 1950?

GS Around 1950–51. I graduated from Reed in '51. By the time I graduated from Reed, I had been talking this stuff, especially Taoist, Confucian, Eastern philosophy, with Phil Whalen a lot and also with Lew Welch. And then with a couple professors—the anthropology guy, David French, and the man who did art and William Blake, Lloyd Reynolds. There was a core of people there that we could talk to. Then Charles Leong, a Chinese American veteran back from World War II, was a GI student at Reed; he was forty-something years old. He did beautiful calligraphy. Taught us all kinds of things. We had really good exposure to East Asian thinking at that time.

DM When did you read the Blyth books of haiku?

GS Not 'til a little bit later. I didn't pick up the four-volume haiku book until the summer of '51, I think. I found them in a bookstore in San Francisco. But I was reading translations of Lao-tzu by Paul Carus. And Chuang Tzu, maybe in Lin Yutang's translation. Confucius. Various Hindu texts, the Bhagavad-Gita, the Upanishads, early Buddhist writings. I absorbed a lot of basic earlier Buddhist and Mahayana Buddhist readings, until I came on Zen via Chinese studies and also from looking at landscape paintings. When I came onto Zen, I said, ah, this is where it all comes together. I got interested in trying to study Zen first hand. Sort of broke off my anthropology career in mid-stream. I was enrolled, and had a fellowship in Indiana University and was studying with Thomas Sebeok, the semiotician, and Charles Voegelin, an Americanist anthropologist and linguist. And Dell Hymes was there—we were roommates. I just quit mid-stream and said, "I'm going out to Berkeley and study Chinese." Took the Greyhound bus and went back to the West Coast. Got into the East Asian languages department. Also took some literature courses. And that's when I started reading Han Shan's texts. In the summer of '55 I started writing some more poems while I was up on trail crew. Those are the poems that are generally considered my earliest poems and are in my first book, *Riprap*.

DM How does immersion in the Japanese language alter your relation to the world you inhabit?

GS That's a really rich question, and I'm not sure. . . . People have been asking themselves for centuries. Japanese has a radically different syntax. It has a lot of qualities that are as far away from English as you can get. But once I wrapped my mind around it I could do it, and I really enjoy it. I really enjoy shifting gears into talking and thinking in Japanese. There's a sheer pleasure in it. Why or what that does for me, I have no idea. I think Japanese allows a certain kind of subtlety that English doesn't. Japanese allows a lot of ambiguity. Also, I just appreciate the manners in Japanese. It has a lot of etiquette built into it. There's something that happens to the mind when the verb always comes at the end. You learn to hold a series of clauses in abeyance—clauses that are sometimes placed within clauses within clauses. And you hold it all in abeyance. And then finally this verb makes it all make sense.

DM You went to Japan in '56 and stayed there for how many years?

GS I had a household and lot of my stuff there for twelve years. But because I went out to India for a while with Joanne Kyger and then back to the States for a while and taught at Berkeley for a year, my actual time of residence in Japan was about ten years.

DM This must have been a profound period in terms of shaping your relationship to Buddhism.

GS I just became very at home in Buddhism. I feel at home in Japan and with Japanese people. My Japanese enables me to get along quite well and to do the manners right, pretty much. In a sense, I'm bicultural. I've gone a considerable distance toward being bicultural.

DM How does one then receive the world of appearances in this bicultural set or frame?

GS In my own case, I don't find anything particularly exotic or striking about it. It's like being at home in several radically different landscapes. At one time, I was primarily at home only in the maritime Pacific Northwest on the west side of the mountains. And felt a little ill at ease if I was too great a distance from Douglas fir trees. The first time I saw the arid zone to the east, the Great Basin, and the first time I saw California, I felt unsettled and uncomfortable. This is not right.

[*laughter*] But a conscious or semiconscious learning exercise, equating yourself with and learning the ropes of a place, can very rapidly conjoin it to you, so you become a switch-hitter. As I say, I'm monogamous in marriage but promiscuous in landscapes. I really like to go into new landscapes now. They turn me on. I'm promiscuous with cultures, too. I got into India pretty fast. What I like is the fact that you can be at home in different cultures if you open yourself up to their manners and modes of doing things and enjoy it.

DM Could you elaborate on your idea of manners or manners as a practice?

GS Well, cultures do have their codes, and even classes have their codes. In regard to which many people are resolutely clueless and remain so, sometimes deliberately, because they think that they're protecting some unique selfhood by not learning how other people do things. I've done that a little bit, and every time it was to my own loss. If I were going to do Japan again, I would dress better. Right away. Whereas I resolutely hung on to West Coast blue-jeans style for several years. That was ideological for me. You have to give up ideology in lots of ways. And when you do that you can find your way into a culture and appreciate what it is that make people feel comfortable or uncomfortable, and what gives them respect. Manners is a sense of the codes of relationship that make things work with people. And allow for status, too. When Americans go to Japan, they're uncomfortable with having to determine status. It's a hierarchical society. Status is built in to grammar in Japanese. Status is built in to personal pronouns. There are different words for "you" for each level of status. If you are older than me and more powerful than me, I use a different word for "you" than if you and I are peers. If that ideologically rubs you the wrong way, you're in trouble. You're going to speak the language that doesn't go well.

. . . .

GS The circle of people I started working with in Japan in the late fifties and early sixties, Nanao Sakaki and his circle, who called themselves "Future Primitive," were doing the same thing as Peter Berg and the bioregionalists were doing when I got back here in the early seventies—making a tradition that loops back to the archaic and choosing to find primary identity in relationship with the land. Ethnicity, race, and religion are secondary or tertiary identities. So that makes the question of community possible. It makes community coherence possible. But it does not discriminate against any variety of human being who would choose to join in that exercise, and the first step would be respect for the land. This is very old.

DM Many people, coming out of an urban culture, don't have respect for themselves and others, let alone the land.

GS But they might have respect for some lingering ethnic tradition of their own. See, when you say "respect for tradition," then you have to ask, "Well, what tradition?" And then you're going to say, "Italian Catholic," "Irish Catholic," "Sephardic Jew," "Exiled Moroccan Sephardic Jew," and so on.

DM How about Mongrel?

GS What is the tradition of Mongrel?

DM It's probably more durable then the rest.

GS But what are the family values of Mongrel?

DM Oh, I see what you're saying.

GS What do you do on your holidays? Do you have a special dish that you cook?

DM I see. I haven't investigated the cult of Mongrel yet.

GS Well, you see, that's what Mongrel is. They don't know quite what to do. So they look at the neighbors and do that. Where I grew up we had Swedish neighbors, so we learned to cook some Swedish dishes during the Solstice holidays because we were Mongrel Anglos. Our closest cultural identity, our closest tradition, was the left. That was what gave us an identity, the left. My mother was a Southerner, from Texas, but she tried to forget it. She did some Southern cooking, though.

ML Were you raised with Christianity?

GS I was raised with atheism. My parents were very disturbed when I mentioned Buddhism.

DM At Reed, the relationship between you, Phil Whalen, and Lew Welch was one of initiation into various forms of poetry. . . .

GS Cultural outlooks. They were more sophisticated by far than I. Phil was an air force vet and was really widely read and could talk with a Bloomsbury accent and could be very bitchy—put up his nose and say bitchy things. I was impressed. [*laughter*] Lew was from California, which is where the girls are fast, and they sell liquor in the grocery store. [*laughter*] He had a lot of sharps. He knew a lot about jazz. I was the youngster, and they were my mentors in those early days. I very much appreciated it.

DM I'm curious about your relationship to certain key words I find in a lot of your essays, like "radical" and "radicality."

GS I use "radical" to mean fundamental change, structural change. At the root.

DM Do you see possibilities for that kind of radical change in relationship to the technology that you've gradually incorporated into your own life? I don't expect you to do a Nostradamus!

GS It's OK, poets are asked these questions all the time. People have the capacity to make a radical change in their own lives, for starters. People can totally quit eating meat, start running a mile a day, quit answering their e-mail. There's any number of things you can do that would amount to a radical change in your life—that's the easiest, because it's just you. The same way a family or a small community can make conscious decisions and choices.

Up to a certain point, change can be accomplished by individuals or small groups, which is a good argument for community and grassroots activism. Because then what you have is a model. Others look at one working model and say, "Hey, they did it! Maybe we can do it!" That's the way watershed consciousness, watershed organizing, and a certain kind of practical bioregional organizing has been. It's done by models. It's spread in a grassroots way around parts of the country—in parts of the world.

I'm in touch with people in Italy and Slovenia who are into bioregionalist organizing. But that has its limits. It runs into the dynamics of the larger system, and then it has to creep around those limits. That's when you shift to talking about structural change from the top. Marx had some pretty brilliant insights, and the idea of interpreting history as basically class warfare was one of the most brilliant. It is to some degree a myth but a very useful myth—one that kept, for example, the Serbs, the Croatians, and the Albanians from beating up on each other for seventy years. For seventy years they lived in peace.

When you look back, that's quite an accomplishment.

DM So in the de-Sovietizing of that area you get different kinds of warfare—which would be what? Tribal warfare?

GS It goes back to ethnic and religious hostilities. The way the Soviets were able to plaster over those divisions was by saying that those were not the real divisions, that history is really a class struggle. It was the landlord class against the peasant class, not the Turks against the Serbs. I'm just using that as an example of the structural differences in the way a government might be administered. It slices things in different ways. But it still is government. What is not government are the radical changes like feminism and the spread of women's consciousness and independence now gradually and not so gradually into all cultures of the world. Feminism is changing the nature of the world.

DM Racism remains deeply ingrained.

GS Different places in different ways, though, and, depending on the economic friction, racism is harder, darker. Different color of skin is not an issue in a lot of countries because they're not in economic competition with each other. The other change that is really radical in the world is the globalizing of the economy. That is advanced capitalism in its purest and finest form.

DM Is it capitalism's final form?

GS It might be its final form.

ML Marx said capitalism would become extinct once it became global.

GS Yeah, but he didn't say what we'd have to go through to get there. [*laughter*]

DM Could you elaborate on this process called globalization and what it implies and how it affects your alternative practices?

GS It makes it very hard for any regional economy to maintain its skill, its crafts, its knowledges, because everything is measured in dollars and cents. A local basket-weaving tradition, a local carving tradition, or a local agricultural tradition that is specialized but not cost effective in terms of the global economy is doomed, so subsistence economies are doomed. Local subsistence economies are doomed.

DM Don't you see that as an obstacle to continuing?

GS Absolutely. One of the things that Doug Tompkins and the Foundation for Deep Ecology are doing is putting money into fighting the global economy. Jerry Mander works with him. At first, I didn't quite catch Jerry's passion entirely, but now I see what he's saying.

DM Curiously enough, as we talk about it the word "globalization" it becomes more and more naturalized and given a certain inevitability. . . .

GS Inevitability, yeah. And people will say "these struggles in the Balkans are terrible—the global economy will straighten that out!" [*laughter*] Here's a new book, *False Dawn: The Delusions of Global Capitalism* by John Gray, Professor of European Thought at the London School of Economics. He was converted to opposing globalization after having been in favor of it for a long time. He says that the conservative agenda is no longer viable. He says America has forgotten that the market works best when it is embedded in society. When it is not embedded in society it becomes a monster. That's basically correct, I think.

We have to walk a path between local integrities and local cultures on the one side and the possibilities of their prejudices and the idea of some kind of utopian cosmopolitanism. Most intellectuals that I run in to, East Coast or West Coast, are still pretty much caught up in a vision of a cosmopolitan urban world society that is the intellectual version of the global economy.

DM In one of your essays you have this phrase: "our post-industrial pre-collapsed world." Your use of "the wild" makes it a radical key word, too. Any thoughts about the "nature" or "wildness" of cyberspace?

GS Good question. I do think that the technology of cyberspace and the Internet is a wild card. Stewart Brand and I talked about this some years back. It has the potentiality of enhancing centralized power. It also has the capacity of decentralizing information and public engagement. I know for the people I work with that we're dealing with a speeded-up and increasingly dangerous situation. The only thing that keeps us up is our e-mail. I'm on the list for a dozen passionate environmental groups that are sending out information from the Los Angeles Ballona wetlands to logging plans in British Columbia to what's going on in Brazil. Everybody's typing this stuff, and it's getting sent around the world. There's a lot more information accessible, more quickly.

DM How much information can one absorb quickly?

GS That's something we have to learn. That's something we have to master. Not being swept downstream by it. By picking and choosing, and getting what you need to know, not seeing any more than you have to, forming your picture. I have a friend who subscribes to about forty periodicals, and I asked him, "What are you doing with all those?" "I just glance through them and then I pass them on. This is how I keep up with things," he said. He feels that that's the way he keeps on top. Well, that's the old-fashioned way.

DM No, it's not. It's scanning.

GS Scanning—but you would do the same thing with Internet stuff.

DM That presumes that you already have a picture. But what if you're going to it for that picture to emerge?

GS I don't think people are going to get their values off the Internet. I think they're going to have to get their values in communities with their peers, with their workmates, and form their agenda that way.

DM The technology has both the capacity to unify but also to isolate and privatize. You receive lots of information, but it has a way of pacifying you, too.

GS Or just numbing you. What about some young person who simply watches TV six hours a day? What picture do they form of the world?

DM A very limited one, if they can remember it. Do you have a Web page?

GS I do, but I didn't set it up. Somebody else set it up.

DM Like stars, there are billions of Web pages out there.

GS I do send around an occasional e-mail to some of my e-mail group addresses—it's a quick way to share ideas.

DM That's true. I coordinated a very interesting seminar that was student directed and student taught. We called it "Techno-ontology"—we were trying to see if one could resolve some of these issues. It was fascinating—the subject couldn't be dichotomized. As soon as you were sure it was Satan incarnate, someone else would very compellingly show that it was one of the avenues for community building and idea sharing. It's become too commercial. No, not really. You can find countercommercial, counterhegemonic sites, and so forth.

GS Hmm. Sounds like we should go to a monastery.

DM Is a monastery possible on line?

GS No. A monastery's possible in the real world.

DM There's much more attention and much more privilege being paid to the concept of a "virtual" rather than "actual" for a lot of people.
GS I can't make any sense of virtual. I guess a virtual monastery would be to turn off your TV.
DM In the postwar era there was interest in America in Zen Buddhism through certain texts of the time like Suzuki's, Blyth's, and Paul Reps's *Zen Flesh, Zen Bones*. A lot of it came by accident in some people's lives, but a lot came from reading some of the writers, like you, who have been ghettoized as Beat writers. What seemed to characterize that conjunction was an intense spiritual involvement, spiritual absorption. I'm thinking of Kerouac, for instance. When I read his letters there's something profoundly heartbreaking and hopeful about this person who was a kind of Catholic mystic.
GS He kind of was, wasn't he? You really see that?
DM Yes, a Catholic mystic. I think he enjoyed Buddhism because of his attachment to mystic Catholicism.
GS I totally agree. He went for the Catholic part of Buddhism with its big glorious spaces and its saints and figures and hierarchies. It was like an expansion. Tibetan Buddhism is really like Catholicism, with its appreciation of ritual and ceremony and its willingness to deal on all levels of spiritual accomplishments simultaneously. Like a high lama will hand out a little amulet to a peasant woman who's standing in line to talk to him and, at the same time, give a discourse on high-level metaphysics to somebody standing next him. Hand out another amulet. Say a few words. That's like the Church in the Middle Ages.
DM I'm curious about the relationship to today's flourishing of Buddhism and the emphasis on the split between Tibetan Buddhism and Zen Buddhism. I believe Tibetan Buddhism was not really introduced— there wasn't any conscious move to the States—
GS Not until Trungpa came. He and the guy in Berkeley, Tarthang Tulku. Those were the first.
DM You must forgive me, but I see a class dynamic to much of American Buddhism—you seem to need a certain wherewithal to be able to afford it. And there's the fact that it's something that can be afforded. What do you think about the current revival in these two forms of Buddhist practice in the middle and upper classes?

GS Well, Buddhism has been gradually finding its way around in American society. Very slowly and, as you say, basically not from the top down but from the upper-middle down. What bothers me is that American Buddhists, people who call themselves Buddhists in America, are bringing a lot of their old agendas with them. Basically Protestant liberals. Or Jewish liberals. They have a problem with their parents. So they say, "I'm going to be a Buddhist." But they don't make a big shift in the way they see or think.

DM Looking at the Buddhist magazines and at New Age magazines, they're populated with an awful lot of white faces participating in the joys of all of these ineffable pleasures available for a price.

GS You know where the black people are? They're in the martial arts schools. That's where they learn to do zazen. I've said this to the Zen guys: "Do you want to have more black people at the zendo, have a martial arts class once a week." But it's true. That's one place where East Asian spirituality reaches into the minority community. See that neat movie, *Ghost Dog*.

One of the ways to keep Buddhist practice clear is not to soften it, not to make it easier. Some white teachers want to make it open and comfortable and soft and nice for anybody who comes. And that's what you get. You get anybody.

DM Then again, "anybody" constitutes sentient beings.

GS Yes, but this is a practice. It's uncomfortable and it's hungry and it's cold. That does not appeal to people of any particular class unless they're motivated. It definitely doesn't appeal to Hollywood yuppies. It's serious and it's difficult.

DM Other key words that you use—and you use them dialectically— are "discipline" and "freedom."

GS You've been reading my work very closely. Well, you're right. I like to think about the dialectic of "discipline" and freedom."

DM Can you elucidate a little bit more? The notion was "in discipline there is freedom and in freedom is discipline." Something like that.

GS Taking freedom as empowerment and capacity, you have to have a focus for it to work, for it to mean anything.

DM What are the similarities and differences between anarchism and Buddhism?

GS When I say anarchism, I think of the variety of communitarian anarchism that sweetly used to argue that communities can govern themselves without a centralized state or leader. Obviously, the only way to do that would be to have people who knew themselves, who were in touch with themselves, and who had cultivated both wisdom and compassion. An anarchist society would have to be a society where people could accomplish these things; in the deepest sense of the word, it could be self-governing. The next most effective thing is a well-established tradition that people agree to. The tradition becomes the mode of helping them steer their lives and makes it unnecessary to have a large legal system and political system imposed on them from the outside. So that's culture.

DM Aren't traditional cultures conservative by nature?

GS Oh yeah—and that's not a bad word. Once you've got something going that's working, you don't change it right away. You know, change is here anyway. The nature of the world is impermanence. Change is gonna get you no matter what! [*laughter*]

DM So then, "wisdom." That's a large and elusive word that probably means all things to all people. What does it mean to you?

GS It means the capacity to make good use of what you know. Distinguishing information from knowledge, first of all. The right configuration of information might be knowledge, and then the right configuration of knowledge, be wisdom. And wisdom is knowing how to live. That's universal.

DM Knowing how to live?

GS Knowing how to live also means knowing how to treat others. And then there's another term in Buddhism—"transcendental insight" or "transcendental wisdom"—which is insight into the nature of becoming and disappearing into birth and death, the question of your ultimate disappearance from the Earth. How to be comfortable and to have equanimity in the face of death.

DM Is this articulated in the moment or the reception or perception? Is this when what's once known becomes added to the way one lives with others and oneself?

GS They would say it becomes a way of living. Confucian wisdom is knowing how to live and knowing how to live with others. Buddhist wisdom is knowing being and not being, comfortable with questions of being and not being.

DM But with living with oneself and others?

GS And nothing.

DM In a materialist society this nothing of nothing can be either something heavily desired or heavily feared.

GS Either way, you get it. [*laughter*]

DM I know.

GS You will pay a great deal for your death. [*laughter*]

DM You knew Alan Watts, who was a real bridge figure for introducing Zen Buddhism to the postwar generation.

GS Yeah, he was the bridge between D.T. Suzuki and, so to speak, the Beats, etc. He was first a Buddhist. Started at about sixteen or seventeen, as a young disciple and helper to Christmas Humphreys. Humphreys introduced him to D.T. Suzuki when Suzuki came to London. Alan was around Suzuki a lot, heard him give talks a lot, helped him out a lot, understood a lot, wrote his first book on Zen when he was in his early twenties. Then he came to the United States when the war was breaking out, and studied with the Zen Master Sokei-an in New York City. He met the American woman who was supporting and helping Sokei-an, Ruth Everett. He was part of that circle. Ruth then married the Roshi, and Alan married Ruth Everett's daughter, Eleanor, the daughter of Mr. Everett, who had died. Now somewhere in here, Alan decided that to have credibility in America—and also possibly to make a living—it would work better if he was a Christian. The Anglican Church being the way it is, he very swiftly was declared an Episcopal minister. He got a job at Northwestern University as the Episcopalian chaplain, but he basically taught a Buddhist version of Episcopalianism.

Like anybody who grew up in England, he knew a lot about Christianity, anyway. He was a very, very smart young guy. He was so quick in reading and understanding, putting things together, and he had many friendships that he developed all over. When the marriage with Eleanor fell apart, he left Northwestern and cast off his Episcopalian robes, and he came out to San Francisco to join up with the Academy of Asian studies. It was shortly after that that I first met him. He was on the West Coast until he died.

A bunch of the young folks who were around then started something called the East-West House, which was a circle of artists and students. Joanne lived there. Lew Welch and Lenore Kandel were there for a while. There's a whole little story there. When I was living in Kyoto, Alan started leading trips for Americans who were interested in Buddhist culture and taking them around Kyoto. He would always get rid of them for one night and come out and hang out with me in my little place in northern Kyoto, and we would go and sit in the Daitoku-ji zendo.

DM Before I get to the easy questions: you talk in many of your essays not only about your comrades in the fifties and their relationship to the institution of education, but you also indicate the irony of how so many wound up in the institution that they were defying or challenging. Is this inevitable?

GS I don't think there's anything wrong with it. I always enjoyed universities. I enjoyed going to college, graduate school, both at Indiana and Berkeley. Universities have many things to be said for them, including lots of hot water and lights that stay on late and toilets that aren't locked.

DM Sounds like prison. [*laughter*]

GS Yeah, but the toilets aren't locked. Sometimes they have free movies. Not to mention poetry readings. The university is one of the more benign institutions in Western culture. It has the potential to serve the people. They have libraries. It's true, their major mission is to prepare new cogs for the industrial global economy, in one form or another. They create the people who will do that. But almost as a reflex to that, in evolutionary terms, as if making side bets—they sponsor people who do literature and philosophy, too. To sort of keep themselves honest, they have historians and political scientists who look at what's been going on. Some of these are fiercely critical. The institution is dedicated to some small extent to the idea of free exploration of ideas—which, in evolutionary terms, is a very good idea, to have alternative probes out there, just in case your major probe is wrong. [*laughter*] That's the niche that I see myself occupying. I and a few others are here because the university has institutionalized the possibility of a few alternative probes.

DM At a time where poetry is more removed from visibility, what's the work of the poet, and how does the poem work outside of the poet? What's its task or its tasks?

GS Well, there must be more than one task because there's more than just one kind of poetry. I think on a spiritual and psychological level the task is to keep our minds awake and fresh and to break through stale and rigidified perceptions of the world and the sense of oneself, and to enlarge the imagination thereby, and to make the heart of compassion and empathy possible, to help us get past the rigidities of ego and personal realities. That can happen with simple beauty. A haiku can help do that. It doesn't have to be ideological to help us see the world better.

DM Don't tell me, show me.

GS Show me. Exactly. I like that poem of Diana di Prima's that says, "the only war is the war against the imagination"—that, in a sense, our problems boil down to a lack of imagination. A lack of a sense of playful and gentle and compassionate alternative possibilities.

DM The ability to imagine something other than—

GS Yeah, exactly.

DM You answered that pretty easily. I thought that was going be a tough one.

GS Well, you can get into more elaborate ideas about poetry, but I think that to see the value of all of the arts as opening our senses, our imagination, our hearts, in keeping our hearts available is their deepest role. This is something we learned from long ago and in countless places.

DM What did Pound say? Poetry is always the news.

GS It's the news that stays news that counts.

Lew Welch (1969)

© Christina Fleischmann; courtesy SFSU Poetry Center & American Poetry Archives

Summer 1969: Jack Shoemaker and I drove up into the hills of Marin City to Lew and Magda's house. It was late in the afternoon, and Lew was waiting and anxious to begin. He was a tall, skinny, lantern-jawed redhead man who looked like a baseball pitcher. He said he'd been thinking about the interview for a week and knew what he wanted to say and where he wanted to go with it and that it was important to him to get it right. He'd been drinking and offered us some jug wine. Plugged in the Sony and began. As the interview intensified, it started getting dark outside. The green oscillator light on the tape recorder was our only light source as Lew reached an intensely emotional diatribe against his mother; in the darkness it seemed to gather volume and rage. When he was done, we fell silent, and he, suddenly aware of the darkness in the living room, turned on a light and went to the record player to put on an LP of Charlie Parker. More wine, cigarettes. End of first interview. The second time we went to Marin City, it was to talk about Lew's poetics, which he did with that same singing precision in his poems. I was very pleased with this interview. Of all the poets in The San

Francisco Poets, *Welch was the least known and felt unjustly left out of the fast-breaking pantheon of Beat bards. As I've written earlier, my hope was that the mass-market paperback publication of* The San Francisco Poets *would enhance his visibility as a poet. Ironically, on May 23, 1971, just weeks before the book came out, Lew left a farewell note in the cabin he was living in on Gary Snyder's property in Grass Valley. He was never seen again, and his body was never found.—DM*

Lew Welch (**LW**)
David Meltzer (**DM**)

1

LW My mother was the daughter of a very famous surgeon in Phoenix. And her friends were President Hoover, Alan Campbell, the Goldwaters. The father and mother of Barry Goldwater killed my grandfather. Quite accidentally and sorrowfully. They would liked to have had it be any other way.

The story is this: you have a proud-born only daughter of a family, the Brownfields. . . .

Six boys came from Ulster, Ireland, and it appeared that they had to come there because of some kind of political necessity. They were the Brownfields. They were peasants, and their names came from peasant stock, and somehow or other they had to come to America. And they did. And there were six of them, and they were all men, and the entire issue was my mother. Six men could have made a lot of children, but there was only one and that was my mother.

My mother married a man named Lew Welch, and he had one sister, and she died when she was forty-four, and he died when he was forty-seven. So you have in my life a thing very much like *Buddenbrooks,* where you have the end of a very strong line. My sister will never have a child. I have never had a child from my loins. (I have and enjoy having two stepsons, but have none of my own.) My mother had myself and my sister, and so it is over. The father is dead. The grandmothers on both sides are dead. There is nobody alive in my family, except my mother, me, and my sister. And we are both barren.

My father was called Speed Welch because he was very fast in high-school football. In Redfield, Kansas, he was a very good football player and ran very fast. And how he met my mother, I have no idea. He really was very handsome. He looked like Tyrone Power and Cary Grant. I can show a photo to prove it. My mother, naturally, fell terribly in love with him. She really loved my father. It was a good love match. My mother had all the money, however. He didn't have a nickel.

He was the kind of guy that would play in the high sixties and low seventies in golf and knew everybody and didn't have a nickel unless it came from my mother. And she held on to her money. . . .

My grandfather looks exactly like me. It's spooky. You look at the goddamn photo and it's weird. My mother's father. A man named Robert Roy Brownfield. He was a man of great parts. He invented, among other things, the way of pulling out tonsils instead of cutting them. He was the first man to invent a decent machine to test hearing ability. He was a very fine surgeon. And he was also a sort of John Wayne–type cat. Seriously, he was an unbelievable man.

Robert Roy Brownfield never weighed more than 168 and was the heavyweight champ of the state of Nebraska. He put himself through school and got to be a doctor, got his M.D. His father wanted him to be an engineer, and when he wanted to be a doctor, his father disowned him.

Bob Brownfield was a real gutty cat. He not only had to put himself through college, and did, but he became the amateur heavyweight champion of the state while doing it . . . *while* earning the money to get through school. A tough dude. I regret that I never met him.

He married a woman named Sims, Edith Sims, who came from a Pennsylvania Dutch family. They met in Nebraska, and their only issue was my mother. His brothers all were without issue, except one, and that issue, whoever he was, disappeared. There is nobody left. Six strong boys came over from Ireland, and six strong girls came out of Pennsylvania. And the whole thing produced only me and my sister.

My grandfather was probably the best surgeon in the West in 1920. Bob Brownfield knew more about the problems of cataracts than anyone. He operated on something like 4,000 cataracts in a year, and few had ever done forty in a whole lifetime. He would write papers about it, and they would get published. Here it is 1910 and he was the first cat to want to buy an airplane.

You know what happened? My grandfather, Bob Brownfield, and his wife, Edie, and the Goldwaters, the parents of Barry, went to a country-club dance. And Bob had an operation to do the next morning, and he didn't drink a drop. He said, "Please let me drive." And Mrs. Goldwater said, "I am all right, I'll drive." Bob Brownfield couldn't win the day and she drove. She made a mistake, rolled in a ditch, and he was dead at thirty-eight years old. His neck snapped.

And Mrs. Goldwater was so ashamed of herself. She was very lovely about it. The Goldwaters were very lovely. (Barry was my mother's schoolmate, about two years younger. He was a fat little Jewish boy that nobody liked. Spoiled rotten. The only Jew in Phoenix. The whole bit.) And Mrs. Goldwater would rather have died herself than to have killed Bob Brownfield. She loved him that much. He was a beautiful man. You could give him any musical instrument, and he could learn it in a half-hour and would sing on it and make up the lyrics. I have whole books by Bob Brownfield. Short stories he wrote. They are terrible. But he was in there working. And he was a goddamn good doctor.

2

LW My father, Lew Welch (I am a "junior"), was the son of a very simple Kansas farmer and his wife. Real good, straight, go-to-church-every-Sunday American, Kansas people. I met them once when I was five. We spent a whole summer with them. And my grandfather had lost four fingers on his hand. He was a fuck-up. The Welches were fuck-ups. My grandfather was respected and loved by everybody in his county, but you wouldn't want to take him on a dangerous mission. That kind of thing.

You know what they finally did with Frank? (Frank Welch was my grandfather's name.) They finally made him a district judge because they respected him so much. They knew he could not make an immoral decision about anyone. He would be a great judge, even though he was stupid enough to cut all his fingers off on his right hand. And he always sold the land cheap when he should have sold it dear. And his cows always died. When he bought a bull it would always be sterile. Frank Welch had bad luck, they called it. But the community still loved this man so much they made him a judge and lived by his decisions. He lived the rest of his life, with his bum hand, as a judge. And no one ever pretended he ever read a book. He never did.

My father was so bad, you can't believe it. He was an embezzler against the family which gave him a job only because he married my mother. He was a teller in the bank. The reason he was a teller was because my mother got hot pants for him. This beautiful man who looks like Tyrone Power, who comes from Kansas, Speed Welch. Bam! He comes in and she can't believe it. And when the dance is through they are married. My grandfather is already dead. My grandfather would have seen this. That this man was a phony. But the kid came up to her, and he was very handsome and very sharp.

My mother had $100,000, American big ones, in 1922. She was rich. I mean superrich. And her friends were all superrich. Well, Lew Welch, my father, was a poor man who was very clever. And he really loved my mother, there is no question about that. This is a very interesting part of it. My mother really loved that man, and that man really loved my mother. And the stories that go to prove it are really intricate and probably not worth going into. Suffice it to say that I know I was not born into a wedlock of hate.

This should be put into this. It is very important. I went to the loony bin when I was fourteen months old.

DM I don't understand.

LW I know you don't. It is the world's record. Even among my Beat Generation friends. I have the world's record. I copped out, I went crazy, split, I said, "Forget it! No, I don't want it," when I was fourteen months old. I'll tell you why.

It's a very simple thing. I refused to eat. And I would have died unless I got really strict attention. My mother was a twenties flapper, pretty, and high-style, who had little breasts and probably taped *them* down. Anyway, there wasn't enough milk, and to this day, when I go into rages like I do, she'll say, "You used to look like that when you were a little baby. You used to pound on my chest and turn red and scream." She made feeding so awful, I cracked up.

When I was six, I remember her sticking enormous bowls of oatmeal in front of me. It was disgusting. She'd scream, "Eat! Eat!" I still have trouble eating. I'm a classic case of the alcoholic with an eating problem. To this day I suck on the tit of the bottle. I try to control it, but the scars are very deep.

It's awful to be born to a rich, selfish shiksa. It wasn't her fault, but whose bad habits of mind are purely their own? It's still awful. Growing up was something I'd sure never want to do, that way, ever again.

Let's get out to the positive part of it. All I have done correctly in literature, if I have done anything correctly, was done because I resisted a terrible mother who was the absolute form of Kali, death. Even her pets die inside of a year or two. And then you can see why I praise the planet so highly. Why I take other goddesses.

The thing is that my need for the woman, my mother, was very deep and frustrated. So I hated my mother very strongly for not being able to give it to me. Though she tried. God, did she try! But maybe because of this I admire all of the great feminine traits in the world, such as the mountains, or my present wife, Magda. I am especially sensitive to how beautiful it is when it comes.

So this is why if I sound like I am exaggerating about Mount Tamalpais, it is just that I have taken Mount Tamalpais as my goddess in a very real way, like a priest takes a vow. I mean it.

I ask her, Mount Tamalpais, about this, about that, and I listen to what she tells me. A lot of people think I am being goofy about it, you know, or being poetic about it, but I mean it. I really mean it, and the only way to say it is in the poetry. The praises. Prayers.

How did I get out of it? When I was eleven years old I wanted a pair of tennis shoes very badly. And this was a way out of it. My mother explained to me that I had very bad feet, because when I was in kindergarten, that was in Santa Monica, she got in the grips of some idiot who made a steel-trap shoe that ruined my feet so bad . . . you know, if you put anything into a cast long enough it becomes atrophied. When I was in the seventh grade, my feet were atrophied because I had to wear high shoes. I insisted on tennis shoes, and there was a big scene, and luckily we were in a school where we had a good coach. I was very fast. And we would run barefooted. We didn't have any shoes and I won. I was the county champion at fifty yards in the sixth grade, and I was really a small tad then. I really ran faster than anybody else in the whole county and broke my arches doing it. Because my mother had put my feet in those iron shoes. But I won it, anyway. Because I took them off and did it. And when it got to be that way, when my feet were really broken and I couldn't walk, I had a confrontation with her and I won it. And the doctor did what was needed.

I had to walk backward for the entire time I was in the ninth grade. Backward, because I could not walk any other way, and I would not let my mother give me another crutch. And there were exercises to do, which I did, and my feet got fairly normal.

In Chicago, about 1954, I got a poem out of a dream I had. I often dream poems, and if everything is just right I can go back in there and dig the poem out by re-dreaming it. It is a poetic skill I'm proud of and on which I work very hard. I hope to be able to have a mind, finally, which has the thinking of sleep (which we call dreaming) and the thinking of waking (which we call thinking) be the same available thing.

I was dreaming, in Chicago, on a hot summer afternoon nap, that I was reading a book called *Expediencyitis*. Isn't that a great word? And the book was written by a German whose name I can't remember. The book was written as Cocteau writes, and as Wittgenstein, the form I feel is the finest form for the true mind transmission: the form is little paragraphs separated by dots, and the paragraphs have no obvious connection with one another, but the whole form finally comes through. You can see it in Cocteau's *Opium* and in Wittgenstein's *Philosophical Investigations* (originally his *Brown and Blue Books*) and in that book about Huang Po—*On the Transmission of Mind*. It's also in Stein's lectures and, I hope, somewhat there already, in this piece we're doing here.

Anyway, I am dreaming I'm reading this perfect book, *Expediencyitis*, which has this perfect form and is very wise, and I realize, while dreaming, that this is not written by any German but is being dreamed by me, therefore written by me. I'm dreaming this thought about the dream. So it is so fascinating that, when I awake, I say to myself: "Let's go back in there and get some of that." And I rolled over and forced myself back into sleep and that dream, and came up with this:

Through the years of her speech
a persistent gong
told us how grief had
cracked the bell of her soul.

It was months before I realized this poem exactly said what I felt about my mother's agony and her language. When I wrote it down upon recovering the dream, I had no idea what it meant.

3

LW When you come into a new school, the first guy that comes up to talk to you is the guy that is suspicious. If he has to come up to you and you are the only new kid, then he can't be any good, can he? The second thing that happens is that there are games in the yard. And it turns out that I was gifted with very swift legs. I could always hang back, play very quiet. I have already rejected the first kid that came up to me, because you know he was no good because he had to come up to the new kid. He doesn't have any friends, so who the hell wants to know him, right? Then there gets to be this day, and I remember it with really great pleasure.

They had a game called "Pom-Pom Pull-Away." It was very simple. One guy is "it" and he stands in the middle of the football field, and everybody runs by him, and everybody he tags is also "it." And finally everybody is "it," and there are a few people who try to work through.

OK, I am the new kid. Nobody knows who I am, and we are playing Pom-Pom Pull-Away, and we have only an hour to do this. So there is a guy named "it," and everybody runs across the football field a couple of times, and then everybody is on the football field, and there are about fifteen of us, and I was one of them. And they say: "Who are you?" and I say: "I am Lew Welch."

And we ran through the next time, and nobody could catch me. And we went through the next time, and still nobody could catch me. I will never forget this triumph. This was a real triumph. Finally, the entire school was "it." And I was the only guy that wasn't, and nobody knew who I was. I made it three times through all of them, and the coach came up and said: "Do you want to come out for football?" And I said: "Yeah." That's a true story. And I did it, man.

There was a very beautiful man named Robert Rideout, who was a teacher in the seventh grade, and he had a very simple thing going. He said, "If you ever like a book, you will probably like another book by the man that wrote it." He would lay books on us.

I must say this in defense of my mother. One of the best things she said to me was, "You know, all the knowledge of the world is in the library, and I will show you how to use it." And she did. She took me to the library, and we walked in, and she showed me how the card catalog worked, and she introduced me to the lady who worked there, and I spent a very beautiful summer there and was very proud of it. Like, I could really go up to the card catalog, look up books, get authors, pull the books off the shelves, and so on. It was too much, man.

DM Did you teach yourself to read, or were you taught to read?

LW No, like most of us, the real readers, it all happened accidentally. My mother was a very good reader . . . this is in defense of my mother. She was very good about that. She would always read us stories when we were very young. I started reading when I was five or six, because she sat us on her lap as she read *Dr. Dolittle,* or whatever it was, and she would move her finger over the words, and I learned accidentally how to read. No, it wasn't accidentally. Not really. It was because of her good grace. She really loved books. So all blessings to her.

I am going to mention right out in my author's preface to my new book, *Ring of Bone* (Grove Press, 1971), you know, where it says: thank you. I don't even know where he is now, but Robert Rideout was a seventh-grade teacher in El Cajon, California, and he had this little thing about how books were to be used.

I am on a pirate kick, so he gets me *Falcon of France.* Nordhoff and Hall wrote *Mutiny on the Bounty.* Hall was really a World War I pilot. Rideout had the sense to see that if the kid liked pirates, he would certainly like this. So then, bang! I go into all the World War I airplane books.

Rideout said: "Every time you read a book, write it down. Write down the author and tell whether you liked it or not." He had a five-star system. One star for bad, two, etc. You know what I did? I read 160 books in one year under Rideout. Most of them were about pirates or airplanes. He was too much.

He got me into Ernest Thompson Seton. He got me into all the Lassie books, the dog and animal bit. But Ernest Thompson Seton was a really important writer, and Nordhoff and Hall were great. And, most of all, Will James.

DM When did you start reading poetry?

LW Ha! Right then! In the middle of all this reading, I read "Trees" by Joyce Kilmer. I ran into and out of the pirate thing. I ran into and out of the Ernest Thompson Seton thing. And suddenly I got into poetry, and believe it or not, it was Joyce Kilmer's "Trees" first, and more importantly, Robert Service. No kidding. This is true, man. That son of a bitch is a terribly good poet.

I got *Rhymes of a Red Cross Man* when I was about eleven years old. And when he talks about the man on the wire—I said: *"There!"* That was the great thing that drove me to poetry. Service never cheats. And his *On the Wire,* that man is festering on the wire and people are shooting at him and it is getting hot . . . whew! I got it! I got truth! So Robert Service is a super-American poet.

DM No doubt about it. He is incredible. He is tremendous to read aloud to people.

LW Right ! When I was on my hermitage, and it really was a hermitage, we would sit and weep with bad sherry wine. Me and a bunch of bad-ass drunk Indians. And we would read a poem about a dog by Service and we would break up. It was relevant. It was truly relevant. I would like to have poetry be the kind of thing that a man can say with good friends in a mountain cabin. And Robert Service can do it.

DM How did you become interested in language? For instance, you talk about your speed, being able to move . . . when did you realize that language was a way of moving, too?

LW That's a well-put question.

When you say something right, "with your finger on the throttle and your foot upon the pedal of the clutch," you are doing something in language that becomes almost abstract to most minds, but to my mind this is the supreme act.

The difference between the ordinary kind of language that we use every day and the language that we call poetry is very slim when we have great poets working. Example. Take Burns's "Loch Lomond." You think that's language, and you can actually sing it. But you don't realize how complicatedly the man has bent language in order for it to be said that way.

I would like to be the kind of singer that is respected by his tribe in the way Bobby Burns is respected. I would much rather have that kind of a feeling from my people than anything else I can think of.

What I would really like to do . . . say, wouldn't it be wonderful to write a song or a story that anybody would say, *"That* is art," on any given evening just because he loved the way it went? And that is what I want to do. And that is what I think poetry is about. And I think at times that some of my poetry has done that.

DM Do you remember when you wrote your first poem. Can you remember what it was about?

LW "Skunk Cabbage" was my first poem.

I began to be a poet at Reed College, and one day I was walking around the pond they had there . . . a very lovely lake . . . and there is also a swamp behind it where you could get laid by your girl. I saw this thing, and it was really weird. It was a skunk cabbage. I believe this was my first poem.

1
Slowly in the swamps unfold
great yellow petals of a
savage thing, a
tropic thing—

While no stilt-legged birds watch,
no monkey screams,
those great yellow petals
unfold.

2
Rank plant.

I really thought that then. I saw that then. That is when I started to be a poet.

The way I went to Reed College is a long story. I went to the war and got through it, and that's not interesting. World War II. No, I didn't fight. It was just a big bummer. I tried very hard to fight. I wanted to be Errol Flynn. Let's get back to that later. I want to tell you how I got to Reed College, and it takes about eight hours from one point to the other. I mean, like World War II was not interesting at all. A bummer. I want to tell you what I feel about poetry. I can do it easily with a poem of mine.

I WANT THE WHOLE THING, the moment
when what we thought was rock, or
sea
became clear Mind, and

what we thought was clearest Mind really
was that glancing girl, that
Swirl of birds . . .

(all of that)

AND AT THE SAME TIME that very poem
pasted in the florist's window

(as Whalen's *I wanted to bring you this Jap Iris* was)

carefully re-typed and
put right out there on Divisadero St.

just because the florist thought it
pretty,

that it might remind of love,
that it might sell flowers . . .

The line

Tangled in Samsara!

4

LW I want to get into that now. The thing about poetry that is usually wrong is that the people who tend to be writing it are not poets. They don't know what their tribe is speaking, and they don't have anything to talk about themselves.

I met William Carlos Williams in 1950. I had graduated in June and waited all summer, with a fine redheaded girl, to meet him in September. I remember I put all my poems together, I was only about twenty-four, and added great long explanations, so I'd be ready for him.

Whalen, Snyder, and I were asked by the school—Reed was really a groovy place then—to go meet him at the airport. After all, we were the poets of Reed, and the faculty was sort of embarrassed about it all. So we got him into his hotel and rapped with him, it was like meeting a saint, a really important man, and he came on like a Middle Western hick, really, shy and everything. I always think of him as looking like President Truman.

He was so sweet and humble, and we loved him so much. He had saved our lives. And when we told him how he had truly defeated T.S. Eliot, he was really touched. That young men, poets, would come to him and say he had won the battle of his life.

We took him to our pad, where Whalen and Snyder and I lived, and we played poetry games and talked, and we gave him our stuff. And when he gave his reading at Reed, he began by saying, "It's good to be in a place where they will give a degree for a thesis on Gertrude Stein." I was so overwhelmed, after nobody wanted me to do the Stein thesis, and then my hero said that! He was the first poet I had met. He asked me to visit him in Rutherford. Again, I was overwhelmed. But I did it. I went to see him at his home maybe three or four times. I was pure mind transmission. I really became a poet only because of Williams. Williams and Gertrude Stein.

One day we were waiting for the dinner, served as "supper" in New Jersey at two in the afternoon, and Williams invited me upstairs to wash up. On the way we stopped at a three-drawer file cabinet, and he said, "That's my autobiography in there." And then he took me into a large room with a big oak table in the middle of it, and on the table was a funky old typewriter. Very neat. No clutter at all. And he said, to me, the punk, "This is where I work."

I felt like I was somebody in the baby trade, that I had come to investigate a foster father, and that he was saying: "See, I am raising it with love." I could hardly eat.

Years later he wrote to me: "I knew you were cracking up in New York, but it's like a concentration camp, one look of recognition and you too are done in. Thanks for the book. Sometimes it's a long time coming."

I had sent him *Wobbly Rock,* and he was into his fourth or fifth stroke, dying, and I wanted to thank him for what he had done for me.

Maybe five meetings altogether, but the result is total mind transmission, when the man is that great, and I hope I carry it well.

You have to know what the tribe is speaking, and you have to have something to talk about yourself. This is a two-part argument. Let's take the first part.

You have to have a sense of what the tribe is speaking. This takes ear training. You have to go out into the street and listen to the way people talk. You have to really listen to the kind of things that people say. You have to listen to the birds that are in the air, the helicopters, the big rush of jets. . . . Listen to this, you can't even talk in my living room without the din of it. You have to have your ears open. You have to have your goddamn ears open or you are not going to be a poet. Or you are not going to be a writer of any importance whatsoever.

I am sick and tired of all these punk kids trying to tell me how sad they are every time they walk through a park. Come on. Step one.

We have two things . . . you have to hear what is. You have to hear how your mother talked. You have to hear how your mother talked in a way that is so straight that it will almost kill you. Not only what she said, but how the language moved in what she said. And how the language affected the people around her. Because that is what is going to affect you. And you have to know what the people in the town talk like. How it is said. You have to know it so perfectly that you can never ever make an error. Even Hemingway made errors, and we must not, if we are poets, ever make an error. It is a very precise art and a strong and a good one. I die behind it . . . its strength and its purpose.

I had the privilege of seeing a poem of mine pasted in the No Name Bar window. I was asked by the owner of that bar to partake in a small demonstration to protest against the misuse of the beautiful area that the city of Sausalito is. It's being badly misused. You have this gorgeous beach that is nothing but asphalt and parking meters. So we had this demonstration, and it was really touching to me, and a source of great gratification, to be asked by an innkeeper in one's own village to partake in such a thing because of the fact that I am a poet. He wanted me to write a prayer and speak it. And I did. And then he published it . . . it's just a little short poem. We published it by going to the public library and for a dime apiece Xeroxed it until we got forty copies, and we gave them to the press and gave them to the people in the crowd, and they could read behind me. And then it was pasted in the window of the bar for the people on the street to see.

Sausalito Trash Prayer

Sausalito,
   Little Willow,
Perfect Beach by the last Bay in the world,
   None more beautiful,

Today we kneel at thy feet
   And curse the men who have misused you.

I think that poetry should be at least as lively as Robert Burns is. Where it can be used by the tribe in moments of need. When the chips are down, it's the turn of the New Year, and you are drunk and you can't even move, but you still sing "Auld Lang Syne."

DM I remember, back a few years ago, you were involved with trying to organize a fund to feed the poets of America. . . . You were planning to put out a magazine called *Bread* that would contain material showing how hard it is to survive economically as a poet in America. . . .

LW A big organization called Bread, Inc. All I would have needed was $10 million, and then we would be able to support all the poets that would be in America, ever. I figured $10 million would be the capital. You would have a half-million a year, 500,000 bucks, and also a hospital fund so poets could have babies and fix their wives' teeth and the other things that we need. The rest would be doled out. . . .

See, the trouble with most grants is that the grants are either for a book that is going to be written, or not written, or it's for going to Italy and doing something. Nobody just gives you bread. I don't need any grants. I know what I am going to do next year. What I need is $4,000! Like maybe I'll just sit here and spend it all on bourbon, but that's my goddamn right. If I am a poet I need bread to go, just like a car. You have to put gas in it. So that was the idea behind Bread, Inc. The fortunes of life have gone in such a way that I now have a way to get bread by myself, but it's very time-consuming and it's a big drag. But at least I have it.

DM What work do you do now to earn a living?

LW I work on the docks as a longshoreman's clerk. And I also get fees for going around and reading poetry. I ask for $500 and I get about $350. I work for as cheap as $100, if it is close, like Davis. At American River I went for $100 because it is in Sacramento. In fact, in the last two years, I have covered every part of the U. of California except UCLA.

I want poetry to be as useful as singing "The Star Spangled Banner" at a baseball game. I want it to be right in there. It is really strange to see that's possible, even in a culture as vulgar as America. It has happened. Like Phil Whalen's poem was really pasted in that florist's window. I didn't make that up. And my poem was really stuck up in a bar window.

I got two free drinks from a guy in Riverside just a few weeks ago. Before the poetry reading there, I asked the guys that were driving me from the airport to the reading to stop at a bar and we would all have a drink together. And as we had a drink, I got all excited . . . I am getting ready for the reading and I happen to mention this to a very groovy bartender why I was in town, and would he like to have a book of mine. He said: "Why sure." And I said, "You can't have it unless I can read it out loud, right here." And he got very nervous because he expected some gloomy poem . . . "I-love-the-night" bunch of bullshit to come out of me. Here it was, eleven in the morning, and who was ready for poetry? Who was ready for poetry in a bar in Riverside at 11 a.m. in the morning?

And I read *Courses* to him from start to finish, and he broke up. He thought it was the funniest thing he had ever heard. So I laid the book on him and said, "See, I work. Like Bobby Burns worked. I am trying to get the poem back into the bar." And he said, "That's a good idea. You should hear most of the shit these people talk around here!"

It could easily follow from such a position that, therefore, poetry would be quite mundane, watered down, made popular. Pop art instead of great art. Now, I think that Bobby Burns wrote as fine a set of lyrics as any poet ever wrote. Or even more heavily, probably the greatest poet that ever lived was Milarepa, the great Tibetan Buddhist. All of his teachings are in the form of songs. They are poems that he sang out loud to his students, his disciples, the people in the town.

The poetry of Homer, after all, are simply the songs of a blind old man in a time when there weren't printed books. Men would go around and tell the kings what their history was. Chaucer is the same thing. Chaucer is the man who made poetry of the streets, just as Han Shan's poetry would be scribbled on shit-house walls . . . . People found them on the rocks. Han Shan wrote them on the rocks on the mountains. People would run down to town and say: "Han Shan's written a new poem!" They would write it on the walls.

Po Chü-i, the great Chinese bard . . . his poetry was memorized by all the harlots in China and was sung by all the whores and pimps. I am not talking about writing down something. I believe if a poem is really well made, it can be strong enough to stand inside the general din of the speaking world.

We do a lot of talking, don't we? And the best talking we call poetry.

If the poem is made right, it will sit well in any room. Now, I believe this is the starkest, most unmundane standard for a poet to set for himself and his work. The opposite is . . . you take a guy like Rod McKuen, he is not a poet at all. He is not doing anything that is even interesting. Contrast him to a real poet like Bob Dylan, whose poems are in every living room.

I remember when I read my taxicab poem in a pool hall I used to play in when I was a cabdriver. I got to know these guys very well. This is a problem in America because America is such a vulgar place. I mean vulgar in the real sense, like coarse. If you are a cabdriver and you have cabdriver friends and they finally get to know and like you and then you say: "I am a poet" . . . they instantly think you are a goddamn queer. It is very hard to be a virile man going about his life when the main part of your life is being a poet. The main part of my life, the part I hold closest to my sense of self, is Lew Welch, the poet. I am also a father and a lover and a husband and a worker and a good shot or whatever it is that I think about myself, but always riding over it is: I am really Lew Welch, poet. Now you find you have to say to your cabdriving, pool-playing buddies that you are a poet, sooner or later. You have to tell them, you have to let them in on it, you have to. Otherwise, you are cheating them of your friendship. And when you do, you get this: "Mm-mm, uh-uh, oh, yeah. . . ."

Anyway, I told them at this pool game. I said, "By the way, do you know that I am a poet? If you don't mind, I would like to read you one." And I read them "After Anacreon." And they stopped chalking their cues, and they stopped playing, and they really started listening. And when I finished, they said: "Goddamn, Lewie, I don't know whether or not that is a poem, but that is the way it *is* to drive a cab."

I said, "Thanks, I am just testing it."

Now, Po Chü-i used to do that, too. He was a very great poet that used to have a peasant lady who was illiterate yet very, very smart. She was a peasant lady who ran a good garden down the road, and he would go and engage her in conversation. And then he would dump the poem on her, and if she didn't recognize that he had just said a poem, he figured that he had written it right. If she had a little "huh?" about it or something, if it seemed awkward to her or wrong, some-how ungraceful, then Po Chü-i would go back and fix it. At the same time, that very poem would have more literary references in it for the literate reader than we can imagine today. Po Chü-i is a real master at this, a super T.S. Eliot. He can put more echoes of old poems into four or five lines than any Chinese ever did before or after, and that is really something. He tested it against this lady who never read a poem in her life or wanted to. That's a standard, and that's the way I feel about that standard.

Let's get a little more technical about it. Talking about it like a poet talks to another poet.

You have a sense of language where language is held as a music, where that music is the sound of a taut soul singing. You have this kind of sense of language for some mysterious reason. It is a mystery. I don't understand it. There are people who write and sometimes make a poem. But then a weird thing happens to those of us who have this sense of language with this kind of intensity. It causes us to train ourselves as carefully as a flutist will. It is very, very close to music where you have to learn how to practice and practice. You have to learn how to shave the reed just right—you have to learn how to breathe just right. . . .

The poem should be able to be spoken so that the performance is just as much a part of it. . . . In other words, what you do when you write down a poem is that you are transcribing a voice. You are not learning how to read the poem, you are learning how to write the song. For me, poetry is the sound of a man in words. And it partakes of song, of chanting, of prayer, of all the things we do when we really intensify language.

Learning the art of poetry also becomes learning the art of hearing. Ear training and voice training, just as surely as a musician does it.

I have always respected Rexroth's opinions on these matters. I have never found him to be incorrect. He put it this way once. He said he likes translating poetry when the muse isn't with him. He was going back to the old thing . . . that the muse wasn't there. You haven't got a poem of your own, and you are getting restless. You are saying, "My God, I am a poet and I have no poem. What will I do today?" You know how awful it is? Rexroth says, "Keep your hand in by making translations." He says, "More often than not, halfway through the translating, a poem comes out." The muse . . . that crazy little chick running around and rapping at a bunch of idiots who don't under-stand what she is saying . . . and she goes over and sees you are work-ing very hard, and she says, "Sweet old Lewie," and goes over and says, "Bark," in your ear, and pretty soon, bang! you have a poem. And the translation falls by, or it comes out close enough to the guy so that you say "After Anacreon" or "After William Blake."

It's fun to translate English poets. For example, like Yeats has a poem that could be a very great poem, but he wrote it badly because he took the wrong meter. Yeats was really kind of meter-dumb. He is, I think, the greatest English-writing poet of the century, but he had a funny trick ear.

5

LW The art of poetry, in my mind, is connected with the art of music, because in my life it was. I sometimes ask myself: when did you start being a poet? I remember when I was four years old, running in to my mother: "You should have heard what Milton the gardener said," I said. "'I ain't got nothing.'" And I laughed because I thought that was the funniest thing I had ever heard. My mother had a very quick ear for language, up to a point, and she could see that that was a very unusual thing for a four-year-old boy to hear. To hear a funny word structure and to laugh at it. But my mother took it to mean that I was a natural scholar or that I knew right from wrong. I wasn't hearing "wrong," I was hearing what he said. Like, "can't hardly" always hits my ear with a very funny ring.

You see, the stuff of poetry insists that you have this kind of sense, somehow or other, and it is quite a mystery. It's just there or it isn't there. There is no way of teaching it. There is a way of honing it down, refining it, sharpening it up.

John Handy told me that after a few weeks he could play horn, alto sax; he already knew the clarinet, almost perfectly, not to his ear, but to everybody else's ear. He had to go into the hard work of it. Practicing scales over and over again. Long slow tones.

The second thing was that we had a jug, which I still have on my desk, to remind me of my sources. And on this jug is a little poem that I think was the start of it. It goes:

Do the work that's nearest
though it is dull at whiles,
helping when you meet them
lame dogs over stiles.

I found myself at twelve or thirteen reading that poem on the jug and thinking that those people needed some help. It's almost like a parody of Thelonious Monk. "Helping when you meet them" . . . what a funny meter! I'd see it every morning. The jug was on what my mother called a Welsh dresser, which is a piece of furniture that you put in the dining room and display all your pretty plates on.

DM Can you remember your first interest in music, specifically in jazz?
LW It was so early that I can't even figure it out. My mother reports once that I was about three or four and I was walking through a store in San Diego and I was singing something I had just heard on the phonograph or the radio. I had remarkable retention. And I could sing right in tune and with great pleasure.

I did play clarinet but never had the patience to learn an instrument. I've always been a very impatient person, and this business of embouchure, lingering, the little black notes, always stopped me. I started on clarinet, accordion, piano, bass, and now my music is entirely singing.

I used to call myself the best jug player in America, but I realized just yesterday that I wasn't. I was playing with an Okie chick that really knows that kind of music. Do you know Peter Coyote's old lady with a tattoo on her tit? She's the best Jew's-harp player in the whole world! God, she's good! I was playing with her, and she said, "You don't play jug, you play bottle." And it's true. Jug players play big three-quart ceramic instruments that have a tuba sound to them. But I play a glass bottle which has a high frequency and a high resonance. The best general jug, believe it or not, is a quart Coca-Cola bottle. Something about the curves in it, I guess.

I remember that the only way my mother could make me wake up happy was to put on Cootie Williams. I just loved Cootie Williams! Do you know, he played a trumpet in such a way that you could *taste* the notes. Really chewy. Chu Berry I dug. He had that bite, that mouth thing going, like Hawkins did. So it was people like Cootie Williams, Hawkins, Prez, and of course, the real capper was Charlie Parker. Goddamn! That man astounds me to this day! When I listen to his records, I still can't believe it.

DM It's sad to note that only a small percentage of Parker's total record output is available in his country.
LW Is that so? I wouldn't doubt it. America is so vulgar! Americans just can't see heroes!

I had the great privilege of hearing that man "live" every single night for nearly two years. Because I went to the trouble to go hear him. The blessing was that he was there. I was also very grateful that somehow or other my hearing and my sense of the importance of this man was such that I availed myself of the opportunity.

I was at the U. of Chicago, in '51, '52, '53, and '54, and at that time Charles was damn near dead. I really enjoy calling him *Charles* Parker. There is something about "Charlie" that doesn't fit the man. He was Charles. He was dying, and none of us realized it.

He was working in a little joint on Sixty-Third Street in Chicago, and all of his side musicians were high-school kids. Just a thrown-together band: a piano, bass, drum, and Parker. That's all. The kids would be eighteen, nineteen, twenty, maybe twenty-one . . . if they weren't old enough, they would fake their age or something. But really nowhere. I mean the kind of group you would expect to find in an after-hours joint in San Francisco. Really dedicated, really young musicians who knew who the hell Parker was. Boy, did they know! They just played their asses off.

And he would come up after a set . . . oh, I remember him so well! He always wore double-breasted brown suits—God, or a brown double-breasted gabardine coat with blue pinstripe pants and bad shoes, just terrible. The cat just didn't give a fuck how he looked, he just didn't care at all. And his horn always hanging from his neck, and he had these funny walleyes . . . the one eye was high and to the outside. . . .

He would come after a set, you know, one of those fantastic tunes [*Lew scats "Scrapple from the Apple"*], and the kids are trying to stay in there with him, and they are staying as best they can because they know who they are playing with. They know it. (I'd like to run into a couple of those kids now. I bet they are big guys now. Real heavy.) After the set was over—and here was everyone, a bunch of Okies in a Chicago bar giving you so much *crap*. No one was even listening, man . . . just nothing going on . . . there would be maybe eight people there: me and seven pimps and whores. Weird, man, because it was really a down Chicago bar scene. One of the places was called The Beehive. Charles Parker revolved around four joints within six blocks on Sixty-Third Street, which is a famous old jazz street. Apparently, he had a good contact for his heroin. That is the reason why he stayed there. Because he had a big name, Jesus, he could have made three or four thousand a week!

You know who he reminded me of? The only person I have ever met that reminded me of Charles Parker was Jack Spicer. They were the same man. They were just hell-bent on self-destruction. They were both six feet plus and heavy. They were big and strong. Jesus, Charles Parker had hands like a fucking farmer! Big hands. He had a working body, and it turned all into mind at a terrible price. They were very similar men, and they both had the same approach to their art.

Parker used to get up after a set and walk over to the piano player, and he would be so sweet . . . his horn hanging from his neck like a big necklace. He was big enough, he was really a strong man, his horn just hung and swung around. He didn't hold it like other guys do. And he leaned over and showed the kid how the chords should have gone. And the kid would sit there like: "Oh yeah, oh yeah . . . of course . . . B flat 7th . . . oh, B 9th minor . . . wow. . . . " And the next time Charles would say: "Let's do 'Salt Peanuts.'" And these tremendous tempos he would lay on these poor kids. Tremendous tempos that he would take with great ease and brilliance. . . .

The great breakthrough for me was of a structural nature. My ear began to hear things in terms of structure, not in terms of meaning. Almost as far back as I can remember, I was hearing structures. The big breakthrough came when I was freaking out as a twenty-year-old college student will freak out. I had this dear teacher who understood everything, I thought, and I had to see him.

I was really freaking out . . . I was on a $600-a-year track scholarship, wearing the saddle shoes, a fraternity boy at Stockton Junior College. And I have all that going for me . . . fraternity houses where I can't get laid . . . my head's breaking . . . and I had to talk to this man who is named James Wilson and is now a teacher at San Francisco State . . . a very dedicated teacher, one of those rare men who regards teaching as an art. He really got through to me, and I had to talk to him. I don't know what I wanted to say to him . . . you know how it is when you are that young. I go into his office, and he is not there. His desk is very littered, and there are lots of books and most of them are open, and I decide I am going to sit there and wait until he comes back, no matter how long it takes.

I picked up a book called *Three Lives* by Gertrude Stein, and I read

Melanctha, And I became a writer. It's the damnedest thing. It's like Malraux reports in *The Voices of Silence:* "We are brought to art by an artist. We are not brought to art by a natural wonder." I read *Melanctha*, and the impression was really wonderful. She is not so hard to understand. Everyone has been telling me that Gertrude Stein was "A rose is a rose is a rose. . . ."

DM You had been writing, hadn't you?

LW No, I was only twenty then. Oh, yes, I was sports editor for the paper. I did all the writing for the tribe. When they needed somebody, it was: "Lew, will you do this, Lew would you make a speech?" I always did it, but I thought of myself as a painter, a singer, and a track star. I was a voracious reader. I never read less than four books a week since I was about nine. And then in college I ran the 440 in 49.7 seconds.

Suddenly, reading *Melanctha* I felt as though I had been invited to a very distinguished party, a weekend party in the country, and at this party there were Shakespeare, Poe, Stein, Joyce, Dickens, Chaucer, all of the people that I had admired. And because of Stein's story *Melanctha*, it was like an invitation. "Why don't you come out to the country and spend a weekend with us?"

I came to that house, and I came with great humbleness. And I didn't say a word. I just listened. I listened for a long time, and it was a good long party. Now I am forty-three and I do most of the talking. After all, they are tired, but the same people are there. And that is who I am talking to, and it is wonderful to want to listen once in a while. I don't know how I see them. Do I see them as a monkey in a zoo with the visitors or what? But I must do my talking, my poetry, to them, the hosts of the party. That is my real audience.

Anyway, there was this moment in my life reading this one story, and I suddenly said: "Goddamn, writing is not only a good thing to do, it is very easy. The thing you have to do is to put your words down absolutely true like Gertrude Stein is doing here." It wasn't so much that I loved the story better than other stories or that I liked the writing more, it was a moment of revelation. A vision. The mystical part, the mystery of it, is contained in an experience like that.

That was my presence at the great garden party. I worked for them for nearly ten years to learn exactly what Gertrude Stein had going for her and why. And I still believe that Gertrude Stein is probably the best writer if you just want to take writing as a supreme exquisite art. Nobody ever did it as purely as Gertrude Stein, because everybody gets the story in the way somehow or other, or gets themselves in the way. She really went word, word, word, word, word. You know how musicians talk about Mozart? Well, that is the way Stein is as a writer, in my mind.

I know writers I prefer to read now, but I don't know of anybody who can write better than Gertrude Stein, ever. She is just a supreme master of this business of getting what is in your head out of your head and into words. Writing as opposed to storytelling. Making a *poem* instead of "making it up." Anderson I respect at the same level and Hemingway, too, but I really think that Gertrude was right, that Hemingway learned from Stein, not vice versa. She also said: "But I have a weakness for Hemingway." She saw that. She also said that, and she's right: "The first person that ever wrote an American sentence was Sherwood Anderson."

Sherwood Anderson is another very wrongly placed person in the literary fable. This man was a real giant, and you never hear anybody talking about him anymore. I think Gertrude was a little wrong about him being first, because the opening of Mark Twain's *Life on the Mississippi* has, for me, the first American sentences. One after the other. Hundreds of them, and they are all perfect and big.

DM What about Thoreau?

LW Thoreau, Melville, Hawthorne, Emerson, and Whitman . . . they are very great Americans and great writers, but they didn't write in this funny diction that has now become the major language of the Earth. But Twain did, and Stein did, and Sherwood Anderson did, and Hemingway did.

But Hemingway did it as if he had heard Sherwood Anderson and Stein do it so perfectly that he could not miss. No, he wasn't cheating any more than Shakespeare was cheating when he came onto his Elizabethan English because Marlowe and Sidney had done so much hard work that he could do it easily without thinking about it. He didn't cheat. In other words, it gave him the strength of confidence he needed in order to write it truly in the way that he spoke. I don't think Hemingway could have done it by himself. It was Stein, Twain, and

Sherwood Anderson that rapped it in his ear and gave him the freedom to work with it.

You see, Marlowe made up the line that Shakespeare was free to use. This doesn't put Hemingway down to say it, at all. It just places him in another order of creativity.

I find myself in this role. There is a lot of hard work that I don't have to do because men like William Carlos Williams did it for me. Stein did it for me. Also Hemingway did it for me, and Sherwood Anderson did it for me. I find that when I read Whitman I feel I am reading a translation. . . .

You see, you have a tree, and you have the real limbs and leaves, and always you have the sports. Now, at times these sports are the most prized. They are really beautiful. I think Robert Duncan's work is very beautiful. But it is utterly useless and will not have any heirs. And it will not go anywhere, and it came from part of the trunk that I don't understand—but I respect it. It's really a strong piece of the tree. But it is a sport. It is a sucker that comes off the side. I don't know or care where it comes from.

T.S. Eliot would be in the same class. He had nothing to do with English literature, at all. He is a sport off the side of it. While T.S. Eliot is fumbling around with his imitations of seventeenth-century sermons, the real work is being done by Hart Crane, William Carlos Williams, Fitzgerald, e.e. cummings, Gertrude Stein, Hemingway. Emily Dickinson is right there in the heartwood of the tree; so are Rexroth and Patchen and Miller. But not Pound and certainly not Eliot.

The thing about the sucker, the sport, was that Eliot captured the imagination of so many people and made so many people look away from the real tree for so long. Eliot didn't say one thing pertinent to the twentieth century. He simply is a recording of the best of the seventeenth-century sermon writers. Where the hell is the twentieth century? His language is an absolute failure. Pound's language is even worse. I love Pound, but. . . .

Those who seek to find poetry in the library, as Duncan and Eliot do, are ultimately doomed to failure. Duncan's language at a cocktail party is very lively. He is wonderful, but why the hell can't he get it into his poetry? He doesn't get it in there, and therefore his poetry is dead.

Robin Blaser suffers from the same thing. Robin Blaser is one of the most erudite, witty, charming, good men that I have ever known, and I can't understand why he uses poetry like some kind of shield between himself and reality. He uses it like I use chess in my life. I play chess as well as Robin writes poetry. He writes exquisite things that don't matter at all. There is no matter in them.

I find myself very uncomfortable talking against Duncan because I don't want to talk against Duncan, you know what I mean? But it evolves into an example, because he is so strong. He is so strong in doing whatever he is doing. But whatever he is doing does not, finally, matter.

6

LW Let's get to the mystery. As I see it, it is like this. A vision is what you see with the mind's eye; which is to say, a vision is what you see. Of course, we see everything with the mind's eye, don't we? And the word "seer" is simply see-er. A person who sees.

We talked about how there are people who have an absurdly tense understanding of the way that language moves, and we call them poets. But then there are some people who have that gift and don't have anything to say. Like, W.H. Auden would be one. He is just impeccable in his ability to handle word problems, yet he hasn't ever said one interesting thing to us, nor has Eliot, where William Blake really did.

Now a vision is what you see with the mind's eye; which is to say, a vision is what you see. A seer is a man who can see things that others cannot see. He is Prometheus, a man who goes into the void, and brings back something and shows it to you, so that that kind of void is forever illuminated. After he has done that, anybody can look into that void, and they can see it because the man brought it back. He illuminates something that anyone *could* see, but they don't see it. He does it some way. He paints it, he dances it, he writes it down.

Blake put it his way: "I do not distrust my corporal or vegetative eye any more than I would distrust a window for its sight. I look through it, not with it." That is the source of vision. That is a man who *sees*. A vision is what you see with the mind's eye; which is to say, a vision is what you see.

In my life I have never found a need to wonder about whether or not there is a God, let alone believe in it. The whole idea of another power has always seemed to me the most outrageously unnecessary and dangerous human idea that ever was. Yet I have always worshipped this planet, which is, of course, another power.

There is something that is not us, right? Now for me, it is this earth that I stand on, these trees, this sweet air, the lovely water I drink, the fish that swim in it . . . all of this is a source of endless wonder. But it is the see-er in us who, as Stein put it, can "know themselves knowing it." We are the poets. When I was six years old, I used to take my bicycle to the ocean because my household was filled with very nervous women and I had to get out of there and my friends were nowhere, just kick-the-can bullshit friends . . . so I would go to the ocean and sit on an ocean rock and sit for hours and get all the sound of that ocean and pick those mussels and eat them raw—knowing that they are going to "poison you . . . impossible to eat them, you better not eat them . . . "—fuck it! And I taught myself how to swim in it and rub sand on my arms, and I figured out how to catch minnows with a little orange-juice strainer, which I did because I was that patient. I didn't get very many, but I got them. And I saw an octopus as big as a coffee cup, a real octopus, and I got him and I put him in the tub and I looked at him and I said: "Shit, I am not going to take you home, baby." And I put him back, but I got him. That was my God, and still is my God, and I really deeply believe that if it can be that simple a God for everybody, then all the troubles we have would go away.

When you start talking to me about trinities and Christs and virgin births and saints and Buddhas, like, forget it, man. That's all words. That's all shit, shit. That's trash. That's mind trash. Because it is right there under your feet, see? And it is not only your feet and your eyes that let you "know yourself knowing it." It's God.

Those are visions. They are things that you can see. You can see them. They are not special states of mind, although when I see them at times, the ecstasies get to the point that it is physically painful. I actually writhe like I am in a fit and I weep and I bellow. And that is the source of my poems. And I don't write from any other source, because the rest of it is just shit, trash. Mind trash.

You read poems by people who are always crying about how their girl left them or some kind of crap. I got a poem the other day from a student. A very nice poem about the moon. He had some good things in it. It looked like he really looked at it a little. A little bit. Then he looked inside his own squirmy gut and he said: "Oh, it is sad!" He puts it in Spanish that the moon is sad. What a goddamn cop-out lie! The moon is not sad! When I look at that moon, I get so high, I blow my mind. Now don't tell me the moon is sad, because it isn't sad. Even Shelley wasn't that bad!

These ecstasies that I suffer have been suffered by every real poet that ever lived. And if you can't know them, you probably don't have a source strong enough to write a poem from.

You know my poem called "Ring of Bone"? I will let you in on a little secret. Here's what really happened.

I had to leave Lenore Kandel because she was corny, and our life was not getting on together because of that. I have an exquisite kind of fineness to my life that she could not meet. She could not meet the other stuff that I needed desperately with perfection. She was a perfect helpmate. A goddamn good wife. But I didn't need it. I needed some other goddamn thing.

By this time I am thirty-eight, I am no punk, anymore. It is really hurting. And how can you give up the most beautiful girl in San Francisco, who you need? But I had to go. I had to split, and I remember the split. It was really wild. She is weeping at the top of the stairs, and I am weeping at the bottom of the stairs, and like there are no words left. And we are both poets. And she knows I've got to leave, yet she really doesn't know why.

Ferlinghetti loaned me his cabin in Big Sur. I went to him and said: "Look, man, it's really freak-city time. Can I borrow your cabin?"

He's beautiful that way. Sure. And bang, here's the key. OK, so down I go. I take enough groceries to last about two weeks and a typewriter and a lot of paper, and I just thrashed around in it. And one day, I got it.

I woke up after a wine drunk—I had brought a lot of red wine with me—I woke up about three in the afternoon and I saw it.

I saw myself
a ring of bone
in the clear stream
of all of it

and vowed
always to be open to it
that all of it
might flow through

and then heard
"ring of bone" where
ring is what a

bell does

And in the middle of it I got an erection and put my dick out the open
window, and I came without even touching it. And that's the kind of
ecstasies I am talking about. It's like that old joke, you know, a girl has
a cunt that is too big, and you say it is like sticking your prick out the
window and fucking the world. That was it. I stuck my prick out and
I fucked the world.

And I freaked out. And I knew I am not kidding now. I didn't make
this up. I had to recover that experience, and I made this neat tight
little poem, out of it. If I didn't have the chops now after twenty years
of hard work getting the chops down, I couldn't capture it. People
read that poem, and they see and sense a strange power. And they
can't figure out why.

Now you heard the vision, and now you have heard the poem. Now
these two things are terribly important. Without the practice I could
not have captured it. I would have said: "I sure had a bad freak-out in
Big Sur, David. I think I had better go to Langley Porter."

But if you are a poet, you can snag it, put it down, and then you
look at the poem, and then you look at your wet prick, and you look
at the earth you just came on, and you say, "Goddamn, it is all right,
isn't it?" You get a big up out of it. And I am *that* crazy.

It's the vision brought back. And it is not the vision, either. The
poem is not the vision. The vision is the source of the poem. The

poem is the chops, but the real chops are being able to go across that river and come back with something that is readable.

The ecstasies get to a point where they are usually unbearable. That one was on wine and despair. *Wobbly Rock* was done on despair. Period. And rain. We are in a drug era now. Everybody asks you, "Like, what did you do it on?" Well, you do it cold sometimes. When ecstasies hit me, they hit me so hard sometimes that I wouldn't even entertain the idea of taking so much as a drink of wine, if it would mess with it.

The danger is that you begin to like them very much. The ecstasies. You require that every day you have one. This is, of course, a drag. No one could survive it. It is really debilitating. As Saints Teresa and John pointed out, as Huang Po does. All the big mystics have pointed out that ecstasies are dangerous. They really are. I mean they are all right, and it is certainly wrong to deny yourself ecstasies if you happen to be available to them. Apparently, some people are not available to ecstasies. . . .

Philip Whalen (1999)

© Nancy Victoria Davis

June 26, 1999: Reconnoiter with the interview crew, Marina and Jim. We meet at the Muni Metro Castro Street station the day before the Gay Pride Festival. The neighborhood is already pulsing with pre-party partying. We jump-start with coffee at a Castro rocket-launcher coffee shop and then amble to the Hartford Zen Center, where retired abbot Philip Whalen lives. Knock on the door, punch some buttons, wait and mutter, and finally Whalen opens the door to let us in. We ask, to break the ice, "How are you?" He answers: "Fat and out of breath." Barefoot, in T-shirt and loose-fitting pants, Whalen escorts us into a dining room where we set up the tape recorder. We find our places around the table and begin. Whalen and I share a history and disparate community. No matter how fractured and contentious it might appear, there was always a weird undertow of unity and regard. (Because of Philip's health problems in the months that followed, we were unable to ask his help in correcting the text of the interview.) —DM

Philip Whalen (**PW**)
David Meltzer (**DM**)

PW I was born to poor but honest parents in Portland, Oregon, on October 20, 1923, which was my mother's birthday. At that time and for many years thereafter, my father worked for the Honeyman Hardware Co. in Portland as a traveling salesman. Shortly after I was born—I was maybe two or so—we moved up to Centralia, Washington, for about two years. From there we were transferred to The Dalles, on the south bank of the Columbia River about eighty miles from Portland. That's where I grew up more or less and went to grade school and high school.

After my mother died, my father and I moved to Portland, where I lived with him for a year or so, and then in 1943 I got drafted into the U.S. Army. They were collecting people to be air corps ground crew folks, so I was lucky I got selected into that group. I couldn't do very active things because my eyesight was very bad—and it hasn't improved. I had basic training at Keesler in Biloxi, Mississippi. We moved from there after about two months up to Sioux Falls, South Dakota, where I went to radio school. I learned Morse code and learned about doing simple repairs on radio equipment. I was kept on to be trained as an instructor, and later on I worked at different bases as either a radio mechanic or as a radio mechanic instructor. I got to do some flying when I was stationed at Yuma. God, flying over the desert was beautiful! Over the desert and over the Salton Sea and over the Gulf of California and around all the mountains—it was very beautiful.

I was discharged in 1946 and came back to Portland. I wanted to come down here to go to the University of California and study Chinese. But that didn't work out because I squandered all the money I had, somehow. The next thing to do was to apply to Reed College, so I could get taken care of on the GI Bill. I went there for five years. I was thrown out of college for about one year because I wasn't doing enough scholarly work and wasn't attending enough classes, but I got readmitted and graduated in 1951. I should have graduated at the same time as Lew Welch in 1950, but I missed that boat. Gary Snyder and I were in the same class in '51.

That summer I moved down to San Francisco. Things didn't work out terribly well. So I went down to L.A., where a friend of mine was living out at Venice Beach. He and I both got jobs at North American

Aircraft. I wasn't there too long, probably less than a year, I dare say, because it was too busy. I came back up here and floundered around trying to find work and so on—and getting some, a little bit, but not very much. It was very hard—I was "overqualified," they kept saying—and that was very discouraging. Anyway, at some point I went back down again and wandered around, and then I came back up here and joined Gary, who had found an apartment on Telegraph Hill that he could share with me.

Gary had started at Cal as a special student in Chinese and Japanese because he wanted to find what the Zen business was about from the inside and that took a lot of language. Anyhow, there were various moves and switches and whatnot. . . . In 1955 Ginsberg and Kerouac showed up, and we began "the revolution"—which had been started by Robert Duncan and Jack Spicer and everybody earlier on. We were all carpetbaggers, which did not set well with the locals.

I was living in Berkeley, and through a friend I got a job at the Poultry Husbandry Department, where I washed laboratory glassware. I was able to live and eat food and so forth. And every once in a while they gave me a free dead chicken to take home or a laboratory creature that had lost its life. I also got many eggs. Very cheap. I was eating, which was very interesting. And presently Allen got his job with the Military Sea Transport Service and was off on a trip to Alaska. He gave me the cottage on Milvia Street, where he had been living. I lived there for several years and worked for the university.

And then my friend, Richard Anderson, who had been practicing law in Newport, Oregon, was appointed to the circuit court bench by the new governor, the first Democratic governor of Oregon in a long time. He was going to have to run for the office in the next election, the following year, and he asked me to come up and help with all that and do publicity and paperwork and travel around and meet all the local yokels and talk to them because they wanted to look at him. Apparently, he impressed people, because he won the election. That was about 1957.

Around 1959 LeRoi Jones/Amiri Baraka wanted me to give him a book manuscript. I sent him the book that became *Like I Say*. And at the same time Dave Haselwood of Auerhahn printed up a broadside poem of mine—"Self-Portrait from Another Direction"—that later appeared in *Memoirs of an Interglacial Age,* so I could go on a trip with Michael McClure to New York to do readings at colleges. Everything sort of went billowing up after that, a reckless and lovely bohemian life. Sometimes it was nice and sometimes it was a little too rackety— I was older than most people.

Anyhow, I got into the business of having readings arranged for me at different colleges. They would buy me an airplane ticket, and I would go out and see them and talk to them and read poems and talk to students and do a seminar on poetry. I was making money for the first time. That was a grand period. Meanwhile, Gary heard from a friend of his who still lived in Kyoto that the Kyoto YMCA school wanted teachers, and would I be interested in going over and teaching there for a year. So I said, fine, because I was totally broke here in San Francisco. It all got magically put into place. First of all, I did a short movie of myself reading poetry and walking around in the Palace of the Legion of Honor and so on. Richard Moore of KQED asked me to participate in this shoot. Gary and I, and Duncan, I guess, all did a bit part in this series about American poetry. That was right when I needed money, and I got $300. Then Allen promoted me into a grant from the American Academy, which came up with $1,000. So I was able to move by boat to Japan to stay with Gary temporarily 'til some other friends helped me find a place to live.

I liked the Japanese aesthetic very much. I enjoyed living in Japanese houses in Japan and walking around through Kyoto and through the old temples and shrines and things. I miss it. It's really a wonderful place. I think I like it better than Paris. Maybe Rome has a lot of stuff that I would still like to poke at and look at. Still, as a living continuous tradition, since the year 700 and something, there it is. It's wonderful to be there and read *The Tale of Genji* on the spot, as it were. Lady Murasaki had a real eye for the look of things and for weather. Her accounts of what it smelled like and felt like and looked like were really marvelous.

DM In interviewing Gary we talked about the experiences in Japan, especially the hard work of Zen. I asked him what were some of the things he found so useful. And he said, "One of the great lessons was manners." There's so much stress on formality, but there's a comfort there, too.

PW Yeah. Oh yeah. Japanese buildings feel good and smell good, and then out of doors there are other smells in the morning. People are grilling dried fish, and there are black fumes floating around, or they're setting fire to one of those big briquette things that they put inside of the heating hibachi. They have to set fire to it out of doors because the starter has all sorts of vile chemical mess hooked up to it.

DM Were you studying Zen there as well?

PW No. I was reading and I was visiting all those lovely temples. I started sitting seriously when I returned there in '68. Doing it every morning in my place, no matter what. As Issan used to say, "No matter how late, no matter how drunk, get up and do it."

DM What time in the morning?

PW Oh, it wasn't very early. It was probably about seven or so. I would get up and sit, and then I would take a trolley over to this coffee shop that I like, which is across the street from Kyoto University, and eat croissants and drink coffee, the delicious coffee that they make in small quantities. I was doing a lot of writing. I would write every morning. I would go out, after I had been sitting, I would go out to the coffee shop, take a blank notebook with me. What I was doing at that time was writing *Imaginary Speeches for a Brazen Head*.

It was great: I had a job, and I was living in an elegant house in Kyoto, which is a gorgeous city. If you have to have a city, that one's a real success, I think. I was there in something like '66 until about the end of '67, and I came back here to work on the publication of *On Bear's Head* because I didn't want to do it by overseas mail. That was a mistake, because it wasn't very long before I was homesick for Kyoto. I had to race around and sell things, to raise money to go back and get my job back in Kyoto. It all came together. I went back there in 1969 and stayed until 1971. That was just wonderful because I could spend a lot of time writing, looking at things, and writing, reading a lot, and writing. At some point, not too late after I got back in '71, I had a poetry manuscript and sent it to Donald Allen. One of the books that Don Allen had taken came out before I left, and maybe even two—I don't remember.

John Martin, from Black Sparrow Press, wrote to me and asked if I had any poetry to print. I wrote back and said, "No, but I have this prose manuscript that I've been lugging around for a while." And he said, "Well, let's see it." And so I sent him *Imaginary Speeches for a Brazen Head.*

In the beginning of 1971 the school that I was working at decided that all the people who were teaching there had to have a master's in teaching English as a Foreign Language because these two bright guys came over from America and sold the school on that idea. About thirty-five of us were left out on a limb. I was going to have make arrangements to come back to the United States, and my friend Margot Patterson Doss found out through a friend of hers that I could rent a tiny apartment in the basement of her house in Bolinas. I removed from Kyoto to Bolinas in one fell swoop.

The main floor of the house was rented by Joe Brainard. He was doing a huge quantity of work, and everybody else was in town and writing everything. Lewis MacAdams and Tom Clark and Joanne Kyger were there, and God knows who all—a huge crowd of old-time poets. It was very comfortable and pleasant.

At some point, Donald Allen told me that he had a space in his house to rent. It was a much more private and elegant arrangement than living in that basement. I moved up there on the hill. Up on the mesa.

On New Year's Day of 1972, Richard Baker came out—he and his wife Virginia were visiting Mike Dickson, who lived right near to Don—to say happy New Year, and he asked me, "What are you doing?" I said, "Well, I'm thinking about moving to the city for more peace and quiet because up here there's a party about once every five minutes. People get mad if you don't come, and people get mad if you do. It's not interesting." He said, "Well, why don't you come look at the Zen Center and see if you could live there." "Oh, all right, when can I come?" And he said, "Oh, any time. Call up Yvonne Rand and tell her you want come." She was one of the big bosses. He had only recently moved into that building up there on Page Street. I went up there and looked around, and it looked very nice. He gave me a conducted tour and talked. And finally I said, "Well, when can I move in?" And he said, "Any time." I say, "OK, I'll come by next week."

I found out a couple years later that the usual way anybody came to live in that building was that they came to San Francisco and got a job; they hired an apartment in the neighborhood there around Page Street and lived there; and then went every minute they could spare to the Zen Center to do meditation and ceremonies. You had to do that at least for a year or so before you could be on the list of candidates to live in the building.

I was terribly embarrassed when I found out Richard had railroaded me in there. It was even more embarrassing when I asked him in the fall if I could go to Tassajara because I wanted to see what the monastery was like, because I had already asked to be made into a monk. He said, "There's a truck leaving on Saturday morning." And I said, "That's fine." Yvonne helped me pack up all my books and put them in the basement of that house that's right next door. Was it 310? Where the big rubber tree was? Early the next morning I was off to the monastery. Richard came down later and asked how I was doing. I said, "I felt overtrained. It's too much like the army." But at the end of that practice period, the fall of 1972, I came back up to San Francisco for the ordination ceremony and was here for about a year acting as Richard's attendant. At the end of the following year, I went back for another training period at Tassajara. It was awful.

DM Why was it awful?

PW You know, I was bucking the system. I was quarreling with the system, which is ridiculous. It wasn't until the next year that I gave up and said, all right, if you just follow the schedule and shut up, everything is going to be fine. After that, I did about seven more practice periods in just one summer. Ten practice periods in the summer.

DM What was the practice period?

PW Three months.

DM What does it encompass?

PW Hours of meditation, a little bit of studying time and working time. Mainly, I took care of the library.

DM That's appropriate.

PW In 1973 I was ordained. I guess it was '74 when I first went down there as a monk; 1975 was the year that I was head monk in the autumn practice period. That was a marvelous experience. And, I don't know, I finally got used to it.

DM What are the functions of the head monk?

PW Oh, you have to do all of the ceremonies every day.

DM How many are there?

PW First of all, you preside over the morning meditations—there are three of them. And then there's the incense offerings service that follows. You have to lead that. At some point you start lecturing—hardy-har. At the end of that practice period when you're *choshu,* you have to sit up in front and face all the people who are the former choshus and answer whatever questions they ask. Then all the people who have participated in the practice period also get to ask you a question that you are obliged to answer in some way or another. You get two tries to each question. It's very hard.

DM Is there a possibility of striking out?

PW Oh yeah, I struck out. A guy called Bob asked me some question or another, and I had no idea what the answer was or if there was an answer. I didn't know. I think that in a regular place they would have thrown your ass out.

That's what I was doing between 1972 and 1984. Some of that time, of course, I was going out to do college readings, fussing over having things published, having to do proofreading. And it was satisfactory. Then in 1983, there was the grand hoopla at the Zen Center when Roshi Baker was made to resign. Early the next year, he had arranged for a zendo in Santa Fe. He asked me if I would go down and look at it and see if I could help out. I went down and looked at it and said, "It's just fine. I'll come down." That year I was supposed to go to Naropa Institute to teach. I had to pack up my apartment and store stuff and sail off to first to Colorado and then to New Mexico. That was in 1984. I stayed there until 1987, continuing to study the Zen business with Richard and going through the transmission ceremony with him, which gave me authority to teach.

DM What is the transmission ceremony?

PW The Zen lineage—the succession of patriarchs—is passed on from teacher to student. They say "from warm hand to warm hand," which means from the eldest to the eldest, without interruption. In other words, the teaching, the understanding, the Buddhist understanding of the teacher is passed on to the student, and the student understands that that's what's happening. It's a private ceremony, very elegant, very elaborate; it takes hours and hours, and endless quantities of equipment. It's a huge affair that goes on a week. Culminating in all-night, all-day, all-night sessions and ceremonies, after which you are added to the list of patriarchs of the Zen school. Then I came back here for a year, during which time I did a lot of traveling back around the United States and went to Europe to help Roshi do a *sesshin* in Germany. I got to see Paris on that trip, briefly. It was wonderful.

DM You'd never been to Europe before?

PW It was 1980 or a little later that I got invited to an international poetry festival in Rome. That was my first trip to Europe. I really dug it. I really dug Rome because I was hung up on it when I was a kid and studied Latin assiduously. In 1989 we went to a Buddhist Center outside of Undernach on the Rhine, after which we went and visited Heidelberg, where Roshi had some friends.

In '92 I came down with endocarditis—an infection inside the heart. There were all sorts of staph bugs in there tromping on the heart valves. Sandor Burstein bumped me into the hospital at Mount Zion and dropped in gallons of all sorts of exotic antibiotics and pills. It was terrible because it gave me nightmares. You can't imagine what kind of exquisite, horrible nightmares you can get from antibiotics. That was pretty nasty.

After I got out of the hospital, Sandor was worrying about me and fussing and telling me, "You're still in heart failure." I thought, "This is wonderful. It's like being in Peoria." [*laughter*] I had to take pills and things.

It was the next year that he said—he and several other people said—that I had to have a heart-valve replacement operation. I said, "Come on, this is too fancy." Rick Levine introduced me to a celebrated heart specialist who was then at the county hospital, a guy who had been President Eisenhower's cardiologist. He looked at me and looked at the records and said, "If you don't do an operation, you're going to have liver failure, kidney failure, heart failure, and everything is going to hell. You'll be in bad trouble." So I went in for the surgery.

You know they kill you? First of all, they refrigerate you. You don't know about that, because they anesthetize you; they refrigerate you and bring your body temperature down to some wonderfully low level where the life functions decline and fall; everything comes nearly to an end, and then they get out their electricity and pop you with that and hook you up to a heart-lung machine. You don't breathe anymore. Your heart isn't leaking anymore.

DM The machine is breathing for you.

PW The machine is doing everything, and you're deader than a doornail. It's very interesting. I didn't know anything about it. The next thing I knew—well, first I was being anesthetized, which was a very good job. The next thing was that I was waking up in the intensive-care unit with people pulling tubes and whatnot out of my person. I have arthritis in my knees. I have the rotary cuff trips going in my shoulders. I can't see anything. So it's all wonderful. I suppose it would be gracious of me to mention along the way that the Merritt Academy gave me an award for inventive modern poetry, or something. It's named after some guy; I forget what it is called. I'm sure it was engineered by Allen, anyway. Books are published; things are published. I haven't been able to read anything for years now.

DM Can you write?

PW No.

DM That's a difficult turn, isn't it, for a poet and a person of letters?

PW It's very frustrating.

DM I've heard that Leslie Scalapino, who wrote the introduction for your new collection, *Overtime*, comes and reads to you. Do you have other people, besides Leslie, who—

PW Sporadically, yes. Lou Hartman, from the Zen Center, comes on Wednesdays and reads to me out of Buddhist texts.

DM What have you heard lately?

PW Well, most recently it was a book that Leslie discovered. Lou read it to me, most of it, anyway. It's all about Dogen's poetry. Lou also read to me the entire volume called *Crooked Cucumber*, which is the life and times of Suzuki Roshi. It was very funny and very interesting. All the trials and tribulations that that fellow went through to get to where he was.

DM Is most of what you listen to Buddhist material?

PW Yeah. It's what I want to know about. Of course, Leslie reads me her own writing, which I admire immensely, and Michael McClure reads stuff of his to me, the new stuff. Every other week. whenever it's possible, Michael and Diane di Prima and I have lunch together, and yak and carry on at the sushi restaurant on Church Street.

DM *Overtime* has just been published by Viking Penguin. . . .

PW Yes, that was done with an immense amount of work by Michael Rothenberg. We went through all of my books page by page, practically, to pick out what would be a manuscript for Penguin and decided what we could use and what we could throw away. And then we went through it again to throw away some more, because they were only going to give us 300 pages plus Leslie's essay, which is remarkable.

DM Are you through with poetry?

PW Not really, no. I hear things and see things and think about things.

DM You relationship to music is interesting. In fact, I think that of all the poets we've interviewed, you're probably the only one who's had any kind of background in music or is familiar with the language.

PW Yeah, that's sort of busted, because I can't remember anything, and I can't read music now. I was always reading music and playing, and I certainly miss doing that. I miss having a radio that will pick up the classical music station. I have three radios. One is a Sony with two speakers in it, and I have another little one that has a CD player in it, and I have a Sony Walkman. Somehow or another, if you hold the Sony Walkman in the right position, you can pick up that classical music station when none of the other equipment will.

DM If I can change channels for a moment, how did you first receive poetry? When did you get it?

PW Oh, when I was in high school. I was fifteen or so, and I wrote out four or five lines and handed it to the girl ahead of me. She thought it was wonderful—that was very encouraging. And there was a lively teacher who gave me a lot of encouragement in his creative writing class. So I kept reading more and more in an anthology of American poetry. There was one of Pound's cantos, which I thought was terrific. And e.e. cummings was very funny. I realized that poetry didn't have to be like Edgar Allan Poe. I got into the idea of trying to do experiments, trying to write as freely as possible. . . . The next really encouraging thing happened when I was in college, after I got out of the army. William Carlos Williams came up to read for a week, and we got to hang out with him and talk with him and hear him read.

DM How was his health then?

PW He had had the first couple of strokes, but he was able to get around pretty good, and he had a lot of energy at that time. When I saw him, maybe five years later, at the University of Washington, I was up there on my way up to Lookout Mountain and went to the university to hear him read, and then I talked to him after the reading. He was really sort of gimpy by that time, slurring, and one of his hands was sort of bent.

DM Did Williams give you a kind of permission, as it were, as a poet?

PW Well, just that. He looked at our stuff; all the students who were interested in writing came to hang out with him. He would put in time reading your stuff and marking it up and making comments on it and so on, which was very useful. The thing was, he accepted us in a way as writers. That was permission, I guess.

What was important to me at that time was the *Paterson* material that was coming out. I think I got the first volume of it before I got out of the army. I took the rest as it came along. I think that *Paterson* III had come out by the time he was up there. It was very exciting to talk to him about some of it, especially one point about some punctuation. He bestowed a semicolon on the text, which was very nice. I don't know whether it survived into the later copies of the poem.

DM I can see *Paterson* in relationship to your work with its streams and strands of heard language and written language and also this notion of the concreteness as the source of this mystery.

PW "No ideas but in things." The trouble is, I no longer believe in concreteness. I think that everything is fluid. Maybe that has a lot to do with where my head is at now. I'm very embarrassed when people don't know I'm blind, and they want me to come and read to them in various places in various venues, and I have to tell them I can't do it. Although I would like to.

DM For the record, you were a participant in the famous Six Gallery reading and also had a friendship with Kerouac. I wonder if you could speak to the reading event and the friendship with Kerouac.

PW Well, that's hard because Kerouac was such a difficult character. Sometimes he was very open and funny and telling stories, and other times he would just be kvetching and cranky and fussing about various people and things and so on, and moaning about how nobody loved his poetry or his books, and he was unhappy. I tried to cheer him up once in a while, but I was not very successful at it. I think that Gary and I were strange creatures that he had never seen the like of before in his part of the world. These people who spent a lot of time in the woods or outdoors caught his attention. He went out and got a job as a lookout one year. We were sort of responsible for that. He did a lot of writing, I guess, up on the lookout, and he wrote me into several books, which is embarrassing. But it's all right because he always was very gentle about what he said and did. I never really could pick up on his poetry very well, somehow, and I don't know why. But the prose books are marvelous. And he was very religious. You know, he did that funny book called *Some of the Dharma* and *The Scripture of the Golden Eternity*, but he never stopped being a Catholic. I never supposed that he became a Buddhist, but he was certainly interested in the teaching, and I think especially in the language of the translators. He had quite a lot of insight into Buddhist writings, actually. I don't know how it was he could set all his favorite saints off in one corner and really plug into all of this Buddhist stuff that he did.

DM Maybe as a Catholic, as a sort of mystic Catholic, he could see the hierarchies and structures as similar yet removed.

PW Yeah, I think you're right. He had all these favorite things about Catholicism that he enjoyed, particularly various saints and—what's her name?—the one who was called the Lily Flower of Jesus? She was one of his favorite persons. Sometimes he would draw pictures of Jesus in various ways and sometimes of the Virgin. He never talked very much about her. He had this wonderful relationship with his mother. Which people seem to have misconstrued or misunderstood. His mother was this wonderfully lively Canadian, and she was a great cook and a great storyteller. He says that's where he learned to tell stories. She was a bouncy, lively lady, and she was very devout. She wore little religious medals pinned to the straps of her slip, and so on. He was much attached to his father, who apparently was not a very nice man. In many ways, perhaps, when he was into his curmudgeon mode, he was probably being his father. But his mother would tell stories, and he would say, "Well, Ma, Phil and I are going to San Francisco." And she'd say, "Oh, Jackie, why don't you stay home? I will cook dinner for you." "Ahh, Ma." And so on. So we would go off into the wild sweet bop neon American night, run around North Beach, and hang out in Chinatown.

We'd be out running around, and he'd be busy asking me did I see this or that, and he'd be writing in his notebook. He was very perceptive. He saw lots of things. His eyes were real good, which mine are not. He told me he was out walking with Williams in Rutherford, and Williams pointed out to him that there was moss growing on the underside of the railroad tracks. He thought that was kind of wonderful.

Wherever he went he was always writing back to his mother and telegraphing for money. She was always bringing him back from wherever he was. And he appreciated it. When he was able to take care of her, he did. He bought that little house in Northport to take care of her, and she didn't like it. So they went down to North Carolina for a while and then to Florida, and then back to someplace, maybe back to New England, and then back to Florida again. I guess it was maybe when he got back to New England that he married Stella Sampas.

I didn't see much of him after 1960. I think that was the last time he was out here, and he wrote *Big Sur.* It was very funny. We were supposed to go on this great expedition with Lew Welch and Lily Carr and everybody. We were all supposed to drive down to meet Henry Miller at Big Sur in some such place, and have dinner with Emil White. It kept getting later and later and later, and there was more and more wine, and more and more grass, and more and more everything. God knows what time it was when we left, and we arrived down there many hours after we should have. So we never met Henry Miller or Emil White or anybody. It was very embarrassing. But we did stay at what was then Larry Ferlinghetti's cabin, which was a very rough piece of carpentry. Big doors that could open out into the deck on the outside—it was very pleasant. It was by a creek in Bixby Canyon. Later, he built it into a real house. One time, Allen Ginsberg, his father and stepmother, and I, went down there and stayed for a weekend. Thinking about Jack hearing the ocean and being scared. Golly, he sort of went to pieces there, too.

DM Do you want to talk about Lew Welch?

PW Yeah, all right. I first met him in the Reed College coffee shop. I think it was 1947, spring. I was sitting with somebody or another, and in the next booth there was this guy spouting off all sorts of wonderful nonsense. I kept listening to it. I heard him say, "Red glass birds! In brass dome!" I said, "Wait a minute!" I got up and went over to the next booth where this redheaded guy was, talking to people. I said, "What was all that about red glass birds?" "Oh," he says, "no, no." It was a song that he had been working on that had to do about how "She hollered and roared and tore all of her hair. And I carved my initials on her thin breast bone." "Thin breast bone" is what I heard as "bright brass dome" or something like that. We continued talking, and I told him, "You ought to write things down, for God's sake." He said, "Well, that's no good." We went on from there talking about Gertrude Stein and about Williams and all sorts of things. He was very funny. He was like Jack in that he was sort of bipolar. He would be fine sometimes, and other times he was down. You knew him well enough to know when he was down.

DM Inconsolable.

PW Yeah. It was very funny. We would go to the mail room on the main floor of Elliot Hall at Reed College, where the student mail came in. I wouldn't have any letters, but he would come out with a package. I said, "What d'ya got there?" And he said, "I got another goddamned sports coat. My mother goes out and spends $200 on this sports coat, which I don't need, and I do need the $200. Why don't she send me the money?!"

It was just terrible. He'd grouse around about how he was broke and was having a hard time, and then, you know, presently, a couple of hours later he'd be sparkling all over everything and having a grand time. He had had this marvelous life in California but was always his mother's child.

Dorothy was a funny lady; she was very talkative and lively, bustling around. When Lew went to college up in Portland after having been down in Stockton, where he knew Brubeck and Desmond and all those people and sang with them, his mother was inspired to return to college and complete her education. And what does she do? She gets a degree in home economics or something, over at the University of Utah. And she parlays that into a fantastic job working in a lunatic asylum—or, no, it was a home for bent babies or something like that. The state paid her immense sums of money to do the cooking or arrange the cooking or something. She was happy and making lots of money.

Lewie would fuss because he said she would go down to Macy's and buy some "goddamned porcelain shepherdess." She would take it home, all wrapped up pretty in a box, and then she would put the box, with the shepherdess in it, up in the closet. Never bothered to unwrap it. "Goddamn it! She has all that money!" Lew was absolutely tortured by the fact that his mother, who was born rich and had her money removed from her variously by certain nefarious husbands and so on, even then made a big comeback on her own as a successful home economics lady.

The two of them together in one room was something else because they were both talking at once. He'd be mooching around town here, driving a cab or not, and going broke and whatnot, and finally he would say, "Goddamn it! I guess I'll have to call up mother and go and see her!" He would leave on the appointed day and come back at the appointed time with $100 and all wore out and crazy. Of course, he would drink the $100 as soon as possible. This was tragic.

But he could also get out from under—something could pull him out, I don't know whether it was the hypoglycemia or what; he'd eat a candy bar or something and be turned on for a week afterward.

He was very funny and lively and smart, and had all sorts of ideas about writing and about everything else. He would say, "You know, I've got this idea for a poem. It's gonna go: 'Do-do-Da-do-Dee-do Pop-Pop-a-Dop-Doop-Zep- Zep.'" "Well, that's great, Lewie. Why don't you write it down?" "Ahhh, I don't know. I haven't finished it yet." You'd see him two weeks later or so, and he would say, "You know that poem I told you about? That goes 'Da-do-da-da'?" And I would say, "Yeah." "Well, it continues like 'So-so-So-So Sa-sa-Sa-Sa Zoop-ze-Zip-pah-pah.'" "Well, great, Lewie. Why don't you just write it down?"

"Ahhh, it's no good." Maybe three weeks later he would come up with some sort of typewriter version of it to read, and we'd say, "Well, that's great. Why don't you sell it or something, or do something with it?" "Ahhh, it's no good. It's no good at all."

But he would, like Williams taught us, put it away in a shoe box and save it, not throw it away. I thought that was very remarkable how he did all his composition and these rather complicated things in his head without recourse to paper and pencil. And keep it there and be able to resurrect it and tell you what it was and so on. And then later on write it down, and then tell you it was no good.

DM When was the first encounter with Buddhism?

PW Oh, I think when I was still in high school. First of all, I ran into the writings of Helena Petrovna Blavatsky. I wanted to see where was she coming from—where is she getting all this stuff? Then I found translations of the Vedanta writings—the Upanishads and the Vedas and so on. It was very satisfying that this system was really there, and it made sense to me; the Christian religion never did. That led me into Lin Yutang's big anthology, *The Wisdom of China and India*. And to a very obscure little book by a friend of Yeats's, A.P. Sinnet, called *Esoteric Buddhism*. It was sort of a rundown on tantrism, but very interesting and clear. I ran into Evans-Wentz's translation, which he calls *The Tibetan Book of the Dead*. But I couldn't read it. I couldn't get past about the second page because of the density of the footnotes. I had not yet learned the joy of reading footnotes. They were in a tiny print that was hard to understand. I couldn't do anything with it. But the pictures were interesting. [*laughter*] I thought that Buddhism was interesting but overcomplicated compared to Vedantism. For a long time I might well have been a Vedantist. I was also very interested in the idea of being a Christian—to fit in, sort of, with the world. I couldn't do it.

First of all, I had to decide what was real. I finally decided, well, all right, the Roman Church has all of the backing for being real, although it was pretty clear that the Russian Church was a kinder, gentler Christianity. Their emphasis was on the resurrection, whereas the Catholic business was about blood and tears and nails and so on. That was rather unattractive. I couldn't do the Christianity on any level, even in spite of the Christian mystics—it was too sticky to me. Too many little gummy things, infantine damnations, and so forth.

I gave up on that and stuck pretty much with Vedanta. When I got out of the army and was looking in Portland, I found that there was a local Vedanta society operating there. It took me a long time to get up the courage to go and visit one of their evening lectures. I was very surprised because it all was about stuff I had read, the Upanishads, Swami Vivekenanda, Sri Ramakrishna, and so on. I thought that was very nice, but it was depressing because it was a collection of elderly people sitting around this room. We got to sit on straight chairs later, and they had this lady play sad songs on the piano while they were waiting for the swami to come in and lecture. He would come in and lecture on some aspect, which was very good. I enjoyed him; I thought he was really a cool guy. I finally went through another crisis of trying to get up the nerve to go see him and talk to him. Which I did, and I thought, "Well, that's very good." So I thought, "Well, I'll just keep on trying to meditate at home and come over here and see this guy." But after a while I couldn't do it. I couldn't get through the middle-class miasma. That was a very interesting trip because I found out—where was I getting off criticizing other people's middle-class miasma? Why wasn't I just going there and shutting up and doing what I did? I didn't go anymore.

And then there's a great controversy about whether Snyder had found something about Zen in the Reed College library. He denies it categorically. But I have a recollection about, at some point, about everybody talking about what is the sound of one hand clapping, what does *kwatz* mean, and all sorts of stuff. But he says, "No, no, no. We didn't know anything about it till we all moved down here." So that's a mystery. He was busy seeing Alan Watts over at the American Academy for Asian Studies, which was then on Broadway. Listening to lectures by him and by other visiting Japanese folks. That was where he met a painter—Chiura Obata—he tells about it in the introduction to *Mountains and Rivers Without End*—and getting the idea of writing a long poem based on a Chinese scroll. And he was busy, as I say, studying Japanese and Chinese over at Berkeley. I found this very interesting. Especially when he turned up with the translations of haiku poetry by R.H. Blyth, whose first volume is almost entirely devoted to commentaries and great revelations about Zen. And then there were the writings of D.T. Suzuki . . . the next thing that happened was that we started reading the essays in his *Zen Buddhism*. That converted me, I think, pretty much to the idea that Buddhism, and certainly Zen, was a much more free and unbent kind of operation. That one could live in the mountains and be crazy and be fine. Nobody would care. I thought that was a swell program. Of course, misunderstanding the whole point. But anyhow, we were all sort of trying to sit around that time.

And the next thing is we met, out in Mill Valley, friends of ours who were friends of Albert Saijo. Albert showed us how to sit because he had worked with Nyogen Senzaki for a number of years. He set up a funny zendo in an unfinished house up there on the hill behind Locke McCorkle's place. He showed us how to sit on pillows, how to chant the Heart Sutra in Japanese, and how to drink tea. That was very helpful and made me feel like something was happening. You sat down and did zazen and then went outside and did some fast walking up and down through the brush and timber out there and came back and sat down some more. It just blew away a lot of the theoretical stuff that I had read. It changed your mind a little bit about things, and I thought that was a good idea. Because I learned that I had a great many idées fixes I could jettison, and I still have too many. Albert was very helpful, and he was a very creative guy. He wrote a funny little book about hiking. He made that trip with Lew and Jack Kerouac back to New York in the Willy car, and they put together that little book called *Trip Trap*.

The next big bop was when Gary was leaving for Japan and had that monumental party at Locke's place in Mill Valley, which Jack wrote about in *Dharma Bums*. What was entertaining, to me, was to see what he was writing about, and who was there, and what I thought was happening, what I thought it was all about, and then Jack's version in writing about it, which was extremely carefully selected. I thought it was really terrific how he had boiled so much nonsense away and kept particular track through the midst of all this confusion and hoopla and blah-blah. He could make a sequence of stuff and people and so forth out of it, that held still on the page, and yet it was lively. I thought that was quite an accomplishment. And so Gary went off to Japan. The next year, Joanne Kyger went over, and they got married. In 1962 he and Joanne went to Vietnam and to Ceylon and up into Northern India where they connected with Allen Ginsberg and Peter Orlovsky up in Delhi. Together they all went visiting celebrated lamas. The Dalai Lama and endless other marvelous creatures up there.

DM Much of your work is generated out of your notebooks, isn't it?

PW Well, sometimes it's lifted. Maybe very small changes or large cuts.

DM The practice of writing in a notebook—

PW It was very hard to start. I used to try and do it, and I would get hung up about trying to do it—with the lines on the paper. It wasn't until Bob LaVigne turned me on to some kind of artist pad thing, book thing, that had blank pages. He used them because they would take ink, paint, color, whatever. I used those for a long time. And then in Japan, the stationers had these marvelous bound books and whatnot that were very cheap, but the paper was very good. It could take anything and not lose it. That's probably why I scribbled so much, because it was fun working with these blank books. The ones that LaVigne turned me on to were bound. They were about yay thick and had a heavy binding, so they were a little hard to open at first. I had been using small notebooks, and that didn't work as well, although I filled up a lot of them. And, as I say, in Kyoto you had all these papers and books, blank books, and then also Pentel pencils, colored stuff to play with.

DM You also have a calligraphic style you learned from Lloyd Reynolds at Reed, which is dependent on having good fountain pens, as I recall. I was interested in the notion of writing by hand. It's so much different than working on the keyboard. I wonder if you have any thoughts on that?

PW Yeah, and the idea of what the page, what the whole page would look like, and the spacing, how much space to use here and there, or adding stuff on the side.

DM Your pages would be filled with various sizes of lettering, caps, drawings, and so forth, all part of an interesting process of thought.

PW Well, it was fun to do them. It was entertaining to me, and sometimes people thought it was nice. One poem in *Memoirs of an Interglacial*

Age I dictated to McClure, who typed it, and it came out all right. It was called "A Press Release" because Elsa Dorfman was rigging up a series of readings for Mike and me back east and she wanted a press release. Michael said, "C'mon, you have to write." "I don't have anything to say. I don't know anything about it." "I'll go write it on the typewriter." All right. I started talking. I think there were some bits and pieces that I actually wrote on the typewriter but very, very few.

DM You took the material out of the notebook and then you would type it?

PW Yeah. And at one point McClure told me, "You shouldn't do that. You should get them to print it the way you wrote it, because it's beautiful." But it's impracticable, apparently.

DM There was a book of yours that was published in facsimile.

PW Yes, *Highgrade,* which was all short poems and doodles and stuff. That was one of the books Coyote Press published. Zoe Brown did a very good job on the cover and the layout and the insides.

DM An important absence, felt in all these interviews, is Allen Ginsberg.

PW Allen was just great, you know? He was a brother, and he took endless bother to get my stuff published. When people would ask him for things, he would say, "All right, I'll give you some, but you have to print something of Phil's and Gary's, too." His head was going 500 miles a minute. He had huge quantities of English poetry by memory, which he could quote if he wanted to. He and I had an endless argument about how to pronounce the name of Shelley's poem, "Epipsychidion." I'd call it "Epi-psych-idion" and he'd call it "E-pipsi-chidion." He had a real wild passion for Blake and other writers. When I first met him and Jack, they were selling Melville's novel *Pierre,* which I had never read. Of course, their big drive when they were in college was Dostoyevsky, whom I had read and admired, but not with the passion that they had for him and thinking of it as a model for something. I always thought it was funny that Dostoyevsky's model was Charles Dickens. [*laughter*]

Allen was always helping me all the time. Sometimes he would cook, and we would have dinner together, or we'd go running around North Beach together. He was tremendously good company. He was seldom down, crying, or moaning. He was usually operating. He was too fucking smart to take time off to be sad. He could be sad enough, being that he was by nature a Russian, but he kept out of it as much as possible. He was always writing—writing and talking at the same time. One time he made up this lung stew, if you can imagine such a thing. But it was quite good. At the time we were running around together he wasn't reading much. He was very hung up on writing. The only time he really got suddenly interested in reading something was when his mother died, and he tried to get a minyan together to read Kaddish for her. He couldn't do it. He couldn't find enough people. But he wanted to know how to do it, and so he got a hold of all the literature, and he bantered in everybody's ears from here to New York trying to find out how to do it.

Allen had an endless string of applications to him from various friends, old and new, about how they were broke and needed money, and could they please have $200 right away. He always answered, and he always sent money. He had a real motherly instinct. He was very tough, too. He had a very clear head and a very precise vision of himself and about what it was he wanted to do. What he wanted to do was to be famous. If he was famous, then a whole lot of people would go to bed with him. [*laughter*] So that's what he did—he contrived to become famous. And he contrived to go to bed with a lot of people, which amused him and pleased him and made him happy. His long relationship with Peter was sometimes very hard for him because Peter had periods of total insanity and had to be taken care and was a mess. Later on, a few years ago, Peter just got totally crackers, and Allen paid to put him in some expensive sanitarium in Wisconsin. When Peter got out he was just fine until he'd get a drink of liquor, and then he would go bananas. It was terrible.

I don't think I ever met Allen's brother, who was a lawyer. I did meet his father, Louis, who was a lively fellow and whose conversation was entirely made up of puns. Which was a little stressing. Allen's step-mother, Edith, is a very pleasant person who still lives in part of his apartment in New York some of the time. She lives in New Jersey most of the time, I guess. I think his brother had two or three sons that Allen kept track of and helped out in various ways. He knew so many people, and would tell wonderful stories about all these famous people, literary people and so on, and places that he went, and things that he saw and did and smelled, tasted, and touched. He could project so much excitement and so much force and so much life, that it was incredible. Jack had every bit as much talent and could tell you what he wanted and could do things, but he was so bottled up with that Catholic education, it just absolutely squashed his personality or his mind or something in some terrible way. That made it hard for him to get out and do things. He could, but then he would also have to get drunk to get out from under all that stuff. It was very hard, because he had a theory about how if you had just enough alcohol, you would feel good and be able to do things. And if you waited until it was not too late, you had just a little more, and then you would get back to where you were at, and so on. Of course, later, there you were, plotzed.

DM I remember seeing a letter that Jack wrote to Don Allen in which he outlined very seriously his regimen for writing, which would include very methodically drinking so much alcohol, and then taking half of a benny, and so on. If you just kept on, taking a little of this and a little of that, you could go on for days and days and days and write at this incredible speed. You once talked about how "spontaneous bop prosody" was not necessarily as stated—that Jack had been filling up notebooks and, when it came time to write, there was so much material already there that he could extract it in the process of translating it into type.

PW The typewriter would somehow make it possible for him to expand on the notes and go to bop, maybe half a page. Or he would make a mistake in typing, and say, "Oh," and it would drive him another line or so.

DM In one of your interviews, you talk about the regard that you have for Kerouac as a writer. Often it's forgotten that he was writing very interesting, and in some cases, very radical, experimental writing. So much of this mytho-poeticizing bypasses the fact that he was a very serious and innovative writer. I think Clark Coolidge is one of the only other poets I know who sees Kerouac as a great feast of writing that instructs him.

PW You know Clark himself has done remarkable stuff. I haven't seen any of his stuff since he wrote *At Egypt,* which I thought was terrific.

DM He's prolific.

PW That's what you have to be, you know, to get anywhere. You have to get a lot of words on paper. Kerouac used to say that writing was like having a dope habit. You just keep on doing it.

DM Can we talk about another absence—Kenneth Rexroth?

PW He was a fascinating talker and very good poet. The long poems, like *The Phoenix and the Tortoise* and *The Dragon and the Unicorn,* are terrific and much neglected. His shorter things are very beautiful, and I don't know why people don't read them. Kenneth was always very encouraging. He would have these soirées at his Scott Street apartment where all sorts of visiting firemen would appear and be available for talking. It was interesting. A few times we got to see wonderful folks at Ruth Witt-Diamant's house. Kenneth was always very helpful—he tried and tried to get New Directions to print me. They wouldn't do it. Didn't like it. I guess it was too much like James Laughlin's own writing. Anyway, he was instrumental in getting them to print McClure and Snyder, which is great, and because in any airport or drugstore you'd find New Directions books.

I thought his ideas in the long poems were always very interesting, and his interpretation of the *Genji* story is wonderful, and some of his other critical writings are very useful and entertaining. He wrote a great quantity of stuff that is fairly high quality; I mean, it's as tough and as good as somebody like Ford Maddox Ford in his critical writing. I never read his *Autobiographical Novel.*

Kenneth was a great cook, and he would have me to dinner sometimes. Then later on, when Snyder and I were in Kyoto, he and Carole Tinker showed up. We sort of carted them around to see various treasures and whatnot. He was very grumpy. "They nickel and dime you to death!" He had a great appreciation for Kyoto, for Japanese history, and so on. He wrote a great book that nobody ever read—*Communalism*—all about utopian communities. Funny, it's the kind of thing that anybody else would get a Ph.D. for writing.

Mainly, you know, you hear him; I can hear his voice telling stories. Either edifying or totally scandalous things would come out. He had a great number about the Duke of Windsor and Wallis Simpson. Wasn't charitable in the least.

DM What other poets of that time did you find interesting?

PW Certainly Robert Creeley. On another generational bend, Gregory Corso, who I think is a really inventive guy. Inventive in a different way, but in the same league as Clark Coolidge. Whenever I would see things of yours, they would just seem to be getting better and better, and I thought it was wonderful. Ted Berrigan's work had a lot of marvels in it. When I got a copy of *The Sonnets* I thought, "Wow, this is really something!" Frank O'Hara was always very nice to me, but I never could really get excited about his writing. It didn't send me, as they say. I am totally unable to read John Ashbery. Kenneth Koch is very funny, and he hates to be funny.

DM How about Charles Olson?

PW Oh, I thought Olson was a wonderful creature. He was a terrific guy, and his way of handling a class in school—at the poetry conference up at Vancouver—was terrific. He would get people up off their asses, and get them to try and do things and get going and move. This was a great talent. His own work was very interesting. At the same time, I felt that a lot of it was so parochial that it didn't do so much for me. He was a wonderful talker, and he would tell stories and theorize endlessly. I have been told that he had a great feud with Buckminster Fuller because Buckminster Fuller could talk longer. Charles would get tired at some point, and Fuller would go on. Olson had this funny way of projecting energy and power. It was like being in front of a dynamo. He was always into so many things—all these offbeat scholars he liked because the academy hated them: Cyrus Gordon, Velikovsky, Harry Hooton. . . .

DM You can't play music, but you can hear it. What are you listening to?

PW Nothing. I told you, I can't get the damned machine to work. I can't play the CD player—can't read the fine print on the buttons.

DM When you played, which composers did you like playing?

PW I like everything. I like pretty things, like Rachmaninoff, which I can't play. I like small, complicated things, like the Bach inventions, which I can't play—*The Well-Tempered Clavier*, *The Goldberg Variations*, and *The Art of the Fugue*. This is all because of a man I met in the army who'd been trained to be a pianist. He knew all about all this Bach stuff that I had never heard of before. When I was younger I doted upon the French Impressionists like Debussy and Ravel—that was all in vogue. I like Gershwin and all sorts of obscure creatures.

DM Did you ever improvise?

PW Not really, no.

DM Is there a reason?

PW Yes, I don't know anything about it. I used to make noise. [*laughter*] To my mind, improvisation would have some sort of shape to it.

DM Do you have any thoughts about the successive waves of Buddhism in America?

PW I don't know. Some days I think that it's like fashions—fashions in dress or fashions in art or fashions in whatever. It just gets co-opted into everything until there's nothing left of it. I have this vision that in twenty or twenty-five or thirty years there'll be small elegant buildings where people will meet to listen to lectures—it'll be like going to a Lutheran church. I don't know if there'll be any Buddha energy to it.

On the other hand, I like to think that places like Tassajara and other places that Suzuki Roshi built will persist and still carry on that tradition of sitting and working and studying. It's something that people can do instead of playing together in gangs at the mall or spending their time at the store choosing movies to take home and watch. I can't feature doing that. Maybe if I could see better, I might.

The question is whether Buddhism will persist in the U.S. in a form that's close to the traditional teaching. It would be nice if it did. It might have some chance of affecting our funny heads or funny ways or prejudices. I still suspect that, in the long run, there will be an absorption—all the edges of Buddhism will be blurred. I don't know how well the Tibetan teachers are getting things going. That may be where it will last. I don't know.

DM There are great differences between Tibetan Buddhism and Zen. . . .

PW Yes, but underneath it all there's the same business about, "Who are you?" "How are you doing?" "How are you treating other people?" "How are you treating yourself?" "What are you doing to the world?" "Are you out there cutting down trees or planting them?"

The thing that's important is that Buddha was a human being—he was a man. He wasn't a metaphysical creature—that was added on later. He was a man who figured out something and taught other people who were interested in how to start figuring things out. It's what you do with it, you know? "How are you living?" "What are you doing with life?"

We are still a puritan culture and this is not so useful, at heart. The idea of work—the work ethic—we get so involved in it. You can use up a lot of energy in doing Buddhist practice and in living the monastic way, but it can also get wound up too tight with progress and accomplishment and so on.

DM Does one have to be on one's toes all the time?

PW No, of course not. You just have to watch where your toes are. Whose are they and what are they doing? [*laughter*]

Bibliographies

These bibliographies include important books by the poets interviewed in San Francisco Beat. Not included is the profusion of chapbooks, broadsides, audio and video recordings, edited volumes, and magazine and anthology publications.

DIANE DI PRIMA

Poetry

This Kind of Bird Flies Backwards. New York: Totem Press, 1958.
Dinners and Nightmares. New York: Corinth Press, 1961.
The New Handbook of Heaven. San Francisco: Auerhahn, 1962.
Haiku. Los Angeles: Love Press, 1966.
Kerhonkson Journal. Berkeley: Oyez, 1971.
Revolutionary Letters. San Francisco: City Lights Books, 1971.
Selected Poems: 1956–1975. Berkeley: North Atlantic Books, 1975.
Pieces of a Song: Selected Poems. San Francisco: City Lights Books, 1990.
Loba. New York: Penguin, 1998.

Prose
Memoirs of a Beatnik. New York: Penguin, 1998.
My Life as a Woman. New York: Penguin, 2001.

WILLIAM EVERSON (BROTHER ANTONINUS)

Poetry
These Are the Ravens. San Leandro: Greater West, 1935.
The Masculine Dead: Poems 1938–1940. Prairie City: James A. Decker, 1942.
Poems. Waldport: Untide Press, 1942.
Poems of Nineteen Forty Seven. Reno: Black Rock Press, 1968.
The Residual Years: Poems 1934–1946. New York: New Directions, 1948.
The Crooked Lines of God: Poems 1949–1954. Detroit: Univ. of Detroit Press, 1959.

The Hazards of Holiness: Poems 1957–1960. New York: Doubleday, 1962.

Single Source: The Early Poems of William Everson, 1934–1940. Berkeley: Oyez, 1966.

Man-Fate: The Swan Song of Brother Antoninus. New York: New Directions, 1974.

The Masks of Drought. Santa Barbara: Black Sparrow Press, 1980.

The Integral Years: Poems 1966–1994. Santa Rosa: Black Sparrow Press, 2000.

Prose

Robinson Jeffers: Fragments of an Older Fury. Berkeley: Oyez, 1968.

Earth Poetry. Berkeley: Oyez, 1971

Birth of a Poet: The Santa Cruz Meditations. Santa Barbara: Black Sparrow Press, 1982.

The Excesses of God: Robinson Jeffers as a Religious Figure. Stanford: Stanford Univ. Press, 1988.

LAWRENCE FERLINGHETTI

Poetry

Pictures of the Gone World. San Francisco: City Lights Books, 1955. Rev. ed. 1995.

A Coney Island of the Mind. New York: New Directions, 1958.

Starting from San Francisco. New York: New Directions, 1967.

Back Roads to Far Places. New York: New Directions, 1971.

Open Eyes, Open Heart. New York: New Directions, 1973.

Who Are We Now? New York: New Directions, 1976.

Landscapes of Living & Dying. New York: New Directions, 1979.

Wild Dreams of a New Beginning. New York: New Directions, 1988.

These Are My Rivers: New and Selected Poems 1955–1993. New York: New Directions, 1993.

A Far Rockaway of the Heart. New York: New Directions, 1997.

Prose
Her. New York: New Directions, 1960.
Tyrannus Nix? New York: New Directions, 1969.
Love in the Days of Rage. New York: E.P. Dutton, 1988.

Plays
Unfair Arguments with Existence: Seven Plays for a New Theatre. New
York: New Directions, 1963.
Routines. New York: New Directions, 1964

JACK   HIRSCHMAN

Poetry
A Correspondence of Americans. Bloomington:
Indiana Univ. Press, 1960.
Interchange. Los Angeles: Zora Gallery, 1964.
Yod. London: Trigram Press, 1966.
William Blake. Topanga: Love Press, 1967.
London Seen Directly. London: Goliard Press, 1967.
Black Alephs. New York: Phoenix Bookshop; London:
Trigram Press, 1969.
Scintilla. Bolinas: Tree Books, 1971.
Lyripol. San Francisco: City Lights Books, 1976.
The Arcanes of Le Comte de St-Germain. San Francisco:
Amerus Press, 1977.
The Jonestown Arcane. San Francisco: Poetry for the People, 1979.
The Proletarian Arcane. San Francisco: Amerus Press, 1980.
Class Questions. San Francisco: Retribution Press, 1981.
The David Arcane. San Francisco: Amerus Press, 1982.
The Bottom Line. Willimantic: Curbstone Press, 1988.
The Satin Arcane. Oakland: Zeitgeist Press, 1991.
Endless Threshold. Willimantic: Curbstone Press, 1992.
The Back of a Spoon. San Francisco: Manic D Press, 1992.
The Arcane on a Stick. San Francisco: Roadkill Press, 1995.
The Green Chakra Arcane. San Francisco: Deliriodendron Press, 1996.
The Grit Arcane. West Yorkshire, England: Spout, 1997.
Arcani. Salerno, Italy: Multimedia Edizioni, 1999.

Prose

KS: An Essay on Kabbala Surrealism. Venice, CA: Bayrock & Beyond
Baroque Press, 1973.

Translations

Vladimir Mayakovsky. *Electric Iron.* Trans. from the Russian with
Victor Erlich. Berkeley: Maya, 1971.

René Depestre. *A Rainbow for the Christian West.* Trans. from the
French. Los Angeles: Red Hill Press, 1972.

Antonin Artaud. *Love Is a Tree.* Trans. from the French. Los Angeles:
Red Hill Press, 1972.

Ait Djafer. *Wail for the Beggars of the Casbah.* Trans. from the French.
Los Angeles: Papa Bach Bookstore, 1973.

Johann Maier. *The Book of Noah.* Trans. from the German. Berkeley:
Tree Books, 1976.

Jean Cocteau. *The Crucifixion.* Trans. from the French. Bethlehem,
PA: Quarter Press, 1976.

Jabixshak: Albanian Poets Today. Trans. from the Albanian.
San Francisco: Amerus Press, 1982.

Sarah Kirsch. *Poems.* Trans. from the German. Santa Cruz: Alcatraz
Editions, 1983.

Katherine Gogou. *Three Clicks Left.* Trans. from the Greek.
San Francisco: Night Horn Books, 1983.

Roque Dalton. *Poemas Clandestinos/Clandestine Poems.* Trans. from
the Spanish. Willimantic: Curbstone Press, 1990.

Paul Laraque. *Fistibal/Slingshot.* Trans from the Haitian Creole.
San Francisco: Seaworthy Press; Port-au-Prince:
Editions Samba, 1989.

Amber Past. *The Sea on Its Side.* Trans. from the Spanish. Sausalito:
Post-Apollo Press, 1994.

Rocco Scotellaro. *Seven Poems of Rocco Scotellaro.* Trans. from the
Italian. San Francisco: Deliriodendron, 1994.

Ferruccio Brugnaro. *Fist of Sun.* Trans. from the Italian. Willimantic:
Curbstone Press, 1998.

Alexei Kruchenych. *Suicide Circus.* Trans. from the Russian. Los
Angeles: Green Integer, 2000.

JOANNE KYGER

Poetry
The Tapestry and the Web. San Francisco:
Four Seasons Foundation, 1965.
Joanne. Bolinas: Angel Hair, 1970.
Places to Go. Los Angeles: Black Sparrow Press, 1970.
All This Every Day. Bolinas: Big Sky, 1975.
The Wonderful Focus of You. Valais: Z Press, 1979.
Going On: Selected Poems. New York: E.P. Dutton, 1983.
Phenomenological. Canton, NY: Institute of Further Studies, 1989.
Just Space: Poems 1979–1989. Santa Rosa: Black Sparrow Press, 1991.
Some Sketches from the Life of Helene Petrovna Blavatsky. Boulder:
Rodent Press & Erudite Fangs, 1996.

Prose
Japan and India Journals 1960–1964. Bolinas: Tombouctou Books,
1981. Reprint. *Strange Big Moon: Japan and India Journals 1960–
1964*. Berkeley: North Atlantic Books, 2000.

PHILIP LAMANTIA
Erotic Poems. Berkeley: Bern Porter, 1946.
Ekstasis. San Francisco: Auerhahn Press, 1959.
Destroyed Works. San Francisco: Auerhahn Press, 1962.
Touch of the Marvelous. Berkeley: Oyez, 1966.
Selected Poems 1943–1966. San Francisco: City Lights Books, 1967.
The Blood of the Air. San Francisco: Four Seasons Foundation, 1970.
Becoming Visible. San Francisco: City Lights Books, 1981.
Meadowlark West. San Francisco: City Lights Books, 1986.
Bed of Sphinxes: New and Selected Poems 1943–1993. San Francisco:
City Lights Books, 1997.

MICHAEL MCCLURE

Poetry
Passages. Ashland: Jargon Society/Jonathan Williams, 1956.

Hymns to St. Geryon and Other Poems. San Francisco:
    Auerhahn Press, 1959.
The New Book/A Book of Torture. New York: Grove Press, 1959.
Dark Brown. San Francisco: Auerhahn Press, 1961.
Love Lion Book. San Francisco: Four Seasons Foundation, 1966.
Little Odes and the Raptors. Los Angeles: Black Sparrow Press, 1969.
Star. New York: Grove Press, 1970.
September Blackberries. New York: New Directions, 1974.
Jaguar Skies. New York: New Directions, 1975.
Selected Poems. New York: New Directions, 1986.
Huge Dreams: San Francisco and Beat Poems. New York: Viking/
    Penguin, 1999.
Pain Mirror: New Poems. New York: New Directions, 1999.

Theater
Gargoyle Cartoons. New York: Delacorte Press, 1971.
Gorf; or, Gorf and the Blind Dyke. New York: New Directions, 1971.
The Beard; and Vktms: Two Plays. New York: New Directions, 1985.

Prose
Meat Science Essays. San Francisco: City Lights Books, 1963.
Freewheelin' Frank, Secretary of the Angels. With Frank Reynolds. New
    York: Grove Press, 1967.
The Mad Cub. New York: Bantam Books, 1970. Rev. ed. New York:
    Book of the Month Club, 1995.
Scratching the Beat Surface. Berkeley: North Point Press, 1982.
*Lighting the Corners: On Art, Nature, and the Visionary: Essays and
    Interviews.* Albuquerque: Univ. of New Mexico Press, 1993.

DAVID MELTZER

Poetry
Poems. With David Schenker. San Francisco: n.p., 1957.
Ragas. San Francisco: Discovery Books, 1959.
The Clown. Larkspur: Semina, 1960.
The Process. Berkeley: Oyez, 1967.
Round the Poem Box. Los Angeles: Black Sparrow Press, 1969.

Yesod. London: Trigram Press, 1969.

Luna. Los Angeles: Black Sparrow Press, 1970.

Tens: Selected Poems. Ed. by Kenneth Rexroth. New York: McGraw-Hill, 1973.

Hero/Lil. Los Angeles: Black Sparrow Press, 1973.

Blue Rags. Berkeley: Oyez, 1974.

Six. Santa Barbara: Black Sparrow Press, 1976.

The Art, the Veil. Milwaukee: Membrane Press, 1981.

The Name: Selected Poetry 1973–1983. Santa Barbara: Black Sparrow Press, 1984.

Arrows: Selected Poetry 1957–1992. Santa Rosa: Black Sparrow Press, 1994.

No Eyes: Lester Young. Santa Rosa: Black Sparrow Press, 2000.

Fiction

The Agency Trilogy. North Hollywood: Brandon House, 1968. Reprint. New York: Richard Kasak, 1994.

Orf. North Hollywood: Brandon House: 1969. Reprint. New York: Masquerade Books, 1995.

The Martyr. North Hollywood: Brandon House: 1969.

The Brain Plant Tetralogy. North Hollywood: Brandon House, 1969–1970.

Star. North Hollywood: Brandon House, 1970.

Under. New York: Rhinoceros Books, 1997.

Essays

We All Have Something to Say to Each Other: Kenneth Patchen. San Francisco: Auerhahn Press, 1962.

Bazascope Mother. [On Robert Alexander.] Los Angeles: Drekfesser Press, 1964.

Isla Vista Notes. Santa Barbara: Christopher's Books, 1970.

Two-Way Mirror: A Poetry Notebook. Berkeley: Oyez, 1977.

Edited Volumes

The San Francisco Poets. New York: Ballantine Books, 1971.

The Secret Garden: An Anthology in the Kabbalah. New York:
Continuum Press, 1976. Reprint: Barrytown, NY: Station Hill
Press, 1998.

Birth: Anthology of Ancient Texts, Songs, Prayers, and Stories. Berkeley:
North Point Press, 1984.

Reading Jazz. San Francisco: Mercury House, 1996.

Writing Jazz. San Francisco: Mercury House, 1999.

JACK MICHELINE

River of Red Wine and Other Poems. Intro. by Jack Kerouac. New York:
Troubadour Press, 1958.

I Kiss Angels. New York: Interim Books, 1962.

In the Bronx and Other Stories. New York: Sam Hooker Press, 1965.

Low Class. New York: Midnight Special Editions, 1972.

Poems of Dr. Innisfree. San Francisco: Beatitude Press, 1975.

Street of Lost Fools. Mastic, NY: Street Press, 1975.

North of Manhattan: Collected Poems, Ballads, and Songs: 1954–1975.
South San Francisco: ManRoot, 1976.

Skinny Dynamite. San Francisco: Second Coming Press, 1980.

Acapella Rabbi: A Jack Micheline Sampler. Pueblo, CO:
Quick Books, 1986.

Imaginary Conversations with Jack Kerouac. Oakland:
Zeitgeist Press, 1989.

Outlaw of the Lowest Planet. Oakland: Zeitgeist Press, 1993.

A Dagger at Your Heart. San Francisco: Midnight Special Editions,
1997.

Sixty-Seven Poems for Downtrodden Saints. San Francisco: FMSBW,
1997.

KENNETH REXROTH

[NB: Many Rexroth texts and a bibliography are available on the
Bureau of Public Secrets Web site at http://www.bopsecrets.org.]

Poetry

Collected Shorter Poems. New York: New Directions, 1966.

Collected Longer Poems. New York: New Directions, 1968.

Selected Poems. New York: New Directions, 1984.

Flower Wreath Hill: Later Poems. New York: New Directions, 1991.

Sacramental Acts: The Love Poems. Pt. Townsend, WA: Copper Canyon, 1997.

Swords That Shall Not Strike: Poems of Protest and Rebellion. Warner, NH: Glad Day Books, 1999.

Complete Poems. Pt. Townsend, WA: Copper Canyon, forthcoming 2001.

Plays

Beyond the Mountains. New York: New Directions, 1951.

Essays

Bird in the Bush: Obvious Essays. New York: New Directions, 1959.

Assays. New York: New Directions, 1961.

The Alternative Society: Essays from the Other World. New York: Herder & Herder, 1970.

With Eye and Ear. New York: Herder & Herder, 1970.

American Poetry in the Twentieth Century. New York: Herder & Herder, 1971.

The Elastic Retort: Essays in Literature and Ideas. New York: Seabury, 1973.

Communalism: From Its Origins to the Twentieth Century. New York: Seabury, 1974.

Classics Revisited. New York: Avon Books, 1968. New ed. New York: New Directions, 1986.

World Outside the Window: Selected Essays. New York: New Directions, 1987.

More Classics Revisited. New York, New Directions, 1989.

Autobiography

An Autobiographical Novel. New York: Doubleday, 1964. Rev. and expanded, ed. by Linda Hamalian. New York: New Directions, 1991.

Kenneth Rexroth and James Laughlin: Selected Letters. New York: Norton, 1991.

Translations

[*NB:* Rexroth's translations have a complicated publication history; these editions are either the most recent or best known.]

One Hundred Poems from the Japanese. New York: New Directions, 1955, 1964.

Thirty Spanish Poems of Love and Exile. San Francisco: City Lights Books, 1956.

One Hundred Poems from the Chinese. New York: New Directions, 1956, 1971.

Poems from the Greek Anthology. Ann Arbor, MI: Ann Arbor Press/ Univ. of Michigan Press, 1962.

Pierre Reverdy: Selected Poems. New York: New Directions, 1969.

Love and the Turning Year: One Hundred More Poems from the Chinese. New York: New Directions, 1970.

One Hundred Poems from the French. Cambridge, MA: Pym-Randall, 1972.

One Hundred More Poems from the Japanese. New York: New Directions, 1974, 1976.

Complete Poems: Li Ch'ing-Chao. New York: New Directions, 1979.

Women Poets of China. New York: New Directions, 1982.

Women Poets of Japan. New York: New Directions, 1982.

Fourteen Poems by O.V. de Lubicz-Milosz. Pt. Townsend, WA: Copper Canyon, 1983.

Seasons of Sacred Lust: Selected Poems of Kazuko Shiraishi. New York: New Directions, 1997.

GARY SNYDER

Poetry

Riprap. San Francisco/Kyoto: Origin Press, 1959.

Myths & Texts. New York: Totem Press/Corinth Books, 1960.

Riprap and Cold Mountain Poems. San Francisco: Four Seasons Foundation, 1965.

Six Selections form Mountains and Rivers Without End. San Francisco: Four Seasons Foundation, 1965.

A Range of Poems. London: Fulcrum Press, 1966.

The Back Country. London: Fulcrum Press, 1967.
Turtle Island. New York: New Directions, 1974.
Axe Handles. Berkeley: North Point Press, 1983.
Left Out in the Rain. Berkeley: North Point Press, 1986.
No Nature: New and Selected Poems. New York: Pantheon Books, 1992.
Mountains and Rivers Without End. Washington, DC:
    Counterpoint, 1997.

Prose
Earth Household. New York: New Directions, 1969.
*He Who Hunted Birds in His Father's Village: The Dimensions of a Haida
    Myth.* Bolinas: Grey Fox Press, 1979.
The Old Ways: Six Essays. San Francisco: City Lights Books, 1977.
Real Work: Interviews and Talks 1964–1979. New York: New
    Directions, 1979.
The Practice of the Wild. Berkeley: North Point Press, 1990.
A Place in Space: Ethics, Aesthetics, and Watersheds. Washington, DC:
    Counterpoint, 1996.
The Gary Snyder Reader. Washington, DC: Counterpoint, 1999.

LEW WELCH

Poetry
Wobbly Rock. With drawing by Robert LaVigne. San Francisco:
    Auerhahn Press, 1960.
Hermit Poems. San Francisco: Four Seasons Foundation,1965.
On Out. Berkeley: Oyez, 1965.
The Song Mt. Tamalpais Sings. San Francisco: Cranium Press, 1969.
Redwood Haiku & Other Poems. San Francisco: Cranium Press, 1972.
Courses. San Francisco: Dave Haselwood Books, 1972.
Ring of Bone: Collected Poems 1950–1971. Ed. by Donald Allen.
    Bolinas: Grey Fox Press, 1973.
Selected Poems. Preface by Gary Snyder; ed. by Donald Allen. Bolinas:
    Grey Fox Press, 1976.

Prose

Trip Trap: Haiku Along the Road from San Francisco to New York. By
  Jack Kerouac, Albert Saijo, Lew Welch. Bolinas: Grey Fox Press,
  [1959] 1973.
*On Bread & Poetry: A Panel Discussion with Gary Snyder, Lew Welch &
  Philip Whalen.* Ed. by Donald Allen. Bolinas: Grey Fox Press,
  1977.
I, Leo: An Unfinished Novel. Ed. by Donald Allen. Bolinas: Grey Fox
  Press, 1979.
I Remain: The Letters of Lew Welch & the Correspondence of His Friends.
  Ed. by Donald Allen. Bolinas: Grey Fox Press, 1980.
How I Read Gertrude Stein. Ed. with an intro. by Eric Paul Shaffer. San
  Francisco: Grey Fox Press, 1996.

PHILIP WHALEN

Poetry

Self-Portrait from Another Direction. San Francisco:
  Auerhahn Press, 1959.
Memoirs of an Interglacial Age. San Francisco: Auerhahn Press, 1960.
Like I Say. New York: Totem Press/Corinth Books, 1960.
Every Day. Eugene: Coyote's Journal, 1965.
Highgrade: Doodles, Poems. San Francisco: Coyote's Journal, 1966.
*The Invention of the Letter: A Beastly Moral History, for the Edification of
  Younger Readers.* New York: Irving Rosenthal, 1967.
On Bear's Head. New York: Harcourt, Brace & World, 1969.
Severance Pay. San Francisco: Four Seasons Foundation, 1970.
The Kindness of Strangers: Poems 1969–1974. Bolinas: Four Seasons
  Foundation, 1976.
Enough Said: Fluctuat Nec Mergitur: Poems 1974–1979. San Francisco:
  Grey Fox Press, 1980.
Canoeing up Cabarga Creek: Buddhist Poems 1955–1986. Berkeley:
  Parallax Press, 1996.
Overtime: Selected Poems. Ed. by Michael Rothenberg. New York:
  Penguin Poets, 1999.

Prose

You Didn't Even Try. San Francisco: Coyote, 1967.

Off the Wall: Interviews with Philip Whalen. Bolinas:
Grey Fox Press, 1978.

The Diamond Noodle. Berkeley: Poltroon Press, 1980.

Two Novels. Somerville, MA: Zephyr Press, 1985.

CITY LIGHTS PUBLICATIONS

Acosta, Juvenal, ed. LIGHT FROM A NEARBY WINDOW: Contemporary Mexican Poetry

Alberti, Rafael. CONCERNING THE ANGELS

Alcalay, Ammiel, ed. KEYS TO THE GARDEN: New Israeli Writing

Alcalay, Ammiel. MEMORIES OF OUR FUTURE: Selected Essays 1982-1999

Allen, Roberta. AMAZON DREAM

Angulo de, G. & J. JAIME IN TAOS

Angulo, Jaime de. INDIANS IN OVERALLS

Artaud, Antonin. ARTAUD ANTHOLOGY

Barker, Molly. SECRET LANGUAGE

Bataille, Georges. EROTISM: Death and Sensuality

Bataille, Georges. THE IMPOSSIBLE

Bataille, Georges. STORY OF THE EYE

Bataille, Georges. THE TEARS OF EROS

Baudelaire, Charles. TWENTY PROSE POEMS

Blanco, Alberto. DAWN OF THE SENSES: Selected Poems

Blechman, Max. REVOLUTIONARY ROMANTICISM

Bowles, Paul. A HUNDRED CAMELS IN THE COURTYARD

Bramly, Serge. MACUMBA: The Teachings of Maria-José, Mother of the Gods

Brecht, Bertolt. STORIES OF MR. KEUNER

Breton, André. ANTHOLOGY OF BLACK HUMOR

Brook, James, Chris Carlsson, Nancy J. Peters eds. RECLAIMING SAN FRANCISCO: History Politics Culture

Brook, James & Iain A. Boal. RESISTING THE VIRTUAL LIFE: Culture and Politics of Information

Broughton, James. COMING UNBUTTONED

Brown, Rebecca. ANNIE OAKLEY'S GIRL

Brown, Rebecca. THE DOGS

Brown, Rebecca. THE TERRIBLE GIRLS

Bukowski, Charles. THE MOST BEAUTIFUL WOMAN IN TOWN

Bukowski, Charles. NOTES OF A DIRTY OLD MAN

Bukowski, Charles. TALES OF ORDINARY MADNESS

Burroughs, William S. THE BURROUGHS FILE

Burroughs, William S. THE YAGE LETTERS

Campana, Dino. ORPHIC SONGS
Cassady, Neal. THE FIRST THIRD
Chin, Sara. BELOW THE LINE
Churchill, Ward. FANTASIES OF THE MASTER RACE:
    Literature, Cinema and the Colonization of American Indians
Churchill, Ward. A LITTLE MATTER OF GENOCIDE: Holocaust
    and Denial in America, 1492 to the Present
Cocteau, Jean. THE WHITE BOOK (LE LIVRE BLANC)
Cohen, Jonathan. APART FROM FREUD: Notes for a Rational
    Psychoanalysis
Cornford, Adam. ANIMATIONS
Corso, Gregory. GASOLINE
Cortázar, Julio. SAVE TWILIGHT
Cuadros, Gil. CITY OF GOD
Daumal, René. THE POWERS OF THE WORD
David-Neel, Alexandra. SECRET ORAL TEACHINGS IN
    TIBETAN BUDDHIST SECTS
Deleuze, Gilles. SPINOZA: Practical Philosophy
Dick, Leslie. KICKING
Dick, Leslie. WITHOUT FALLING
di Prima, Diane. PIECES OF A SONG: Selected Poems
Doolittle, Hilda (H.D.). NOTES ON THOUGHT & VISION
Ducornet, Rikki. ENTERING FIRE
Ducornet, Rikki. THE MONSTROUS AND THE MARVELOUS
Eberhardt, Isabelle. DEPARTURES: Selected Writings
Eberhardt, Isabelle. THE OBLIVION SEEKERS
Eidus, Janice. THE CELIBACY CLUB
Eidus, Janice. URBAN BLISS
Eidus, Janice. VITO LOVES GERALDINE
Fenollosa, Ernest. THE CHINESE WRITTEN CHARACTER AS
    A MEDIUM FOR POETRY
Ferlinghetti, L. ed. CITY LIGHTS POCKET POETS
    ANTHOLOGY
Ferlinghetti, L., ed. ENDS & BEGINNINGS (City Lights
    Review #6)
Ferlinghetti, L. PICTURES OF THE GONE WORLD
Finley, Karen. SHOCK TREATMENT
Ford, Charles Henri. OUT OF THE LABYRINTH: Selected
    Poems
Franzen, Cola, transl. POEMS OF ARAB ANDALUSIA

Frym, Gloria. DISTANCE NO OBJECT
García Lorca, Federico. BARBAROUS NIGHTS: Legends & Plays
García Lorca, Federico. ODE TO WALT WHITMAN & OTHER
    POEMS
García Lorca, Federico. POEM OF THE DEEP SONG
Garon, Paul. BLUES & THE POETIC SPIRIT
Gil de Biedma, Jaime. LONGING: SELECTED POEMS
Ginsberg, Allen. THE FALL OF AMERICA
Ginsberg, Allen. HOWL & OTHER POEMS
Ginsberg, Allen. KADDISH & OTHER POEMS
Ginsberg, Allen. MIND BREATHS
Ginsberg, Allen. PLANET NEWS
Ginsberg, Allen. PLUTONIAN ODE
Ginsberg, Allen. REALITY SANDWICHES
Glave, Thomas. WHOSE SONG? And Other Stories
Goethe, J. W. von. TALES FOR TRANSFORMATION
Gómez-Peña, Guillermo. THE NEW WORLD BORDER
Gómez-Peña, Guillermo, Enrique Chagoya, Felicia Rice. CODEX
    ESPANGLIENSIS
Goytisolo, Juan. LANDSCAPES OF WAR
Goytisolo. Juan. THE MARX FAMILY SAGA
Guillén, Jorge. HORSES IN THE AIR AND OTHER POEMS
Hammond, Paul. CONSTELLATIONS OF MIRÓ, BRETON
Hammond, Paul. THE SHADOW AND ITS SHADOW: Surrealist
    Writings on Cinema
Harryman, Carla. THERE NEVER WAS A ROSE WITHOUT A
    THORN
Herron, Don. THE DASHIELL HAMMETT TOUR: A Guidebook
Higman, Perry, tr. LOVE POEMS FROM SPAIN AND SPANISH
    AMERICA
Hinojosa, Francisco. HECTIC ETHICS
Jaffe, Harold. EROS: ANTI-EROS
Jenkins, Edith. AGAINST A FIELD SINISTER
Katzenberger, Elaine, ed. FIRST WORLD, HA HA HA!: The
    Zapatista Challenge
Keenan, Larry. POSTCARDS FROM THE UNDERGROUND:
    Portraits of the Beat Generation
Kerouac, Jack. BOOK OF DREAMS (complete unabridged edition)
Kerouac, Jack. POMES ALL SIZES
Kerouac, Jack. SCATTERED POEMS

Poe, Edgar Allan. THE UNKNOWN POE
Porta, Antonio. KISSES FROM ANOTHER DREAM
Prévert, Jacques. PAROLES
Purdy, James. THE CANDLES OF YOUR EYES
Purdy, James. GARMENTS THE LIVING WEAR
Purdy, James. IN A SHALLOW GRAVE
Purdy, James. OUT WITH THE STARS
Rachlin, Nahid. THE HEART'S DESIRE
Rachlin, Nahid. MARRIED TO A STRANGER
Rachlin, Nahid. VEILS: SHORT STORIES
Reed, Jeremy. DELIRIUM: An Interpretation of Arthur Rimbaud
Reed, Jeremy. RED-HAIRED ANDROID
Rey Rosa, Rodrigo. THE BEGGAR'S KNIFE
Rey Rosa, Rodrigo. DUST ON HER TONGUE
Rigaud, Milo. SECRETS OF VOODOO
Rodríguez, Artemio and Herrera, Juan Felipe. LOTERIA CARDS
    AND FORTUNE POEMS
Ross, Dorien. RETURNING TO A
Ruy Sánchez, Alberto. MOGADOR
Saadawi, Nawal El. MEMOIRS OF A WOMAN DOCTOR
Sawyer-Lauçanno, Christopher. THE CONTINUAL
    PILGRIMAGE: American Writers in Paris 1944-1960
Sawyer-Lauçanno, Christopher, transl. THE DESTRUCTION OF
    THE JAGUAR
Scholder, Amy, ed. CRITICAL CONDITION: Women on the
    Edge of Violence
Schelling, Andrew, tr. CANE GROVES OF NARMADA RIVER:
    Erotic Poems from Old India
Serge, Victor. RESISTANCE
Shepard, Sam. MOTEL CHRONICLES
Shepard, Sam. FOOL FOR LOVE & THE SAD LAMENT OF
    PECOS BILL
Solnit, Rebecca. SECRET EXHIBITION: Six California Artists
Tabucchi, Antonio. DREAMS OF DREAMS and THE LAST
    THREE DAYS OF FERNANDO PESSOA
Takahashi, Mutsuo. SLEEPING SINNING FALLING
Turyn, Anne, ed. TOP TOP STORIES
Tutuola, Amos. SIMBI & THE SATYR OF THE DARK JUNGLE
Ullman, Ellen. CLOSE TO THE MACHINE: Technophilia and Its
    Discontents

Kerouac, Jack. SCRIPTURE OF THE GOLDEN ETERNITY
Kirkland, Will. GYPSY CANTE: Deep Song of the Caves
Lacarrière, Jacques. THE GNOSTICS
La Duke, Betty. COMPAÑERAS
La Loca. ADVENTURES ON THE ISLE OF ADOLESCENCE
Lamantia, Philip. BED OF SPHINXES: SELECTED POEMS
Lamantia, Philip. MEADOWLARK WEST
Laure. THE COLLECTED WRITINGS
Lavín, Mónica. POINTS OF DEPARTURE
Le Brun, Annie. SADE: On the Brink of the Abyss
Lucarelli, Carlo. ALMOST BLUE
Mackey, Nathaniel. ATET A.D.
Mackey, Nathaniel. SCHOOL OF UDHRA
Mackey, Nathaniel. WHATSAID SERIF
Martín Gaite, Carmen. THE BACK ROOM
Masereel, Frans. PASSIONATE JOURNEY
Mayakovsky, Vladimir. LISTEN! EARLY POEMS
Mehmedinovic, Semezdin. SARAJEVO BLUES
Meltzer, David, ed. SAN FRANCISCO BEAT: TALKING WITH
     THE POETS
Minghelli, Marina. MEDUSA: The Fourth Kingdom
Morgan, William. BEAT GENERATION IN NEW YORK
Mrabet, Mohammed. THE BOY WHO SET THE FIRE
Mrabet, Mohammed. THE LEMON
Mrabet, Mohammed. LOVE WITH A FEW HAIRS
Mrabet, Mohammed. M'HASHISH
Murguía, A. & B. Paschke, eds. VOLCAN: Poems from Central
     America
Nadir, Shams. THE ASTROLABE OF THE SEA
O'Hara, Frank. LUNCH POEMS
Pacheco, José Emilio. CITY OF MEMORY AND OTHER
     POEMS
Parenti, Michael. AGAINST EMPIRE
Parenti, Michael. AMERICA BESIEGED
Parenti, Michael. BLACKSHIRTS & REDS
Parenti, Michael. DIRTY TRUTHS
Parenti, Michael. HISTORY AS MYSTERY
Pasolini, Pier Paolo. ROMAN POEMS
Pessoa, Fernando. ALWAYS ASTONISHED
Pessoa, Fernando. POEMS OF FERNANDO PESSOA

Valaoritis, Nanos. MY AFTERLIFE GUARANTEED
VandenBroeck, André. BREAKING THROUGH
Vega, Janine Pommy. TRACKING THE SERPENT
Veltri, George. NICE BOY
Waldman, Anne. FAST SPEAKING WOMAN
Wilson, Colin. POETRY AND MYSTICISM
Wilson, Peter Lamborn. PLOUGHING THE CLOUDS
Wilson, Peter Lamborn. SACRED DRIFT
Wynne, John. THE OTHER WORLD
Zamora, Daisy. RIVERBED OF MEMORY